KEEPIↄ SHTUM

AND OTHER COMMUNICATION STRATEGIES

A disruptive look at public relations,
reputation and crisis management
that redefines communication strategy

STEVEN OLIVANT

Steven Olivant

Keeping Shtum and Other Communication Strategies
A disruptive look at public relations,
reputation and crisis management
that redefines communication strategy

Copyright © 2016 Steven Olivant

ISBN-13: 9781517312381
ISBN-10: 1517312388

For Izabella

ABOUT THIS BOOK

Why do I need a communication strategy?

All leaders face these questions:
1. What is the state of our organization?
2. What opportunities and threats does the environment present?
3. What options do we have?

The answer – deciding on an option and how to make it happen – is strategy. Communication plays a vital part in successful strategies, answering these questions:

- What is our position (our story)?
- When do we need to communicate it? (And when is it better to keep quiet?)
- To whom?
- How?

Anyone in the public eye (institutions, businesses and people) needs a communication strategy that helps achieve their objectives. Without a communication strategy, you risk everything spinning out of control. Without a communication strategy, you can't mobilize the people you need to put your strategy into effect. (Napoleon had a communication strategy – see chapter 9.) Without a communication strategy, you may not have a position worked out, and you certainly don't know when, to whom, or how to tell your story.

Yet communication strategy has been neglected.

Accentuating the positive, eliminating the negative

You could try the simple-sounding communication strategy of accentuating the positive and eliminating the negative.

That would be a start but it's like saying a great business strategy is to raise revenues and cut costs. OK but how?

What if accentuating the positive raises your profile and

makes you a target for critics or competitors? You may think you want your name in the media. You may think you want people talking about you and tweeting about you. But what if you look bad? How do you keep control of your story? And how do you stop other people spoiling it? Without a communication strategy, you don't know how to control your profile, and whether to seek a high profile or a low profile.

What's new about this?

There are thousands of books on public communication but:

- Most of them are about tactics, not strategy. They tell you how to publicize a new product or run a campaign. They don't tell you where communication fits into your strategy.
- Most of them are too idealistic, preaching openness and transparency. They advise always telling the truth – the whole truth. They want you to have "symmetrical" relationships with myriad stakeholders.
- Most of them assume that publicity is a Good Thing. You won't find this advice in mainstream books but one of the secrets of top professionals is that it's often better to say less.

Instead of telling you what you ought to do (or what the author did), this book tells you what works.

How to use the book

Part I looks at what happens when things go wrong because the communication strategy is inappropriate, inadequate or non-existent.

If you want to go straight to how to do communication strategy, read part II, especially chapter 7 (short introduction), and chapter 17 (how to put communication strategy into practice in 100 days).

Each chapter ends with a bullet point summary. There is an executive summary at the end of the last chapter.

The author

Steven Olivant learned about public communication with one of the world's largest corporations (BP) in New York and London. He has worked for a number of major businesses as a communication executive or consultant. Since 2000, he has served as director of corporate affairs at the world's leading airport company (BAA), and as director of communications and investor relations director at two of the world's largest travel companies (MyTravel and Thomas Cook).

Most recently, he has made a study of communication strategy. This book is the product of that study and lessons learned over more than thirty years in the business of communication. He holds a bachelor's degree in law and a master's degree in public relations.

He can be reached at stevenolivant@icloud.com.

These pages intentionally left blank

Contents

List of figures and tables

GUIDE

Communication Strategies Discussed in This Book

Everyone's communication strategy is unique.

As with business strategy, no one should simply take a generic communication strategy and apply it uncritically. An appropriate strategy is likely to involve features from more than one generic strategy and features that are distinctive.

However, identifying common and/or effective strategies that have been adopted in particular circumstances is a useful way to explore the subject.

Allies	Chapter 12 reviews the concept of reputation and how organizations communicate with audiences (often termed stakeholders). It concludes that the most effective strategy is to choose strategic (priority) stakeholders and focus on them. Some examples of this strategy in practice may be found in chapters 8 (Apple), 13 (Exxon), 15 (Carnival) and 16 (BAA).
Control/ Controlled disclosure/ Targeted profile	These aspects of communication strategy are summed up colloquially in the title of this book as "Keeping Shtum." Keeping shtum is used as shorthand for careful control of communication and a targeted (differentiated) profile, rather than literal silence. The steps to take are set out in full in chapter 17, with examples throughout the book. Controlled disclosure is explained in chapter 3, using examples from Apple, AstraZeneca, eBay and Pfizer.
Crisis	There is a summary of key points for crisis communication strategy at the end of chapter 13. Chapters 13, 14 and 15 examine the crisis cases of Exxon, BP and Carnival, respectively.
Critical path	Critical path is proposed as a control mechanism at the core of communication strategy in chapter 17, with examples including the European Central Bank,

J. C. Penney and Ryanair.

Focus on objectives	The purpose of all communication strategy should be to help deliver the objectives of the overall strategy, i.e., the corporate or business strategy. Chapters 7 and 17 explain and chapter 18 is a plea for focus.
High profile advocacy	The most powerful exponent of this communication strategy was Mobil, the giant oil company. As shown in chapter 10, its communications were innovative and eye-catching but it is debatable whether the strategy was successful or would be transferable.
Keeping shtum	See Control (above) and Surprise (below).
Narrative	Narrative is not a communication strategy but the use of strategic narrative is an essential element in most communication strategies, as set out in chapter 9, with examples throughout the book.
Normative stakeholder strategy	An attempt to engage wholeheartedly with all stakeholders. For the reasons discussed in chapter 12, such a strategy is not a wise use of resources.
Optimism	The communication strategy of promising a better future in spite of everything. Chapter 6 explains that it is only advisable if circumstances require outright promotion, as when a start-up is seeking funds. Even then, it is a short-term strategy that often ends in failure. It is not appropriate for established, publicly quoted companies.
Personality	Building communications around promoting the leader. As chapter 2 explains, although there are clear advantages to this strategy, in most cases, the disadvantages are likely to outweigh the advantages.
Pragmatic reputation strategy	One possible communication strategy toward stakeholders is to engage with them issue by issue while employing pro-stakeholder rhetoric. This strategy is explained fully in chapter 12. It is widely used but is less likely to be effective than the Allies strategy.

Surprise | Keeping shtum about actions or intentions and then springing a surprise such as launching a new product or service or changing a business model, often with a view to disruption. This can be a highly effective communication strategy. Alphabet (Google), Amazon, Apple and Facebook are among those who have surprised and succeeded. See chapter 8.

Telling It All | Another alternative to communication strategy, telling it all (and telling it now) is advocated by many public relations scholars and professionals. Rejected by this book as often prejudicial to the client's interests. Contrast the strategy of truth. See chapters 5 and 6.

Truth, Strategy of | When someone promises to tell the truth even though information revealed is damaging to their position. (Not to be confused with telling the truth for its own sake.) In an adversarial situation, where the other side has low credibility, this can be an effective strategy. Examples are drawn from international relations. See chapters 5, 6 and 9.

Two-way symmetrical communication | Two-way symmetrical communication is both shorthand for a theory and, at its simplest, the argument that there is one excellent way for organizations to communicate and that is symmetrically, paying attention to the interests of audiences or stakeholders as well as the organization itself. An alternative to communication strategy which has been influential in public relations. See chapter 4.

INTRODUCTION

Apple's shock strategy

Apple's iPad was a secret project for eight years. Then Apple launched the iPad in a blaze of publicity. And when the pyrotechnics came, they were carefully controlled — a performance, not a free-for-all.

Before 2010, most people knew tablet computers only in science fiction. Apple changed all that. The story of how Apple created and sold the iPad is not the story of how a company designed and made a great product. Nor is it about a PR campaign to launch a product. It is the story of how Apple sold over 200 million units of a revolutionary product thanks to a *radical communication strategy*.

Relegated to Page 16

Until 2010, technology cognoscenti regarded tablets either wistfully, as the world-changing innovation that might have been, or derisively, as a dead end. Against this background, in July 2009, the *Financial Times (FT)* put a report about Apple on the front page of its American edition. It was about selling more music albums, rather than single tracks, by bundling extras with album downloads.

The editors relegated a second story about Apple to page 16. This was that Apple was planning a tablet in time for Christmas.[1] This new tablet might have a touch-sensitive screen, like the hugely successful iPhone, but measuring up to 10 inches diagonally. It would be capable of connecting to the internet and to Apple's online stores for software and entertainment.[2]

The article on page 16 cited unnamed sources. One said it was a portable device for watching movies. Another speculated that it might cost between $600 and $1,000. The *FT* had assembled enough information from various sources to be comfortable publishing its report, despite having no confirmation from Apple. (Sometimes, unattributed articles are the result of controlled and deniable leaks. There is no reason to believe that this was the result of such a leak by Apple.)

When the article appeared, Apple said nothing. But the story of the iPad had begun.

Tiniest niche

A tablet is a portable computer in one piece, without the separate keyboard of a laptop. The Hitch Hiker's Guide to the Galaxy was an imaginary tablet encyclopedia. In book form, it would have filled several large buildings.[3]

Bill Gates of Microsoft showed a prototype tablet at Comdex 2000 and predicted that tablets would become the most popular type of personal computer (PC).[4] Years later, tablets using Microsoft's operating system were "the tiniest of niches... heavy and expensive... A few people swore by them. More swore at them. Most ignored them."[5] Computer makers could not find a consumer market for tablets.

There was a persistent view in the industry that tablets had a bright future. Someone just needed to work out what it was.

"No plans to make a tablet"

Meanwhile people talked about what they were working on. There is a tale that, back in 2002, such loose talk needled Apple CEO Steve Jobs and stimulated his determination to make a great tablet.[6] Whatever its genesis, Apple kept quiet about its Project Purple — to build a portable machine with an interactive touch screen.[7] When Jobs was asked about a tablet in 2003, he said, "We have no plans to make a tablet." This was true but not the whole truth. (See chapter 8.)

Apple went to a lot of trouble to develop its products in secret, rigorously controlling information. It was rumored that when focus groups tested the iPod, for example, they had to operate it with wires in a sealed box. They had no idea what it was really like.[8] Apple juggled code names like a conjuror.[9]

Meanwhile, a successful tablet needed a viable touchscreen. Apple's iPhone project resolved the technical problems and the iPhone's commercial triumph from 2007 reduced the cost of the screens.

It took eight years from 2002 for Apple to admit to any interest in tablet computers.

Guessing

Analysts gradually surmised that a tablet could be in the works.[10] But they could only guess at its capabilities, launch date and price. Apple had long been the subject of countless rumors and there had been rumors about a tablet ever since 1993, when Apple produced the Newton proto-tablet. Newton was not only ahead of its time in concept but also ahead of the software, processing power and touchscreen that would have made it work well.

While Apple worked away silently, speculation mounted about the hypothetical tablet. At last, it was reported that Apple had rented space for an event in San Francisco that was expected to be a product launch.[11]

David Pogue (*New York Times*) concluded that: "The only thing we know for sure about the Apple tablet is that we don't know anything for sure."[12] On January 18, 2010, Apple invited the press by email to come see its latest (unspecified) creation on January 27.

And success was far from certain. The *FT*'s Lex column pointed out on the eve that manufacturers had flirted with tablets for decades without the mass market taking off. Since Microsoft had only been able to sell a million tablets a year, maybe Apple, a niche player, would sell a few thousand. The *FT* did not believe that Apple would achieve the same lead as it had with the iPhone because competitors were ready to retaliate. Apple would charge $800-$1,000 and copycat tablets would sell for half of that.[13]

Day of the iPad

"iPad creates and defines an entirely new category of devices that will connect users with their apps and content in a much more intimate, intuitive and fun way than ever before," said Apple.[14]

It turned out that the *FT* report of July 2009 was fairly accurate, except about the price, only $499. And the *FT* piece had given no idea what the product was actually like.

Immediate reaction was mixed. Critics said that the iPad lacked a camera, a phone and the ability to run applications simultaneously.[15] Technology columnist John C. Dvorak said: "Apple's iPad — what is it good for? Absolutely nothing!"[16]

The name reminded some people of feminine hygiene products. "The first impression of every single woman I've spoken to is that it's cringe-inducing," said one tech PR expert.[17] (Perhaps they had never used a notepad.) In a flash, the name's sanitary connotations were trending.[18] A feeble-minded CEO might have thought this was a crisis.

But it was only a social media panic. The years of secrecy had produced the conditions for Apple to launch with a big bang. There was no lead-up of delays, complaints and failures, common in consumer technology. The presentation sparked overwhelming enthusiasm and drowned out the nitpickers and complainers.[19]

9½ weeks

Even after the launch, Apple took extreme care over what information was released, using the 9½ weeks before it was due to go on sale to show it to selected journalists. At one demonstration, Alan Murray of the *Wall Street Journal (WSJ)* tweeted: "This tweet sent from an iPad. Does it look cool?"[20] The tweet was quickly deleted. Afterwards Murray said: "I would love to talk about this, but can't... I will say that Apple's general paranoia about news coverage is truly extraordinary."

Few had access to anything beyond media reports and Apple's own communications. Developers had access in secret, with the new machine chained to a desk.[21]

One of the few was the actor and "fanboy" Stephen Fry, who wrote: "I am finally left alone with an iPad… When I switch it on, a little sigh escapes me as the screen lights up. Ten minutes later I am rolling on the floor, snarling and biting, trying to wrestle it from the hands of an Apple press representative."[22]

Apple did not try to please everyone but concentrated on delighting the customer. Wall Street had to guess. Analysts' forecasts for first year sales at the time of the launch ranged wildly from 1 million to 10 million.[23] (In late 2014 and early 2015, there was a similar guessing game about the prospects of Apple's new watch.)

Instant disruption

The iPad went on sale on April 3, 2010. Apple now proudly announced that the first day's sales of 300,000 surpassed the iPhone. In nine months, sales reached 14.8 million, far more than the highest guess.[24] It was the opposite approach to tech companies that talk up what they are going to do but are cagey with hard figures.

Walt Mossberg (*WSJ*) predicted that the iPad could change portable computing profoundly and challenge the laptop.[25] He said the interface was alluring and intuitive. Although Apple had carefully curated the user's experience, access to the internet and the breadth of apps meant there was a sensation of being pampered rather than patronized.

 Apple's share price rose 21% from January 1 to May 31 in a declining market. It overtook Microsoft to become the world's most valuable technology company, on the way to becoming the most valuable company of all.

Competitors were wrong-footed. They had expected the new tablet to be twice as expensive, with half the power and half the battery life. It took months for serious alternatives to appear. Microsoft had shown a tablet in January 2010 before the iPad announcement but it did not ship until October. Competitors brought more than 100 different tablet products to the Consumer Electronics Show in January 2011. None succeeded. H-P, the world's leading PC manufacturer, soon discontinued its Touch-

Pad tablet and sold its inventory on eBay.[26]

Microsoft and Google (now Alphabet) announced tablets using proprietary hardware and software in June 2012, two and a half years after the iPad.[27] They entered a market dominated by Apple. By then, the iPad was causing havoc across the PC market. Laptop assemblers were switching from portable computers to servers and the tablets that access them.[28] And when real tablet competition did emerge, Apple could argue that competitors had snatched its ideas.

Behind the success

It was one of the most successful product launches in history, and the iPad needed to be a remarkable product. Marc Andreessen, the influential tech entrepreneur, believes that Apple deserves more credit for its technological achievement, which is effectively offering consumers the portable equivalent of a multimillion-dollar supercomputer for a few hundred dollars.[29]

But being an outstanding innovation has never guaranteed commercial results. Whenever a new technology works, it stimulates fierce competition for the new market. Who wins is determined by competitive strategy, not technological superiority.[30]

As well as technology, the iPad relied for its success on Apple's communication strategy, which was to focus on the consumer, work in secret in order to keep competitors guessing, and then launch with a big bang.

Apple described its 1984 Macintosh computer as "insanely great." Macintosh and its descendants have all been superior products with a devoted fanbase. But they did not win significant market share and profits until the 2000s. Only the new communication strategy adopted after Jobs returned to the company as CEO in the late 1990s enabled it to launch great products that conquered markets: iPod, iPhone and iPad.

It was a communication strategy of surprise, lying low and launching with a big bang, that gave the iPad a huge lead, with long lasting market dominance. Apple has taken the apex predator's share of the profits from the new product category.

Questions raised by Apple's example

This is not another book about Apple. But being impressed by Apple was what first prompted this book to be written. Studying Apple provoked a number of questions the book seeks to answer:

- By conventional wisdom, excellent communication means openness and transparency, not secrecy and surprise. In theory, keeping shtum, as Apple did for years, should have been bad for business. Is surprise, the strategy that launched the iPad, effective or even legitimate in the 21st century? See chapter 3.

- Despite being arguably the most successful company of the past two decades, Apple has been ignored or derided by communication experts. So is Apple one of a kind — such an extreme case that all the rules it broke stand unaffected — or can lessons be learned from Apple and applied by others? Chapter 8 has the answers.

- Apple is renowned for its attention to the customer. What about other stakeholders? Who are they and how should they be treated? Chapter 12 proposes an unorthodox solution to the stakeholder problem.

Apple was the starting point but the book looks at many other examples, such as:

- Mobil, the giant oil company, sought a high profile. Exxon, the largest of all, kept a low profile. Which worked better? Should you seek a high or low profile? And why do textbooks ignore that question? See chapters 10 and 13.

- Experts advise that, in a crisis, the CEO should rush to the scene and apologize. When a ship owned by Carnival sank, losing more than thirty lives, the CEO stayed in Florida. What should he have done? See chapter 15.

- And chapter 1 looks at two interviews that changed the lives of the interviewees (a CEO and a four star general) — for the worse. It explains why these were not just gaffes but strategic errors. How could the situation have been handled for better results?

In Summary

- By innovating in secret, controlling communications, and using its strategy of surprise to outflank competitors and delight customers, Apple won a huge competitive advantage and sold over 200 million copies of the iPad, the first mass market tablet computer.
- The story of the iPad shows the impact communication strategy can have — and raises awkward questions for communications driven by tactics or normative public relations theory.

_____

References

[1] Front page story: Joseph Menn, Kenneth Li & Matthew Garrahan, 'iTunes Push Aims to Recreate Heyday of the Album,' *Financial Times*, (US edn.), July 27, 2009. Page 16 story: Joseph Menn, Matthew Garrahan & Kenneth Li, 'Apple Targets New Player Revolution,' *Financial Times*, (US edn.), July 27, 2009.

[2] Matthew Garrahan, Kenneth Li & Joseph Menn, 'Apple joins forces with record labels,' *Financial Times*, July 27, 2009.

[3] Douglas Adams, *The Hitch Hiker's Guide to the Galaxy*, (London: Pan, 2009, 22).

[4] Mark Ward, 'Gates Hands Down His Tablet,' *BBC News*, (November 13, 2000), <http://news.bbc.co.uk/1/hi/sci/tech/1021270.stm>.

[5] Charles Arthur, *Digital Wars: Apple, Google, Microsoft and the Battle for the Internet*, (London: Kogan Page, 2012), 222.

[6] Walter Isaacson, *Steve Jobs*, (London: Little, Brown 2011), 467.

[7] Brent Schlender & Rick Teztzeli, *Becoming Steve Jobs: The Evolution of a Reckless Upstart Into a Visionary Leader*, (London: Sceptre, 2015), 299-302.

[8] Jeffrey S. Young & William L. Simon, *Icon Steve Jobs: The Greatest Second Act in the History of Business*, (Hoboken, NJ: John Wiley & Sons, 2005), 282.

[9] Owen Linzmayer, *Apple Confidential 2.0: The Definitive History of the World's Most Colorful Company: The Real Story of Apple Computer, Inc.*, (San Francisco: No Starch Press, Inc., 2004), 26.

[10] See e.g., Bill Shope, Elizabeth Borbolla, Vlad Rom & Thompson Wu, *Apple Inc.*, Credit Suisse, August 7, 2008.

[11] David Gelles, 'Apple to Host Event in January,' *Financial Times*, December 23, 2009.

[12] David Pogue, 'The Apple Guessing Game,' *New York Times*, January 23, 2010.

[13] Lex, 'Tablet Computers,' *Financial Times*, January 26, 2010. A Few Thousand: Arthur, *Digital Wars*, 226. Pricing: Richard Waters & Chris Nuttall, 'The Gadget Gamble,' *Financial Times*, January 8, 2010.

[14] 'Apple Launches iPad,' Apple Inc. news release, January 27, 2010.

[15] 'Steve Jobs and the Tablet of Hope,' *The Economist*, January 30, 2010.

[16] John C. Dvorak, 'Apple's Good for Nothing iPad,' *PC*, February 2, 2010.

[17] Claire Cain Miller, 'The iPad's Name Makes Some Women Cringe,' <http://bits.blogs.nytimes.com/2010/01/27/the-ipads-name-makes-some-women-cringe/>.

[18] 'iPad: Worst Name Ever?' *Ragan's PR Daily*, January 25, 2011, <http://www.prdaily.com/Main/Articles/4680.aspx?>.

[19] Steve Kemper, *Code Name Ginger*, (Harvard Business School Press, 2003), 256.

[20] Ryan Tate, 'The iPad Tweet That Enraged Steve Jobs?' *gawker.com*, February 8, 2010, <http://gawker.com/5466906/the-ipad-tweet-that-enraged-steve>.

[21] Shira Ovide & Suzanne Vranica, 'Magazines Use the iPad as Their New Barker,' *Wall Street Journal*, March 29, 2010.

[22] Stephen Fry, 'The iPad Launch: Can Steve Jobs Do It Again?' *Time*, April 1, 2010.

[23] Lex, 'iPad Launch,' *Financial Times*, April 1, 2010.

[24] Apple Sells Over 300,000 iPads First Day, Apple Inc. news release, April 5, 2010. 'Apple Says It Sold More Than 300,000 iPads First Day,' *Bloomberg*, April 5, 2010. 14.8m: Adam Satariano, 'Apple Profit Rises 78% on Demand for iPads, iPhones,' *Bloomberg*, January 18, 2011.

[25] Walter S. Mossberg, 'Apple's Sleek iPad Opens a New Frontier,' *Wall Street Journal*, April 1, 2010.

[26] Industry expectations: 'IPad Prompts Scramble for Second at Samsung, Hewlett-Packard,' *Bloomberg*, May 14, 2010. Microsoft: Richard Waters, 'Microsoft Beats Apple in Unveiling Slate PC,' *Financial Times*, January 7, 2010. Khidr Suleman, 'HP Launches Slate 500 tablet,' *V3*,

<http://www.v3.co.uk/v3-uk/news/1947217/hp-launches-slate-500-tablet>, October 22, 2010. Consumer Electronics Show: Chris Nuttall, 'Tablets Set to Steal the Show at CES,' *Financial Times*, January 3, 2011. Chris Nuttall, 'Tablet Contenders Vie for iPad's Crown,' *Financial Times*, January 5, 2012. eBay: Sara Kimberley, 'HP Dumps its Apple iPad Rival Tablet on eBay,' *Marketing*, December 13, 2011.

[27] 'Microsoft Announces Surface: New Family of PCs for Windows,' Microsoft Corporation news release, June 18, 2012. Walter S. Mossberg, 'From Google, the Toughest Challenger to the iPad,' *Wall Street Journal*, July 10, 2012.

[28] 'iPad Onslaught Sends Taiwanese Laptop Makers to the Cloud,' *Bloomberg*, April 24, 2012.

[29] Schlender & Teztzeli, *Becoming Steve Jobs*, 365.

[30] Alasdair Nairn, *Engines That Move Markets: Technology Investing from Railroads to the Internet and Beyond*, (New York: John Wiley & Sons, Inc., 2002), 476.

PART I

Myths about Communication and Strategy

In part I

Part I explores six myths about communication and strategy that cause people to fumble their communications:

- Chapter 1 starts with errors, from a slip of the tongue to a disastrous interview. The myth is that the answer is to eliminate these errors. It shows that the more significant problems are strategic.
- Chapter 2 looks at the part psychology plays in public communication problems. The myth is that the ideal is a high profile focused on a big personality. It examines the personality strategy and finds it flawed.
- Chapter 3 examines the mounting social pressure for transparency and openness. The myth is that openness and transparency are both desirable and inevitable. How should organizations respond?
- Chapter 4 turns to the professional communicators. The myth is that the best way to communicate is by mutually beneficial, so-called symmetrical, two-way communication. Theory, good intentions and the desire for excellence often get in the way of effectiveness and strategy.
- Chapter 5 confronts the problem of truth. The myth is that there is a simple answer: tell the truth, tell it all, tell it now.
- The myth in chapter 6 is that optimism is not only a healthy state of mind but a long-term communication strategy. It also examines credibility and the *strategy* of truth.

Each chapter broadens the focus from tactical errors to strategic failures of policies, programs and projects that are misconceived.

CHAPTER 1

Out of Control: Tactics and strategy

"Once you have spoken a word, taking it back is like hurling a stone at someone and then trying to stop it in mid-air."
— After Menander

"Nothing is so contrary to good counsel as these two, haste and anger, whereof the one is ever accompanied with madness [folly] and the other with want of judgment."
— Thucydides, translated by Thomas Hobbes, "History of the Peloponnesian War"

No one wants to be embarrassed, shamed or humiliated when they open a newspaper, turn on the television or look at social media. No one wants to be seen to fail in their career or personal life. No one wants their family, friends, business associates, investors or the wider world to think badly of them.

Maybe that is not entirely true. Some people are just plain silly and silliness inoculates them against embarrassment, shame or humiliation.

Jane Austen found the epitome of silliness in the character of Lydia Bennet in "Pride and Prejudice." The Bennet family divided between the wise Bennets — Mr Bennet, Jane and Lizzie — and Mrs Bennet and their three "uncommonly foolish" daughters. Lydia, the youngest, who ran off with Mr Wickham, "always unguarded and often uncivil," would have made rich raw material for reality TV. "Imprudent, self-willed, ignorant, idle and vain... She seldom listened to anybody for more than half a minute" but gossiped uncontrollably as she "never heard nor saw anything of which she chose to be insensible."[1]

Surprise is still expressed that celebrity should accrue to people without talent even though Daniel Boorstin identified the phenomenon in 1961: "Until very recently, famous men and great men were pretty nearly the same group," whereas now "celebrities are known primarily for their well-knownness."[2] Jane Austen provided a prototype in Lydia.

For the rest of us, embarrassment, shame or humiliation are a horrifying prospect, the inevitable result if things go out of control and we say or do the wrong thing.

It sometimes feels as though public life is a parade of these blunders that we often call gaffes. By making it easier to propagate inane remarks, Twitter has increased the flow of gaffes — racist comments, compromising photos, scurrilous slurs, and all the rest.

Silliness is one thing but why does it happen to the rest of us? How do things go out of control? And what can be done about it?

Let's start at the top.

All the presidents' gaffes

Some believe it was a gaffe that decided the 2012 American presidential election. Mitt Romney's campaign veered out of control when he was secretly filmed speaking dismissively of Americans who would vote for Obama, "who believe they are victims." A leading Republican commentator wrote ahead of the election that the recording "killed Mitt Romney's campaign for president... Romney already has trouble relating to the public and convincing people he cares about them. Now, he's been caught... saying that nearly half the country consists of hopeless losers."[3]

All recent presidents of the United States have said the wrong thing from time to time. Jimmy Carter told *Playboy* magazine that he had "committed adultery in my heart many times," losing 15 points in opinion polls ahead of the 1976 presidential election.[4] Bill Clinton declared: "I did not have sexual relations with that woman."[5] Barack Obama spoke of a "Polish death camp," when he meant a Nazi death camp in what became Poland.[6]

And on the Republican side, Ronald Reagan joked: "I just signed legislation which outlaws Russia forever. The bombing begins in five minutes."[7] George Bush senior said: "I'll never apologize for the United States of America. Ever. I don't care what the facts are."[8] George Bush junior made a speech on an aircraft carrier in May 2003 beneath a large "Mission Accomplished" banner. As war in Iraq dragged on, the cover of *Time* magazine a few months later read: "Mission Not Accomplished: How Bush misjudged the task of fixing Iraq."[9] And every nation could assemble a hall of fame for gaffes — although, in many less fortunate countries, public discussion of gaffes is censored.

One compendium of recent political gaffes runs to several thousand.[10] They are hard to avoid. The fact that recent American presidents, highly intelligent and experienced to a man, were nevertheless unable to avoid making multiple gaffes, suggests how difficult it may be.

The media are striving to make it harder. And that is just the conventional media. The Wild West freak and horror show of social media is far worse.

The nitty-gritty of tactical errors

The tactical errors that are a magnet for comment tend to be controversial and entertaining.

In public communication, tactics is the doing and saying — the nitty-gritty — the cut and thrust. It is comparable with tactics in warfare, meaning the fighting itself. Tactical communication activities are such things as issuing a press release, issuing a photo, and answering a journalist's question. A tactical error is saying or doing the wrong thing.

Thus Reagan's bad joke about bombing Russia was a tactical error. It was not part of a plan. It was an accident. He never intended it to be heard outside the studio where he was getting ready for a radio broadcast. This type of gaffe, to which political leaders are especially prone because they haunt radio and television facilities, is a microphone gaffe. Speakers lower their guard because they believe they are in private but a microphone picks up what they say. It is then broadcast around the world.

Microphone gaffes can be particularly damaging in an election campaign. During the UK's 2010 parliamentary elections, prime minister Gordon Brown was campaigning with the usual crowd of journalists when he had an unsatisfactory but insignificant encounter with a voter about immigration. When he returned to his car, he described the voter to an aide as "a bigoted woman."[11] Brown had forgotten to take off his lapel microphone, his comment was broadcast, and this became the lead story on the news. Jon Stewart quipped: "You actually see the moment when a man's political career leaves his body."[12]

Microphone gaffes are damaging because they are thought by many to reveal what the speaker really thinks, especially in one who is professionally economical with the truth. If someone is caught with their guard down, perhaps what they say goes to the heart of who they are and what they really stand for. "A gaffe is when a politician tells the truth," according to Michael Kinsley.[13] Those at risk from predatory microphones can eliminate these gaffes to a large extent by being wary. George Bush senior reportedly warned future California Governor Arnold Schwarzenegger, pointing to broadcast microphones: "These, they're very dangerous. They trap you. Especially these furry ones... it's these furry guys that get you in real trouble. They can reach out and listen to something so — keep it respectful here."[14] Doubtless haunted by the Brown/bigoted woman stumble, major parties in the UK's 2015 elections made a repetition less likely by restricting unscripted contact with voters.

Speaking *off the record* is another situation in which the speaker believes that he or she is in private but may turn out to have been in public. According to Seth Lipsky, then a senior journalist on the *Wall Street Journal*, Otto von Habsburg told him in 1986: "I don't have the slightest doubt that [Kurt] Waldheim was a Soviet spy throughout his entire time at the United Nations." This was just before Waldheim was elected president of Austria. Lipsky respected a promise that the conversation would be off the record and kept the confidence until the death of Habsburg in 2011.[15] Bravo! But speaking off the record is dangerous. The safer course is either to withhold sensitive information (see chapter 3) or to communicate it in such circumstances that it is deniable.

Both Presidents Bush were prone to *linguistic gaffes*. These occur when the speaker is aware of being in public but accidentally says the wrong thing. Like the microphone gaffe, a lapsus or slip of the tongue — an involuntary linguistic mistake — has been thought by some psychologists (Freud, Lacan) to reveal an unconscious desire but may be purely mechanical. However inconsequential linguistic gaffes may be, they are amusing and make good stories.

Tactics and strategy

Tactical errors such as microphone gaffes, off the record remarks that are reported, and careless use of words, can be avoided much of the time by taking tactical measures. The ways of the media can be studied and exploited. Common traps can be avoided. The correct procedures can be followed. Speakers can train and rehearse for their encounters. (See also chapter 17.)

But there will always be faux pas, which can be moments of inattention or foolishness but which can also be the result of *strategic errors*.

What is strategy, as distinct from tactics, in public communication? Strategy is large-scale and long-term planning toward an objective. Crudely, action is tactics, planning is strategy.

The concept of a campaign is central to public relations as it is to warfare. When a person or corporate entity launches a product, promotes a service, reports financial results, or seeks a political change, for example, they typically mount a public relations campaign to help reach their goal. These campaigns are strategic in the limited sense that they involve planning toward a desired end. Thus, in this sense, a strategic error would be one caused by a plan that is misconceived or flawed.

One of the most common and simple strategic errors is the poorly planned media interview as part of such a campaign. Interviews are high risk because they expose the speaker to interrogation by a journalist. (Even if the interview is a radio or television interview recorded for later broadcast, the conversation usually takes place in real time and on the record. An interviewee rarely says to the journalist in mid-interview, "Hold on a minute while I look up the answer, or consult my advisers, or think about how I want to respond to that question.") Saying the wrong thing in the course of an interview can be devastating, so interviews should only be granted as part of a plan, in pursuit of an objective. This book contains numerous examples of interviews that should not have taken place. For example, Carter made a gaffe in his *Playboy* interview but it was a strategic error for him to give an interview to *Playboy* at all.

It is particularly dangerous to communicate in public when you are not in the right mental condition, for example, if you are in the grip of strong emotions. The effects of visceral factors such as emotions, drive states (e.g., hunger), and feeling states (e.g., pain) on behavior have been underestimated not only by economists but also in communication.

For all speakers, the rule should be that encounters with the media and other important communications only take place when they are in a cold state emotionally. Otherwise, poor decisions are likely to be made, so poor as to be sometimes incomprehensible under later rational scrutiny. Communicators who are in the grip of visceral factors are out of control.[16] See chapter 2 for more on the psychology of decision-making.

There is an exception to this rule in a situation where emotion is positively required to be in the foreground, such as a televised appeal for a missing family member, or when speaking about disaster (see chapter 13). This is part of the trend since the 1990s for media content to become more emotional, as public emotion has become more acceptable or even demanded.[17] Previously, good quality news journalism sought to report the facts: what happened, when, where, to whom and why. Now, broadcast news especially is likely also to report the emotion: how people felt about it.[18]

In both of the following two examples, someone who was highly respected fell from grace as a direct result of what they said to the media. They were pilloried for what they said, which was a tactical error, but they also made a strategic error when they decided to give the interview at all.

The purpose of examining these cases is not to criticize the interviewees, nor to gasp at their gaffes, but to understand what it means to be strategically wrong.

Key points
- No one wants to be humiliated by a public misstep or misstatement.
- Yet gaffes are hard to avoid, even for professionals.
- Tactical errors — saying or doing the wrong thing — can be avoided by taking tactical measures.
- Strategic mistakes — the wrong plan — are harder to prevent and are often obscured by the tactical fog.

Wrong Man, Place and Time

Tony Hayward was CEO of BP at the time of the Gulf of Mexico oil spill in 2010. In line with almost all expert thinking on crisis management, he went to the scene and thrust himself into the media spotlight — or had the spotlight thrust upon him.

Inevitably, the resulting coverage was not entirely free from gaffes. The media gleefully enumerated, retold and rebroadcast the gaffes. Perhaps the most egregious was saying, when asked by television reporters for his message to people in Louisiana: "We're sorry for the massive disruption it's caused their lives. There's no one who wants this over more than I do, *I'd like my life back.*"[19] ...Especially since the explosion that caused the spill killed eleven people. It gave the false impression that Hayward was more concerned with his personal inconvenience than the human tragedy. He was trying to convey how keen he was to contain the oil spill but the unfortunate choice of words made it look as though he didn't care.

Saying the wrong thing was a gaffe — a tactical error. And the gist of the media commentary on the interview was how crass it was. But the tactical error of saying the wrong thing only came about because of the strategic error of giving the interview. There was no necessity for the CEO of BP to be on that shore, at that time, in front of that camera and that microphone.

Hayward was not ideal for the role of BP spokesman in the

crisis for two reasons. First, and contrary to most expert opinion, precisely because he was the CEO. (See chapter 14.) Second, because he was not an American, spoke with an English accent, and was not intimately acquainted with domestic culture, media and politics.

Even after choosing Hayward to speak for the company, BP could have deployed him more cautiously. Someone who is competent, well-trained and adheres to a number of well-established practices, such as using lines set out in a comprehensive Q&A brief, and exercising good discipline in interviews, is less likely to make gaffes. But high pressure makes it harder for anyone to communicate safely. "Mr Hayward is getting in front of the cameras as much as possible in an effort to put the best light on his giant oil company."[20] The active leadership for which Hayward was once admired meant that he was overloaded and overexposed.

From the end of April 2010, he was subjected to the extreme pressure normally reserved for someone running for a major political office. Every move he made, every step he took, and every word he said were subject to intense scrutiny in the media. For example, when he dropped in to say hello to a group of employees having dinner, "A beer appeared in front of him [that] might have been sent over by a tabloid photographer." At lunch one Saturday, while watching sport, the barman took his photo sitting next to "an attractive young woman... the photo soon appeared on the internet alongside [spurious] claims."[21] And when he spent a Saturday with his son at a yacht race, the *New York Post*'s headline was: "As oil spews in Gulf, BP's CEO at UK yacht race."[22]

Few outside the highest reaches of politics are prepared for the degree of scrutiny to which Tony Hayward was subjected in 2010. For the president of the US, "The glare of publicity is now so merciless as to have been unimaginable in Washington's day."[23] Herb Schmertz, the most high profile corporate PR man of all time, wrote that three decades ago, before rolling 24-hour news and ubiquitous cameras linked to the internet. The biggest factor in the number of presidential gaffes is simply that presidents are constantly in the public eye. Like all democratic leaders, they depend a continuous dialog with the public and do not have the alternative of staying out of sight.

Business leaders only come into such a harsh glare in a major crisis. It follows that, in a crisis, it is important that whoever speaks for the firm should be the right person and appear only in the right place at the right time. (See chapters 13-15.) The media encounters should be avoided when speakers are unwell, under-prepared, over-tired or over-stressed.

(However, mad dogs and over-confident tycoons still go out when the glare is as bright as the tropical midday sun. Chapter 2 looks at the part personality plays in communication meltdowns.)

"Shut the fuck up"

One of Barack Obama's priorities on taking office as president of the US in 2008 was the war in Afghanistan. A key step, in March 2009, was the appointment of General Stanley McChrystal as NATO's commander. The following year, McChrystal's team allowed Michael Hastings from *Rolling Stone* magazine to follow them around at close quarters over the course of a month in Afghanistan, Europe and the US. The resulting article claimed that the general and his associates had ridiculed senior civilians including Vice-President Joe Biden.[24] According to Hastings: "Part of it was the circumstances... They were in Paris."[25] Allegedly, the protagonists thought they were speaking off the record, highlighting once again how dangerous this can be.[26]

Obama said: "The conduct represented in the recently published article does not meet the standard that should be set by a commanding general."[27] McChrystal and his colleagues had said the wrong thing. McChrystal made a dignified statement apologizing: "It was a mistake reflecting poor judgment and should never have happened."[28] The gaffe was sufficiently serious that Obama summoned McChrystal and fired him.[29] It was a tragedy for a man Robert Gates, defense secretary, later said was "perhaps the finest warrior" he ever met to be derailed by one lousy interview.[30]

It was a tactical error to say the wrong thing to the reporter. But the *Rolling Stone* profile was also a strategic error. Saying the wrong thing was tactical but creating the opportunity for the wrong thing to be said was strategic. It was strategic in the most basic sense that it must have been part of a plan.

What then was the plan behind the *Rolling Stone* profile? McChrystal later said it was "designed to provide transparency into how my command team operated."[31] (Transparency? See chapter 3.) The reporter duly witnessed the "brotherhood" among the command team but the end result was clearly not as hoped for. The article was said to be unfair.[32]

Damn right it was unfair but it was a riveting story. The only safe assumption to make when setting up a project for a journalist to accompany senior people at close quarters, not only in a war but in any field, would be that fairness comes no higher on a journalist's agenda than it does on the Taliban's.

This project was particularly high risk both because it involved encounters strung out over several weeks in disparate circumstances and in view of the recent history. On September 21, 2009, nine months before *Rolling Stone*, the *Washington Post* published an expurgated version of McChrystal's initial assessment of the war, with the agreement of the Department of Defense, following a leak.[33] On October 1, 2009, McChrystal made a speech in London urging against scaling down the war in Afghanistan, which was seen as conflicting, controversially, with the views of Vice-President Biden.[34] President Obama met McChrystal the following day in Copenhagen. It was widely surmised that the general had been rebuked. As *Rolling Stone* put it later in the profile, the message had been: "Shut the fuck up, and keep a lower profile."[35]

Putting what happened in 2010 in the most innocuous light, perhaps the *Rolling Stone* project was intended simply to support the war effort but, if so, insufficient consideration was given to the difficulty of implementing that plan.

A plan that looks beautiful on the drawing board may prove to be a practical impossibility. The problem is what military strategy calls *friction*. In war, friction is the accumulation of difficulties such as weather, orders going awry, lost or spoiled supplies, and so on. Whereas plans can be made to take account of many problems, the problems cannot be entirely foreseen. What is inescapable is that such unforeseen problems will occur. In communication, friction is a similar accumulation of difficulties such as the speaker making a poor choice of words, unguarded remarks, untimely revelations from other sources, a headline writer creating a headline that casts the article in a harsher light, and so on. Communication strategies are plagued by friction in a similar way to military campaigns. This friction is the subject of much of Part III.

The chances of a magazine publishing a favorable article that would make a general's case without any damaging revelations or annoyance to the administration were unknown. It was a gamble. Events proved that the risk of this plan, to invite a journalist to report on the commander and his team on their mission, outweighed any possible reward and it was therefore strategically unsound.

Fig. 1.1 Tactical Errors vs. Strategic Errors

	TACTICAL ERROR	PROXIMATE CAUSE	STRATEGIC ERROR
BP	CEO: "I'd like my life back"	Overload	- Wrong man. - Too many interviews.
NATO	Colorful criticism of civilian leaders	Loss of control: Hard to control encounter over a long period, in a war, and at times of relaxation	Risk of interview going out of control was too great

Tactics, strategy and grand strategy

So far, General McChrystal's interview has been critiqued first, for saying the wrong thing — the tactical level — and, second, for making the wrong judgment to do the extended interview — at the level of campaign strategy.

Now imagine that, instead of the loose, extended interview with *Rolling Stone*, the general had written a carefully considered and crafted article for a policy journal over which he had total control. This approach would have been less newsworthy but would have neutralized both the dangers discussed so far — the detail of saying the wrong thing and the wider problem of the profile being out of control.

But it would still have been a bad idea. Why? Because it would not have supported a sound strategic objective.

Above the level of campaign strategy, there is a higher level of strategy most often described in the realm of war and international relations as grand strategy. It is also known as national strategy or major strategy. Grand strategy is the direction of all the diplomatic, economic, military and other resources of a state or alliance to achieve its long-term objectives. Here it will usually be referred to as overall or macro strategy. Grand strategy is too closely associated with world war, conjuring up a mental picture of Roosevelt, Churchill and Stalin meeting at Tehran or Yalta.

The (less exalted) equivalent to grand strategy in management is corporate strategy or business strategy, that is the strategy of the whole firm. Similarly, in communication, overall strategy is the top level strategy of an organization, not merely the plan for a campaign.

Fig 1.2 compares key characteristics of tactics, campaign strategy and overall communication strategy.

Fig. 1.2 Communication Tactics and Strategy

	TACTICS	STRATEGY (CAMPAIGN)	STRATEGY (OVERALL)
TIMESCALE	Immediate	Short term	Medium-long term
SCOPE	Event	Campaign	Policies, plans and positions for whole organization
TYPICAL OBJECTIVES	Today's TV. Tomorrow's newspaper	Change perception of a product or brand	Support and enable the strategic objectives

Tactics are communications that take place now, in the context of an event or incident, and obtain coverage on TV or social media today or in tomorrow's newspaper. Campaign strategy involves a campaign, perhaps to change consumer perceptions of a product or brand, usually in the short term. Overall strategy encompasses the policies, plans, and positions of the whole organization over any timescale.

The importance of tactics is usually exaggerated. Gaffes, soundbites, photographs and tweets are the lifeblood of television news, front pages, newspaper columns and wherever people gather to gossip and chatter in real and virtual worlds. The bulk of comment, even from the most authoritative sources, is at this level because media demand reaction to what has just happened or what has just been said. Most of it is gone in a flash, largely forgotten though probably archived somewhere on the internet. Most of it leaves little lasting impression. But immediate public attention is devoted 99% to these ephemera, 1% to the big picture.

Grand strategy

The *Rolling Stone* article provoked a storm. Some bemoaned the infighting they thought it revealed. Some thought it called the entire Afghanistan operation into question once again. Perhaps the most common reaction was that the issue was a military challenge to the civilian leadership. According to this view, McChrystal was following in the footsteps of Douglas MacArthur, the commander in Korea who was fired by President Truman in 1951. For several months, MacArthur and Truman disagreed over the strategy in the Pacific and subsequent congressional investigations established that MacArthur had been insubordinate. As Truman summed it up: "General MacArthur is unable to give his whole-hearted support to the policies of the United States Government."[36] It had been a challenge to the authority of the President.

A thoughtful contribution from Hew Strachan to the debate about McChrystal suggested that the general was certainly not another MacArthur. The general was simply exasperated with the failure of the political leadership to provide a clear direction in the form of a grand strategy.[37] The point was that operational strategy, for which the military leadership is responsible, can only work properly in the context of grand strategy. When there is a vacuum where there should be a grand strategy, and the operational (campaign) strategy is built from the bottom up, as it was in Afghanistan, everything is apt to go awry.

There is an analogy between military and business strategy. From much of the public relations literature, it would appear that a communication campaign is a self-contained, separately justified project. But a campaign only makes strategic sense in the context of a sound overall communication strategy. A central proposition of this book is that sound communication strategy has to be derived from the corporate or business strategy.

There are clear differences between tactics, campaign strategy and overall strategy, illustrated in fig. 1.3.

As chapter 7 (Introduction to Communication Strategy) explains, the overall communication strategy is derived from and fits into corporate or business strategy. It sets the communication policies, makes the plans, decides the positions (what is our story?) and strategic ideas which make each communication strategy unique.

Within the communication strategy, there may be various campaigns or projects, each with its own plan. In the same way as a military campaign only makes sense if it is implementing a grand strategy, such communication campaigns and projects only make sense if they are giving effect to some aspect of the communication strategy.

Tactical actions, such as answering questions from journalists and others, issuing news releases, holding press conferences, placing advertising, and tweeting, attract most of the attention, and are frequently seen to constitute gaffes, but should be seen in the context first of the campaign or project and, ultimately, in the context of the communication strategy.

Fig. 1.3 Levels of Strategy

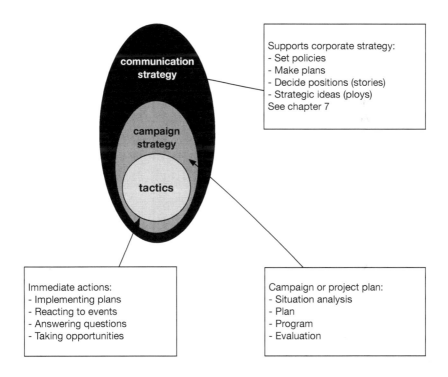

Communication strategy is a hybrid of communication and strategy. It concerns all aspects of communication — audiences, messages, issues, narratives and so on — but is equally integral to strategy. (See chapter 7.) The purpose of communication strategy is to enable and support the achievement of the corporate or business objectives.

In Summary

- Loss of control can be embarrassing to the point of ending a career. And losing control of communications greatly reduces the chances of achieving your objectives.
- Communication problems need to be viewed not only from a tactical perspective but from a strategic perspective, on two levels: campaign and overall. Tactics are subordinate to campaign or operational strategy, and campaign strategy is subordinate to overall strategy.

References

[1] Planet eBook.com, 160, 265, 277, & 389.

[2] Daniel J. Boorstin, *The Image: A Guide to Pseudo-Events in America*, 1961, (New York: Vintage Books, 1992), 46 & 74.

[3] Josh Barro, 'Today, Mitt Romney Lost the Election,' *Bloomberg*, September 17, 2012. See also David Corn, 'Secret Video: Romney Tells Millionaire Donors What He Really Thinks of Obama Voters,' *Mother Jones*, September 17, 2012.

[4] Robert Scheer, 'Playboy Interview, November 1976,' in *Conversations with Carter*, ed. by Don Richardson, (Boulder, CO: Lynne Rienner Publishers, Inc., 1998). J. Brooks Flippen, *Jimmy Carter, the Politics of Family and the Rise of the Religious Right*, (Athens GA: University of Georgia Press, 2011), 99.

[5] James Bennet, 'Clinton Emphatically Denies an Affair With Ex-Intern,' *New York Times*, January 27, 1998.

[6] Jennifer Rubin, 'Obama's Polish Death Camp Gaffe,' *Washington Post*, May 30, 2012.

[7] 'Reagan Said to Joke of Bombing Russia Before Radio Speech,' *New York Times*, August 13, 1984.

[8] Michael Kinsley, 'Essay: Rally Round the Flag, Boys,' *Time*, September 12, 1988.

[9] 'Mission Not Accomplished,' *Time*, October 6, 2003.

[10] David Macfarlane, *The Little Giant Encyclopedia of Leadership Gaffes*, (New York: Sterling Publishing, 2005).

[11] Philippe Naughton, 'Brown Calls Voter Bigoted Woman,' *The Times*, April 28, 2010.

[12] Jon Stewart, quoted in Charles Moore, 'Election Watch,' *Sunday Telegraph*, May 2, 2010.

[13] Michael Kinsley, *Curse of the Giant Muffins and other Washington Maladies*, (New York: Summit Books, 1987), 272.

[14] <http://politicalhumor.about.com/od/funnyquotes/a/georgehwbushism.htm>

[15] Seth Lipsky, 'Lunch With the Holy Roman Emperor,' *Wall Street Journal*, July 6, 2011.

[16] George Loewenstein, 'Emotions in Economic Theory and Economic Behavior,' *The American Economic Review*, Vol. 90, No. 2, (2000), 426-432. George Loewenstein, 'Out of Control: Visceral Influences on Behavior,' in *Advances in Behavioral Economics*, ed. by Colin F. Camerer, George Lowenstein & Matthew Rabin, (Princeton University Press, 2004), 689-723.

[17] Theodore Dalrymple, *Spoilt Rotten: The Toxic Cult of Sentimentality*, (London: Gibson Square, 2011), 124-155.

[18] Mervi Pantti, 'Disaster News and Public Emotions,' in *The Routledge Handbook of Emotions and Mass Media*, ed. by Katrin Doeveling, Christian von Scheve & Elly A. Konijn, (Abingdon, UK: Routledge, 2011).

[19] Jessica Durando, 'BP's Tony Hayward: I'd Like My Life Back,' *USA Today*, June 1, 2010.

[20] Clifford Krauss, 'For BP, a Battle to Contain Leaks and an Image Fight, Too,' *New York Times*, May 6, 2010.

[21] Tom Bergin, *Spills and Spin: The Inside Story of BP*, (London: Random House Business Books, 2011), 175.

[22] 'As Oil Spews in Gulf, BP's CEO at UK Yacht Race,' *New York Post*, June 19, 2010.

[23] Herbert Schmertz, 'The Media and the Presidency,' *Presidential Studies Quarterly*, Vol. 16, No. 1, (Winter, 1986), 11-21.

[24] Michael Hastings, 'The Runaway General,' *Rolling Stone*, June 22, 2010.

[25] Andrew Bast, 'How Rolling Stone Got Into McChrystal's Inner Circle,' *Newsweek*, June 22, 2010.

[26] Giles Whittell, 'Bob Woodward: Scourge of the White House,' *The Times*, October 16, 2010.

[27] Barack Obama, 'Statement by the President in the Rose Garden,' The White House, Office of the Press Secretary, June 23, 2010.

[28] Peter Spiegel, 'McChrystal on Defensive for Remarks,' *Wall Street Journal*, June 21, 2010.

[29] Helene Cooper & David E. Sanger, 'Obama Says Afghan Policy Won't Change After Dismissal,' *New York Times*, June 24, 2010.

[30] Robert M. Gates, *Duty: Memoirs of a Secretary at War*, (New York: Alfred A. Knopf, 2014), 254.

[31] Stanley A. McChrystal, *My Share of the Task: a Memoir*, (New York: Portfolio/Penguin, 2014), 387.

[32] Stanley McChrystal, 'Career Curveballs: No Longer a Soldier,' LinkedIn post, April 22, 2014.

[33] 'COMISAF Initial Assessment (Unclassified) – Searchable Document,' *Washington Post*, September 21, 2009; Bob Woodward, 'McChrystal: More Forces or "Mission Failure,"' *Washington Post*, September 21, 2009.

[34] John F. Burns, 'McChrystal Rejects Scaling Down Afghan Military Aims, *New York Times*, October 1, 2009.

[35] Hastings, 'The Runaway General.'

[36] Harry S. Truman, *Memoirs of Harry S. Truman, Years of Trial and Hope*, 1956, (Boston, MA: Da Capo Press, 1987), 449.

[37] Hew Strachan, *The Direction of War: Contemporary Strategy in Historical Perspective*, (Cambridge University Press, 2013), 210-234.

CHAPTER 2

The Great Communicator

"What great ones do the less will prattle of"
— William Shakespeare, "Twelfth Night," Act I, Scene 2

Ferrero SpA is the world's fourth largest confectionery business with revenues of €8 billion (2013). Its late patriarch, Michele Ferrero, who died at 89 in February 2015, was said to have been Italy's richest man. In a long life he only ever gave a single newspaper interview, and that was released posthumously.[1] His policy was to put the products, not the owners, in the spotlight.

Personality strategy

The pivotal role of the leader, exemplified by the interviews discussed in chapter 1, is so obvious, so natural, that it has led many institutions down the ages to favor a communication strategy founded on personality. A *personality strategy* is to zoom in on and publicize the personality of the leader. It is to integrate the image of the organization (or polity) with the leader. It is indeed to say that "l'état" — or l'entreprise — "c'est moi." The personality strategy is the second of a series of generic communication strategies to be examined. (The first one was the strategy of surprise, as employed by Apple — see Introduction.)

There is nothing new about this strategy. Its incidence through history can be correlated closely with the fortunes of monarchy, a form of government by one person in which the form and substance of power are united. It was defined by Edward Gibbon as "a state, in which a single person, by whatsoever name he may be distinguished, is intrusted with the execution of the laws, the management of the revenue, and the command of the army."[2]

When the security and prosperity of the state are inseparable from the health and statesmanship of the monarch, and when the head that wears a crown lies uneasy, it is inevitable that the personality communication strategy should be employed. A personality strategy may also be appropriate and, to some extent, unavoidable, for fame-seeking pop singers, actors and others in the entertainment business.

The question is whether such a strategy, ideally suited to an absolute monarchy, is also suitable for a modern business. In the business version of this strategy, the thematic personality, usually the CEO, both speaks for the business and is perceived to symbolize and represent the business.

Five possible advantages of spotlighting the CEO could be:

- MEDIA APPEAL. There is no need to fret over the tiresome media habit of reducing difficult issues to gossip about celebrities. Instead, this strategy panders to the media by offering them a ready-made celebrity to cover. (This assumes that a high media profile is desirable.)

- DIFFERENTIATION. If the public perception is that all airlines, banks, oil companies or whatever are the same, the one with a flamboyant personality at the helm is likely to stand out.

- SIMPLE COMMAND STRUCTURE. With a personality strategy, everything revolves around one person. It resembles an old Woody Allen movie, in which a solitary genius writes the script, directs the movie and stars in it.

- FAMILIARITY. According to John D. Graham, it provides groups that particularly like to interact with the CEO, such as investors and employees, with "a sense of the CEO."[3]

- GUARANTEE. Related to this last possible advantage, consumers may be attracted and reassured by what can be

presented as a personal guarantee. In times past, entrepreneurs routinely endorsed their own products and then
endorsed the companies that grew up to make and sell
those products. Associating a product or service with a
celebrity remains a common marketing ploy to this day.
The celebrity may be someone who has nothing to do
with running the business, in the way that William Shat-
ner has personified Priceline. Or it may be the boss of the
company. Taking charge of Chrysler when the firm was at
a low ebb, Lee Iacocca starred in its advertising and pro-
motions, inspiring confidence in customers and dealers.

Although *Fortune* noted in 2013 that seven of the companies
voted "most admired" by business executives in 2013 were what
it called "one-man companies,"[4] it does not follow that glorifica-
tion of the CEO is the right strategy. A personality strategy also
has potential shortcomings:

- DESPERATION. First, the flipside of the differentiation
  advantage. There is a tendency to use a personality strategy when inspiration falls short – when there is little to distinguish a business from competitors apart from the
  personality of its leader. But there should be real differences. See chapter 17.

- RISK. Second, the media are especially fickle toward per-
  sonalities. A change of sentiment toward the personality
  would mean a change toward the firm. One study suggested that the returns are asymmetric: the risk of adverse
  coverage outweighs the advantage of positive coverage.[5]

- SUPERFICIALITY. Contrary to the argument about
  having a sense of the CEO, some audiences, notably
  many investors, expect a business to be more than a personality cult. Personality is too superficial.

- SUCCESSION. If any problem develops with the leader,
  and the company's main message to the world has been

that the company and the leader are one and the same, there is no easy way forward. For Louis XIV, personality was an appropriate communication strategy, pithily expressed. Does a business really want its leader to take as his motto: "I am the firm"? Doing so invites the suspicion that the long-term future, without the boss, is likely to fall short. Narcissism nourished by media adoration makes for difficult dynamics in the management team. Management succession is tricky anyway (see below) but the personality strategy ratchets up any change of leadership from tricky to traumatic.

One final observation, neither an advantage nor a disadvantage but double-edged, is that since celebrity is probably a factor in newsworthiness, making a celebrity of the CEO is likely to lead to more media coverage. See chapter 10 for a discussion of newsworthiness (news factors) in relation to the adoption of a high or low media profile.

Strategy or ego

The biggest problem of all with a personality strategy, and the clinching reason why the disadvantages outweigh the advantages in most cases, is the very personality of the leader around which the whole strategy revolves. Charisma is the key qualification for a personality that is ideal for projection but charisma tends to go hand-in-hand with self-belief to the point of delusion and attention seeking to the point of obsession. Shakespeare's portrayal of Julius Caesar is probably close to the truth, Caesar comparing himself with the brightest star in the sky just before he is assassinated.

One day, the CFO of a large listed company, my client, was asked a relatively obscure question on a call with an analyst and gave a number that sounded plausible in response. It was one I didn't know and at the end of the call I queried it, to be told that it wasn't his policy to admit to not knowing. He had made the number up. He only told me this, of course, because the opportunity to show how clever he was, impressing the analyst, trumped the enforced admission of ignorance.

The CFO's behavior is explained by cognitive dissonance. He believed it was necessary in his position to appear to be an expert and indeed omniscient about the company. His lack of knowledge was inconsistent with this and therefore made him uncomfortable. He resolved the inconsistency by inventing a plausible answer.

In the psychology of motivation, pioneered by William James, people who think of themselves as experts and believe that they are viewed by others as experts are satisfying the important need for esteem. James explained this with his concept of "the social self" —

"A man's social self is the recognition which he gets from his mates. We are not only gregarious animals, liking to be in sight of our fellows, but we have an innate propensity to get ourselves noticed, and noticed favorably, by our kind. No more fiendish punishment could be devised, were such a thing physically possible, than that one should be turned loose in society and remain absolutely unnoticed by all the members thereof. If no one turned round when we entered, answered when we spoke, or minded what we did, but if every person we met 'cut us dead,' and acted as if we were non-existing things, a kind of rage and impotent despair would ere long well up in us, from which the cruelest bodily tortures would be a relief; for these would make us feel that, however bad might be our plight, we had not sunk to such a depth as to be unworthy of attention at all."[6]

"Our social self-seeking… is carried on directly through… our desire to please and attract notice and admiration, our emulation and jealousy, our love of glory, influence, and power, and indirectly through whichever of the material self-seeking impulses prove serviceable as means to social ends."[7]

James proposed a hierarchy of selves. At the bottom is the material or bodily self, whose needs include clothing, family, home and property. Then comes the social self, as just set out. At the highest level is the spiritual self, "a man's inner or subjective being."[8] This idea of a hierarchy was developed by Abraham Maslow into the familiar hierarchy of needs, in which esteem — both self-esteem and the respect of others — is the highest level of a person's basic needs. The idea was also taken up by Dale Carnegie in his popular classic, "How to Win Friends and Influence People," which highlighted the extraordinary lengths to which people will go to feel good about themselves and justify unjustifiable conduct.[9] He cited Al Capone, who said: "I have spent the best years of my life giving people the lighter pleasures, helping them have a good time, and all I get is abuse, the existence of a hunted man." He wasn't joking.

There is an element of self-delusion when the need for esteem goes this far which may perhaps be explained by memory metamorphosing over the years into a narrative with heroes (including ourselves) and villains.[10] (The significance of narrative in communication is examined in chapter 9.) Some observers of the financial bubble of the 2000s believe that self-importance and self-delusion were intrinsic to the development of the global financial crisis.[11]

The need for esteem is often at the root of interviews that go out of control. The interview itself involves intense one-on-one attention for the needy subject. Media coverage feeds the needy subject. People we know are likely to read the interview or watch it. We believe that they are likely to be impressed by it, compliment us on it, and talk to other people about it. The combination of the interview and its follow-up in print or broadcast can be irresistible. As a result, all too often, decisions to do interviews are not made as part of a carefully worked out strategy.

For many people, doing interviews becomes virtually automatic. Attention — from the media and the resulting public attention — may be a temptation they cannot resist. Or attention may meet a psychological need. Whichever it is, seeking attention is never a good reason for seeking a higher profile. (Another communication strategy that tends to be adopted in response to psychological pressures, and is sometimes combined with the personality strategy, is a strategy of optimism, discussed in chapter 6.)

There must always be a suspicion that the leader promotes himself as the face of his company, (it is nearly always a man), not as a sound strategy but to satisfy his need for esteem. This corporate despot is typically an absolute ruler in all but name and has the power to do indulge it. Another common symptom of corporate egotism is the grandiose new headquarters building.

An agency I worked for (in the years before YouTube) came across an opportunity to show external material on a cable channel at unsocial hours but for a relatively small fee. The chairman of one of my clients had a planet-sized ego. Naturally, one of his responsibilities was to preside and make a speech at the annual stockholders meeting, at which there was never any dissent. I suggested broadcasting the meeting. The night-time broadcast performed a public service by relieving insomnia as well as a private service by soothing the chairman's ego but did nothing for the client company. This escapade took place before I recognized the need for strategic focus (see chapter 18).

It is worst of all if the leader's spotlit personality is also in heat. The incendiary reaction between ego and libido, which readily trigger visceral factors, has been one of the causes of leadership problems since time immemorial.

Key points
- The pivotal role of the leader has led many organizations to base their communication strategy on the personality of the leader.
- The advantages of this strategy include simplicity, the appeal of celebrity for the media that helps achieve a high profile, and (possibly) increased personal contact.
- On the other hand, the personality strategy has disadvantages. It may be seen by critics as a last resort, it gambles everything on one personality, and it is superficial.
- If personality goes out of control, there will be damaging consequences.

The Augustus Paradox

A personality strategy is more likely to succeed if the leader does not have the typical assertive, confident, energetic CEO/field marshal personality (ENTJ in the Myers-Briggs typology). This is the *Augustus Paradox*. Consider two contrasting role models from Ancient Rome.

Julius Caesar was the ancient world's most obvious model, with Alexander the Great, for leaders considering a personality strategy. Assertive, confident and energetic, he was a great commander ("Veni, vidi, vici") and had a genius for self-promotion. He was an exceptionally gifted speaker, judged by no less an orator than Cicero to be peerless. In his first book, "De Bello Gallico," he dazzled Romans with his exploits in Gaul. In his second book, "De Bello Civili," he cast himself as the victim of a conspiracy and explained why (according to him) he had been forced to make war on the Senate.

But Caesar was a gambler ("Alea iacta est"), continually risking everything and gambling again. The ensuing civil war would decide whether he would rule the Roman world or lose — at best a hunted exile, at worst a corpse. He joined battle at Pharsalus as an enemy of the Senate with an exhausted, depleted army outnumbered two to one by Pompey the Great. Not for the first time in his career, the game was almost lost. But the charismatic adventurer won the battle and became dictator for life.

He yearned for public recognition and reveled in the most magnificent triumphs, spectacles and celebrations yet seen in Rome, including a naval battle staged in a specially built lake.[12] He had the most prominent statues, a golden seat in the Senate house and the month of July was renamed after him. The Republic had never granted such honors before.

Caesar, a man in a hurry, was unable to forge an enduring regime, and was assassinated ("Et tu, Brute.") Less than four years after Pharsalus he fell at the base of Pompey's statue. Gibbon said: "Caesar had provoked his fate, as much by the ostentation of his power as by his power itself."[13]

Caesar's great nephew, Octavian, later took and is generally known by the name Augustus. At the age of 18, Augustus found himself Caesar's heir. Like Caesar, he obtained power through force of arms and political maneuvering. But, unlike Caesar, he kept it and died in bed at what was then the very old age of 76. "In the life of Augustus, we behold the tyrant of the republic, converted, almost by imperceptible degrees, into the father of his country, and of human kind."[14]

As Augustus made his way to supreme power, he did so cautiously and modestly. Make haste slowly — "festina lente" — was the motto that served him well throughout his career, including over forty years in government. He managed the state and personal relations to nurture the impression that, although his personal status was matched only by Caesar's, he was not an autocrat but first among equals. "To resume in a few words, the system of the Imperial government, as it was instituted by Augustus... it may be defined an absolute monarchy disguised by the forms of a commonwealth."[15] For this to have any credibility, it was necessary for his behavior to be carefully controlled.

Although the communication strategy of Augustus has been described as "a great assault on the psychology of a generation,"[16] by the standards of ancient monarchs, it was a subtle and targeted assault. "He wished to deceive the people by an image of civil liberty and the armies by an image of civil government."[17] As Macaulay said, "The policy of wise rulers has always been to disguise strong acts under popular forms. It was thus that Augustus and Napoleon established absolute monarchies, while the public regarded them merely as eminent citizens invested with temporary magistracies."[18] The cult of personality was relatively subdued. "The imperious spirit of the first Caesar too easily consented to assume, during his lifetime, a place among the tutelary deities of Rome. The milder temper of his successor declined so dangerous an ambition."[19] His friend Agrippa built the Pantheon in Rome (not the present building) and wanted to dedicate his new temple to Augustus. Augustus declined the honor and asked that it should contain no statue of himself. This may have been an orchestrated opportunity for Augustus to show how modest he was but the point is precisely that modesty was an aspect of the image he projected.[20] (The Romans named a month after Augustus but not until he had been in shared or sole power for half a century.)

Instead, he promulgated the attractive narrative of a new age of Augustan Peace, partnership between the heritages of Greece and Rome, and, less convincingly, moral reconstruction. Augustus encouraged the flowering of art and literature and, remarkably for an autocrat in all but name, tolerated humor at his own expense. Alternative narratives that would have been less helpful to his regime were allowed to wither and die. His most characteristic move was made in 27 BC when, aged 35, and having eliminated all rebels and pacified all provinces, instead of raising himself to a new authority, he went to the Senate, gave back to it the formalities of power, and officially restored the republic. This was not a sudden impulse. He had chosen the moment, the audience was prepared, and from then on, the customs and appearances of the republic continued while he remained the ultimate authority.

Discretion, consistency and control contributed as much in the long run as actively spreading the word. Everything he communicated was crafted, from what he said to what his statues looked like.

According to Daniel Kahneman's book summarizing advances of behavioral psychology in understanding how decisions are made, "Thinking, Fast and Slow," thinking takes two different forms, which he refers to using the metaphor of two agents, sometimes referred to as System 1 and System 2.[21] System 1 is the fast, unconscious and automatic thinking that enables us to remember, recognize and react instantly. System 1 takes a shower, drives the car, recognizes the neighbors, and so on. System 1 controls most of what we do, most of the time. System 2 is the much slower, conscious, deliberate, laborious process that enables us to think. System 2 is the in-house strategist. System 1 handles most of our communication and most of the time it does a good job. But System 1's communication style is colloquial, spontaneous and unstructured. System 1 produces knee-jerk reactions, jokes, flashes of inspiration, and rough guesses, rather than accuracy, rigor or sophistication. In poorly ordered minds, System 1 is in charge of tweets and Facebook comments. This is all very well for those who are not in public life. But in the high risk, high stress situation of a media interview or a press conference, it is the System 1 messages, and sometimes the individual words, that get people into trouble. The solution is to ensure that System 2 rather than System 1 handles these critical, sensitive events.

Where Caesar relied on the automatic system, Augustus preferred deliberative thinking. How can we possibly know this? Because he was reported by Suetonius to be in the habit of writing everything down in advance of a meeting to make sure that he said what he planned to say, no more and no less. The habit became so ingrained with Augustus that he made notes before speaking to his own wife. This makes him sound grim and cold.

In fact, he had a hot temper that he found difficult to restrain. It was because he recognized the present danger of saying or doing something he would regret that he took the precaution of writing himself an aide-mémoire or script. It was thanks to his self-control and planning that he appeared to rise above human failings and maintained this superhuman image for decades.

Succession

In the ancient world, succession was an abiding problem. The ruthless struggle for succession, to obtain the power conferred by the most important magistracies, ultimately brought the Roman Republic to an end. Under the empire, the transition from one reign to the next should have been a matter of inheritance but continually gave cause for insurrection. Although succession is nowadays supposed to be on the basis of merit, it remains troublesome. Communication issues arise, particularly when the selection process is protracted or contested, or when the departure of the incumbent is involuntary.

Yahoo! Inc. is on its fifth (interim or permanent) CEO since co-founder Jerry Yang stepped down in 2009. On September 6, 2011, the company removed Yang's successor, Carol Bartz, without explaining why.[22]

Bartz was swiftly interviewed by *Fortune* magazine. Telling *Fortune* about the firing, she reportedly said: "These people f—ed me over." She said that the board still expected her to grow revenue even though they had been told there would be no growth before the next year. And she said that the board was haunted by its decision not to sell the company to Microsoft before her arrival. "'The board was so spooked by being cast as the worst board in the country,' Bartz says. 'Now they're trying to show that they're not the doofuses [idiots] that they are.'"[23]

She risked that her legacy would be the manner of her departure rather than her achievements in the job.

When an executive is forced out, without justification in his or her view, one possible plan is to try to put the record straight, and possibly even take revenge on the employer. Once the immediate shock of being fired has receded, it may become clear that a better plan than "putting the record straight" is to ask the question: "How can I repair the damage to my reputation and find a way to take my career forward again?" The reality is that this is a damage control situation. No communication strategy can deliver the emotional need for revenge without making the rational objective of career recovery more difficult to achieve.

Succession is a difficult time for organizations as well as the people who are involved. It is often fraught with communication problems including the behavior of departing executives, the behavior of disappointed candidates, and the behavior of dissenting directors. When the succession is likely to be anything other than a coronation, the best communication strategy is careful orchestration of silence. It can be done. If absolute silence can't be achieved, any sound should at least be pianissimo. The sound to be avoided is one like the fortissimo response to the 2014 change of editor at the *New York Times*: "World reacts to Abramson's ousting with vitriol, dismay."[24] (See also page 64.)

Loud or quiet?

Doubts about the assumption that the CEO needs to be a charismatic leader like Julius Caesar have been borne out by modern research. Rakesh Khurana argued that boards have been selecting CEOs under the illusion that charisma is the key to performance.[25] Another study of the CEOs of 128 companies concluded that the perception that a CEO was charismatic was not correlated with the performance of the business.[26]

Well, surely businesses at least need someone who is both comfortable and accomplished at going out and talking to the media or to large audiences, someone stentorian and confident, someone with John Wayne's on-screen personality?

In view of the prejudice in favor of extrovert CEOs, it would be surprising if a majority of CEOs were not in fact extroverts. But it is not at all hard to think of highly successful CEOs who are said to be introverts. In case of difficulty, consult Susan Cain's book, "Quiet: The Power of Introverts in a World that Can't Stop Talking."[27] Many CEOs who are not household names are quietly and effectively getting on with the job. If you have never heard of them, they probably don't care. They don't need a high profile for their businesses to flourish.

A high profile in business comes partly from deliberate action and partly from circumstances. A low profile CEO can suddenly become a household name in a crisis. And for substantial businesses, one corporate action guaranteed to mean more scrutiny is going public. The late Michele Ferrero's low profile was possible in part because Ferrero remained a private company. When one of the world's largest private companies, Glencore, sought a stock market listing in 2011, it was thrust into the limelight. Its prospectus alone ran, transparently, to 1,637 pages. The media suddenly wanted to know everything. As result of its new status, Glencore is in the thick of issues that have been raised about large mining companies including treatment of indigenous peoples, workers' conditions, and environmental performance, whose public airing its public company status unintentionally promotes.[28]

Whether to seek a high profile or a low profile is an important but neglected question on which there is more in chapters 8, 10 and 16. And chapter 5 discusses the option of silence.

The critics of public companies like Glencore, and other institutions, call for greater transparency. To what extent should you embrace openness and transparency? That is the subject of chapter 3.

Over-exposure

The quality of management is a critical success factor for any business. Although it is therefore true that no company can escape at least a partial identification with its leader, it is open to each company, as it was to the leading figure in post-Republican Rome, to determine how far this goes. Intensive use of social media in the name of the personality, prominent appearance on websites with photos — "a personal message from our CEO" — frequent quotes in the media, and so on are evidence of a personality strategy. This cult of personality is a symptom of excess that many believe accompanied the long bull market in equities and contributed to the global financial crisis.

Public relations advisers often encourage corporate leaders to spend time with journalists but would they be better advised to spend that time with strategically important people such as the owners of large amounts of stock or political leaders? (See chapter 12.) For a few, schmoozing and manipulating journalists is a special skill. But for the majority, there is little point. Many years ago, I accompanied a well-known CEO to a memorably depressing lunch with a business editor. The CEO took no interest in his guest and had no product to promote or story to sell. Instead, he told the editor his favorite anecdotes and lectured him on his pet management theories. The lunch helped him to feel important and maintain status but achieved little for his business.

Hobnobbing with journalists can be dangerous if the chemistry is poor or the CEO is indiscreet. Although some journalists feel vicariously important when they spend time with business leaders, all journalists want a story or, at least, interesting background information. It is in their nature. Set-piece interview or profile formats, such as Bloomberg Television's "Eye to Eye," *The Globe and Mail*'s "The Lunch" and "Lunch with the FT" (*Financial Times*), are a case of symbiosis between public relations and journalism. For the media, it can be an easy way to manufacture interesting content. For public relations departments and consultants, it can be an easy way to glorify and flatter the leader. However, like any interview, these pieces can easily go wrong because journalists are not hunting for the CEO's taste in breakfast cereal or regurgitated material from a PowerPoint presentation but for news.

Broadcast interviews also cause exposure problems. Television and radio news programs routinely incorporate interviews. Most come and go in a flash and are swiftly forgotten. Some are upgraded to news. The interviewee says something that is quickly picked up and repeated in the next news bulletin, both on the station that did the interview and on other stations, perhaps around the world. This is no problem if the CEO has gone on the program with a carefully prepared message, intending to deliver a sound bite, and avoiding questions on unwelcome subjects, and is delighted when it trends. If not, it is a problem.

Social media activity is even more dangerous. How much damage can someone do in 140 characters? The answer is —

more than in ten times as many. In our brave second decade of the 21st century, every person with access to the internet has the opportunity to display our scintillating intelligence — or show how dumb we are — in front of millions of people, so long as we confine ourselves to 140 characters or less. The sensitive ego may be flattered by the number of followers Twitter recruits. Twitter encapsulates the dangers of social media, though other social media may be just as dangerous:

- It is easy for sensible thinking to be converted into foolishness by being compressed into 140 characters.
- Anyone can dash off a tweet, without the vital second opinion that removes a high proportion of the errors from more conventional communications.
- In the prevailing atmosphere of informality, tweeting is ever so tempting.
- A dodgy tweet, even from someone with a handful of followers who may all be known to the writer, often escapes and finds its way around the world within minutes.

Key points
- The natural assumption is that the ideal candidate for a personality strategy is a charismatic leader such as Julius Caesar. Actually, the subtle, cautious and self-controlled personality of Augustus offers a better role model — "Festina lente."
- The assumption that the extrovert leader should also be a high profile evangelist is also incorrect.
- Whatever profile an organization adopts, the leader faces the danger of over-exposure.

In Summary

- A common communication strategy when the boss is larger than life is to focus on personality. The personality strategy has certain advantages but it is fraught with danger. Augustus may be a better role model for leaders than Julius Caesar.
- The advantages of a high profile are obvious. But there are also disadvantages, explored in later chapters, which develop the idea that profile should be designed to fit the strategy.

References

[1] Rosie Scammell, 'Italy Mourns Nutella Creator Michele Ferrero,' *The Guardian*, February 16, 2015. Rachel Sanderson, Michele Ferrero, Confectioner & Nutella Creator, 1925-2015, *Financial Times*, February 15, 2015.

[2] Edward Gibbon, *The History of the Decline and Fall of the Roman Empire*, Vol. 1, edited by J. B. Bury,1776-1788, (New York: Fred de Fau & Company, 1906), 75.

[3] John D. Graham, 'Making the CEO the Chief Communications Officer: Counseling Senior Management' in *The Handbook of Strategic Public Relations & Integrated Communications*, ed. by Charles L. Caywood, (New York: McGraw-Hill, 1997), 279.

[4] Geoff Colvin, 'The World's Most Admired Companies: Built for Brilliance,' *Fortune*, March 18, 2013.

[5] Youngju "YJ" Sohn, Ruthann Weaver Lariscy & Spencer F. Tinkham, 'The Impact of CEO Reputation: Negative News and Economic Decisions,' *International Journal of Strategic Communication*, Vol. 3, No. 1, (2009), 1-18.

[6] William James, *The Principles of Psychology*, (London: Macmillan and Co., Ltd., 1890), 293-4.

[7] James, *The Principles of Psychology*, 308.

[8] James, *The Principles of Psychology*, 296.

[9] Dale Carnegie, *How to Win Friends and Influence People*, 1936, (New York: Simon and Schuster, 2009), 4-20.

[10] Carol Tavris & Elliott Aronson, *Mistakes Were Made (But Not By Me): Why We Justify Foolish Beliefs, Bad Decisions and Hurtful Acts*, (Orlando, FL: Harcourt, Inc., 2007), 76.

[11] Gretchen Morgenson & Joshua Rosner, Reckless Endangerment: How Outsized Ambition, Greed, and Corruption Led to Economic Armageddon, (New York: St Martin's Griffin, 2012).

[12] David S. Potter, 'Spectacle,' in *A Companion to the Roman Empire*, ed. by David S. Potter (Oxford: Blackwell Publishing, 2010), 400.

[13] Gibbon, *Decline and Fall*, Vol. 1, (1906), 90.

[14] Gibbon, *Decline and Fall*, Vol. 3, (1906), 170.

[15] Gibbon, *Decline and Fall*, Vol. 1, (1906), 86.

[16] J. A. Crook, 'Augustus: Power, Authority, Achievement,' in *The Cambridge Ancient History*, Vol. X: The Augustan Empire 43 B.C. - A.D. 69, ed. by Alan K. Bowman, Edward Champlin & Andrew Lintott, (Cambridge University Press, 1996), 113-146.

[17] Gibbon, *Decline and Fall*, Vol. 1, (1906), 90.

[18] Thomas Babington Macaulay, *History of England from the Accession of James II*, 1848 (London: J. M. Dent & Sons Ltd, 1953), 55.

[19] Gibbon, *Decline and Fall*, Vol. 1, (1906), 88.

[20] Adrian Goldsworthy, *Augustus: First Emperor of Rome,* (Yale University Press, 2014), 259.

[21] Daniel Kahneman, *Thinking, Fast and Slow*, (New York: Farrar, Straus and Giroux, 2011).

[22] 'Yahoo! Announces Leadership Reorganization,' Yahoo! Inc. news release, September 6, 2011.

[23] Patricia Sellers, 'Carol Bartz Exclusive: Yahoo F—ed Me Over,' *Fortune*, September 8, 2011.

[24] Claire Atkinson, 'World Reacts to Abramson's Ousting with Vitriol, Dismay,' *New York Post*, May 16, 2014.

[25] Rakesh Khurana, *Searching for a Corporate Savior: The Irrational Quest for Charismatic CEOs*, (Princeton University Press, 2002).

[26] Bradley R. Agle, Nandu J. Nagarajan, Jeffrey A. Sonnenfeld & Dhinu Srinivasan, 'Does CEO Charisma Matter? An Empirical Analysis of the Relationships among Organizational Performance, Environmental Uncertainty, and Top Management Team Perceptions of CEO Charisma,' *The Academy of Management Journal*, Vol. 49, No. 1, (February 2006), 161-174.

---

[27] Susan Cain, *Quiet: The Power of Introverts in a World that Can't Stop Talking*, (New York: Crown Publishers, 2012). This book is full of examples of successful people the author believes to be introverts.

[28] Jim Armitage, 'Is It Wrong to Buy Glencore Shares?' *The Guardian*, May 21, 2014.

CHAPTER 3

Stripping Business: Pressure to reveal all

"The transition from private to public can be brutal, as many of us discover each morning."
— Antoine Prost, "Private and Public Spheres in France"[1]

October 25, 1983, dawned with the news that American forces had landed on Grenada, where there had recently been a military coup backed by Cuba. President Reagan recalled in his autobiography: "We decided not to inform anyone in advance about the rescue mission in order to reduce the possibilities of a leak."[2]

Operation Urgent Fury was launched with such stealth that Reagan did not even admit what was going on to his closest ally, Margaret Thatcher, until it was too late. With anti-imperial revulsion at its peak and Soviet influence still strong, there would have been no chance of winning international support for an intervention in Grenada. The United Nations General Assembly duly voted 108-9 to deplore it.

Journalists were not allowed into Grenada for three days and television news had to rely on official footage that did not show any fighting.[3] The media were initially outraged to have been excluded but the invasion soon came to be viewed as a success.[4] Operation Urgent Fury, now seen as little more than a footnote to the history of the cold war, highlighted the crude advantage to be gained by keeping the enemy, and everyone else, in ignorance and controlling the news.

But secrecy is out of fashion. Openness and transparency are in fashion. What to do? That is the subject of this chapter.

Strategic considerations

In his eclectic history of strategy, Lawrence Freedman stressed that it has always involved an element of deception. Guile and stealth have been used as alternatives or adjuvants to force. The Greeks only captured Troy, after the ten-year siege, when Odysseus deceived the Trojans with the wooden horse. Freedman put the wooden horse on the front cover of his book.[5]

Countless campaigns and battles down the centuries involved an element of surprise. In the second world war, for example, pre-emptive strikes, bluffs, feints and intrigues played a vital part in the most decisive actions:

Fig 3.1 Second World War: Some Decisive Surprises

Soviet invasion of Poland from September 17, 1939	… in accordance with secret provisions of the Nazi-Soviet Pact. Only three Polish divisions were guarding the 800-mile long border.
German invasion of France, May 1940	Panzer divisions crossed the Meuse and broke through near Sedan instead of invading Flanders as expected.
German invasion of Russia, June 22, 1941	Despite warnings, Barbarossa took Stalin completely by surprise.
Japanese attack on Pearl Harbor, December 7, 1941	The surprise that was successful but suicidal.
Battle of Midway, June 4-7, 1942	American ambush and sinking of the core of Japan's fleet, made possible by the decryption of enemy signals.
D-Day landings, June 6, 1944	Made in Normandy rather than the obvious Pas de Calais, after deception on a large scale.
Victory in the Atlantic over the U-boats	Code-breaking enabled the Allies to read enemy communications.

Surprise has been a key element in political and business strategy as well, although it tends to be neglected. Business strategists prefer to talk about the closely related idea of disruption but, according to the leading textbook by Arthur Thompson and colleagues, one of the principles of the best offensive strategies is "employing the element of surprise as opposed to doing what rivals expect and are prepared for."[6]

In contemporary business strategy, surprise is perhaps most prominent in the blue ocean strategy proposed by Chan Kim and Renée Mauborgne. They imagined a market universe divided between red oceans, representing the known market space of existing industries, and blue oceans of untapped market space. The essence of blue ocean strategy is to develop a new market in that free space where there is no existing competition.[7] This is what Apple did with the iPad. Surprise is not explicit in blue ocean strategy but it is inherent because market space is unlikely to remain unoccupied if you announce to everyone that you are planning to occupy it.

Secrecy and surprise in warfare began to be more difficult with the appearance in the mid-19th century of war correspondents, sending eyewitness accounts to newspapers by telegraph. Battles could no longer be fought entirely beyond public scrutiny. The military developed increasingly sophisticated machinery to control and influence the images and messages reaching the public.[8] But this attempt to manage the news was contrary to the zeitgeist of the late 20th century. Public opinion increasingly pressed for institutions to abandon secrecy in favor of openness and transparency.

And the public relations industry professes to have embraced openness and transparency. The leading public relations textbooks all invoke transparency.[9] Transparency naturally involves rejecting surprise as a stratagem. It is argued that public relations is about relationships, relationships depend on trust, and unexpected actions destroy trust. A more balanced view would be that relationships of trust are important but no guarantee, and surprise can be highly effective. (See chapter 4 on the role of the PR industry.)

Society has rightly set limits to how far deception can be used without breaking the law. But some have further argued that business also has an ethical obligation to be open and transparent. Everyone must act within a framework of law but to what extent should businesses have additional social obligations? Additional, extralegal obligations would be a constraint on strategy when performance in business, politics or any other strategic game is often enhanced by playing one's cards close to one's chest. This chapter examines to what extent organizations should accede to the demand for openness and transparency.

The opening of information

Secrecy is the default status for information in autocratic societies but, in the West, secrecy has been going out of fashion for centuries, at least since the unsuccessful attempt to suppress translations of the Bible into the vernacular in the early Renaissance.

Steadily increasing access to all kinds of information has been one of the most important long-term trends of the modern era. It has become hard to believe, for example, the extent of Portuguese control of information about Asia in the 16th century.[10] The centuries of struggle for religious freedom and toleration, for freedom of scientific inquiry and exchange, for freedom of the press, and for democratic government, with brief interruptions in times of total war, created a climate in which secrecy came to be viewed with deep suspicion.

The Vietnam War was open like no previous war, as a result of the collapse of military censorship and the presence of hundreds of American journalists on the ground.[11] Rising public opposition to the war made the media more receptive to dissent. The pivotal moment may have been in 1968, when a South Vietnamese general was filmed executing a bound Vietcong prisoner in the street.[12]

Three developments heralded a new public attitude to the use and abuse of information:

- The disintegration of the Soviet Union after 1989 ended the cold war and closed down the secret police (in theory). Some expected a new epoch of peace and openness.

- Richard Nixon, the secretive president who paradoxically arranged for himself to be bugged, was ruined by the Watergate break-in. The cover-up loomed larger in the media and popular imagination than the original crime. It was a subversive novelty for journalists to be cast as heroes played by movie stars, while the head of state was the villain.[13] (See also chapter 5.)

- The internet not only made available an undreamt-of quantity of information but fostered an assumption that information would always be available.

The volume of information is exploding so that most of the data is new within the last couple of years. Quintillions of bytes are added each day.[14] The sheer quantity of new data is of little value if hardly any of it adds to the sum of human knowledge, thinking of mass social media activity. Some of the world's greatest thinkers have lamented what they see as quantity supplanting quality. The internet is indiscriminate. It sometimes seems like a museum where there are no exhibitions, just immense piles of artefacts no one has sifted through. And data can even conceal.

"Secrecy is repugnant"

President John F. Kennedy captured the prevailing mood: "The very word 'secrecy' is repugnant in a free and open society."[15] Secrecy is a Bad Thing. Freedom of information, transparency, openness, and all that jazz is a Good Thing. Governments, businesses and other institutions should aim to be completely open and transparent. The new public attitude to information precipitated the passage of freedom of information laws (also known as open records or sunshine laws) in most advanced economies. Apart from being wrong to keep secrets, it would be futile to try, in an age of the internet, Facebook with a billion members, Twitter and the ubiquitous camera phone.

This is an oversimplification. The above Kennedy dictum, taken out of context, is a travesty of what the president intended. For in this 1961 speech, he called for both greater public information and greater respect for official secrecy. The purpose of the speech was to plead with the press for restraint, asking themselves in relation to any story not only "Is it news?" but also "Is it in the interest of the national security?"

Quoting Kennedy in "Necessary Secrets," Gabriel Schoenfeld dismantled much of the conventional wisdom on secrecy by examining the evolution of the complex relationship between press freedom and national security in America over three centuries. The new model democracy recognized from the outset that government must be with the informed consent of the governed. However, the Founding Fathers tend to be cast as promoters of unrestrained freedom of speech, which was far from the case. In fact, from the oath of secrecy taken by the members of the Second Continental Congress onwards, the young republic took measures to protect the secrets necessary for its national security.[16] In the present day, Barack Obama began his presidency promising that his administration would be "the most transparent of all time," but soon stated: "I have fought for the principle that the United States must carry out covert activities and hold information that is classified for the purposes of national security and will do so again."[17]

Subversive media conduct was taken to its recent extreme by WikiLeaks, which exists "to bring important news and information to the public," and specifically by what has often been called the biggest leak in history (at least in quantity of data). This was the publication on the internet in November 2010 of 500,000 military and diplomatic cables from SIPRNet, the US government's private network. (Although the repercussions of the "biggest leak" were mainly political and diplomatic, there were also consequences for business. For example, Shell feared it could lose valuable oil interests in Nigeria after a leaked diplomatic cable shed unwelcome light on its activities.)[18]

Leaks continued, notably with *The Guardian*'s publication in 2013 of details of American and British government surveillance programs, provided by Edward Snowden.[19] This leaked security measures rather than who said what to whom. Many professed to be dismayed. They were dismayed even though it came 15 years after the Hollywood movie, "Enemy of the State."[20] In the movie, Gene Hackman's retired spy showed Will Smith's lawyer that the only way to keep out of sight of the US National Security Agency (NSA) — even back then — was to avoid all networks, including the phone and the internet. They were dismayed even though Hollywood is not normally out in front of the news. And they were dismayed even though some of them were politicians who preside over their own states' surveillance programs.[21]

The head of Britain's Security Service warned of the damage caused by exposing "the reach and limits of [surveillance] techniques... Such information hands the advantage to the terrorists. It is the gift they need to evade us and strike at will. Unfashionable as it might seem, that is why we must keep secrets secret."[22]

Julian Assange, leader of WikiLeaks, encapsulated the extreme anti-secrecy position: "All institutions — all — are engaged in unjust activities... We look for that information which the institution does not want to be released."[23] WikiLeaks apparently saw no contradiction between distributing stolen information and complaining of others' infringement of privacy.[24]

There is no reason for national security leaks to be beyond prosecution. Whatever its ideals, WikiLeaks is not defending but damaging the democracies. Governments will be reluctant to risk prosecuting the media, in a public trial of Secrecy vs. Openness, in the current climate of opinion, but may need to resort to more subtle measures.

Business under pressure

Business is under almost as much pressure as government to be open and transparent. By the mid-1970s, a relatively benign business environment had been replaced by widespread hostility among politicians, journalists and the general public. Whereas some professional communicators saw it as their duty to protect secrets, leading experts were moving in the opposite direction.

More and more information is becoming available. Critics are becoming better and better organized. Some critics rejoiced that, as a result, "The corporation is becoming naked."[25] Translated into business English, this means that groups that would once have been dismissed as extremists, on the fringes of society, have reinvented themselves as "stakeholders," often a euphemism for stake*scroungers*, and now demand the same consideration from businesses as major shareholders, say, or large customers. (See chapter 12.) Their main weapon is information that can be manipulated to damage a business in the service of their own ideological ends. They are being aided by those who believe in transparency for its own sake. And some believe that resistance is futile because soon everything will be known about every institution. Resistance is not futile but may be more effective when it does not hit headlines.

Transparency is almost certainly here to stay. Organizations have to come to terms with persistent pressure for transparency. But that does not mean that they should strive for total transparency. The *appearance of transparency* may be expedient but businesses don't need to practice corporate naturism. They should control disclosure carefully (see below). They should take measures to protect commercial confidentiality, especially intellectual property, to protect customer data, and to prevent defamation and other unfair criticism.

Are secrets facing extinction?

Has technology made any attempt at keeping secrets futile? Is it true, as one leading PR textbook says, that: "Technology makes transparency mandatory; it is simply foolish to think that bad news can be hidden, mistakes can remain secret, and misdeeds will not get reported"?[26] We now live in a world of 24-hour news with instant reporting both by professional journalists and, increasingly, by people who happen to witness events or wish to express opinions. Misbehavior by members of the armed forces has been revealed to the world when soldiers used their phones to take incriminating photographs. Pictures, film and written accounts of the Asian tsunami in 2004 were distributed immediately by tourists caught up in it.[27] In the Arab Spring protests of 2011, people wielding cameras and phones evaded the news blackouts of dictatorships,[28] although more traditional weapons have come to the fore as idealism has given way to terror and civil war. And realization has dawned that what *Time* called the "surveillance society" has "the ability to collect and store billions of pieces of data forever."[29]

Yet the essential arithmetic of news is unchanged. Collecting and storing data is one thing: noticing a particular piece of information and doing something about it is something else entirely. What makes news is mass interest, traditionally determined by news editors. Now the mass audience sometimes chooses for itself through social media but this is not the same as information coming to public attention being unavoidable. Of all the billions of tweets, blog items, Facebook updates and so on, only a minuscule proportion become news. But the key change is that if they do become news, they do so quickly, and there is no longer any chance of control with a word in the editor's ear.

If, from the depths of some remote war zone, pictures or film can emerge of soldiers, militia or secret police mistreating prisoners or civilians and be seen around the world, surely it would be futile to think that what goes on in the center of a city like New York or London can go on in secret? Secrets can not only be passed on but exploded on the internet. But contrast this notion of instant explosive transparency with the horror story of the sinister television entertainer, Jimmy Savile, who allegedly abused hundreds of children in a 40-year career. Much of the abuse took place in rooms next door to a television studio but was not unmasked by the media or investigated by the police until after his death in 2011, far into the supposed age of transparency.

In the global internet café, distance or proximity is a poor guide to the chances of keeping a secret. Isaac Asimov's allegorical science fiction "Foundation" series imagined, back in the 1950s, that the safest hiding place for the biggest secret in the galaxy would be in plain sight.[30]

The belief that we already inhabit a world where secrets have been abolished is naïve. If secrets had been abolished we would also, for example, have abolished crime and criminals. The detection rate would have risen to 100%. And if that sounds like utopia, call to mind the nightmare world of 1984.

Total openness and transparency would be no more tolerable than total secrecy.

Privacy, the blind spot in transparency

Even as the clamor has risen for openness and transparency, the demand for privacy has also grown. Some people have believed that there should be a private realm, initially in opposition to the state, since the advent of individualism in Greece.[31] But full freedom from the unwanted attention of other people, is a recent invention.

It was still quite normal in 1776 for Benjamin Franklin and John Adams to share a bed while traveling together. They spent the night arguing about whether the window should be open or closed.[32]

Privacy is problematic since it is "a restraint on freedom of expression"[33] yet closely linked to liberty, concerned as it is with protection from surveillance, from the interception of private communications, from the storage and use of information about them, and from the publication of confidential or personal information. Modern readers who may deplore secrecy and welcome transparency still sympathize with Winston and his lover in "1984" when they seek privacy from the omniscient state. And there has long been some protection of privacy in law, more recently strengthened in America by judgments in tort cases and in Europe by the European Convention on Human Rights (ECHR).

Freedom of the press is usually seen as intrinsic to liberty and is enshrined in law by both the 1st amendment to the American constitution and Article 10 of the ECHR. In lawsuits against media groups, the defendants usually argue that publication of newsworthy information is in the public interest. But the press itself is also capable of oppression and it is ironic that the seekers after truth rather than the guardians of secrets have carried out the invasions of privacy which led to its becoming a major issue, at least in the UK. In real life, as in "1984," people want privacy for their relationships — and everything else — not just from the state but also from intrusive media.

A series of recent events have shown the range and strength

of this feeling. Complaints about the invasion of travelers' privacy from full-body scanners screening them for arms and explosives eventually led to the announcement that full-body scanners would be removed from airports.[34] Although Facebook was designed to be a vehicle for revealing, not concealing, personal information, user control of information sharing became an issue, particularly with the accidental and unwelcome outing of gay users.[35] Some believe that the tech industry still has not taken sufficient action to reflect the strength of public feeling about privacy.[36]

And, in Britain, News Corporation journalists were accused of illegally snooping on messages left on the phones of their prey. Accessing the phone of a murdered teenager was seen as particularly heinous. The scandal led to a number of prosecutions, staff changes, a newspaper closing, and a public inquiry led by a judge. Public opinion was on the side of privacy campaigners and the British government decided to introduce a new regulatory framework.

Burglars

Given that total privacy, confidentiality and security are unattainable, should should we just give in to the pressure for total openness and transparency?

There is an analogy with the predicament of the householder who worries about burglars. Absolute security is unattainable. It is almost impossible to prevent a burglar with enough time and resources breaking into any home. Does this make security measures futile? In practice, few leave their doors and windows wide open with their valuables on display. Residents know that most burglars are on the lookout for easy targets. They know that burglars are usually unaware either what valuables they own or where the valuables have been hidden. They know that burglars can be deterred with locks, bars at the windows, "Cave canem" signs, and so on.

So it is with the media. The average journalist operates like a casual burglar, looking for easy pickings. They are not likely to conduct the equivalent of an intensive floor-to-ceiling search of every room. They do not have unlimited time and resources to follow leads, they are generally ignorant of the existence of a secret unless they are tipped off, and they can be deterred by various defenses. Just as there is no need to invite burglars in to have a look around for booty, there is no need to invite journalists to have a look around for stories by, for example, submitting to interviews. Just as there is no need to leave doors open, there is no need to omit confidentiality clauses from employment and supply contracts. The prudent take measures to protect valuable information as well as valuable goods. Never mind your daughters, lock up your information.

Confidentiality and surprise

While organizations do not benefit from the human right to privacy, they do have compelling incentives to seek an equivalent. Commercial confidentiality feels to business much like privacy does to citizens. They are minding their own business. Just because a corporation is a public figure does not mean it should be fair game.

Leaks are neither always right nor always wrong. If a leak reveals a crime then it is justified "whistleblowing." But in many cases a leak is, as Herb Schmertz, the distinguished public affairs chief of Mobil Oil, used to say, a euphemism for theft.[37] Leaked material is stolen. There is no difference between stealing goods and stealing information, and no difference between stealing from a person or an institution.

Commercial rivalry is natural, desirable and often intense to the point of obsession, when it becomes a good subject for satire. The movie "Duplicity" sent up firms obsessively protecting their own secrets while snooping on the enemy, in a competition between two corporations making personal care products, "Burkett & Randle" and "Equikrom." But secrecy — and the surprise it makes possible — has genuinely been a factor in the achievements of numerous businesses, from technological innovators to hedge funds.[38]

Key points
- The very long term trend toward openness gathered pace thanks to the end of the Cold War, Watergate and the digital revolution. Yet there is still a place in public life for "necessary secrets."
- General revulsion toward secrecy has put pressure on institutions, including businesses, to be more open and transparent, which poses a problem for communication strategy.
- The solution is not extreme transparency. Privacy is rightly valued by business as well as citizens. Confidentiality is strategically important to business.

Fair disclosure

In the contest between openness and confidentiality, the front line runs through the communication between listed companies and capital markets. In many jurisdictions, these relations have ceased to be a free-for-all and are now governed by sophisticated regulations. In the US, these began with the Securities Exchange Acts of 1933 and 1934. But selective disclosure, whereby some people are provided with information they use to make investment decisions while the rest of the market is in ignorance, remained widespread until the Securities and Exchange Commission's (SEC's) Regulation Fair Disclosure of 2000 (Reg FD).

Reg FD put all investors on an equal footing for the first time, at least in theory. After Reg FD came into force, further financial scandals, for which Enron became the byword, led to the Sarbanes-Oxley act of 2002 that tightened up accounting practices. Similar legislation to Reg FD has been enacted in other jurisdictions. For example, in Britain, under the Financial Services and Markets Act 2000, the Financial Conduct Authority has its Disclosure Rules and Transparency Rules (DTRs).

The terminology varies between "material information" in America and "inside information" in Britain but they amount to much the same thing.

"*Material information* is knowledge that would cause an ordinary person to make a decision to buy, sell, or hold a stock."[39] The National Investor Relations Institute (NIRI) has suggested some of the kinds of material information that ought to be disclosed, such as financial results, changes in forecasted profits, "the launch of a new product or business; a pending or prospective merger, acquisition or tender offer; the sale of significant assets, or a significant subsidiary; the gain or loss of a substantial customer or supplier; and major changes in senior management."[40]

Inside information is normally defined by the Financial Services and Markets Act 2000 as "information of a precise nature which — (a) is not generally available, (b) relates, directly or indirectly, to one or more issuers of the qualifying investments or to one or more of the qualifying investments, and (c) would, if generally available, be likely to have a significant effect on the price of the qualifying investments or on the price of related investments."[41] The DTRs state that the purpose of their chapter 2 is to "promote prompt and fair disclosure of relevant information to the market," (and to specify circumstances in which a delay is acceptable).

Timing is everything

The regulations appear to be a charter for transparency. Nowadays, in principle, listed companies should announce material changes. There is a maxim for this: "When in doubt, put it out." The regulators' propaganda is all about immediate disclosure, fair disclosure, and full disclosure. Disclosure is sometimes equated with transparency. Yes, the rules have severely restricted, if not entirely eliminated, the old, unfair practice of selective disclosure. But they have not fully introduced transparency.

Inside information has such a bad name that the myth has developed that it is inherently bad, whereas it can be normal and legitimate so long as it stays within the circle of those who need to know and is necessary for business to go forward. Hence DTR 2.5.1 R provides that: "An issuer may, under its own responsibility, delay the public disclosure of inside information, such as not to prejudice its legitimate interests provided…" that delaying the disclosure would not be likely to mislead the public and that the information stays confidential.[42]

Consider some of the categories identified above by NIRI:

1. New products

"The launch of a new product or business." The introduction has already shown how Apple developed a major new product for eight years without any disclosure. No rules were broken. Apple did nothing wrong.

2. M&A activity

"Pending or prospective merger, acquisition or tender offer." In January 2014, Pfizer Inc, the giant drug maker listed in New York, held informal talks with AstraZeneca, listed in London, about the possibility of a merger. Neither disclosed this possibility. On April 20 (Easter Sunday), rumors of Pfizer's interest in acquiring AstraZeneca reached the *Sunday Times* and the rumored target's share price then rose. At this point, neither company had disclosed anything. On April 26, Pfizer renewed its approach and was rebuffed. Then, on April 28 at 0208 EDT, Pfizer made an announcement that put the record straight. But, for well over three months, neither company was obliged by the rules to tell investors what was going on.[43] Pfizer and AstraZeneca did nothing wrong.

3. Disposals

"The sale of significant assets, or a significant subsidiary." Also in January 2014, Carl Icahn, the activist investor, took a stake in eBay and publicly urged it to spin off its PayPal business into a separate listed company. There was some acrimony: "Stick to the Facts, Carl…"[44] eBay was adamant that the two businesses were "more competitive and more successful" as part of the same company.[45] Icahn fought a proxy battle in an attempt to convert eBay to his way of thinking. The proxy fight was settled with Icahn withdrawing his proposal and eBay appointing a new independent director to the board.[46]

Behind the scenes, at some stage, the board must have begun seriously considering a change of direction. Eight months after

Icahn's original stake, on September 30, eBay announced it would, after all, split into two separate listed companies in 2015.[47] There was no obligation to inform investors during several months of any discussions in private about the structure of the company. Neither Icahn nor eBay did anything wrong.

4. Management change

"Major changes in senior management." Although a material change has to be disclosed without delay, in practice, there is always a period in which the change is under consideration or pending and must be kept secret. And this can be a long period. The process of appointing a new CEO, for example, can take several months. I once advised a large company that approached three people, one after another, to become its CEO. There was no leak of either the names or how the selection process was going. Key people have to be in the know well in advance, however, providing confidentiality is maintained, the obligation to disclose does not arise until the moment the appointment is made. (It is also vital to have a contingency plan in case of a leak.)

The same considerations apply to structured disclosure, the information that must be provided periodically according to a set protocol. The SEC's number one enforcement priority has been selective disclosure of expected earnings.[48] In the US, the terms of these structured disclosures are specified in SEC documents such as the form 10-K, the annual financial report, or 10-Q, the quarterly financial report. Results announcements command investors' rapt attention. They are normally scheduled weeks or months in advance. Missing or delaying a scheduled announcement raises awkward questions and so happens rarely. The final stage before announcement is for the results to be approved by the board of directors or other appropriate authority once they are finalized. First drafts are typically prepared weeks ahead of the scheduled date. What must be included is prescribed. What may be included is discretionary. These drafts are bound to contain information that would be valuable in the hands of a trader in the company's shares. For the results to be announced at the scheduled date and time, the material must be prepared in more or less final form days before they are approved and stay strictly confidential until its release. This breaks no rules.

Beyond the limits?

Executive health is perhaps the issue that applies most pressure to the interpretation of the rules. The health of those in public or corporate office is more than just a personal matter. And for a public company, the more a CEO is identified with the company, the more closely investors will pay attention to his or her health. The question therefore arises as to what companies should disclose if the CEO's health is under threat, and when. The transparency reflex of disclosing everything immediately is unhelpful because it would be impractical, potentially misleading and intrusive to attempt to disclose every medical development.

When a key person becomes a complicated and evolving medical case, the decision about what to disclose and when can be excruciating. Take the case of Apple's visionary leader, Steve Jobs, who was diagnosed with cancer of the pancreas in October 2003. Some would argue that, in the interests of transparency, the company should immediately have announced this. They would argue that the diagnosis was material to investors, given Jobs' record and close identification with the company, and especially as the disease is usually fatal, with a five-year survival rate for all stages of only 6%, although Jobs may have had a form of the disease that was potentially curable.[49]

The case for disclosure is partly ethical, partly legal (that material information has to be disclosed), and partly practical (that the truth will come out anyway). The case against disclosure is partly ethical — the right to privacy. But the clinching, practical argument against it is that disclosure of the wrong thing at the wrong time may damage the business. In such a case, the wrong thing at the wrong time would be an open-ended announcement of the "we have a major problem and we don't have a solution" type. This tends to be followed by a loss of confidence, often accompanied by the stock going into a tailspin.

In July 2004, Jobs had an operation to remove the tumor. It was initially successful and Apple then disclosed both the cancer and the operation — the problem and its solution.[50] Jobs did not claim he had been cured, telling Stanford students in the 2005 commencement address: "Remembering that I'll be dead soon is the most important tool I've ever encountered to help me make the big choices in life."[51]

However, the disclosure dilemma recurred when it became clear to Jobs' medical team in early 2008 that his cancer was spreading, and his health then gradually deteriorated.[52] In January 2009, he went on "medical leave of absence until the end of June," and he reluctantly agreed to a liver transplant, which took place in March 2009.[53]

At what point(s) should Apple have made disclosure(s)? Apple said nothing through 2008 while Jobs' health was deteriorating. But, at the beginning of 2009, Jobs released two consecutive open letters about his health in quick succession. The first was misleading, (perhaps inadvertently), saying that the cause of his ill-health had been a mystery but had now been found to be a "hormone imbalance."[54] The second letter said that, "My health-related issues are more complex than I originally thought," and announced the medical leave. The liver transplant was not mentioned until the *Wall Street Journal* reported it in June 2009.[55] Once again, disclosure was limited until after the treatment, with Jobs returning to work and the scope for speculation largely eliminated.

Some were aghast. "When I learned Steve Jobs had a liver transplant two months ago, my first thought was, 'Wow! If I were on his PR team, I'd quit.'"[56] Paul Argenti argued that the law requires full disclosure of material information, and "if a CEO's liver transplant isn't material, what is?" He predicted that it would affect customers and employees who "were lied to or kept in the dark."[57]

There was no discernible effect on customers. Even so, should the market have been informed? The answer is that there has to be some room for maneuver. For example, when Jobs went on sick leave he could not have known when or even whether he would have the transplant. How would it have helped anyone to announce that he was *hoping* to have a transplant? When he did have the transplant, it would have been unknowable at first whether it would succeed. Again, how would it have helped to make an announcement, as soon as the surgeon put down his instruments? Imagine if Jobs' surgeon had spoken candidly, on the record, saying something like, "He's had a transplant but, at this point, we can't be sure if it will work, or even if he'll make it through the next couple of days." Looking back, former Vice-President Al Gore, who was an Apple director, told Jobs' biographer that the board had taken external advice (essential) and had acted "by the book."[58] The SEC investigated whether Apple had complied with the law. No action was taken.

In a thorny situation, Apple may have taken the best course for all concerned. However, this issue contributed to a view among some people in PR that Apple's communications have not been of the highest standard, whereas chapter 8 suggests that, on the contrary, Apple's communications have been of an outstandingly high standard.

Controlled disclosure

All this means that public companies are now operating in a regulatory framework that enjoins both confidentiality and controlled disclosure.

Controlled disclosure is a more accurate description than "fair disclosure" for what happens in practice at well-run companies. Controlled disclosure falls short of the ideal of transparency but balances the need to inform everyone simultaneously with the strategic need for confidentiality.

The need to comply with securities regulations has far-reaching effects on the totality of communications for public companies. In theory, communications with people other than investors are unregulated but, in practice, they are constrained by the obligation to avoid selective disclosure. This has made public companies more disciplined and circumspect. Yet it has made little impact on the debate about transparency. And it has made little impact on the profession and study of communications.

The communications professionals with most involvement in managing controlled disclosure are those charged with investor relations, the shorthand term for communications between public companies and their financial audiences, (current and prospective shareholders, bondholders, lenders and the capital markets at large). Investor relations may have been begotten by public relations in its own image but the two activities became estranged. Many of those working in investor relations have no background at all in conventional communications but are finance professionals or former stockbroking analysts.

And matters of disclosure and confidentiality, the daily bread of those involved in investor relations, are beyond the ken of many of those employed in or writing about public relations. Academic journals from the fields of communication and public relations virtually ignore investor relations. PR textbooks don't have much room for investor relations. Only one of the leading public relations textbooks (see chapter 4) makes a fair attempt to summarize the regulatory requirements for corporate disclosure.[59] The others treat investor relations mostly as a subject for careers advice.

A 1996 survey of Public Relations Society of America members examined their knowledge of legal issues.[60] Half of those surveyed, by their own admission, were "not at all" familiar with "SEC Regulations." They were less well informed about SEC regulations than any of the other aspects of law affecting public relations practice. Since then, securities regulations have become much more important. Has there been a commensurate improvement in the knowledge of communication professionals.

Controlled disclosure has had an interesting side effect on the business media. In the bad old days when selective disclosure was the name of the game, there was a practice in London known as the "Friday Night Drop." Financial PR agencies waited until the end of the week and then gave the best stories to pet journalists on Sunday newspapers. These Sunday newspapers were indispensable reading in the business world because they would unfailingly break news of important developments at leading companies. The story would be given a positive slant by the newspaper in return for the scoop. Now that this practice is illegal, Sunday business sections are shadows of their former selves, enlivened occasionally when an interviewee blurts out a secret. Rumor and speculation are of course alive and well, particularly on internet bulletin boards, and newspapers still predict ten out of every two takeover bids. But most company news is based on the companies' own announcements. The media then report these stories with their distinctive emphasis, analysis and comment.

Key points
- Legal reforms banned selective disclosure of material information by publicly quoted companies, under the banner of "fair disclosure."
- The reforms have put investors on a more equal footing but are not a charter for transparency.
- It remains strategically important for businesses to be very careful what information is revealed, when, and how. Fair disclosure is the mantra of politicians and regulators. The mantra for business should be controlled disclosure.

Conclusion: The professionals

People say things that land them in trouble for three main reasons. The first is that they make mistakes, of which the most important is poor strategy. The second is that psychological factors drive them to communicate in ways that are not in their best interests, or even employing a personality strategy. These two factors were discussed in chapters 1 and 2.

The third reason is that they are subject to social, political and sometimes regulatory pressure to communicate truthfully and openly. Complete transparency — a world without secrets — is an unattainable ideal. Telling everybody everything immediately would be impracticable and, at a personal level, verge on insane.

Some people harm their own interests by talking unwisely. Some are troubled by external foes. When critics call on business to be more open and transparent, often this is code for giving them the information they need to pursue their own campaigns against business interests. Some of those who counsel businesses on public issues have joined hands with critics in advising transparency. And businesses themselves are sometimes confused, almost feeling ashamed of keeping secrets.

The professionals use a variety of terms to describe what they do: public relations/affairs, corporate communications/affairs, reputation management, investor relations, media relations, crisis communications and even spin doctoring. The professionals should be working hard to eliminate gaffes and counteract the psychological and social pressures to over-communicate. They should advise a strategic approach to openness. But the PR industry has officially embraced openness and is dominated by theory and professional bodies that tend to encourage communication. Far from mitigating dangerous pressures, professional doctrine has become an additional pressure to communicate. The next chapter examines how this happened.

In Summary

- Social change has created an atmosphere in which transparency is revered and secrecy is reviled. Yet secrecy remains essential to strategy. Surprise is a vital weapon in the arsenal of communication strategy.
- Businesses should resist attacks on confidentiality, which is the commercial equivalent of privacy.
- Securities regulations prohibit selective disclosure. Regulators talk about fair disclosure. Public companies should practice *controlled disclosure*, balancing the need for simultaneous access to information with commercial confidentiality.

References

[1] Antoine Prost, 'Private and Public Spheres in France,' in *A History of Private Life: Riddles of Identity in Modern Times*, ed. by Antoine Prost & Gerard Vincent, (Belknap Press of Harvard University Press, 1991), 103.

[2] Ronald W. Reagan, *An American Life*, (New York: Pocket Books, 1990), 451.

[3] Jonathan Mermin, *Debating War and Peace: Media Coverage of US Intervention in the Post-Vietnam Era*, (Princeton University Press, 1999). John Anthony Maltese, *Spin Control: The White House Office of Communications and the Management of Presidential News*, (Chapel Hill, NC: University of North Carolina Press, 1994).

[4] Phil Gaily, 'U.S. Bars Coverage of Grenada Action; News Groups Protest,' *New York Times*, October 26, 1983. Robert M. Gates, *From the Shadows: The Ultimate Insider's Story of Five Presidents and How They Won the Cold War*, (New York: Simon & Schuster, 2006), 275-6.

[5] Lawrence Freedman, *Strategy: A History*, (Oxford University Press, 2013), 10-29.

[6] Arthur A. Thompson, Margaret A. Peteraf, John E. Gamble, A. J. Strickland III, Alex Janes & Ciara Sutton, *Crafting and Executing Strategy: The Quest for Competitive Advantage*, (Maidenhead, UK: McGraw-Hill Education, 2013), 183.

[7] W. Chan Kim & Renée Mauborgne, *Blue Ocean Strategy: How to Create Uncontested Market Space and Make the Competition Irrelevant*, (Harvard Business School Press, 2005).

[8] Philip M. Taylor, 'Third Wave Info-Propaganda: Psychological Operations in the Post-Cold War Era,' in *Propaganda: Political Rhetoric and Identity 1300-2000*, ed. by Bertrand Taithe & Tim Thornton, (Stroud, UK: Sutton Publishing, 1999), 331.

[9] See for example: Glen M. Broom & Bey-Ling Sha, *Cutlip and Center's Effective Public Relations*, 11th (international) edn., (Harlow, UK: Pearson, 2013), 395 et seq. Doug Newsom, Judy VanSlyke Turk & Dean Kruckeberg, *This Is PR: the Realities of Public Relations*, 11th edn., (Boston MA: Wadsworth Cengage Learning, 2013), 219. Fraser P. Seitel, *The Practice of Public Relations*, 12th edition, (Upper Saddle River, NJ: Pearson Education, 2013), 106. Dennis L. Wilcox & Glen T. Cameron, *Public Relations: Strategies and Tactics*, 10th edn., (Harlow, UK: Pearson Education Limited, 2013), 396.

[10] Donald F. Lach, *Asia in the Making of Europe*, Vol. I, (Chicago, IL: University of Chicago Press, 1994), 154.

[11] Taylor, 'Third Wave Info-Propaganda,' 269.

[12] Martin Gilbert, *Challenge to Civilization: A History of the Twentieth Century 1952-1999*, (London: HarperCollins, 1999), 375.

[13] *All the President's Men*, directed by Alan J. Pakula, Wildwood Enterprises, 1976.

[14] IBM, 'What is Big Data: Overview,' <http://www-01.ibm.com/software/data/bigdata/> (2013).

[15] John F. Kennedy, *The President and the Press*, Speech to the American Newspaper Publishers Association, 1961.

[16] Gabriel Schoenfeld, *Necessary Secrets: National Security, the Media and the Rule of Law*, (New York: W. W. Norton & Company, 2010), 58.

[17] Schoenfeld, *Necessary Secrets*, 19. Barack Obama, Presidential Letter to the Men and Women of the CIA, April 16, 2009, https://www.cia.gov.news-information/press-releases-statements/release-of-doj-opinions.html, quoted in *Necessary Secrets*, 19.

[18] James Herron & Will Connors, 'WikiLeaks Touches Shell,' *Wall Street Journal*, December 10, 2010.

[19] Glenn Greenwald, Ewen MacAskill & Laura Poitras, 'Edward Snowden: the Whistleblower Behind the NSA Surveillance Revelations,' *The Guardian*, June 10, 2013.

[20] *Enemy of the State*, directed by Tony Scott, Touchstone Pictures, 1998.

[21] Hugh Carney, 'France Steps up Internet Surveillance,' *Financial Times*, December 11, 2013.

[22] Andrew Parker, *Address to the Royal United Services Institute*, Whitehall, London, October 8, 2013 <https://www.mi5.gov.uk/home/about-us/who-we-are/staff-and-management/director-general/speeches-by-the-director-general/director-generals-speech-at-rusi-2013.html>.

[23] *Secrets and Lies*, The Oxford Film Company, 2011.

[24] Ofcom, *Ofcom Broadcast Bulletin*, No. 213, (September 10, 2012), 80 et seq – complaint about film of its founder.

[25] Don Tapscott & David Ticoll, *The Naked Corporation: How the Age of Transparency Will Revolutionise Business*, (Toronto: Viking Canada, 2003), xi.

[26] Broom & Sha, *Cutlip and Center*, 11th (international) edn., 246.

[27] Miguel Ramos & Paul S. Piper, 'Web Waves: Tsunami Blogs Respond to Disasters,' *Searcher*, Vol. 13, No. 5. (May 2005).

[28] David Friend, 'Seeing 9/11 Through a Digital Prism,' *Wall Street Journal*, August 29, 2011.

[29] David von Drehle, 'The Surveillance Society,' *Time*, August 19, 2013, 38-43.

[30] Isaac Asimov, *Foundation; Foundation and Empire; Second Foundation*, (New York: The Gnome Press, 1951; 1952; 1953).

[31] Peter Watson, *Ideas: A History of Thought and Invention, from Fire to Freud*, (New York: HarperCollins, 2005), 146-7.

[32] Bill Bryson, *At Home: a Short History of Private Life*, (New York: Anchor Books, 2011), 382.

[33] A. W. Bradley & K. D. Ewing, *Constitutional and Administrative Law*, 14th edn., (Harlow, UK: Pearson Longman, 2007), 514.

[34] Ron Nixon, 'Unpopular Full-Body Scanners to be Removed From Airports,' *New York Times*, January 18, 2013.

[35] Geoffrey A. Fowler, 'When the Most Personal Secrets Get Outed on Facebook,' *Wall Street Journal*, October 13, 2012.

[36] Richard Waters, 'Tech Chiefs in Plea Over Privacy Damage,' *Financial Times*, September 14, 2014.

[37] Herb Schmertz & William Novak, *Goodbye to the Low Profile: The Art of Creative Confrontation*, (London: Mercury Books, 1986), 78.

[38] *Duplicity*, directed by Tony Gilroy, Universal Pictures, 2009.

[39] Donald Allen, 'Fundamentals of Investor Relations,' in *The New Investor Relations: Expert Perspectives on the State of the Art*, ed. by Benjamin Mark Cole, (Princeton, NJ: Bloomberg Press, 2004), 6.

[40] National Investor Relations Institute (NIRI), *Standards of Practice for Investor Relations*, 2004.

[41] Financial Services and Markets Act 2000, section 118C.

[42] Financial Conduct Authority, Disclosure Rules and Transparency Rules, Release 153, September 2014.

[43] 'Pfizer Confirms Prior Discussions with AstraZeneca Regarding a Possible Combination and Its Continuing Interest in a Possible Merger Transaction,' Pfizer Inc. news release, April 28, 2014.

[44] 'Stick to the Facts, Carl: eBay Inc. Responds to Carl Icahn,' eBay Inc. news release, February 26, 2014.

[45] 'PayPal + eBay Better Together,' eBay Inc. news release, March 19, 2014.

[46] 'eBay Inc. and Carl Icahn Settle Proxy Fight,' eBay Inc. news release, April 10, 2014.

[47] 'eBay Inc. to Separate eBay and PayPal into Independent Publicly Traded Companies in 2015,' eBay Inc. news release, September 30, 2014.

[48] Allen, 'Fundamentals of Investor Relations,' 10.

[49] American Cancer Society, *Cancer Facts and Figures 2013*, 17; Liz Szabo, 'Book raises alarms about alternative medicine,' *USA Today*, July 2, 2013.

[50] Peter Burrows, 'Apple's Cancer Scare,' *Business Week*, August 1, 2004.

[51] Steve Jobs, 'You've Got to Find What You Love, Jobs Says,' *Stanford Report*, June 14, 2005.

[52] Isaacson, *Steve Jobs*, 476.

[53] 'Apple Media Advisory,' Apple Inc. news release, January 14, 2009.

[54] Hormone imbalance: 'Letter from Apple CEO Steve Jobs,' Apple Inc. news release, January 5, 2009.

[55] Yukari Iwatani Kane & Joann S. Lublin, 'Jobs Had Liver Transplant,' *Wall Street Journal*, June 20, 2009.

[56] Gini Dietrich, 'Should Apple Have Disclosed Jobs's Liver Transplant?' *Spinsucks*, June 22, 2009, <http://spinsucks.com/uncategorized/should-apple-have-disclosed-jobss-liver-transplant/>.

[57] Leander Kahney, 'Apple Broke the Law By Lying About Steve Jobs Health,' *9to5mac.com*, June 23, 2009.

[58] Isaacson, *Steve Jobs*, 482.

[59] Newsom et al, *This Is PR*, 176-182. See also Broom & Sha, *Cutlip & Center*, 2013, 40-42; Wilcox & Cameron, *Public Relations*, 10th edn., 408-410. Fraser P. Seitel, *The Practice of Public Relations*, 12th edn., (Upper Saddle River, NJ: Pearson Education, 2013), 132-134. A chapter on law has one page on insider trading and one page on disclosure.

[60] Kathy R. Fitzpatrick, 'Public Relations and the Law: A Survey of Practitioners,' *Public Relations Review*, Vol. 22, No. 1, (1996), 1-8.

CHAPTER 4

The PR Industry Says It's Good to Talk

"Before them there were no such locusts as they, neither after them shall be such. For they covered the face of the
whole earth, so that the land was darkened."
— Exodus 10: 14-15[1]

**PR is riding high. The number of professional communica-
tors has soared since the second world war. And when there
is such a vast number of communicators there is bound to
be a vast amount of communication. There has never been
more PR than there is today.**

"PR is on a roll… The PR boom means more jobs, higher
salaries, and opportunities across the broad spectrum."[2]
The US Department of Labor estimated that in 1950, there
were 19,000 people working in public relations in America, compared with 126,000 in 1980.[3] By 2008, the number had risen to as
many as 320,000.[4] There are thought to be six times as many public relations people as journalists in America, and a multitude beyond the core of full-timers.[5] By 1992, around the world, millions
of people could be involved, suggested James Grunig, the leading
public relations scholar.[6]

Edward Bernays, the first person to lecture on public relations at a university, went to agricultural college before making a
trend-setting career change. Now, laments Jim Rogers, the investor, more Americans study public relations than agriculture.[7]

Alongside the huge number of people employed in public
relations is an increasing number of public relations bodies — PR
agencies, PR departments in businesses and the public sector, political groups and professional associations.

Critics have scented conspiracy. Vance Packard in "The
Hidden Persuaders" was provoked by a saying of Bernays to the

effect that events that make the news don't happen by accident but are deliberately planned to achieve an objective.[8] Daniel Boorstin agreed that the public relations industry was "one of the most powerful forces in American life."[9] Noam Chomsky feared it could "control the public mind."[10] A long line of critics, stretching through Chomsky to John Stauber, Sheldon Rampton, and Douglas Rushkoff, possibly exaggerated this power and cast public relations in a malevolent role.[11]

PRs produce PR

The more PRs there are, the more vocal, high profile PR there is likely to be. Kevin Moloney called it "a great Niagara of PR."[12] In the main, these legions of people are employed to communicate actively, not to be silent. Communicators have a built-in bias to communicate in the same way as legislators have a built-in tendency to legislate.

And they have been programmed to communicate. It is a question of mentality and upbringing. How do all these professional communicators know how to behave? As in other professions, they enroll in vocational education, join professional bodies and consume professional books, journals and web materials. The academic study that underpins the profession broadly encourages active, vocal communication.

This chapter briefly reviews history, theory and practice. It makes reference, as throughout this book, to public relations textbooks. It concentrates on four, selected partly for their longevity, partly according to the recommendations of the leading professional bodies, and partly by the number of copies sold. In order of first publication, these are:

- "Cutlip and Center's Effective Public Relations" by Broom & Sha, 11th (international) edition, 2013 (referred to as "Cutlip"), first published in 1952.[13]
- "This Is PR: the Realities of Public Relations" ("Newsom") by Doug Newsom, Judy VanSlyke Turk and Dean Kruckeberg, 11th edition, first published in 1976.[14]
- "The Practice of Public Relations" ("Seitel"), by Fraser P.

Seitel, 12th edition, first published in 1980.[15]

- "Public Relations: Strategies and Tactics" ("Wilcox"), by Dennis L. Wilcox and Glen T. Cameron, 2013, first published in 1984.[16]

These textbooks come in for criticism in course of the present work. But these are not at all bad books. It is simply that, on a number of matters, we disagree. Each one has its strengths but my own favorite is "Seitel," which I have been using, as edition succeeded edition, since the 1980s. The latest edition is readable, entertaining, irreverent and wide-ranging, a tremendous resource for teachers, students, professional communicators and general managers. Perhaps its strongest point is that it was written by someone who works in public relations, rather than a full-time academic.

Popular books on public relations are even keener on communicating actively and loudly. They are full of advice about how to go forth and spread the word. Among those recently near the top of Amazon's best-selling books on public relations (with heavy emphasis on social media) were: "Word of Mouth Marketing: How Smart Companies Get People Talking;" "Tweet Naked: A Bare-All Social Media Strategy for Boosting Your Brand and Your Business;" and, of course, "Public Relations for Dummies."[17]

Saint Paul the PR Man

The term "public relations" was probably not used in its current sense before the late 19th century.[18] Public relations has ancient roots. The wide-ranging survey, "Propaganda and Communication in World History," established that organized, public communication dates back to the earliest civilizations.[19] But it took a while for the terminology to catch up with events.

Illustrious figures at all times in history have exploited communication. The sketches of history in the leading textbooks feature a number of obvious examples of Great Communicators. Among them are Julius Caesar (but see chapter 2 for a critical view); Saint Paul, author of a substantial part of the New Testament and effective manager of the campaign to spread early Christianity; and Pope Urban II, who launched the First Crusade with an appeal that was copied and distributed across Europe.[20]

Textbooks usually mention the establishment by the Catholic Church of the Congregation for the Propagation of the Faith in 1622, from whose Latin name the word "propaganda" derives. Lastly, they turn to snippets from the story of public relations in America beginning with the recruitment campaign of the Virginia Company and the fund-raising of Harvard College, followed by the activities of the Founding Fathers, first in working for independence and then in the "Federalist Papers."[21]

Later distinctions between public relations and propaganda meant nothing in this period. Were Benjamin Franklin, Samuel Adams and Thomas Jefferson early public relations men or propagandists?[22]

Restless

These historical accounts emphasize the loudest and most public forms of communication. They are all about history being made through sermons being preached, assemblies being addressed, letters being written and copied, bulletins being posted on walls, political or religious campaigns being launched, statues being erected, and missionaries being dispatched across the globe.

The favorite ancestors of PR were all rushing around, hectoring, hollering and scribbling. There is not yet any place in Public Relations History 101 for Augustus (see chapter 2), for Cardinal Richelieu, red eminence behind the Gazette de France by which officially sanctioned news was disseminated in 17th century France, for Napoleon, ("one of the greatest masters of the use of propaganda in history")[23] or for Steve Jobs of Apple. Communication strategies that involved saying little or nothing, or keeping quiet some of the time (keeping shtum) played no part in the mainstream version of public relations history.

Key points
- The last century has seen the rapid and accelerating rise of public relations, now a significant industry that employs millions of people.
- Both popular books on PR and, to a lesser extent, public relations textbooks, advocate speaking out.
- Interest in the history of public relations has focused on dynamic and vocal charismatic leaders such as Julius Caesar and St Paul but has neglected those who communicated more subtly or quietly.

The "evolution" of public relations

When historians began writing the story of public relations they quickly divided PR and its antecedents into periods. This was not only handy but positioned the story as one of "progressive evolution."[24]

This evolutionary account of public relations took its definitive form in the 1984 book, "Managing Public Relations," by James Grunig and Todd Hunt.[25] Although it was written as a textbook that was not updated, it was highly influential. (One study suggested that it was the most cited work in public relations literature.)[26] It was based on a schematic account of the development of public relations as an evolutionary process. According to this scheme, public relations has passed through four conceptual and historical stages, with each stage more sophisticated and more ethical than its predecessor. This concept of evolution supported what was ambitiously envisaged to be a general theory of public relations. This was the symmetry-excellence theory that became dominant in public relations studies (considered later in this chapter).

The four stages of evolution in this scheme could be related to the linear model of communication that was proposed by Aristotle, who said: "Every speech is composed of three parts: the speaker, the subject of which he treats, and the person to whom it is addressed, I mean the hearer, to whom the end or object of the speech refers."[27] Speaker – Subject - Hearer. See fig. 4.1.

Fig 4.1 Simple Communication Model

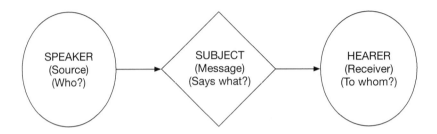

A mechanical version of Aristotle's model was proposed by Claude Shannon at Bell Labs in 1948, envisaging that an electronic communication system involved a source transmitting a signal to a receiver.[28] At around the same time, Harold Lasswell, a political scientist, interested in effects rather than engineering, rephrased Aristotle as "Who? Says what? To whom?" and added, "In what channel? With what effect?"[29] It was all an adaptation of Aristotle's original.

In the past few decades, numerous social scientists have put forward their own models, most of which are modifications and elaborations of the original that added, in effect: "Yes but we need to take account of noise, or context, or results..." Succeeding models included more boxes, arrows and even, sometimes, explication, and were more or less comprehensible and illuminating. Many were helpfully collected into a book.[30] But none was entirely convincing and the originals, while obviously inadequate, at least had the virtue of simplicity.

Returning to the four stages of evolution, these were said to be:

1. Publicity (also known as press agentry), communication from source to receiver;
2. Public Information, also communication from source to receiver;
3. Persuasion (also known as two-way asymmetric), communication from source to receiver with feedback from receiver to source; and

4. Two-Way Symmetric, communication in both directions.[31]

Stage I: 19th century publicity

Evolution began, somewhat arbitrarily, in the 19th century. This was said to be the primitive era of publicity/press agentry, the business of planting stories in newspapers, regardless of their veracity. P. T. Barnum, the showman and con artist, personified it in Grunig and Hunt's account. Others followed their lead.

A dictum from 1882, "The Public Be Damned," is central to the mythology of public relations. Bernays used it as a chapter heading in his 1952 book, "Public Relations."[32] The author of the possibly apocryphal remark was William Henry Vanderbilt, president of the New York Central Railroad. William Henry was the heir of Cornelius Vanderbilt, the steamship and railroad entrepreneur, and one of the extremely wealthy American capitalists who were later labeled "Robber Barons." "It was truly the era of 'The Public Be Damned,'" thundered the leading historian of public relations, Scott Cutlip.[33]

The Public Be Damned is seen as encapsulating attitudes before modern public relations, when big business was supposedly openly contemptuous of the public interest. It was a good story but, truly, the facts were more complicated. Short versions of the tale omit the context. Political interests that supported government intervention in commerce and industry conjured up the colorful image of the "Robber Barons." Some modern historians offer an alternative view which stresses the virtues of the capitalists of the Gilded Age, such as their vision, leadership and philanthropy.[34] Arguably, they were not wholly unlike the buccaneering entrepreneurs of Silicon Valley today.

The interview with Vanderbilt took place as he was on his way by train to Chicago. Two reporters, one from the *Chicago Tribune* and one freelance, boarded the train and joined him. The *New York Times* and others published a report that included the infamous phrase. But the *Tribune*'s version of the interview omitted it. Vanderbilt disowned it.[35] It will never be known for certain whether or not he used that form of words but, far from being a swaggering capitalist, inured to public disapproval, Vanderbilt protested: "I do not, and never have, entertained any such opinions as are attributed to me."

What did Vanderbilt think he was doing giving this two-hour interview in the first place? It seems that he was in the habit of chatting to journalists, not as part of any communication strategy but just doing what came naturally. Largely ignored by Commodore Vanderbilt until he reached middle age, William H. was probably a relative naïf who would have been better off saying less.

II: The Public Information Model

Big business indifference to public opinion was said to have ended and press agentry been superseded around the turn of the 20th century. This saw the advent of the public relations profession and the Public Information model, personified by Ivy Lee, who worked for the Pennsylvania Railroad, then the world's largest publicly traded company, among others. Lee coined the slogan "The Public Be Informed," in contrast with "The Public Be Damned," and persuaded his clients and employers to be more communicative with the press.[36] He expressed what many later public relations people have seen as their mission: "I believe in telling your story to the public." (Not *always* a good idea though.)

In his "Declaration of Principles," Lee said: "Our plan is,... in behalf of business concerns and public institutions, to supply to the press and the public... prompt and accurate information concerning subjects which it is of value and interest of the public to know about."[37]

(I went to learn about communications in the Public Affairs and Information Department of an oil company more than thirty years ago. As late as the 1980s, as its title suggested, this department saw fact dissemination in the style of Lee as an important part of its job.)

Lee raised the "lowly trade of press agentry to the euphonious heights of counselor in public relations."[38] Both he and historians of PR distinguished between his profession of publicity man and the press agents, who were despised as "the only group of men proud of being called liars." Think of Sidney Falco (played by Tony Curtis) in the film noir, "Sweet Smell of Success."[39]

It is significant that both press agentry and public information models were about publicity. Publicity can be powerful but it has the power to harm as well as to help. Public relations may have evolved but the preference for active, vocal communication has been a constant. Other forms of public communication such as marketing and advertising are even more committed to the active, vocal norm. As one leading advertising man put it, the question is: "Where do I place my stories and how do I do so, so that as many people see it and pass it on?"[40]

III: Persuasion

The third stage of evolution, according to the Grunig and Hunt scheme, was persuasive communication. The Wilson administration sought to increase public support for American participation in the first world war, through the Committee on Public Information (CPI, see chapter 6), using science: "psychological principles of mass persuasion."[41] After the war, public relations people such as Edward Bernays, who had worked for the CPI, and advertising agencies such as J. Walter Thompson, used a scientific approach for peaceful purposes.[42]

Persuasion was two-way communication but it was labeled asymmetric, meaning lopsided. It was two-way communication when it involved research and feedback but asymmetrical because it was communication directed by the source to the receiver, not communication in both directions. In this model, the role of the speaker is to send, the role of the audience is to receive, and all the speaker wants or expects from the audience is confirmation or consent, not a dialog. The model did not meet what was seen as the ethical requirement for public relations not to benefit only the source but to be mutually beneficial.

Is it unethical for organizations to communicate for their own benefit rather than equally for the benefit of those they communicate with? Is it legitimate or ethical for them to seek to persuade others, in their own interest?

Common sense would say yes, it is ethical and legitimate, because that is what we all do in our daily lives. As Walter Fisher said, all communication is "manipulative in the sense that communicators intend messages," and help their argument by their choice of subject, materials, style and so on.[43] In public life, this is done by disseminating news, facts and arguments that are favorable to the speaker through the available channels, regardless of whether the speaker is an corporate body or a person. Communications people are usually hired to "advance the interest of the employer."[44] Objectivity is an illusion. (See chapter 9.)

Less visible than this dissemination of news, facts and arguments, but equally important, is constraining information. Cutlip called it "softening and suppressing" information. The information that needs to be constrained, softened or suppressed is what would be unfavorable to the source if it became more widely known, or if it became known at all. Sometimes the best course is to eliminate a problem by cutting off the oxygen of publicity.

The actions of critics or enemies share some of the characteristics of guerrilla warfare. An action may be carried out by guerrillas not merely to damage their opponent, typically a stronger military force or state, but to spread a call for wider insurrection.[45] When a state uses its apparently superior resources to respond to the insurgent's attack, it may play into the enemy's hands, by stimulating groups or people who were not previously committed to join in the insurrection and launch their own attacks. Similarly, a large, successful business may have more financial resources than its critics. But when it reacts to critics, this can sometimes have the effect of bringing new, previously dormant critics into the attack (see chapter 17).

Actively going out and communicating is not the best course of action in all scenarios. Nor is assuming a high profile necessarily the best communication strategy.

IV: Two-way Symmetric Communication

Two-way symmetric communication was presented as the fourth and most advanced stage in the evolution of public relations, beginning in the late 20th century.

Fig 4.2 Symmetrical Two-Way Communication Model

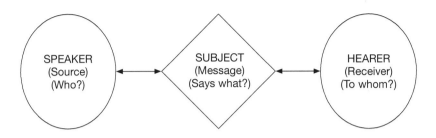

In a model which looked like some version of fig. 4.2, messages pass equally in both directions between an organization and its publics. Without symmetry, the communicator's intention is to persuade. With symmetry, the purpose is said to be "mutual understanding." Its theoretical background included systems theory, with its view of organizations as open systems that have permeable boundaries, adapting to organizational influences, and concern with symmetrical relations in communication theory. The term "two-way symmetric communication" was devised to describe the way systems theorists thought open system organizations ought to communicate.

The concept of two-way symmetric communication was strongly influenced by ethics. Its advocates believed that organizations have a moral obligation to have a dialog with publics.[46] For an organization to use persuasion to get its own way, even though this is what we all do in our daily lives, would be unethical, whereas "symmetrical communication is inherently ethical."[47]

Thus two-way symmetric communication both described a technical analysis of communication in action and an ethical precept, which Grunig later summed up by saying: "Organizations must communicate symmetrically... taking the interests of both the organization and publics into account."[48]

This version of history described a profession advancing steadily like medical science. It began in a primitive state, in which information was manipulated to achieve desired ends and without regard to ethical considerations. It reached its peak in an enlightened state in which public relations enables governments, businesses and other groups in society to achieve "mutual under-standing" and "harmonious adjustment." This vision was seductive for people who had aspirations to be respected as professionals but worked in what some saw as a grubby trade.

But the construct of evolution and, in particular, symmetry as its end result, is only one possible interpretation of the facts. Robert Brown said, "Despite its scientific claims, the symmetry theory of public relations is actually an a-historical heuristic that justifies a belief system that legitimizes public relations."[49] The history of public relations could be seen as reflecting cultural styles that were current at the time it was written. And the evolutionary scheme could be criticized for selecting the facts to fit a theory. For example, research has shown that press agentry probably did not "evolve" into publicity.[50] But the storyline still holds considerable sway.

Key points
- The most influential account of public relations history divides it into four stages.
- According to this account, Stage I was 19th century publicity.
- Stage II was the "public information model"
- Stage III was persuasion or "two-way asymmetric communication," described in these terms as a way of undermining its legitimacy.
- Stage IV, the most advanced model for public relations, was "two-way symmetric communication."
- Throughout, there is undue emphasis on active and vocal communication.

"Excellence"

The evolutionary scheme with symmetry as its goal has never been universally accepted in public relations but its dominance was assured by the largest-ever public relations research project, the IABC Excellence Study. This study was inaugurated in 1985 and funded by the Research Foundation of the International Association of Business Communicators. It lasted seventeen years, and its published reports added up to more than 1,600 pages.

The Excellence Project was so christened in a conscious echo of the best-selling management book, "In Search of Excellence," by Tom Peters and Robert Waterman. Peters and Waterman's research purported to show that excellent businesses share distinct characteristics.[51] The Excellence Project resolved to demonstrate that "the same is true for communication departments."[52] And, by studying excellence in practice, the Project purported to show that two-way symmetric public relations was the only excellent way of practicing public relations.[53]

The first stage of the Project reported as "Excellence in Public Relations and Communication Management" in 1992. This was the first of a series of books, the last appearing in 2013, which developed, expanded and discussed the material, to which many of the leading public relations scholars have contributed.[54] It produced a number of propositions. These were declared to amount to no less than "a general theory of public relations." It studied hundreds of organizations in America, Canada and Britain and participants were asked to complete questionnaires that sought, inter alia, to distinguish which of the four evolutionary models was being used.

The conclusion was that the purpose of public relations is developing good long-term relationships with publics and that these relationships are better when they are symmetrical. Symmetry begets excellence. It argued that the quality of these relationships depends more on an organization's behavior than on "the messages that communicators disseminate." Indeed, professional communicators "have their greatest value when they bring information into the organization, more than when they disseminate information out of the organization."[55]

This was turning the pattern of persuasive communication on its head, making communication into the organization (stakeholder influence — see chapter 12) more important than the organization's own communications (persuasion). Unfortunately, the argument was circular, since the Project set out to find practice that the theory said was excellent and then held this "excellent" practice aloft as evidence to support the theory. "The general theory provides a theoretical explanation for the best current practice of public relations — which our theory says is excellent."[56]

Symmetry-excellence... influential

Symmetry-excellence matters: "Grunig's normative conceptualization continues to enjoy widespread influence on the way public relations is taught, discussed, research, published, and, perhaps to a lesser extent, practiced worldwide."[57] In their comprehensive review of the state of thinking about public relations, Carl Botan and Maureen Taylor said: "The most striking trend in public relations [scholarship] over the past 20 years... is its transition from a functional perspective," that sees communication as a means to achieve objectives, to one that "sees publics as cocreators of meaning... The most researched cocreational theory is symmetrical/excellence theory."[58]

No alternative paradigm has found favor with scholars, notwithstanding the success of reputation management (see chapter 12). Reviewing the state of public relations theory, Carl Botan and Vincent Hazleton said: "Critics... have spoken up, but either the field has failed to see enough merit in what they have said to develop their work into alternative paradigms," or their research has been too limited.[59] However, there is a much older tradition, linked to rhetoric, most notably upheld by Robert Heath, editor of the "Encyclopedia of Public Relations," and on which this book has drawn. This approach is exemplified by his opening survey in "Rhetorical and Critical Approaches to Public Relations II" — "Rhetoric and public relations take their rationale from efforts humans make to influence one another, and to be influenced."[60] In a baffling turn of phrase, the symmetry-excellence school have characterized this as "symbolic, interpretive," in contrast with their own "strategic management, behavioral paradigm."[61] (Chapter 7 will argue a different connection between communication and strategic management.)

And though there has never been a single, universally accepted definition of public relations, after a suitably hip crowdsourcing exercise in 2011, the Public Relations Society of America, the largest professional body, issued a new definition that showed how influential the theory has been on its members. It began: "Public relations is a strategic communication process that builds mutually beneficial relationships between organizations and their publics."[62] (It added: "'Process' is preferable to 'management function,' which can evoke ideas of control and top-down, one-way communications.") This was a clear endorsement of symmetry-excellence ("mutually beneficial").

And symmetry-excellence is central to the leading public relations textbooks. "Wilcox" included a detailed description of the four models and later endorsed two-way symmetric communication and a similar dialogic model. "Newsom" claimed "the internet has shifted the balance of power between organizations and their publics/stakeholders to almost assure symmetric two-way communication." Its second chapter described the "evolution" of PR. "Cutlip" did not explicitly describe the four models but allocated a whole chapter to systems theory, proposing an open systems model of public relations, that "uses 'two-way symmetric approaches.'" Finally, "Seitel" set out the four models and a section on ethics returned to the two-way symmetric model.[63]

Outsiders may see public relations more clearly. Here is one respected historian's alternative definition to provide a reality check: "Euphemism for the professional organization of attempts to secure public understanding and support for the activities of bodies such as governments, political parties, commercial and industrial organizations, professional bodies, etc.... It includes, but is by no means confined to, propaganda."[64]

...but not strategic

Business people generally applaud excellence, going out in their millions to buy the book, "In Search of Excellence." But, asked to choose between effectiveness and excellence, they may choose effectiveness. Peter Drucker clarified at the start of "The Effective Executive": "The executive is, first of all, expected to get the right things done. And this is simply that he is expected to be effective."[65] He went on to say that high effectiveness is unusual and not correlated with qualities such as intelligence and knowledge. An effective business is a successful business, whereas it is possible to achieve excellence on various criteria but still not succeed.

Symmetry-excellence scholars put forward a number of possible social roles for public relations.[66] The first was a "pragmatic" role. In this role, public relations would be a useful tool that could be used by anyone to help achieve their objectives. (Good.) Others included a "conservative" role, in which public relations could be used to help keep society as it is, and a "radical" role, in which public relations could be used to help change society. The final, preferred role was "idealistic." This also saw public relations as an instrument for social change. But instead of using PR for conservative or radical ends, this saw it as a mechanism by which groups in society could manage their interdependence and conflict to the benefit of all. Such an idealistic role could only be fulfilled through symmetrical communications. Public relations that were not symmetrical would fall short of the idealistic social role and, in that sense, could not be excellent.

In its once-fashionable emphasis on excellence, rather than effectiveness, and in its advocacy of an idealistic social role for public relations, symmetry-excellence theory is at variance with what most clients want from their public relations – effectiveness and pragmatism rather than "excellence" and social change. It opened up a divide between theorists and the needs of users. To users, communication was a tool that must play a pragmatic social role. The theorists wanted PR to be idealistic. Their interest in strategy was limited to the role a public relations function might play in "diagnosing" the environment and bringing stakeholders and issues to management attention.[67]

To the extent that scholarship has considered a communication contribution to strategy, it has suggested a focus on social and environmental aspects of strategy rather than the financial aspect (profit).[68] Businesses and institutions, by contrast, are likely to believe that public relations plays a pragmatic role, its purpose being to help them achieve their objectives. Communications departments and agencies are hired not to change the world, nor even to achieve excellence per se, but to help their employers or clients achieve their objectives. "Empirically, public relations is not the search for communicative symmetries, but instead the search for communicative advantages that strengthens the interest of those it services."[69]

From excellence to strategy

The view of strategy to be inferred from symmetry-excellence is one that is out of sympathy with competitive strategy. Its implied view of businesses and institutions is of a steady state. According to this view, how should the organization be different in five or 10 years time? It will be essentially the same, just a little bit greener, a little bit more efficient, with employees who are a little bit better developed and more diverse, and so on. In a competitive world, that is simply not good enough.

The titles of a couple of well-known books on business strategy offer an important clue. Michael Porter called his book "Competitive Strategy."[70] Roger Martin and A. G. Lafley (CEO of Procter & Gamble 2000-09 and 2013 to date) called their book "Playing to Win: How Strategy Really Works."[71] The fields of advertising and marketing understand what much of the public relations field seemingly does not, that success is only achieved through constant renewal and competitive exertion.

Chapter 7 begins to answer the question: what kind of *communication strategy* do you need to win?

Key points
- The Excellence Project was an attempt to show that two-way symmetric communication is the only excellent way of practicing public relations. It has been highly influential.
- However, the idealism of symmetry-excellence conflicts with the pragmatism of management, which is more interested in effectiveness than theoretical excellence.
- Symmetry-excellence does not meet the demands of competitive strategy, which are addressed in chapter 7 by communication strategy.

In Summary

- Huge numbers of people are employed and encouraged to communicate.
- Less vocal styles of communication and communication strategies of silence have been written out of the history of PR.
- Clients need advertising, marketing and public relations to persuade, influence and sell. Yet the normative approaches favored in public relations scholarship lack relevance to these needs. A strategic approach to communication is both legitimate and effective.

References

[1] King James Bible, Exodus, 10: 14-15.
[2] Leonard Mogel, *Making It in Public Relations: An Insider's Guide to Career Opportunities*, (Mahwah, NJ: Lawrence Erlbaum Associates, 2002), xiii.
[3] Scott M. Cutlip, Allen H. Center & Glen M. Broom, *Effective Public Relations*, 6th edn., (Englewood Cliffs, NJ: Prentice-Hall, Inc., 1985), 59.
[4] Bureau of Labor Statistics, *Occupational Outlook Handbook*, <http://www.bls.gov/ooh/Management/Public-relations-managers-and-specialists.htm#emply>.
[5] 'Public Relations,' *The Economist*, January 19, 2013.
[6] James E. Grunig, 'Communication, Public Relations, and Effective Organizations: An Overview of the Book,' in *Excellence in Public Relations and Communication Management*, ed. Grunig, (Hillsdale NJ: Lawrence Erlbaum Associates, 1992), 1.
[7] Jim Rogers, interviewed by Elaine Moore, 'Forget Banking, Become a Farmer,' *Financial Times*, July 19, 2013.
[8] Vance Packard, *The Hidden Persuaders*, (Brooklyn, NY: IG Publishing, 2007), 203.
[9] Boorstin, *The Image*, vii.
[10] Noam Chomsky, *Media Control: The Spectacular Achievements of Propaganda*, (New York: Seven Stories Press, 2008), 22.
[11] John Stauber & Sheldon Rampton, *Toxic Sludge is Good for You: Lies, Damn Lies, and the Public Relations Industry*, (Monroe, ME: Common Courage Press, 1995). Douglas Rushkoff, *Coercion: The Persuasion Professionals and Why We Listen to What They Say*, (London: Little, Brown and Company, 2000).
[12] Kevin Moloney, *Rethinking Public Relations: PR Propaganda and Democracy*, (Abingdon, UK: Routledge, 2006), 1.
[13] Glen M. Broom & Bey-Ling Sha, *Cutlip and Center's Effective Public Relations*, 11th (international) edn., (Harlow, UK: Pearson, 2013).
[14] Doug Newsom, Judy VanSlyke Turk & Dean Kruckeberg, *This Is PR: the Realities of Public Relations*, 11th edn., (Boston MA: Wadsworth Cengage Learning, 2013).
[15] Fraser P. Seitel, *The Practice of Public Relations*, 12th edition, (Upper Saddle River, NJ: Pearson Education, 2013).
[16] Dennis L. Wilcox & Glen T. Cameron, *Public Relations: Strategies and Tactics*, 10th edn., (Harlow, UK: Pearson Education Limited, 2013).
[17] Andy Sernovitz, Guy Kawasaki & Seth Godin, *Word of Mouth Marketing: How Smart Companies Get People Talking*, (Austin, TX: Greenleaf Book Group Press, 2012); Scott Levy, *Tweet Naked: A Bare-All Social Media Strategy for Boosting Your Brand and Your Business*, (Irvine, CA: Entrepreneur Press, 2013); David Meerman Scott, *The New Rules of Marketing & PR: How to Use Social Media, Online Video, Mobile Applications, Blogs, News Releases, and Viral Marketing to Reach Buyers Directly*, (Hoboken, NJ: John Wiley & Sons, Inc., 2011); Eric Yaverbaum, *Public Relations for Dummies*, 2nd edn., (Indianapolis, IN: John Wiley & Sons, 2006).
[18] Scott M. Cutlip, *Public Relations History: From the 17th to the 20th Century: The Antecedents*, (Hillsdale NJ: Lawrence Erlbaum Associates, 1995), ix.
[19] Harold D. Lasswell, Daniel Lerner & Hans Speier, (eds.), *Propaganda and Communication in World History*, (Honolulu, HI: East-West Center, 1979).
[20] Paul: Robert E. Brown, 'St. Paul as a Public Relations Practitioner: A Metatheoretical Speculation on Messianic Communication and Symmetry,' *Public Relations Review*, Vol. 29, No. 2, (June 2003), 229-240. Urban: Robert Brentano, 'Western Civilization: The Middle Ages,' in *Propaganda and Communication in World History*, ed. by Harold D. Lasswell, Daniel Lerner & Hans Speier, (Honolulu, HI: East-West Center, 1979), 552-595.
[21] Cutlip, *Public Relations History*, 10-11 & 40-46.

22 Garth S. Jowett & Victoria O'Donnell, *Propaganda and Persuasion*, 3rd edn., (Thousand Oaks, CA: Sage Publications, Inc., 1999), 78-83.

23 Jowett & O'Donnell, *Propaganda and Persuasion*, 86.

24 Margot Opdycke Lamme & Karen Miller Russell, 'Removing the Spin: Toward a New Theory of Public Relations History,' *Journalism and Communication Monographs*, Vol. 11, No. 4, (Winter 2010).

25 James E. Grunig & Todd Hunt, *Managing Public Relations*, (Orlando FL: Harcourt Brace Jovanovich, 1984), 13-46.

26 Yorgo Pasadeos, R. Bruce Renfro, & Mary Lynn Hanily, 'Influential Authors and Works of the Public Relations Scholarly Literature: A Network of Recent Research,' *Journal of Public Relations Research*, Vol. 11, No. 1, (1999), 29-52.

27 Aristotle, *The Art of Rhetoric*, translated by John Henry Freese, (London: William Heinemann, 1926), Book 1, Chapter 3, 33.

28 James Gleick, *The Information: A History, A Theory, A Flood*, (New York: Pantheon Books, 2011), 11-18 & chapter 7. Claude Shannon & Willard Weaver, *The Mathematical Theory of Communication*, (Chicago: University of Illinois Press, 1949).

29 Harold D. Lasswell, 'The Structure and Function of Communication in Society,' in *The Communication of Ideas*, ed. by Lymon Bryson, (New York: Harper and Brothers, 1948).

30 Denis McQuail & Sven Windahl, *Communication Models for the Study of Mass Communication*, (New York: Longman, 1993).

31 Grunig & Hunt, *Managing Public Relations*, 22.

32 Edward L. Bernays, *Public Relations*, (Norman, OK: University of Oklahoma Press, 1952).

33 Matthew Josephson, *The Robber Barons: The Great American Capitalists 1861-1901*, (New York: Harcourt Brace and Company, 1934). Cutlip, *Public Relations History*, 188.

34 Alternative view: Allan Nevins, *John D. Rockefeller: The Heroic Age of American Enterprise*, (New York: C. Scribner's sons, 1940); Earl Latham, *John D. Rockefeller: Robber Baron or Industrial Statesman?* (Boston: D. C. Heath, 1949); Andrea Tone, *The Business of Benevolence: Industrial Paternalism in Progressive America*, (Ithaca, NY: Cornell University Press, 1997).

35 'Vanderbilt in the West: The Railroad Millionaire Expresses Himself Freely,' *New York Times*, October 9, 1882. *Chicago Tribune*, October 9, 1882, quoted in Cutlip, *Public Relations History*, 189. 'The Vanderbilt Interview; Mr Vanderbilt Denies Its Accuracy,' *New York Times*, October 13, 1882.

36 Dennis L. Wilcox, Glen T. Cameron, Phillip H. Ault & Warren K. Agee, *Public Relations: Strategies and Tactics*, 7th edn., (Pearson Education, Inc., 2003), 37.

37 Telling your story: Scott M. Cutlip, *The Unseen Power: Public Relations. A History*, (Hillsdale NJ: Lawrence Erlbaum Associates, 1994), 54. Wilcox et al, *Public Relations*, 7th edn., 37.

38 Dexter Fellow & Andrew Freeman, quoted in Cutlip, *The Unseen Power*, 42.

39 Will Irwin, quoted in Cutlip, *The Unseen Power*, 51. *Sweet Smell of Success*, directed by Alexander Mackendrick, (Hill-Hecht-Lancaster Productions, 1957).

40 John Hegarty, 'Who's Lighting the Campfire,' *Game Changers: The Evolution of Advertising*, ed. by Peter Russell & Senta Slingerland, (Taschen GMBH, 2014).

41 Grunig & Hunt, *Managing Public Relations*, 37-38.

42 Mark Tungate, *Adland: A Global History of Advertising*, (London & Philadelphia, PA: Kogan Page, 2007), 24-27.

43 Walter R. Fisher, *Human Communication as Narration: Toward a Philosophy of Reason, Value, and Action*, (Columbia, SC: University of South Carolina Press, 1987).

44 Cutlip, *The Unseen Power*, 765.

45 Howard Nothhaft & Hagen Schölzel, '(Re-) Reading Clausewitz: The Strategy Discourse and its Implications for Strategic Communication,' in Holtzhausen & Zerfass, *The Routledge Handbook of Strategic Communication*, 18-33.

46 Shannon A. Bowen, 'Symmetry,' in *Encyclopedia of Public Relations*, ed. Heath, Vol. 2, 837-839.

47 Yi-Hui Huang, 'Is Symmetrical Communication Ethical and Effective?' *Journal of Business Ethics*, Vol. 53, No. 4 (September 2004), 333-352.

[48] James E. Grunig, 'Excellence Theory in Public Relations,' in *The International Encyclopedia of Communication*, ed. by Wolfgang Donsbach, (Malden, MA: Blackwell, 2008), 1620-1622.
[49] Robert E. Brown, 'Myth of Symmetry: Public Relations as Cultural Styles,' *Public Relations Review*, Vol. 32 (2006) 206–212.
[50] Karen Miller Russell & Carl O. Bishop, 'Understanding Ivy Lee's Declaration of Principles: U.S. Newspaper and Magazine Coverage of Publicity and Press Agentry, 1865–1904,' *Public Relations Review*, Vol. 35 (2009) 91–101.
[51] Thomas J. Peters & Robert H. Waterman, *In Search of Excellence: Lessons from America's Best-Run Companies*, (New York: Harper & Row, 1982).
[52] Grunig, James E., ed., *Excellence in Public Relations...*, 3.
[53] Brown, 'Symmetry and Its Critics,' 278.
[54] The first: Grunig, *Excellence in Public Relations....* The rest of the series (so far): (1) David M. Dozier, Larissa A. Grunig & James E. Grunig, *Manager's Guide to Excellence and Public Relations and Communication Management*, (Mahwah, NJ: Lawrence Erlbaum Associates, Inc., 1995). (2) Larissa A. Grunig, James A. Grunig & David M. Dozier, *Excellent Public Relations and Effective Organizations: A Study of Communication Management in Three Countries*, (Mahwah, NJ: Lawrence Erlbaum Associates, 2002). (3) Elizabeth L. Toth, (ed.), *The Future of Excellence in Public Relations and Communication Management: Challenges for the Next Generation*, (Mahwah, NJ: Lawrence Erlbaum Associates, 2007). (4) Krishnamurthy Sriramesh, Ansgar Zerfass, & Jeong-Nam Kim, *Public Relations and Communication Management: Current Trends and Emerging Topics*, (New York: Routledge, 2013).
[55] Grunig, Grunig & Dozier, *Excellent Public Relations and Effective Organizations*, 57 & xi.
[56] Grunig, Excellence in Public Relations..., xiv.
[57] Robert E. Brown, 'Symmetry and Its Critics: Antecedents, Prospects, and Implications for Symmetry in a Postsymmetry Era,' in *The Sage Handbook of Public Relations*, ed. by Robert L. Heath, 2nd edn., (Thousand Oaks, CA: Sage, 2010), 278.
[58] Carl H. Botan & Maureen Taylor, 'Public Relations: State of the Field,' *Journal of Communication*, Vol. 54, No. 4, (2004), 645-661.
[59] Carl Botan & Vincent Hazleton, 'Public Relations in a New Age,' in *Public Relations Theory II*, 2006. ed. by Carl Botan & Vincent Hazleton, (Mahwah, NJ: Lawrence Erlbaum Associates, Inc., 2006), 7.
[60] Robert L. Heath, 'The Rhetorical Tradition: Wrangle in the Marketplace,' in *Rhetorical and Critical Approaches to Public Relations II*, ed. by Robert L. Heath, Elizabeth L. Toth & Damion Waymer, (New York: Routledge, 2009), 17-47.
[61] Jeong-Nam Kim, Chun-ju Flora Hung-Baesecke, Sung-Un Yang & James E. Grunig, 'A Strategic Management Approach to Reputation, Relationships, and Publics: The Research Heritage of the Excellence Theory,' in ed. by Craig E. Carroll, *The Handbook of Communication and Corporate Reputation*, (Chichester, UK: John Wiley & Sons, Inc., 2013), 201.
[62] Public Relations Society of America, 'What is Public Relations? PRSA's Widely Accepted Definition,' <http://www.prsa.org/aboutprsa/publicrelationsdefined/#.VYL-DGDldcQ>.
[63] Wilcox & Cameron, *Public Relations*, 10th edn., 54-60. Newsom, Turk & Kruckeberg, *This Is PR*, 2013, 20. Broom & Sha, *Cutlip and Center*, 11th edn., 172-190. Seitel, *The Practice of Public Relations*, 12th edn., 53, 85, & 120.
[64] D. C. Watt, 'Public Relations,' in *Fontana Dictionary of Modern Thought*, ed. by Alan Bullock & Oliver Stallybrass, (London: Collins, 1977), 513.
[65] Peter F. Drucker, *The Effective Executive*, (New York: HarperBusiness, 1993), 1.
[66] James E. Grunig, 'Communication, Public Relations, and Effective Organizations: An Overview of the Book,' in *Excellence in Public Relations....*
[67] James E. Grunig & Fred C. Repper, 'Strategic Management, Publics and Issues,' in *Excellence in Public Relations....*
[68] Benita Steyn & Lynne Niemann, 'Enterprise Strategy – A Concept that Explicates Corporate Communication's Strategic Contribution at the Macro Organizational Level,' *Journal of Communication Management*, Vol. 14, No. 2 (2010).
[69] Moloney, *Rethinking Public Relations*, x.

[70] Michael E. Porter, *Competitive Strategy: Techniques for Analyzing Industries and Competitors*, (New York: The Free Press, 1998).
[71] A. G. Lafley & Roger L. Martin, *Playing to Win: How Strategy Really Works*, (Boston, MA: Harvard Business Review Press, 2013).

CHAPTER 5

The Truth

"What is truth? said jesting Pilate, and would not stay for an answer." — Francis Bacon, "Of Truth"[1]

"I'm here to tell you I'm deeply ashamed of my mistakes. There's no need to go into the details of how I cheated on my partner (with an intern), used performance-enhancing drugs, misstated my expenses, tipped off my friends about deals, tweeted racist comments, and sent unsolicited pictures of my genitals via social media. I have pledged to cooperate with an independent investigation. But I take full responsibility. I want to apologize to my family, my friends, my employees, my constituents and my Twitter followers. I have seen the light and I'm determined to be a better person from now on. I ask you to find room in your hearts to one day believe in me again."

That is the way some public relations counselors believe someone accused of wrongdoing should redeem themselves. Not priests, not therapists, but public relations counselors. If the words of this statement of apology seem creepily familiar, that is because it is a mash-up of phrases from real life statements. They call it "telling the truth," and that is what conventional wisdom advises.

But what does it mean to tell the truth? This chapter looks more closely at this tricky concept, examining along the way problems of communication strategy faced by John F. Kennedy in his presidential campaign, among others.

(For the avoidance of doubt, the author respects the truth, however hard it may be to establish what it is.)

"Tell the Truth"

Truth is the concept that has bedeviled public relations and its ancestors for two thousand years. The problem, as Alfred North Whitehead said, is partly that: "There are no whole truths; all truths are half-truths. It is trying to treat them as whole truths that plays the devil."[2] Arguably, there is no such thing as the absolute truth in human affairs, only different versions of events, or *narratives* (see below and chapter 7).

The concept of truth looks simple but, on closer examination, is anything but simple. A current book on ethics in PR admits: "Defining what the truth is in public relations, just as in other aspects of our lives… is a challenge."[3] The truth is usually not black and white but everything in between. The question therefore arises: "Which version of the truth should the speaker tell?"

Yet many communication experts see telling the truth as a categorical imperative. One textbook declared: "Honesty is no longer just the best policy, it is the only policy when even painful truths cannot be securely and permanently hidden… Complete candor and forthrightness is the only way to achieve credibility… Businesses must go further than ever before in releasing what was previously considered confidential information."[4]

This purple passage was inspired by Johnson and Johnson's highly regarded handling of the Tylenol crisis (chapter 13). The textbook went on to claim that being open to questions was not enough — businesses should listen to their stakeholders and respond to questions that have not even been formed. Other textbooks (see chapter 4 for details) took a similar line:

- "Seitel" included an account of core values such as honesty, put forward by the Public Relations Society of America, and stated: "Public relations people don't lie."[5] Seitel co-authored a more discursive book, "Rethinking Reputation," that used the word "truth" more than fifty times.[6]
- "Newsom" set out the ethical code of one of the professional bodies. Its first three words were: "Tell the truth."[7]
- "Wilcox" allocated a section to "the ethical dilemma of being a spokesperson."[8]

(And the communiqué from a 2012 global PR conference spoke about "consistently communicating truth.")[9]

Contrast Roger Thornhill, hapless hero of Alfred Hitchcock's "North by Northwest" and probably the most best-known portrayal of an advertising man in drama before Don Draper: "In the world of advertising there is no such thing as a lie, Maggie. There is only the expedient exaggeration."[10]

What is a fact?

Ivy Lee, who has been called "the father of public relations,"[11] was the first PR man known to have advocated telling the truth. His idea "was simple: Tell the truth about an organization's actions; if that truth was damaging to the organization, then change the behavior of the organization so the truth could be told without fear."[12] This confounded the prejudice that professional communicators play fast and loose with the truth. Despite its obvious naïveté, "Tell the Truth" has become a public relations mantra. "Wilcox" described it as the moral imperative.[13] Notwithstanding the mantra, the prejudice lingers that most PR people have a relationship with the truth that is fickle at best.

The trouble is that Lee's truth was not naïve. Stuart Ewen suggested that he donned a "camouflage of facticity."[14] Lee's pitch was that he dealt in facts and told the truth, but he was selective. Lee admitted, when pressed, that the facts he handed out were the facts as management saw them and had not been verified.[15] When he was called before the US Commission on Industrial Relations in 1915, the following illuminating exchange took place:

"Q. You were out there to give the facts, the truth about the strike, the fullest publicity?

"A. Yes, the truth *as the operators saw it.* I was there to help them state their case."

Asked what efforts he had made to check the "facts," he replied: "None whatever." Lee later echoed Pontius Pilate, saying candidly (and quite reasonably): "What is a fact? The effort to state an absolute fact is simply an attempt to... give you my interpretation of the facts."

The effort to state an absolute fact is simply an attempt to give you my interpretation of the facts.

But the doctrine of "Tell the Truth" took hold and has become ever more popular among communication professionals and commentators. Lee's qualification, that the truth is not absolute but the truth as seen by the speaker, got lost along the way. Lee told the truth as an advocate tells it, presenting information and arguments to make a favorable case for his client. Latter day PR commentators tend to see themselves less in the role of advocate for one side and more in the role of moral adjudicator, establishing the facts independently and then presenting them impartially. The call for truth fits right in with the openness and transparency movement, discussed in chapter 3.

The professional bodies tend to have ethics codes that lead with truth. For example, the first principle of the Arthur W. Page Society for senior PR executives and agency directors (incorporated 1983) was "Tell the Truth."[16]

A small minority in public relations has taken a more realistic view. Trevor Morris and Simon Goldsworthy organized a debate at the University of Westminster, London, in 2007, on the motion, "PR has a duty to tell the truth." To the alarm of the PR truth fundamentalists, the motion was narrowly defeated. The organizers' comment was that: "Public figures in business or politics are seldom labeled as liars for denying that they are at loggerheads with their colleagues, or for refusing to admit problems and — when this becomes untenable — minimizing the scale of the problems." Morris and Goldsworthy drew a distinction between soft or white lies, "the sort of thing we all say," and hard lies, intentionally providing false information about important matters.[17]

"You might as well tell the truth…"

In case telling the truth for its own sake wasn't enough, some also made a pragmatic argument for telling the truth. Fraser Seitel, the veteran textbook author, maintained that public relations experts have advised for decades: "You might as well tell the truth… because people will find it out eventually."[18]

Except that people often don't find out the truth… ever. The assassination of President Kennedy is only the most obvious contemporary event this claim brings to mind. The truth about the assassination is tantalizingly slippery. It will probably never be found out in full.

When it comes to telling the truth, timing is everything. A truth that is extremely damaging today may become harmless with the passage of time. Recall the discussion of secrecy and controlled disclosure in chapter 3. After retiring from the US Central Intelligence Agency (CIA), Jack Devine, a former deputy director, said: "Almost all covert action becomes public. Very little I did is still classified."[19] The truth came out eventually but the covert action was effective precisely because, at the time of the action, it was covert, not public. Secrets are necessary in public life and the fact that they may become less secret with time does not diminish the need for them to be secret at the time.

"Tell It All"

In the context of crises, experts expanded the slogan "Tell the Truth," to one that is more far-reaching: "Tell it all, tell it now" (also stated as: "Tell it all, tell it fast"). They claim that the truth should be not just the truth but the whole truth, as in a court of law. And that it should be told straightaway.

Public relations people often allude to a metaphorical "court of public opinion." The expression was used by Edward Bernays in the early 1920s and was commonplace by the early 1950s.[20] This analogy is sometimes used to explain what happens when a public body, business or person is accused of wrongdoing in the media.[21] Legal analogies may sometimes be useful but are also prone to misuse and to erroneous conclusions being drawn. Sometimes PR people give precisely the advice on how to behave in the court of public opinion that is most likely to result in the client ending up in a court of law.

In the courts of legal systems based on English law, witnesses swear or affirm that they will tell "the truth, the whole truth and nothing but the truth." By doing so, a witness takes up a vulnerable position in the interest of justice. Deviation from the court's assessment of the truth risks committing the criminal offense of perjury. Yet, PR experts in the court of public opinion are urging not just witnesses but the defendant to "tell it all, tell it now." Telling it all now may make a good impression on public opinion but could also incriminate the person telling it. What shall it profit a client to escape from trouble with public opinion only to land in jail?

There are many celebrity cases that follow a similar pattern. Each time, a political or entertainment or sporting celebrity is accused of doing something illegal, immoral or both. Rumors mount until there is a direct accusation of wrongdoing. The celebrity then denies the accusation, looking shifty. But eventually, the celebrity admits doing something wrong and suffers various unpleasant consequences. These may include the loss of their partner, their career, their earning power and, of course, their status. Some public relations people suggest that, if only the celeb had made a full confession immediately, along the lines of this chapter's opening mash-up, the media and the public would have forgiven the lapse and the sinner would have enjoyed redemption. Months or even years of painful, pointless denigration and shame could have been avoided. For their advice is that it looks much better to make a full confession straightaway (people will find out eventually) and then, with the baggage cleared away, start rebuilding your life.

Some of the notorious cases have indeed been hopeless. It was a fair cop by the media and the celeb's denial and prevarication just extended the agony. And yet…

Watergate

The ghost of Richard Nixon haunts scenarios of public sin and redemption. The Watergate affair became a template for subsequent scandals, not only in politics. The affair consumed and confused American politics for two years, from the break-in on June 17, 1972, albeit behind the scenes for a few months, to Nixon's resignation on August 9, 1974.

Popular wisdom shares the view attributed to Senator Howard Baker: "It is almost always the cover-up rather than the event
that causes trouble." Why then did the president possibly initiate
the cover-up? Or at least collaborate in it from June 23, 1972, the
day the "smoking gun" tape was recorded? Why did he not confess immediately? He could have made a statement to the American people similar to the opening mash-up. Whenever it is argued
that the cover-up can be as damaging or more damaging than the
original offense, Watergate is exhibit A.

His opponents would say that he should have both confessed immediately and resigned immediately. And of course, in
the interest of justice and clean politics, he should have resigned
earlier.

But would it really have been a better communication strategy for Nixon to have confessed rather than attempted the cover-
up? Even going as far as taking personal responsibility for the
break-in?

Maybe not. Nixon was probably responsible for the cover-up
but not directly for the break-in. The break-in itself was idiotic
and unnecessary as well as criminal. But it took place in the early
stages of the election campaign. Nothing could be permitted to
derail that campaign. A further plausible explanation for the cover-up was that he was involved in a range of illegal activities over
a long period.[22] If the full facts about the break-in had come out
as part of an investigation, this would have been revealed. Without the cover-up, Nixon was finished. Depending on the timing,
either he would never have won re-election in 1972, or he would
have been impeached. He would have faced a prison sentence.
The cover-up gave him a chance of political survival. And although he left office in disgrace, he did manage to stay out of jail.

Finally, it is a fallacy to believe that because we now know
what happened it was always inevitable that the facts would
emerge. The president was involved in illegal activities. But a
number of unforeseeable events were required to catch him out.
First, his own carelessness in effectively admitting to breaking the
law on tape. Second, the accidental revelation of the tapes' existence. Third, the decisions by one of those involved in the break-
in and one of those involved in the cover-up to give evidence.

A full confession to the media is not a cure-all. One alternative to a full confession is a "limited hangout," (the phrase that came into common parlance via Watergate). Someone reveals something to distract journalists or investigators, keeping more damaging material a secret.

And if the alleged wrongdoing is a crime, making such a statement in the court of public opinion, which is an admission of guilt, is likely to lead on to a perilous appearance in the real court.

Contrary to the apparent view of some PR experts, the consequences of appearing in court can be much more serious for the accused than appearing in the media. So to go straight into the court of public opinion and tell not only the truth but the whole truth may be a high-risk strategy. The reward of rehabilitation may be elusive. Adulterers, drug users, fiddlers and exhibitionists may be forgiven (though sometimes after a period in prison). But what about those whose falls have been more extreme? What about murderers, rapists and child-molesters, for example? Their souls may ultimately be saved, since the peace of God passeth all understanding, but it is hard to see a shortcut to redemption for them here on Earth, no matter whom they employ as PR advisers.

And what if the defendant — either a person or a business — does not accept that the accusation is justified? In a court of law, the accused is innocent until proven guilty. Imagine if, when O. J. Simpson was accused of murder, he had been persuaded to confess (on television, naturally) by a "Tell it all" public relations counselor. Simpson was put on trial for murder in both courts — the court of law and the court of public opinion. Public opinion split partly on racial lines, inspired by the conflicting narratives that were eventually put forward by opposing advocates. The intensity of public feeling was linked to conflicting masterplots in American culture, one of which was "the story of the black man who is unjustly punished for stepping 'out of his place.'"[23] The truth was out there somewhere but it was the narratives that prevailed in the court of public opinion. In the court of law, Simpson was acquitted. And in recent years, a private investigator has written a book with the self-explanatory title: "O. J. Is Innocent and I Can Prove It.[24] It is hard to see how he would have been better off if he had confessed and gone to jail.

Key points
- The truth, a concept that is fundamental to communication, looks simple but is slippery.
- Ivy Lee, "father of public relations," advocated telling the truth but actually presented his client's version of the facts. However, the public relations profession officially adheres to what Lee said, not what he did.
- Public relations experts even advise telling the whole truth. (You may need to check with your lawyer before adopting telling the truth as your communication strategy.)

Saying less

Telling it all is said to be both ethical and effective. An alternative communication strategy is some version of saying less (see chapter 11 on saying less in a crisis). This alternative is routinely despised but, when telling it all is undesirable, saying less often works quite well.

Unknown to the general public at the time, Senator John F. Kennedy suffered from Addison's Disease. This is a chronic condition that may progress to severe illness in the form of an Addisonian (adrenal) crisis that is incapacitating and potentially fatal.

In the run-up to the Democratic convention ahead of the 1960 presidential election, questions were raised about the candidate's health. JFK himself said nothing. Robert Kennedy said that his brother "does not now nor has he ever had an ailment described classically as Addison's Disease," only "some adrenal insufficiency" which was "not in any way a dangerous condition." He said, "Any statement to the contrary is malicious and false." And Kennedy's aide, Ted Sorensen, denied that he took the steroids that in fact kept him going.[25]

Some would say that the Kennedy campaign had plainly lied. But Robert Dallek noted that a number of presidents, including Wilson, Coolidge, Franklin D. Roosevelt and Eisenhower, had concealed material information about their medical conditions. (Roosevelt's serious health problems, including congestive heart failure, were concealed from the American public ahead of the 1944 presidential election and he died only a few months into his last term of office.) Dallek added: "There is another way of viewing the silence regarding his health — as the quiet stoicism of a man... performing his... duties largely undeterred by his physical suffering." This cast Kennedy's character in a much better light.[26]

It could be argued that Kennedy's condition made him medically unfit to serve as president. If the truth about his condition had come out during the campaign, he could well have lost the election. The truth did eventually come out. Yet the verdict of history on the Kennedy presidency has not been that it was a fraud.

The extreme version of saying less is saying nothing. This tends to be dismissed with the claim that silence concedes that what the other side is saying is correct. "Silence grants the point."[27] In an argument between two opposing viewpoints like a set piece at a student debating society, this is obviously the case. But much of the present book is about not becoming embroiled in such an argument in the first place. If what appears, at first glance, to be a storm turns out, after a pause for thought, to be a storm contained within the proverbial teacup, treating it like a real storm would be foolish and unnecessary.

Saying nothing does not, of course, mean saying "No comment," like a robot. One survey suggested that two thirds of the US general public are incline to regard "No comment" as an admission of guilt.[28] Fortunately, "no comment" is just the lazy phrase. There are many different forms of words to explain why no statement is being made on the record that may be appropriate for use depending on the situation.

Saying less, (or even saying nothing, without the dreaded "no comment") is often the best approach. The natural reflex to hit back at critics is as strong in organizations, led as they are by emotional human beings, as it is for mere mortals. But hitting back may not be the most effective response. Chapter 1 showed how top executives in difficult situations would have done themselves and their employers a service by saying less. And where a weak adversary takes on a powerful target, responding in kind may be exactly what the critic wants. If the critics' target reacts, that ensures that the attack receives a second airing. Then it gives the critic the opportunity of a third airing, by responding to the response. If you just want the problem to go away, avoid giving a platform to the enemy. (See chapter 12.)

Keep calm and say less (at Goldman Sachs)

Take the case of Goldman Sachs and its ex-employee, Greg Smith. Smith quit his job in 2012, not in the customary way, but on the op-ed page of the *New York Times*, claiming that Goldman did not put its clients ("muppets") first.[29]

The next day, the media gleefully reported that the letter had "wiped more than $2bn off of Goldman's market value." In fact, the stock price rose slightly in the few days after the letter.[30] There was a flurry of intemperate and inaccurate comments. Some said that Lloyd Blankfein would be forced to quit as CEO. And UK Business Secretary Vince Cable was quoted as saying: "This letter has inflicted severe reputational damage on Goldman Sachs and they will pay the price for it."[31] Four years later, Goldman Sachs was thriving and Lloyd Blankfein was still in office.

Goldman emailed staff, briefly reaffirming its commitment to clients, and released the email to the media. This was not a crisis. Smith was one of 12,000 vice-presidents in a staff of 30,000.

A few months later, Smith published a memoir, "Why I Left Goldman Sachs." Now, according to Fraser Seitel, writing for PR newsletter *O'Dwyer's*, the choice for Goldman was between saying nothing, and thereby conceding that what Smith alleged was true, or responding in kind. He praised Goldman for answering back.[32] Goldman launched its own Twitter account in May 2012. When the book came out, Goldman sent a long email to staff.

The choice was not really between conceding and responding. If Goldman traded blows with Smith over the book, it risked increasing interest in what he had to say. Taking the long view, Goldman equally had the option of disregarding the allegations in public and moving on to more important matters, while privately talking round any concerned clients. This strategy of silence could have ensured that those whose opinion really mattered heard Goldman's side of the story without a brouhaha. How much lasting impact would the memoir have had on the world's leading investment bank?

Meanwhile, another storm was brewing in the same mug. For three years in the 2010s, Goldman was taunted and Goldman-watchers were entertained by tweets at the @GSElevator Twitter profile. These purported to be leaks by an anonymous Goldman employee. In January 2014, the stakes were raised by news that the anonymous author was planning a book provisionally entitled "Straight to Hell: True Tales of Deviance and Excess in the World of Investment Banking."[33]

Eventually, the elevator leak was revealed to be fiction. Goldman S. Elevator was not, nor had he ever been, an employee of Goldman Sachs.[34] Throughout this micro-storm, Goldman may have been tempted to answer back. Some PR people may advise those in similar situations to do so, in the mistaken belief that silence grants the point. Those in the eye of a micro-storm are usually best advised to say very little in public and confine their comments to those they need to keep briefed. Micro-storms may not be worth strategic attention.

Here is a model media statement for use in the case of a micro-storm:

"It's a one-sided, inaccurate portrayal of our company and our actions. Beyond that, we don't have anything to say."

That comment was attributed to Procter & Gamble. It was all that the company had to say in public on the subject of a critical 1993 book ("explosive exposé") by Alecia Swasy, a reporter on the *Wall Street Journal*, entitled "Soap Opera."[35] There was some controversy at the time but today Procter & Gamble continues to be widely respected and successful.

Silent communication: keeping shtum

Persuasion is usually seen in the sense of active communication. At its simplest, "Persuasion is something achieved through one person's communicating with another."[36] Professional communications persuade someone to do something or believe something. The advertiser seeks to persuade the consumer to buy the product. The political campaign seeks to persuade the citizen to vote. And so on.

But persuasion can also be used in a broader sense. When the desired response is not an action or a commitment but acquiescence, the hurdle is lower. In the case of Goldman Sachs, the bank did not need people to be outraged on its behalf, either by

Greg Smith or @GSElevator. It just needed them to ignore and forget its critics. Its ideal outcome was for everyone to have the same view of the bank post-Smith/Elevator as before. What is more, it could have settled for just the people who really mattered to Goldman to have an unchanged view of the bank. (Who are those people? See chapter 12.) This level of persuasion can often be achieved by avoiding provocation, saying less and judicious silence.

Few scholars recognize that the study of reputation (again, see chapter 12) has been skewed toward the high profile, active communicators — those who seek the limelight. Most public relations scholars suffer from fear of flying… under the radar. But the fact is that there are many other organizations (and people) that receive little or no public attention. What about those that neither employ professional communicators in-house nor use agencies?

Many organizations don't have a poor reputation but have a small reputation in the sense that they are not well known. Some may even prefer that state of affairs. It could be that aspects of the organization are sheltered from scrutiny by certain audiences. This would be a communication strategy of *keeping shtum*, not for a short time but more or less permanently. Furthermore, for these entities, "Keeping silent… helps the organizations more uniformly manage reputations. We may wish to have a certain reputation among rival groups or in certain industries, but prefer not to be in the general public's eye."[37]

Hermann Simon called the businesses he studied "hidden champions," though they are usually quiet and unobtrusive rather than hidden.[38] However, Palantir, the data analysis company whose origins have been linked to the intelligence community, is a company that has turned secrecy into a marketing message.

Key points
- Another PR adage is "Silence grants the point." But there are many circumstances when saying less or nothing is the best course. In Goldman Sachs' brushes with "whistleblowers," answering back was likely to amplify the original complaints.
- Saying less in order to keep a low profile and quietly go about their business is a successful communication strategy for a surprisingly large number of organizations.

In Summary

- "Tell the truth," the public relations mantra, is simplistic. The stories people tell are their versions of the truth.
- It is often a better communication strategy to say less, or even to say nothing, than to say a lot.

References

1 *Essays or Counsels, Civil and Moral* (1625, original), (Oxford University Press, 1999).
2 Quoted in Watson, *Ideas*, 2005, iii.
3 Patricia J. Parsons, *Ethics in Public Relations: a Guide to Best Practice*, (London: Kogan Page Limited, 2008), 15.
4 Baskin et al, *Public Relations*, 421.
5 Seitel, *The Practice of Public Relations*, 12ᵗʰ edn., 53, 85, & 120.
6 Fraser P. Seitel & John Doorley, *Rethinking Reputation: How PR Trumps Marketing and Advertising in the New Media World*, (New York: Palgrave Macmillan, 2012).
7 Newsom et al, *This is PR*, 145.
8 Wilcox & Cameron, *Public Relations*, 10ᵗʰ edn., 112-113.
9 *Melbourne Mandate*, Global Alliance for Public Relations and Communication Management.
10 *North by Northwest*, Ernest Lehman, Metro-Goldwyn-Mayer, 1959.
11 Baskin et al, *Public Relations*, 33.
12 Grunig & Hunt, *Managing Public Relations*, 31.
13 Wilcox & Cameron, *Public Relations*, 10ᵗʰ edn., 98.
14 Stuart Ewen, *PR! A Social History of Spin*, (New York: BasicBooks, 1996), 78.
15 Newsom et al, *This Is PR*, 11ᵗʰ edn., 33.
16 Wilcox & Cameron, *Public Relations*, 10ᵗʰ edn., 102-104.
17 Trevor Morris & Simon Goldsworthy, *PR - A Persuasive Industry? Spin, Public Relations and the Shaping of the Modern Media*, (London: Palgrave Macmillan, 2008), 49-57.
18 Seitel & Doorley, *Rethinking Reputation*, 113.
19 Belinda Luscombe, '10 Questions,' *Time*, June 16, 2014.
20 Cutlip, *The Unseen Power*, 181. Cutlip & Center, *Effective Public Relations*, 1ˢᵗ edn., 7-8.
21 Seitel, *The Practice of Public Relations*, 12ᵗʰ edn., 128.
22 Keith W. Olson, 'Watergate,' in *A Companion to Richard M. Nixon*, ed. by Melvin Small, (Chichester, UK: Blackwell Publishing Limited, 2011).
23 H. Porter Abbott, *Cambridge Introduction to Narrative*, (Cambridge University Press, 2002), 44.
24 William C. Dear, *O.J. Is Innocent and I Can Prove It*, (New York: Skyhorse Publishing, 2012).
25 Robert A. Caro, *The Passage of Power*, (New York: Alfred A. Knopf, 2012), 357-8.
26 'Says President Is Fit: Vice Admiral McIntire Reports Roosevelt's Health "Very Good,"' *New York Times*, September 26, 1944. Robert Dallek, 'The Medical Ordeals of JFK,' *The Atlantic*, December 1, 2002.
27 Fraser P. Seitel, 'Silence Grants the Point,' *O'Dwyer's*, October 23, 2012.
28 Wilcox & Cameron, *Public Relations*, 10ᵗʰ edn., 243.
29 Greg Smith, 'Why I Am Leaving Goldman Sachs,' *New York Times*, March 14, 2012.
30 Daniel Bates, Simon Tomlinson & Sam Greenhill, 'The £1bn Backlash: Shares Plummet in Goldman Sachs after Disgusted Former Executive Says Bank Rips off Its Clients and Calls Them Muppets,' *Daily Mail*, March 15, 2012.
31 Frederick E. Allen, 'To Save Goldman Sachs, Lloyd Blankfein Must Go,' *Forbes*, March 14, 2012.
32 'Goldman Sachs Response to Greg Smith's Op-Ed,' *Bloomberg Businessweek*, March 14, 2012. Book: Greg Smith, *Why I Left Goldman Sachs: A Wall Street Story*, (New York: Grand Central Publishing, 2012). Answering back: Seitel, 'Silence Grants the Point.'
33 Tracey Alloway, 'Goldman Insider to Cash in on Twitter Fame with Exposé Book Deal,' *Financial Times*, January 22, 2014.
34 Andrew Ross Sorkin, '@GSElevator Tattletale Exposed (He Was Not in the Goldman Elevator),' *New York Times*, February 24, 2014.

[35] 'Procter & Gamble: Hanging Out the Dirty Washing,' *The Economist*, October 16, 1993.
[36] Daniel J. O'Keefe, *Persuasion: Theory and Research*, (Thousand Oaks, CA: Sage Publications, Inc., 2002), 4.
[37] Craig R. Scott, 'Hidden Organizations and Reputation,' in Carroll, *Handbook of Communication and Corporate Reputation*, 554.
[38] Hermann Simon, *Hidden Champions of the Twenty-First Century: Success Strategies of Unknown World Market Leaders*, (New York: Springer, 2009).

CHAPTER 6

Optimism and the Strategy of Truth

"TRUTH, noun. An ingenious compound of desirability and appearance."

"OPTIMIST, noun. A proponent of the doctrine that black is white."

— Ambrose Bierce, "The Devil's Dictionary"[1]

Early in 1940, the Soviet NKVD murdered about 22,000 Polish soldiers and civilians they were holding captive. It took fifty years for that truth to be accepted everywhere.

The incredible truth

The Poles were massacred by the NKVD, the People's Commissariat for Internal Affairs, forerunner of the KGB and today's Federal Security Service (FSB). That was the truth but they concealed the crime in mass forest graves at Katyn and elsewhere in what is now the extreme west of Russia.

The German army overran the area in 1941. They discovered the Katyn graves on April 17, 1943, and immediately publicized their discovery. Despite the evidence, the Nazi claim was open to question because they lacked credibility.

The Soviet Union was not about to admit the shameful truth. The Soviets claimed, plausibly, that the Nazis were responsible for the massacres themselves and that the "discovery" was a ruse to conceal their own atrocity. The Soviets appealed to the truth as zealously as anyone in the West — "Pravda." Their distortion of it had little credibility with critical observers. But they were not seeking to convince critical observers, only the uncritical. For their purposes, it was not necessary to convince the whole world of Nazi guilt and their innocence. They merely needed a version of events that could not be disproved, that would be consistent ideologically, and that would thus provide a story their own people and sympathizers could believe.

Once the Red Army recovered the site later in the war, the Soviets set up a commission headed by the president of their Academy of Medical Sciences to provide their claim with spurious scientific support. The false Soviet version of events stood for decades. It continued to have widespread currency until the 1970s and the Soviet Union only withdrew it in 1990.[2]

The scale of the deception may have been extreme in the Katyn case but it illustrates the gap between the truth and the appearance of truth that occurs frequently in public life. Napoleon is said to have observed that, "The truth is not so important as what people think to be true."[3]

The same applies on a much smaller scale. In 1980, Azaria Chamberlain disappeared in Australia's Northern Territory. Her mother, Lindy Chamberlain, said the baby was snatched by a dingo, but she was wrongly convicted of murder. It took until 2012 for an inquest to conclude: "After 32 Years of Speculation, It's Finally Official: A Dingo Took Azaria."[4]

The cases of Katyn and the "dingo baby" were two among many where the mere fact that something was true did not guarantee belief. This was because: "Truth does not stand on its own hind legs... it must be communicated persuasively."[5] The credibility of the message and the credibility of the speaker or source are more important than truth alone in determining whether a story is likely to be believed.

Propaganda

Knowing the facts about Katyn, we may describe the Soviet version of events as "propaganda." Propaganda has been defined by Garth Jowett and Victoria O'Donnell as "the deliberate, systematic attempt to shape perceptions, manipulate cognitions, and direct behavior to achieve a response that furthers the desired intent" of the communicator.[6]

How does this differ from the non-propaganda behavior of communicators? Until quite recently, there was little distinction either in popular discourse or in the writings of professionals and scholars, between propaganda and public relations. Lee, Bernays and other public relations people in the first half of the 20th century could equally be said to have engaged in a deliberate, systematic attempt to shape perceptions, manipulate cognitions and direct behavior. Bernays even wrote a book entitled "Propaganda." In it, he said: "Whatever of social importance is done today, whether in politics, finance, manufacture, agriculture, charity, education, or other fields, must be done with the help of propaganda."[7] What Jowett and O'Donnell called the "deliberate, systematic attempt" is plainly also the purpose of advertising, marketing and much PR today.

Yet public relations scholars and professional bodies have sought to cast propaganda into the outer darkness. What put propaganda beyond the pale was not only some of its methodology but its use first by the Bolsheviks and then by the Nazis (although Joseph Goebbels disliked the term "propaganda").[8] Both communist and fascist propaganda were immensely persuasive. "Nazi Germany itself was essentially the product of propaganda."[9] And for more than forty years after the War, Soviet propaganda contributed both to maintaining the regime and to distorting political debate all over the world. Throughout the existence of the USSR, many workers, students, politicians, journalists and intellectuals in the West and the Third World saw it through rose-tinted spectacles. The tint was applied by Soviet propaganda. Many were duped into regarding the West and the USSR as equivalent rather than inherently different. It is hardly surprising that the nascent profession of public relations was at pains to distance itself from propaganda. People like Nikolai Bukharin, Mikhail Suslov and, above all, Goebbels would not be welcomed into any of today's professional bodies. And if it becomes hard to fathom the power of totalitarian propaganda, we have only to think of the success of demagogues and religious fanatics in our own time.

Damning all propaganda in mid-20th century because of a man like Goebbels split the study of public communication into two academic disciplines. The majority concern themselves mainly with business, the public sector and charities, and call their subject public relations. A smaller group, with different interests, studies propaganda, concentrating on military and diplomatic affairs. (Yet another military/diplomatic group studies "strategic communication," defined as: "coordinated actions, messages, images, and other forms of signaling or engagement intended to inform, influence, or persuade selected audiences in support of national objectives.")[10] The leading public relations textbooks virtually ignore propaganda, apart from "Newsom," which concedes that: "there is nothing inherent in the nature of propaganda that prevents it from being used to change attitudes and behavior in a constructive way."[11] No one has yet made a convincing case for treating propaganda and public relations as separate subjects but political correctness enforces the distinction.

Requirements of credibility

There is often good reason not to tell the whole truth and the chosen narrative need not be the whole truth. But the verifiable facts are still the essential foundation when composing a position. It needs to resist easy refutation and be consistent with established, recognized facts, unless the whole point of taking a position is to dispute an established "fact."

The importance of source credibility has been known since Aristotle. His "Rhetoric" proposed that one of the keys to persuasion was ethos, the character of the speaker. Or, as Cicero put it: "Feelings are won over by a man's merit, achievements and reputation."

Modern research has established that what is termed source credibility is indeed critical to success.[12] It has been shown to depend chiefly on two perceptions: first, that the speaker can be trusted and, second, expertise — that the speaker knows what he or she is talking about. It has been suggested that a number of less important perceptions such as the energy and sociability of the speaker may also play a part.

Both main aspects of source credibility, expertise and trust, suggest that it is inadvisable to deploy public relations people in broadcast interviews. They lack credibility. As mere staffers, they are not seen as having the requisite expertise unlike, say, the manager of a plant or store. And, despite the efforts of PR's own PR, they are not trusted. To skeptics in the audience, the title, "vice-president, public relations" means professional liar.

In practice, it can be extremely difficult to tell the difference between persuasion and propaganda.[13] In the muddle of ends and means, truth is a litmus test of doubtful value. Ideally, "unlike propaganda, which distorts facts and exaggerate claims, persuasion should be based on information that an organization honestly believes to be true." But it is rarely that simple, especially since in order to be effective, propaganda has to be "convincing, viable and truthful within its own remit."[14] There could be a sliding scale. The more officials were prepared to use deception, the more it would be likely to be considered propaganda. Another possible criterion is bias but bias is hard to define and even harder to avoid. Or the distinction could be whether communications are serving good or evil. This was Bernays' view.[15]

Key points
- "Truth does not stand on its own hind legs" but has to be communicated persuasively.
- For a narrative to be persuasive, the source and the content must be credible.
- By demonizing propaganda, theorists and professional bodies have introduced an ideological distortion into the study of public communication.

Accentuating the positive

Optimism demonstrates every day around the world that truth in public communication is relative, not absolute. Credibility is the problem, ultimately, for the very popular communication strategy of optimism.

The problem with optimism is that one day its distortion of the facts of the case is likely to cause revulsion. The good news for optimists is that there can be a time lapse, sometimes a gap of many years, between the speaker distorting the facts and the audience realizing (or choosing to realize) that the facts have been distorted. Thus many optimists complete their terms of office and move on without being unmasked.

Those who practice optimism have not necessarily made a deliberate choice. More often, people just do what comes naturally, because optimism is a cognitive bias. Most of us believe that the world is better than it really is, that we are better than we really are, and that our prospects are better than they really are. We believe that a glass containing 50% liquid and 50% air is better described as half-full than half-empty. Optimism is normal. It is beneficial both to optimists and for those around them. And because optimism sells, it is rife in public life. In PR, it is the tendency that Ian Verchere described as seeking to put a happy complexion on everything and everyone.[16]

(Denial is a related phenomenon.[17] In the first world war black comedy, "Blackadder Goes Forth," General Melchett says at one point: "If nothing else works, a total pig-headed unwillingness to look facts in the face will see us through.")[18]

But, and it is a significant but, according to Daniel Kahneman, "the blessings of optimism are offered only to individuals who are only mildly biased and who are able to 'accentuate the positive' without losing track of reality."[19] Optimism in moderation is a good thing. When it becomes excessive, it ceases to be a good thing and becomes harmful.

People whose professional lives involve a lot of public communication are particularly susceptible to the temptation of optimism. Whenever the aim is persuasion, the persuader is tempted to exaggerate the advantages of whatever course of action is being urged. This was familiar in the classical world, where they defined the rhetorical device of using exaggeration to make a case and called it hyperbole. And optimism is closely associated with public relations. Edward Bernays, one of the first authorities on PR, whose career almost spanned the 20th century, was criticized for "excessive hyperbole."[20] (He described himself as "US Publicist No. 1").

A climate of optimism, which is a kind of psychological inflation, is good for economic growth. Pessimism, psychological deflation, is bad for the economy. More specific optimism about the benefits of a product or service sells. Constraints have been put in place by law as to how optimistic sellers can be. But there is plenty of scope for optimism within the law. Vance Packard's best-selling 1957 book, "The Hidden Persuaders," used insights from psychology to bring to public attention the impact on society of advertising and marketing that used these insights. One chapter was devoted to "Care and Feeding of Positive Thinkers," using quotes from the industry journal, *Tide*, to explain their aim of boosting confidence so that, "Dealers will keep on ordering goods and consumers will keep on buying goods, at a higher and higher rate, and if necessary go into debt to do it."[21]

Do the record debt levels of our century imply record levels of optimism?

Strategy of optimism

There can be a disposition to optimism, and optimism is built into the process of selling, but optimism can also be a communication strategy. It is never explicit, because that to make it explicit would be to own up to distortion, and those who employ it may not admit it even to themselves.

The *communication strategy of optimism* can be defined as:

Consistently or systematically, and recklessly, promising or forecasting that the future will be better than an objective observer in possession of all the facts and figures would estimate, with the aim of increasing the valuation of the promoter or the promoter's wares.

Of course, there is no objective observer. Leaders always have inside information, especially about their own intentions. The strategy of optimism is the strategy of promising that things will improve when their real prospects are no better than mediocre or uncertain.

Promising recklessly. Optimists are not fraudsters. The optimist does not call for a confidential forecast and then add 10% before publishing it. The optimist's fault lies in not being sufficiently careful. The optimist may not know but recklessly behaves as though he or she does know, like the plausible CFO in chapter 2.

Part of the problem is that people who play the role of constituent (or investor or follower) hunger and thirst for certainty from the political or business leader when there is no certainty. When leaders recognize this uncertainty, one option is to be open about it. The other option, taken by many, is to pretend to a nonexistent certainty. The technical term for this form of communication is bullshit: "Bullshit is unavoidable whenever circumstances require someone to talk without knowing what he is talking about."[22]

The strategy of optimism is prevalent in politics in the run-up to elections. The future will be better — so long as you vote for us. There is little regulation of political communication to keep it in check. Roderick Hart analyzed language used in thirteen US presidential elections for their tone rather than their content. One of the scales he used for analysis was optimism. He found that more optimistic campaigns were more likely to win. Once an election was over, candidates switched from optimistic language to more realistic language.

(Hart threw away a comment to make communication strategists in business pause for thought: "While highly optimistic, politicians are almost dour compared to corporate spokespersons."[23])

However, optimistic strategies are not confined to campaign politics. For example, the Johnson administration's management of the war in Vietnam used an optimistic communication strategy. As time went on, the gap between the optimistic official account of progress in the war and conditions on the ground grew ever wider, against a backdrop of waning public support for the war. "The President seemed to think that if he and his aides spoke long enough and loud enough about Vietnam, he could bend the American public and the North Vietnamese to his will." But unfortunately, "Because so much of what he hoped for in the war was at variance with the realities of the conflict, his expressions of faith, which rested on sincere convictions about what the US military could achieve in Vietnam, made him seem devious."[24] Then, in early 1968, the Tet offensive, in which fighting reached the grounds of the US embassy in Saigon, exposed the realities and snatched away the administration's credibility. Walter Cronkite editorialized: "To say that we are closer to victory today is to believe in the face of the evidence, the optimists who have been wrong in the past."[25]

Optimism about the war continued under Nixon: "Tonight I can report that Vietnamization has succeeded." (April 7, 1971)[26] And the pattern was established for exaggerated claims of success in subsequent conflicts from Iraq ("Mission Accomplished") to ISIL/Daesh.

Political optimism continues unabated. Writing his latest volume of presidential history, Rick Perlstein found that, in the transition from Nixon to Reagan, "something almost like a cult of official optimism… saturates the land."[27]

Key points
- The strategy of optimism is popular in many walks of life.
- Optimism is rooted in cognitive bias. It can be beneficial but only if the bias is limited.
- Systematically promising a better future than can be justified by the facts breaks down when the gap between promise and reality becomes too wide.

Optimism at public companies

The strategy of optimism is also one of the most popular communication strategies in business (and not only with unregulated or unscrupulous salespeople). Optimism is not inherent in any types of business but some do seem particularly susceptible to this strategy, especially when they are seeking investment. Financial services collaborate enthusiastically in the optimism. As Jason Zweig put it: "Wall Street sells stocks and bonds, but what it really peddles is hope."[28] Optimism is organized hope.

- Miners are apt to talk up the potential of their holdings. They are apt to play down hurdles such as the logistical works required to transport ore from a remote corner of some African kleptocracy.

- Oil explorers are apt to talk up the size of a discovery. They are apt to play down obstacles such as the need to negotiate farming out the cost of development.

- Small drug companies are apt to talk up the potential of their product pipelines. They are apt to play down the likelihood of a drug failing clinical trials or the likelihood of the company running out of cash before it can bring a product to market.

- Up and coming tech companies are apt to talk up the scope for their new business models eating the lunches of legacy businesses such as banks, bricks and mortar retailers and IT giants. They are apt to play down the practical problems and the possibility their own lunch will be eaten by someone smarter and hungrier.

An argument can be made that optimistic presentation is essential to obtaining investment in start-ups. A new business needs capital and cannot attract it without explaining why its prospects are good. In other words, it needs a compelling strategic narrative for prospective investors.

In the mid-19th century, railway entrepreneurs formed hundreds of companies and made optimistic cases for capital to build thousands of miles of track. Unfortunately, the optimism was so extreme as to be dubbed "railway mania." Some of these businesses collapsed without building anything. Others built routes to nowhere.

At some stage, reality must intrude. It's my job as the communication expert to warn against the probable consequences of continuing with an optimistic strategy once funding has been secured. A degree of optimism may be irresistible for a minnow coming to capital markets. It is unsuitable for an established, publicly traded business with responsibilities to investors and employees, because it relies on fortune.

Fortuna is fickle. It is possible for a CEO, or a general, or a political leader, to succeed thanks to a run of good fortune rather than good judgment. Sometimes optimistic promises can be kept through gamblers' luck but it always runs out in the end. Perception and reality must eventually come back into alignment, usually not smoothly but with a sickening downward lurch. Once patience and fortune are exhausted and stark reality becomes clear, the story ends in tears for the optimist. (Julius Caesar had an incredible run of luck — until the Ides of March — see chapter 2.)

Optimistic reporting

An important weapon in the armory of the optimistic communication strategist is *optimistic reporting*. There are fundamentally two aspects to this: aggressive accounting and commentary on underlying performance.

First, aggressive accounting techniques which tend to show the business in a more favorable light on a permanent basis — or until they are either rescinded by a more conservative management or outlawed by accounting regulators. An example on the income statement is the timing of recognition of sales. In theory, sales could be recognized when they are booked, when goods or services are delivered, when they are invoiced, or when they are paid for. And when maintenance or upgrades are involved, there is a further complication. Another example is the extent to which employee stock options should be accounted for on the income statement. An example on the balance sheet is how leases are reported. A conservative balance sheet would show lease obligations for aircraft, office buildings, stores and so on as liabilities. Aggressive balance sheets hide these obligations away. There are thought to be $2 trillion worth of off-balance sheet leases in total.[29]

The second group of techniques in optimistic reporting employs the concept of underlying performance. Both investors and managers have a legitimate interest in looking through the figures in annual accounts to try to discern how the business is really performing, which may be better or worse than a glance at the headline earnings would suggest (usually "net income" in the US and "profit before tax" in the UK). Take closing a redundant facility. The one-off cost should reduce earnings in the year of the closure. Yet since the business no longer incurs the running costs of the closed facility, earnings should be higher in subsequent years.

There are various ways of adjusting the reported figures to arrive at underlying performance. Adjusted EBITDA (earnings before interest, taxes, depreciation and amortization) is particularly popular in the US. In the UK, "underlying" or "core" figures, as defined by the company, are popular. Adjustment has been around for a long time. In the 1980s, the terminology du jour in the UK involved the separation of "extraordinary" and "exceptional" items. These items came under the spotlight in Terry Smith's classic critique of "accounting sleight of hand," in which he noted that they were sometimes very large relative to profits, and that in some companies extraordinary events seemed to have become ordinary. There was no suggestion of any breach of the law or accounting rules. The companies may have had justification for using the methods. However, the real issue with these adjusted figures is what happens over time. Underlying figures may be a fair indication of performance when the adjustment is only for temporary factors (and only on a consistent basis). But when a company continually adjusts the accounts to show its performance in a more favorable light, and when underlying and reported figures seem to be perpetually distant from one another, the underlying figures should be viewed with suspicion. Suspicion is increased when cash tells a different story from earnings. As Smith said, "Profits can be manufactured by creative accounting, but creating cash is impossible... Profits are someone's opinion... whereas cash is a fact."[30]

Among his many memorable aphorisms, Warren Buffett is supposed to have said: "I try to buy stock in businesses that are so wonderful that an idiot can run them. Because sooner or later, one will." In this maxim, the words "idiot" and "optimist" should be interchangeable. Buffett also warned against investors in a bull market behaving like "the preening duck that quacks boastfully after a torrential rainstorm, thinking that its paddling skills have caused it to rise in the world. A right-thinking duck would instead compare its position after the downpour to that of the other ducks on the pond."[31] The optimistic manager and the foolish duck are members of the same species. Like the duck, the optimistic manager takes undue credit for benign economic conditions.

Valuation

In the perennial struggle between the growth and value styles of investment, are growth companies optimistic and value companies realistic? Not necessarily. Apple, the large cap growth company of the 21st century par excellence, has been a paragon.

Valuation is a key test of realism versus optimism in communication with investors. Some boards and managements believe that valuation is none of their business, because the market should decide the value of a quoted company. And sometimes pundits, with or without a vested interest, urge that the real value of a business has been grossly underestimated by the market, without encouragement from management.

It is a truism that the market decides the market value of anything. But no one is in a better position than the company itself to estimate its fair value.

Why not take a view of the company's own value as part of its strategy process? "Based on a robust valuation process, a company can identify its fair value corridor [making allowance for variables such as earnings ratings for industry peers] and regularly assess its position in it."[32] Building and maintaining an internal valuation model is a good discipline and superior to the alternative of relying on the model of a favorite analyst. A communication director can help by keeping a record of all forward-looking statements made by management, tracking performance against the statements and advising management about issuing forward-looking statements.

If managers feed the market with optimistic forecasts, it is disingenuous to claim no influence over the resulting share price rises. (Pontius Pilate the CFO.) If the market undervalues the company, management should be able to see what the market is missing and point it out. If the market value has become upwardly detached from fundamentals, management should ask itself whether its communications are sufficiently realistic.

There is no doubt of the importance of sentiment in the stock market, more often bullish than bearish, and individual companies cannot affect how stocks generally are rated. There is frequently exuberance and whether it is rational is likely to be hotly debated. But companies can and do influence how their own stock is rated relative to the equity market as a whole.

When it all goes wrong

Cases of an uninterrupted upward share price trajectory are comparatively uncommon. Few small firms make it to the global stage. Those that do are businesses such as Apple, Berkshire Hathaway, Facebook and Alphabet (Google) whose success really is extraordinary. Andreessen Horowitz, the tech venture capital firm, is approached by 3,000 startups every year. It invests in fifteen of them. Of the fifteen, one becomes a unicorn (a company valued at $1 billion or more), if they are lucky.[33] These unicorns are lionized. Losers are quickly forgotten.

The business of tipping and selling investments is centuries old. It gave us the South Sea Bubble. Around the time that P. T. Barnum was making his name as an impresario and personifying what public relations historians called the era of press agentry, men of a similar stamp were promoting stock market speculations. Finance has come a long way since then. But the global financial crisis served to remind outsiders that while the rules multiply, the promotional game goes on. Company managements need to accept that investors (speculators) may be playing a different game, and work with those playing it, but should never delude themselves that it is their own game, being played for their benefit, and join in unreservedly.

In established companies that employ an optimistic strategy, over-promising and under-delivering, expected results will fail to materialize from time to time. The company suffers a serious or sustained setback. When this happens, investors, lenders and other supporters are disappointed. There is a change of management. The leader who thought that CEO stands for "Chief Executive Optimist" departs. The incoming management is more conservative, committed to taking remedial action, based on a more realistic view of the company's situation and prospects. Then analysis of the previous, discredited management's statements to investors and the media is likely to provide copious evidence of an underlying strategy of optimism, although it is highly unlikely either that the company formally adopted such a strategy or that any laws will be judged to have been broken. There may be shareholder lawsuits but the new management is obliged to defend the company against them, taking the side of the present shareholders against the original shareholders, whose gullibility or inattention may have facilitated the strategy of optimism through their acquiescence.

Key points
- For public companies, a strategy of optimism is most appropriate in the start-up and rapid growth stages.
- Once a company has responsibilities to shareholders and employees, its communications should transition from optimism to realism.
- But many companies either cling to a strategy of optimism for too long or adopt a strategy of optimism anew at a later stage in their life cycle.

Lifting the spirits

When the outlook is bleak, is it not incumbent upon the leader to lift the spirits of the masses? (Or the workforce? Or the shareholders?)

Winston Churchill became British prime minister in desperate circumstances. It was Friday, May 10, 1940, the day Germany invaded France, Belgium and the Netherlands. On the following Monday, May 13, the Germans sweeping all before them, Churchill went to the House of Commons to make his first speech as leader. Surely, if any situation called for an optimistic speech that would give hope to his parliamentary audience and, through the media, the entire people of Britain, this was it? Instead, he said:

"I have nothing to offer but blood, toil, tears and sweat. We have before us an ordeal of a most grievous kind. We have before us many, many long months of struggle and of suffering. You ask, what is our policy? I can say: It is to wage war, by sea, land and air, with all our might and with all the strength that God can give us; to wage war against a mon-

strous tyranny, never surpassed in the dark, lamentable catalog of human crimes."

It was not at all optimistic. But it was inspiring. In a series of
communications in the early summer of 1940, Churchill took the
idiosyncratic view that people can handle bad news. The reports
of Mass Observation showed that the immediate public reaction
to Churchill's somber warning was positive.[34]

Anyone who finds the strategy of optimism irresistible despite all of this might pay attention to the advice attributed to
Abraham Lincoln: "You can fool some of the people all of the
time, and all of the people some of the time, but you can't fool all
of the people all of the time."

The strategy of truth

Statesmen had spent the Thirties in strategic optimism.
Eventually, reality became too insistent to ignore. The "long
weekend" was over. A change in communication strategy was a
by-product of the advent of total war.

A week after America entered the first world war in April
1917, President Wilson set up the Committee on Public Information (CPI) to sell the war to the domestic audience. The CPI
recognized that wartime propaganda had come to be associated
with "deceit and corruption," and determined to follow the lead
of Ivy Lee in supplying information to the public that was
prompt and accurate. George Creel, its chairman, said, "We had
such confidence in our case as to feel that no other argument was
needed than the simple, straightforward presentation of facts."[35]

Between the wars, there was a reaction against government
information in the democracies. And President Roosevelt, among
others, considered the CPI to have fueled too much fear and ha-
tred of the enemy, rather than concentrating on the justice of the
Allied cause.[36]

The second world war saw the apotheosis of Lee's approach.
The Allies' official communication machinery committed itself in
public to telling the truth. Voice of America broadcast (in German and other languages): "Every day at this time we will bring

you the news of the war. The news may be good. The news may be bad. We shall tell you the truth."[37]

This was presented as an ethical commitment but it was actually strategic. Archibald MacLeish gave the policy a name, *strategy of truth*.[38] Roosevelt appointed MacLeish, a former journalist, to head the new Office of Facts and Figures, whose purpose was to disseminate factual information in support of defense.[39] He set out explicitly to combat the Axis "strategy of terror" with an Allied strategy of truth. This meant reporting facts that were not encouraging to the Allied cause in order to be seen as reliable and objective, and thus to achieve credibility.

However, this was not the same as "telling it all." The beneficial effect on Allied credibility had little to do with the innate truthfulness of Allied leaders. It had little to do with Allied respect for truth along the lines advocated by the professional communication bodies of today. Instead, Allied credibility was a result of communication strategy. The Allies had no qualms about hushing up inconvenient events or keeping secrets. For example, the truth about Allied code breaking was covered up not only during the war but for many years afterwards. They simply recognized that *relatively* truthful communication could serve a useful strategic purpose.

The Allies also used propaganda but made a distinction between white propaganda, where information is mostly accurate but serves a hidden purpose, and black propaganda, where the source and the information are false. The strategy of truth did not, of course, mean that the Allies gave up the use of black propaganda as well. While the US Office of War Information disseminated its version of the truth, the Office of Strategic Services was responsible for black propaganda.[40] Soldatensender Calais, for example, was an Allied radio station that broadcast news of sabotage that never happened, fostering the morale-undermining belief among Germans that sabotage was far more widespread than it actually was.[41]

The wartime leadership of the BBC was equally clear that truth was to be used as a strategic weapon. It might be tempting to deviate into untruth for tactical reasons but the temptation must be avoided in order to preserve credibility.[42] The BBC sometimes held back good news that might have lacked credibility with the audience in occupied Europe.[43]

By claiming to establish the truthfulness of the news, the Allies created a more powerful propaganda weapon than if they had been more blatantly selective. Richard Crossman, who worked on political warfare on General Eisenhower's staff, said: "The brilliant propagandist is the man who tells the truth, or that selection of the truth which is requisite for his purpose, and tells it in such a way that the recipient does not think that he is receiving any propaganda."[44] This is fundamentally the same idea as the limited hangout (see page 104).

The strategy of truth continued through the cold war. Although government propaganda within the US was outlawed after the war by the 1948 Smith-Mundt Act and the Office of War Information was succeeded by the US Information Agency, at the height of the cold war in 1950, President Truman launched an anti-communist persuasion offensive entitled the "Campaign of Truth." He promised to overcome communist propaganda around the world "with honest information about freedom and democracy."[45]

"The concepts of truth and objectivity were another way of dividing the world. Democratic governments were portrayed as disseminators of information that was truthful and objective, while totalitarian governments were pictured as distributing falsehoods and propaganda." The US government cultivated the impression that its information was the absolute truth when it was actually relative.[46]

The strategy of truth was employed explicitly by the Western Allies in the second world war and the cold war. It is also used, without being given a name, in situations where credibility is in question. When realistic management has taken over from optimistic management at an business in difficulties, the new management effectively promises key audiences that they will be told the truth (in the sense of the facts, not in the sense of the whole truth), contrasted with the worthless promises of the old regime. There is a bonfire of the vanities that often includes optimistic reporting.

Conclusion: Truth in communication strategy

What then is the right approach to truth in a communication strategy?

- First, forget slogans such as "tell the truth," and "tell it all, tell it now" and resist painting issues black or white.

- Second, there is often the alternative of saying less. Telling all is not essential to a successful communication strategy. Depending on the circumstances, saying less can work equally well.

- Third, construct a *strategic narrative* (see chapter 9) that meets the requirements of an effective and strategic communication, by taking forward the strategy of the communicator. The strategic narrative must be factual but does not have to be the whole truth.

Truth is important but not in the simplistic way some public relations experts claim. Fanatical devotion to the absolute truth is neither practical nor desirable. "Pravda," by Howard Brenton and David Hare, is a brilliant satire of the newspaper industry in the 1980s. But, like Milton in "Paradise Lost," they gave the devil the best lines. Lambert Le Roux, the monstrous proprietor, is made to ask: "What on earth is all this stuff about the truth? Truth? Why, when everywhere you go people tell lies. In pubs. To each other. To their husbands. To their wives. To the children. To the dying — and thank God they do. No one tells the truth. Why single out newspapers?"[47] We should probably jeer but find ourselves thinking, "Well, he's got a point."

In Summary

- Your standing and whether people believe what you say depend not on the absolute truth but on credibility.
- A communication strategy of optimism seems irresistible to many in business and politics but often ends badly.
- A strategy of truth is a better bet in the long run.

References

[1] Ambrose Bierce, *The Devil's Dictionary*, (Cleveland, OH: The World Publishing Company, 1911), 239 & 352.
[2] Andrew Roberts, *The Storm of War: A New History of the Second World War*, (New York: HarperCollins, 2011); George Sanford, *Katyn and the Soviet Massacre of 1940: Truth, Justice and Memory*, (Abingdon, UK: Routledge, 2005); Nicholas J. Cull, 'Poland,' in *Propaganda and Mass Persuasion: A Historical Encyclopedia*, ed. by Nicholas J Cull, David Culbert & David Welch, (Santa Barbara, CA: ABC-CLIO, Inc., 2003), 302-305.
[3] James A. Leith, 'Napoleon,' in Cull, Culbert & Welch, (eds.), *Propaganda and Mass Persuasion*, 260.
[4] Malcolm Brown, *The Age*, June 12, 2012.
[5] Herbert W. Simons, with Joanne Morale & Bruce Gronbeck, *Persuasion in Society*, (Thousand Oaks, CA: Sage Publications, Inc., 2001), 4-5.
[6] Jowett & O'Donnell, *Propaganda and Persuasion*, 6.
[7] Edward L. Bernays, *Propaganda*, (New York: Horace Liveright, 1928), 19-20.
[8] Ralf Georg Reuth, *Goebbels: The Life of Joseph Goebbels, the Mephistophelean Genius of Nazi Propaganda*, (London: Constable & Company Limited, 1993), 173.
[9] L. John Martin, 'The Moving Target: General Trends in Audience Composition,' in *Propaganda and Communication in World History*, ed. by Lasswell et al, Vol. 3, 280.
[10] Christopher Paul, *Strategic Communication: Origins, Concepts, and Current Debates*, (Santa Barbara, CA: Praeger, 2011), 3.
[11] Newsom et al, *This is PR*, 117.
[12] Ethos: Brian Vickers, *In Defence of Rhetoric*, (Oxford: Clarendon Press, 1988), 19. Cicero, 'De Oratoribus,' quoted in Wendy Olmsted, *Rhetoric: An Historical Introduction*, (Oxford: Blackwell Publishing, 2006). Source credibility: Erwin P. Bettinghaus & Michael J. Cody, *Persuasive Communication*, (Fort Worth, TX: Harcourt Brace College Publishers, 1994).
[13] Leonard W. Doob, 'Propaganda,' in *International Encylopedia of Communications*, ed. by Eric Barnouw, (Oxford University Press, 1989), 374.
[14] Persuasion: Ann R. Carden, 'Persuasion Theory,' in *Encyclopedia of Public Relations*, ed. Heath, Vol. 2, 615. Propaganda: Bertrand Taithe & Tim Thornton, 'Propaganda: A Misnomer of Rhetoric and Persuasion?' in *Propaganda: Political Rhetoric and Identity 1300-2000*, ed. by Bertrand Taithe & Tim Thornton, (Stroud, UK: Sutton Publishing, 1999), 2.
[15] Edward L. Bernays, *Propaganda*, (New York: Horace Liveright, 1928), 20.
[16] Ian Verchere, *The Investor Relations Challenge: Reaching Out to Global Markets*, (London: Economist Intelligence Unit, 1991), 1.
[17] Richard S. Tedlow, *Denial: Why Business Leaders Fail to Look Facts in the Face and What to Do About It*, (New York: Portfolio, 2010).
[18] John Lloyd, Richard Curtis, Ben Elton & Rowan Atkinson, *Blackadder: The Whole Damn Dynasty*, (London: Penguin Books, 2009), 413.
[19] Kahneman, *Thinking, Fast and Slow*, 256.
[20] Cutlip, *The Unseen Power*, 161.
[21] Packard, *The Hidden Persuaders*, 209.
[22] Harry G. Frankfurt, *On Bullshit*, (Princeton University Press, 2005), 61-2.
[23] Roderick P. Hart, *Campaign Talk: Why Elections are Good for Us*, (Princeton University Press, 2000), 38 & 19.
[24] Robert Dallek, *Lyndon B. Johnson: Portrait of a President*, (Oxford University Press, 2004), 264.
[25] Walter Cronkite, CBS Evening News, CBS, February 27, 1968.

[26] Richard Nixon, 'Address to the Nation on the Situation in Southeast Asia,' April 7, 1971.Rick Perlstein, *Nixonland: The Rise of a President and the Fracturing of America*, (New York: Scribner, 2008), 558.

[27] Rick Perlstein, *The Invisible Bridge: The Fall of Nixon and the Rise of Reagan*, (New York: Simon & Schuster Paperbacks, 2014), xix-xx.

[28] Jason Zweig, *The Devil's Financial Dictionary*, (New York: PublicAffairs, 2015), xi.

[29] Emily Chasan, 'Lease Accounting Changes May Trip Up Bank Loans,' *Wall Street Journal*, September 2, 2014.

[30] Terry Smith, *Accounting for Growth: Stripping the Camouflage from Company Accounts*, (London: Century Business, 1992), 4, 68, vi & 200.

[31] Warren E. Buffett, Chairman's Letter, 1997 Annual Report, Berkshire Hathaway, Inc.

[32] Mark C. Scott, *Achieving Fair Value: How Companies Can Better Manage Their Relationships with Investors*, (Chichester, UK: John Wiley & Sons Ltd., 2005), 116.

[33] Tad Friend, 'Tomorrow's Advance Man: Marc Andreessen's Plan to Win the Future,' *The New Yorker*, May 18, 2015

[34] John Lukacs, *Blood, Toil, Tears and Sweat: The Dire Warning*, (New York: Basic Books, 2008), 47-64.

[35] George Creel, *How We Advertised America: The First Telling of the Amazing Story of the Committee on Public Information that Carried the Gospel of Americanism to Every Corner of the Globe*, (New York: Harper & Brothers, 1920), 4-5.

[36] John Morton Blum, *V was for Victory: Politics and American Culture during World War II*, (New York: Harcourt Brace Jovanovich, 1976), 21-22.

[37] Martin J. Manning, *Historical Dictionary of American Propaganda*, (Westport, CT: Greenwood Press, 2004), 307.

[38] 'The Administration: The Strategy of Truth,' *Time*, February 23, 1942.

[39] Girona, Ramon, & Jordi Xifra, 'The Office of Facts and Figures: Archibald MacLeish and the Strategy of Truth,' *Public Relations Review*, Vol. 35 (2009) 287-290. (See also Girona, Ramon, & Jordi Xifra, 'From the Strategy of Truth to the Weapon of Truth: The Government Information Manual for the Motion Picture Industry, 1942,' *Public Relations Review*, Vol. 36 (2010) 306-309.

[40] Philip M. Taylor, *Munitions of the Mind: A History of Propaganda from the Ancient World to the Present Day*, (Manchester, UK: Manchester University Press, 2005), 226.

[41] Manning, *Historical Dictionary of American Propaganda*, (Westport, CT: Greenwood Press, 2004), 262.

[42] Philip M. Taylor, 'Psychological Warfare,' ' in Cull, Culbert & Welch, (eds.), *Propaganda and Mass Persuasion*, 326.

[43] Taylor, *Munitions of the Mind*, 224-225.

[44] Propaganda weapon: Doob, 'Propaganda,' 376. Richard Crossman, quoted in Scott Macdonald, *Propaganda and Information Warfare in the Twenty-First Century: Altered Images and Deception Operations*, (Abingdon, UK: Routledge, 2007), 35.

[45] Andrew Defty, *Britain, America and Anti-Communist Propaganda 1945-53: The Information Research Department*, (Abingdon, UK: Routledge, 2004), 144-149.

[46] Joel H. Spring, *Images of American Life: A History of Ideological Management in Schools, Movies, Radio and Television*, (State University of New York Press, 1992), 142-144.

[47] Howard Brenton & David Hare, *Pravda: A Fleet Street Comedy*, (London: Methuen, 1985), 113.

PART II

Elements of Communication Strategy

In Part II

People make gaffes. They talk too much or say the wrong thing. Their communications are sometimes out of control. People in public life and organizations are under increasing pressure to communicate. They may feel inadequate if they don't have a Facebook page with lots of friends. Public figures may feel that they should have a presence on Twitter, with large numbers of followers, to whom they regularly tweet topical comments. Organizations are under pressure to be more open and transparent. And they often lack a communication strategy.

The sheer volume of communication has been stoked by the steady rise of professional communication, usually known as public relations. At its most basic, public relations stands for maximum publicity. Many in the public relations field are stuck in the default high profile position. The avant-garde subordinates effectiveness to social and ethical considerations. And the compulsion to adopt a normative, dogmatic approach to the difficult concept of truth has confused the issue — but see chapter 9 (From Truth to Narrative). Often communication strategy is inadequate or non-existent.

Part II begins with a short introduction to communication strategy. What is it? And where did it come from?

The following chapters look at the elements of communication strategy. Part IV puts these elements together.

CHAPTER 7

A Short Introduction to Communication Strategy

Communication strategy: The use of communication to achieve the strategic objectives through a combination of policies, plans, positions and ploys.

Fig. 7.1 Communication Strategy

Origins of strategy

Thucydides and Sun Tzu wrote strategic works around 2500 years ago. Though Edward Gibbon was ignorant of the word, "strategy," he wrote of policies, systems, designs and plans through the centuries, and declared: "The science of tactics, the order, evolutions, and stratagems of antiquity, was transcribed and studied in the books of the Greeks and Romans."[1] The concept of strategy became widely known and discussed only in the era of Napoleon, whose strategic genius shattered and rearranged the continent of Europe. The Napoleonic wars inspired and provided copious material for both of the modern pioneers of the theory of strategy. First, Antoine-Henri Jomini, who served on Napoleon's staff. Second, and more esteemed today, the Prussian general, Carl von Clausewitz, who was captured at Jena.

Eventually, the new science of strategy percolated from the military domain to other spheres. At first, strategy infiltrated politics at all levels, especially through the strategies devised by activists and revolutionaries to influence decisions or bring about changes of government.[2]

Scientific analysis of business can be traced back to Frederick Winslow Taylor and the foundation of business schools in the late 19th century. However, business strategy only became explicit and prominent in the 1960s. Until then, large businesses had strategies with a small "s," strategies in the same sense as pre-Napoleonic generals. But they lacked the mindset and tools that would bring it all together into a systematic way of moving the organization in a certain direction.

Credit for bringing strategy into the business mainstream has been given variously to Alfred Chandler's "Strategy and Structure," published in 1962;[3] to Bruce Henderson's Boston Consulting Group, the management consultancy that marketed strategy (founded 1963); to Igor Ansoff, through his pioneering 1965 book on strategic planning, "Corporate Strategy;"[4] and to Harvard's basic textbook, "Business Policy: Text and Cases" (1965).[5]

At first, a systematic approach in the largest corporations meant strategic planning, pioneered by Robert McNamara, first at Ford and then at the Pentagon. It was an activity that bore some resemblance to Soviet planning, more about organizational structure than it was about competition. Its fatal flaw was its reliance on stable conditions, whereas it became clear by the early 1970s, with the end of the Bretton Woods monetary system, the oil crisis, and political and social turmoil in the West, that the business environment had become less predictable. When discontinuity came to seem more likely than continuity, planning went into decline. (I worked at a major oil company in the 1980s, witnessing the transition from relatively rigid, bureaucratic planning to leaner, more flexible strategic management.) The decline took some time. It was not until 1994 that Henry Mintzberg wrote "The Rise and Fall of Strategic Planning," commenting, "The mid-1990s is perhaps the right time to publish such a book."[6]

Strategy in vogue

Two decades on, strategy and strategic are vogue words. It is no surprise that the word "strategic" regularly appears in a list of the ten most overused words in career profiles.[7]

Yet genuine strategy is essential. As Lawrence Freedman said, "Everyone needs a strategy."[8] That is the perception anyway. And that is the view of this book. I don't ever expect to read about a CEO who, asked for his strategy, said: "There isn't one."

But strategy is hard to pin down. Many definitions have been advanced; none has gained widespread acceptance. However, it is clear that a strategy embodies a vision of the future or, at its most limited, an objective, and the means of achieving it. It also implies decisions about the use of resources, which are always limited (see chapter 18).

Strategy meets communication

From the 1980s, the wide academic world of business studies and the narrow academic world of public relations traveled in opposite directions.

In management theory and practice, strategy assumed more and more importance. Business scholars and business leaders increasingly saw strategy as the Holy Grail. This was partly because of the influence of investors over the fates of large businesses, since for them strategy is a primary concern. Managements are under more pressure than ever to get it right. Investors who believe that a business could do better are increasingly likely to seek to change the strategy.

Meanwhile, public relations scholarship came to be dominated, and sidetracked, by the symmetry-excellence paradigm (see chapter 4). Scholars tended to advocate an idealistic social role for public relations, as a way for groups in society to manage their relationships. They tended to despise the pragmatism of communication as a tool for achieving objectives.

Communication strategy, which is using communication to achieve the overall business objectives, is therefore an alien concept for the mainstream of public relations scholarship. (See fig. 5.2.)

(One chapter of the first Excellence Project book genuflected toward strategic management, urging that public relations should take part in strategic planning. But they rejected control or manipulation, using strategic as "a symmetrical term." They agreed that: "It is in the strategic interest of organizations to change their behavior when they provoke opposition from the environment.")[9]

Belatedly, and despite the idealistic tendency in public relations scholarship, people working in communications began to catch on to the trend in management. If it was not clear how strategy should be applied to communication, it was at least clear to these masters of perception that it was important to *appear* strategic. Thus they spoke of "strategic communication" or "strategic public relations."

Colin Gray, the distinguished strategic studies scholar recently noted that: "'Strategy' and 'strategic' have attracted up-market and respectful devotees who have discovered that almost random use of 'strategy' triggers positive responses from an audience."[10] As a result, "One word repeated throughout the [PR] literature is 'strategic.'"[11] The vogue words began to be tacked on all over the place.

Fig. 7.2 Scholarship Traditions Poles Apart

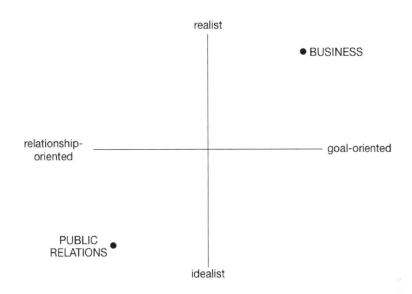

University communication departments, public relations agencies and even individual executives have realized that calling themselves strategic might make them look more serious and important. As a result, consultancies and managers routinely claim to be carrying out strategic research, dispensing strategic advice, drawing up strategies or strategic plans, executing strategic programs, and communicating strategic messages to strategic audiences. The suspicion must be that not much of this so-called strategic stuff deserves the name. "The Economist Style Guide" said: "Strategic is usually meaningless except to tell you that the writer is pompous and is trying to invest something with a seriousness it does not deserve."[12]

The title of the *International Journal of Strategic Communication*, inaugurated in 2007, promised much. But its foundation article disappointed.[13] Although it defined "strategic communication" as "the purposeful use of communication by an organization to fulfill its mission," it celebrated the very wide range of programs and units describing themselves as strategic. The authors rejoiced in the "expanded adoption" of the term, apparently unaware that dilution threatened to make it meaningless. It has been argued that there is a tendency for almost everything to be seen as communication and almost everything to be seen as strategic.[14] To put it bluntly, when everything is strategic, strategy becomes meaningless.

The Public Relations Society of America began a new definition of public relations with: "Public relations is a strategic communication process..." No comment necessary.

Key points
- From the 1960s, strategy became first influential and then pervasive in business.
- Now everyone in public life needs a strategy.
- But people in communication have used it indiscriminately and without understanding it.

What is communication strategy?

What then is communication strategy? My definition is: "The use of communication to achieve the strategic objectives through a combination of policies, plans, positions and ploys." It can be broken down into three parts:

1. The communication strategy takes its direction from the strategic objectives. (This could be the strategic objectives of a business, institution or person.)

2. It involves communication — obviously, but what does that mean?

3. It is more than just a plan but also includes policies, positions and ploys (stratagems).

(1) Direction from strategic objectives

Levels of strategy

Communication strategy is needed to help achieve *strategic objectives*, not limited, short-term or campaign objectives such as a product launch. As discussed in chapter 1, it is about overall strategy (grand strategy), not tactics or campaign (operational) strategy.

Public relations is confused about different levels of tactics, campaign strategy and overall strategy. Carl Botan concluded that scholars had failed to distinguish different concepts, that the literature was sometimes contradictory, and that different assumptions had been made.[15]

As soldiers are concerned with warfare and stop short of grand strategy, so people in communication often stop short of overall or macro communication strategy. Whether corporate executives, PR agency heads or professors, they tend to be concerned with active communication — doing and saying — and campaigns. (And with various aspects of theory, in the case of scholars.)

Strategy is most often used in public relations to mean planning projects and campaigns rather than top level strategy. For example, according to Paul Argenti, "Communication strategy, developed as a concept in the 1980s by communication expert Mary Munter, serves as the basis for all management communication." Munter recommended that, before undertaking any communication, a manager should think strategically about the communicator, the audience, the message, the choice of communication channel, and the culture that is the backdrop. This was all good but it was a how to guide for projects and campaigns, with targets given in her examples such as "update management on department performance" or "increase the number of women hired."[16] Strategy was being used in the narrow sense of planning and problem solving for projects. Genuine strategy was being confused with the nuts and bolts of persuasion. These "persuasion strategies,"[17] such as stimulus-response or a social appeal (seeking to change behavior by bringing attention to social conditions) are campaign strategies, not macro level communication strategy. A 2007 literature review confirmed that this was the prevalent view: "The emphasis [in PR] is on the PR process at the micro or operational level."[18]

Turn to most public relations textbooks and you will find a diagram (or at least a description) of a planning process similar to this one, in which the communicators analyze the situation, decide what their campaign will aim to achieve, run a public relations program to achieve the agreed objective, and then evaluate the program and see whether the objectives have been achieved.

Fig. 7.3 Planning Process

The granddaddy of such diagrams (and more impressive than most) appeared back in 1952, in the first edition of "Cutlip."[19] But it was designed for planning a public relations program, not for strategy.

Books on communication that claim to be strategic similarly operate most often at the micro level of programs or campaigns, for example, when strategic communication was described as "delivering a message to a specific audience to elicit an intended response."[20] Another book on "strategic communication" based itself on a "model of strategic communication" with the following four components: situational knowledge, goal setting, communication competence, and "anxiety management."[21] And a book on "public relations strategy" covered why public relations campaigns fail, how to develop a newsworthy story idea, etc.[22]

Public relations people speak of "strategic communication" or "strategic public relations" but they rarely used the terms "strategy" or "strategic" in the same way as experts in business strategy. We are not speaking the same language.

The study of consumer behavior by psychologists and economists has enabled marketers to use a number of relatively new techniques to persuade consumers to make the decisions they desire. But these are not a strategic breakthrough. The fact that these measures are crafty rather than obvious does not change their nature from tactical into strategic. To see why an effective campaign of persuasion does not amount to communication strategy, imagine the CEO of a hotel company unveiling its new strategy. Now suppose that he or she says: "We are going to take advantage of a context effect. Instead of simply displaying the available room options for booking on our website, we are going to add an additional, irrelevant option to book the same room at a higher price. By doing this we're aiming to persuade customers to make the choice we want them to make. Otherwise things will be pretty much the same." Or perhaps he or she says: "We are going to take advantage of the power of social norms to influence consumer behavior. We have a cunning plan to cut our laundry costs and please environmentalists not by telling customers that they are saving the planet but by telling them that most people re-use their towels. Otherwise things will be pretty much the same." Neither of these techniques is a communication strategy.

Communication strategy is not about campaign solutions or project plans. Here communication strategy is used to mean overall (macro) strategy, not campaign (micro) strategy. Where detailed examples are used in this book, it is always in the context of strategic objectives.

Relevance

The purpose — the sole purpose — of communication objectives is to help achieve the corporate or business strategy. This seems simple and obvious but it is worth emphasizing because so often public relations activities seem to have little connection to strategy. The objectives of communication strategy must support the corporate or business strategy. That does not mean that communication objectives should be vaguely relevant to the strategy. It means that the communication objectives must be essential to the strategy.

If there are no communication objectives that are indispensable to the strategy, maybe its whole communication effort as currently constituted could be dispensed with? More likely, the business strategy has not been fully understood, so that the wrong communication direction is being proposed. Alternatively, communication is misperceived as such a low level service function that it does not matter whether it is aligned with strategy or not.

Disconnected communication strategy sometimes results from professionals developing their own priorities and forgetting that they are only employed to serve the business. It is possible for a function such as human resources or public relations to be professional but strategically irrelevant. Staff or service functions are especially prone to the delusion that their job is to pursue some autonomous professional mission when their only function should be to serve the business by applying their specialist knowledge and expertise. I once managed a press officer who was a former journalist and thought his job was "to get the news out." Our employer was being excoriated in the media and the strategic requirement was for there to be less "news," not more. (And see chapter 18 for more on the problem of distraction.)

Some advocates of symmetry-excellence and academics of the "Critical" tendency lobby for such an autonomy, urging public relations professionals to resist power in their organizations by, for example, "planting rumors or information in the grapevine, leaking information outside the company, [and] constructing counter-narratives."[23] No sensible management should allow this any more than they would allow one of their stores, for example, to stock competitors' products because the store manager believed they were more environmentally friendly. In fact, the communication staff should do the opposite of resisting. The communication agenda should be the management agenda. And the communication function should ensure that its activities are not merely relevant to the organization but critically important — by focusing like a laser on the strategy.

Control

Eliminating distraction and focusing on strategic objectives depends on first achieving control. The story of the iPad, told in the Introduction, showed how control can be critical to a communication strategy. Chapter 1 looked at the devastating consequences of communication that go out of control. It suggested that control is not just a question of not saying the wrong thing but a strategic issue. And now chapter 8 (In Control: Marketing genius or PR misfit?) looks at how Steve Jobs put control at the heart of Apple's communication strategy. Control is the first element of communication strategy set out in chapter 17, which explains how to design a communication strategy.

(2) Communication

Aristotle set out the original speaker-subject-hearer model of communication (pages 79-80). Is it possible to design a better model? An entire field of study grew up to explore "the media, modalities, and messages by which humans exchange, reflect on, and enact different perspectives on reality."[24] Most of this exploration took place in the 20th century, and explorers devised a series of models to explain what they thought was happening in communication. Chapter 4 noted Lasswell's updating of Aristotle (Who says what to whom, in what channel, with what effect?) It also noted Shannon's source-message-receiver model. The model factory has been busy.[25] But although the models became more complicated as they incorporated previously neglected facets of communication, they have not necessarily come closer to its essence. The problem is that communication does involve speakers addressing hearers and any number of analogs of speakers addressing hearers, but there is more to it than that. If it were possible to add up all the messages sent from A to B, and even all the messages from B to A as well, the result would not be the sum total of communication. It would omit a lot of "dark matter."

The usefulness of models like Aristotle's and its derivatives is limited by their starting assumption, with its roots in Greek oratory, that a speaker is addressing an audience. A more sophisticated model would recognize that there may not be a transmission of a message at all. Communication embraces all kinds of transmission and none. It runs the gamut from trumpeting a message as strongly, widely and instantly as possible all the way to total, permanent silence. Communication may mean publicizing information. But it may equally mean disclosing it without undue publicity. Or it may mean withholding it. And if there is a transmission, the audience may vary from one to many. It may be a transmission once only to a single person or a broadcast to many people, many times. And an original transmission may be repeated by third parties, as made supremely easy by social media.

What then is strategic communication? It would surely embrace persuasion but would not be limited to persuasion. There can be strategic communication without trying to persuade anybody of anything. A model of the speaker-subject-hearer type is applicable at best to the simplest communications. Even a tweet is too sophisticated to fit this model. And the model obscures the different modes of discourse such as argumentation, exposition, description and *narrative*.

Narrative

The best fit for strategic communication is not a linear model at all but narrative.

Recent scholarship suggests that narrative can be the most effective, natural mode of communication. Chapter 9 (From Truth to Narrative) applies the concept of narrative in communication strategy. It starts by looking at the concept of truth that is fundamental in communication but also problematic. It goes on to propose that effective communications owe more to the narrative model. Such a model poses a series of questions:

- What is our position (our story)?
- When do we need to tell it? (And when is it better to keep quiet?)
- To whom?
- How?

Profile

This book uses *profile* to denote the cumulative, quantitative effect of all this communication, the total amount of public attention the subject attracts. A closely related term is *prominence:* being well known, which tends to coalesce into familiarity.

"Profile" is an imperfect term because it conflates cause and effect. It is used most often to refer to the way an organization or person is covered in the conventional media. If an organization receives numerous and/or prominent media appearances, it is said to be high profile or to have a high profile. If it makes relatively few and/or obscure media appearances, it is said to be low profile. But it is also used to refer to the way the entity deals with the media. Does it seek a lot of media coverage? Does it publicize a lot of information or disclose a little? And, beyond the media, there is the question of how an entity relates to other groups and people. Does it talk to a lot of people or a few, how much, and how loudly.

As discussed in chapters 2 and 4, it is often assumed that a high profile, meaning a high media profile, is highly beneficial. Chapter 10 (Profile: Mobil and the high profile advocacy strategy) examines the case for a high media profile.

Audiences and reputation

Even for fans of the high media profile, that high profile is not an end in itself. It is a way to establish and maintain a reputation. And it is a way to communicate with those people who are the ultimate targets or audiences — through the media.

Chapter 12 (Allies: Reputation and stakeholders) dissects the concepts involved with the receiving end of communication:

- Brand, image, identity and reputation.
- Audience, target, public and stakeholder.

It is obvious that it is possible to have a low profile in the media but a high profile with a particular audience, achieved by communicating with that audience directly. To achieve such a *targeted profile* requires careful control.

(3) More than just a plan

Look for information about strategic communication or communication strategy and most of what you find will be about planning, not strategy, and low-level planning at that. Yet as Lawrence Freedman said, "To win in war, in business or in sport requires a strategy. That doesn't mean you need a plan, you need flexibility."[26] And, it might be added, creativity is a distinct advantage. Hence planning is only one aspect of communication strategy. There are three others:

a) Policies.

"Grand strategy is the policy-level decisions an organization makes about goals, alignments, ethics, and relationship with publics and other forces in its environment," said Botan.[27] Communication strategy does indeed involve these policy-level decisions but this statement makes it appear that once you have a set of policies, you have a strategy. They are necessary but not sufficient.

b) Positions.

What views does the organization need to communicate (with no implication as to the volume of communication)? These positions are most likely to take a narrative form, see chapter 9.

c) Ploys (stratagems).

A ploy or stratagem is a creative idea, device or trick to gain an advantage over an enemy or competitor.

To take an example from the battlefield, at Austerlitz, Napoleon occupied the strongpoint of the Pratzen Heights, vacated the strongpoint, and then attacked and recaptured it. To the conventional general, schooled in the importance and benefit of holding the high ground, this would have seemed madness. But in the context of Napoleon's audacious idea of how the battle would play out, it was the decisive move that eventually delivered a French victory. It was a stratagem, appropriate only to the circumstances of Austerlitz on that day, not a standard maneuver that anyone could try.

Stratagems that are at the core of communication strategies are not necessarily repeatable but this book discusses several:

- Surprise, as in the case of Austerlitz, and as in the case of the iPad that was discussed in the Introduction.

- The personality communication strategy discussed in chapter 2.

- The communication strategy of optimism that is widely used in politics and business, explained in chapter 6 (From Optimism to Truth).

- The communication strategy of truth which is sometimes as a reaction to the strategy of optimism, also explained in chapter 6.

Combining into strategy

Putting these aspects together then, communication strategy is not any one of the four but a combination of policies, plans, positions and ploys.

Communication strategy is competitive. It is not old-fashioned Soviet-style planning, as though it was a game with only one player. Competition is the antidote to complacency. Without competition, complacency is an ever-present danger.

Businesses need communication strategies that help them to win.

- This means plans such as aligning all communications with the critical path (chapter 17).
- It means policies, such as deciding which stakeholders or audiences are going to be a priority (chapter 12).

- It means positions, expressed as strategic narrative (chapter 9).
- And it means ideas that are particular to the conditions, such as keeping quiet about disruptive technology until it is ready and then springing a surprise (Introduction).

Designing communication strategy

Communication strategy is the use of communication through combination of policies, plans, positions and ploys to achieve the strategic objectives. But how do you design a communication strategy? How do you decide what communication strategy will help you? The next five chapters explain how.

CHAPTER		CONTENT
8	In Control	The introduction took the example of Apple's iPad. Apple's control of communications, combined with surprise, helped it to astonishing achievements. Chapter 8 looks more closely at how this was done and what can be learned from it.
9	From Truth to Narrative	How should communication strategy handle the truth? Chapter 9 suggests that narrative is a more appropriate concept in communication strategy.
10	Profile: Mobil and the high profile advocacy strategy	Do you want a high profile or a low profile? That is a key strategic question. Chapter 10 critiques the most sustained, resourced and purposive attempt, by Mobil, to employ a high profile advocacy strategy.
11	Friction: Troubleshooting issues and crises	Troublesome issues are intrinsic to business. Through effective management, most issues can and should be prevented from escalating into crises.

| 12 | Allies: Reputation and stakeholders | The concept of reputation was taken for granted for a couple of millennia. Then, in the 1990s, it suddenly became fashionable to study, discuss and propagate reputation management. Is this the way forward? And what about stakeholders? Chapter 10 offers a strategic answer. |

Chapters 17 and 18 at the end of the book bring it all together in a guide to creating communication strategy. And there is an executive summary at the end of chapter 18.

In Summary

- By the end of the 20th century, strategy had become all-important in business. But works on public communication lagged behind, concentrating on tactics and planning campaigns, while belatedly using the word "strategy" so loosely as to deprive it of meaning.
- Communication strategy can be defined as: "The use of communication to achieve the strategic objectives through a combination of policies, plans, positions and ploys."

References

1 Gibbon, *Decline and Fall*, (1906), Vol. 8, 76.
2 Freedman, *Strategy*, 245.
3 Freedman, *Strategy*, 462 & 496.
4 Igor Ansoff, *Corporate Strategy*, (New York: McGraw-Hill, 1965).
5 E. P. Learned, C. R. Christensen, K. R. Andrews, & W. D. Guth, *Business Policy: Text and Cases*, (Homewood, IL: Irwin, 1965).
6 Henry Mintzberg, *The Rise and Fall of Strategic Planning*, (London: Prentice-Hall, 1994), 4.
7 Catherine Fisher, 'Brand You Year: How to Brand Yourself Without Sounding Like Everyone Else,' LinkedIn official blog, <http://blog.linkedin.com/2015/01/21/brand-you-year-how-to-brand-yourself-without-sounding-like-everyone-else/> January 21, 2015.
8 Freedman, *Strategy*, ix.
9 Grunig & Fred C. Repper, 'Strategic Management, Publics and Issues,' 123.
10 Colin S. Gray, *The Future of Strategy*, (Cambridge, UK: Polity Press, 2015), 24.
11 Peggy Simcic Brown, 'Communication Managers as Strategists? Can They Make the Grade?' *Journal of Communication Management*, Vol. 5, No. 4, (2001), 313-326.
12 *The Economist Style Guide*, (London: Profile Books Ltd, 2005), 132.
13 Kirk Hallahan, Derina Holtzhausen, Betteke van Ruler, Dejan Vercic, & Krishnamurthy Sriramesh, 'Defining Strategic Communication,' *International Journal of Strategic Communication*, Vol. 1, No. 1, (2007), 3-35.
14 Simon Møberg Torp, 'The Strategic Turn in Communication Science: On the History and Role of Strategy in Communication Science from Ancient Greece Until the Present Day,' in *The Routledge Handbook of Strategic Communication*, ed. by Derina Holtzhausen & Ansgar Zerfass, (New York: Routledge, 2015), 34-52.
15 Carl Botan, 'Grand Strategy, Strategy, and Tactics in Public Relations,' in *Public Relations Theory II*, ed. by Carl Botan & Vincent Hazleton, (Mahwah, NJ: Lawrence Erlbaum Associates, Inc., 2006), 197. See also Freedman, *Strategy*, 206.
16 Paul A. Argenti, *The Fast Forward MBA Pocket Reference*, (New York: John Wiley & Sons, Inc., 2002), 273. Mary Munter, *Guide to Managerial Communication: Effective Business Writing and Speaking*, (Upper Saddle River, NJ: Prentice Hall, 2006), 3-33.
17 Newsom et al, *This Is PR*, 11th edn., 120.
18 Benita Steyn, 'Contribution of Public Relations to Organizational Strategy Formulation,' in *The Future of Excellence...*, ed. by Toth.
19 Scott M. Cutlip & Allen H. Center, *Effective Public Relations*, 1st edn., (New York: Prentice-Hall, Inc., 1952), 87.
20 Barbara Diggs-Brown, *Strategic Public Relations: An Audience-Focused Approach*, (Boston, MA: Wadsworth, 2012), 77-79.
21 Dan O'Hair, Gustav W. Friedrich and Lynda Dee Dixon, *Strategic Communication in Business and the Professions*, (London: Pearson, 2011), 24.
22 Alex Singleton, *The PR Masterclass: How to Develop a Public Relations Strategy that Works*, (Chichester, UK: John Wiley and Sons Ltd, 2014).
23 Bruce K. Berger & Bryan H. Reber, *Gaining Influence in Public Relations: The Role of Resistance in Practice*, (Mahwah, NJ: Lawrence Erlbaum Associates, 2006), xii.
24 Klaus Bruhn Jensen, 'Communication Theory and Philosophy,' in Donsbach (ed.), *International Encyclopedia of Communication*, 839.
25 McQuail & Windahl, *Communication Models for the Study of Mass Communication*; Uma Narula, *Handbook of Communication Models, Perspectives, Strategies*, (New Delhi: Atlantic Publishers and Distributors, 2006).

---

[26] Lawrence Freedman, 'Underdogs, take heart – there is a key to victory,' *Sunday Times*, November 3, 2013.
[27] Botan, 'Grand Strategy, Strategy, and Tactics in Public Relations,' 198.

CHAPTER 8

In Control: Marketing genius or PR misfit?

"[There is not] one of ten thousand, who is stiff and insensible enough, to bear up under the constant dislike and condemnation of his own club. He must be of a strange and unusual constitution, who can content himself to live in constant disgrace and disrepute with his own particular society."
— John Locke, "Essay Concerning Human Understanding"[1]

Apple Inc. is probably the most successful large business of the 21st century. Yet communication experts have been strangely reluctant to learn from it.

Apple's net sales grew from $8.0 billion in 2000 to $182.8 billion in 2013-14, up 23 times. Net income grew 49 times, from $0.8 billion to $39.5 billion. Its market capitalization was $25 billion in 2000, at the height of the dot.com bubble and surpassed $600 billion on April 10, 2012. It became the first company to close worth more than $700 billion on February 10, 2015. Ten years before it became the world's most valuable company, Apple had been merely 287th in America.[2] Apple may be the world's most valuable brand, worth perhaps somewhere north of $100 billion.[3]

Steve Jobs, best CEO of our time

Apple was and remains closely identified with its co-founder and long-serving chief executive, who was probably the most acclaimed business leader of our time. Over a twelve-year period, the "World's Best Performing CEO" achieved a total shareholder return of 3,188%, more than twice his closest rival.[4] He was crowned "CEO of the Decade" by *Fortune* and "Person of the

Decade" by readers of the *Wall Street Journal*.[5]

When Jobs died in 2011, the pages of newspapers, magazines and electronic media were filled with tributes. In that quarter of 2011, Apple received more traditional and social media coverage than any other brand.[6] Between February 15, 1982, and October 17, 2011, *Time* magazine put Apple on its coveted cover no less than nine times. *Fortune* magazine put Apple on its cover twelve times up to 2009. Jobs was hailed not only as a business leader but as a creative genius, technological innovator, turnaround artist and cultural icon. Apple's new CEO, Tim Cook, wrote to employees: "Apple has lost a visionary and creative genius... Steve leaves behind a company that only he could have built, and his spirit will forever be the foundation of Apple."[7] (When this chapter discusses Apple, it is Apple 1997-2011, led by Jobs, unless otherwise stated.)

Amid the adulation, there was also widespread recognition that not everyone loved Jobs. "Bullying, belittling and swearing at people. So why does Steve Jobs deserve to be deified?"[8] The consensus, taking all the published material together, was that Jobs had a hugely beneficial impact on modern life. And Jobs developed. "The cliché that Steve Jobs was half genius, half asshole is based largely on his actions during the nine years that constituted his first tenure at Apple."[9]

This chapter is not making the case for a personality strategy based on Steve Jobs:

- There was much more to Apple than a personality. There was surely never a meeting at which someone said: "Steve is such a wild and crazy guy — all we need to do is use him as front man."
- Jobs was one of a kind, not a template.
- Identification with Jobs had disadvantages for Apple, causing difficult issues with health (see chapter 3) and, above all, posing a question as to whether Apple Without Jobs could succeed.[10] By now, Tim Cook and his team at Apple have of course answered that question with a resounding "Yes we can."

Marketing genius…

Aside from Jobs' obvious impact on technology, there were paeans of praise to his genius for marketing. Probably the most common accolade was "marketing genius." Apple's financial performance, sales figures, brand strength and academic review all provide evidence to support the marketing genius epithet.

Facts and figures (from the 2010-12 period) attest to Apple's marketing prowess. As of February 2010, more than 10 billion songs had been purchased and downloaded from the iTunes Store, "The world's most popular online music, TV and movie store." One million iPhone 4S's were pre-ordered. More than 25 billion apps had been downloaded from the App Store. (The very word, "app," "Word of the Year 2010," if not coined by Apple, was successfully marketed by Apple.) The total number of iPhone, iPod Touch and iPad devices reached more than 315 million. In the first quarter of 2011-12 alone, ending December 31, 2011, Apple sold 37.0 million iPhones, 15.4 million iPads, 5.2 million Macs and 15.4 million iPods.[11] (Apple sets the standard ever higher but these statistics relate to the Steve Jobs era.)

Apple's marketing prowess has been recognized in the trade ever since they launched the Macintosh with the "1984" advertisement, directed by Ridley Scott, and broadcast during the 1984 Superbowl. Thanks to Apple, 1984 was not going to be like Orwell's "1984." Apple's early brand narrative depicted Apple as David to IBM's Goliath. *Advertising Age* eventually declared it the greatest commercial ever and, in 2010, declared that Apple was "Marketer of the Decade."[12] It praised the company for building an exceptionally brand-loyal consumer base, as well as for its advertising that was "like a hit parade of the most memorable ads," for its agency relationships and for its retail stores that: "define the high-end, low-key, over-the-top customer-service shopping experience of the later part of this decade."

Marketing scholars respect Apple's marketing. Apple features prominently in leading marketing texts: "Apple exemplifies the marketing concept in every aspect of its business." One Apple case study was introduced by saying: "From the very start, the tale of Apple Computer is a tale of dazzling creativity and customer-driven innovation."[13]

Although Apple's success is comparatively recent, it has also made its mark on business strategy, as in the case studies that open "Crafting and Executing Strategy" and "Good Strategy/Bad Strategy."[14]

...Public relations misfit?

In view of Apple's success, in view of the high regard in which customers hold it, and especially in view of the acclaim for its marketing communications, it is curious that Apple's public relations have not enjoyed the same respect. The PR trade press has criticized Apple on the rare occasions it has appeared to stumble, such as the way it handled Jobs' health or the "Antennagate" incident (in 2010, when there were reports that the iPhone 4 lost its cellular signal according to how it was held).

Apple has been virtually absent from textbooks on public relations and reputation management. In "Seitel," for example, the only substantive references to Apple were the CEO's pay, the conditions at a supplier, and a tetchy email exchange between Jobs and a student.[15] Major works by public relations scholars have not cited Apple as an example of good practice.[16] Apple has been conspicuous by its virtual absence from the leading journals.

Media darling...

Both the original Apple and the revived Apple of the late 1990s, after Steve Jobs returned from the wilderness, were largely his handiwork. Naturally, one thread in media coverage from the mid-1990s told the Steve Jobs story. The Steve Jobs story neatly exemplified Joseph Campbell's heroic monomyth (which also fits Aristotle's three-act template— see chapter 17):[17]

- A hero hears the call to adventure — Jobs founds Apple in a garage.
- The hero undergoes trials — mounting problems at Apple culminate in Jobs' exile; Apple loses its way.
- The hero returns with a great gift for humanity — Apple

is reborn and gives the world wonderful new products and ways of doing things.

The media loved their version of the Apple story, with products that not only pleased or satisfied but also thrilled its customers, legions of devoted fans, a charismatic leader, rags to riches mythology and counter-culture vibe. (Charismatic leaders are not intrinsically bad, pace chapter 2 — the point is that charisma is not enough on its own.) They bought into Apple's narratives.

…media bête noire

But some hated the way Steve Jobs' Apple conducted its public relations, apparently aiming to control the flow of information. Among the alleged behaviors they hated (but that were highly effective for the company):

- SECRECY. Especially the way it limited access to products. "The in-house PR… could only tell me what the Apple website had already revealed and as for review units, well forget it… This secrecy drives people insane with lust or just plain insane."[18]

- UNRESPONSIVENESS. "Working in Apple's PR team is both a dream job and easy money: All you have to do is not return calls from the press and respond with the same 'no comment' one-liner to email inquiries."[19] (Answering questions on the record is not the only way for a company to arrange for information or a point of view to enter the public domain.)

- MANIPULATION. "I hate Apple's approach to Public Relations… to maintain maximum control through any means possible, over anything that is written or reported."[20] (Control that is fully justified.)

- FAVORITISM. "Apple prefers working with high profile reporters, seating them in the front row at media events and providing them with products for review in advance... At the same time, Apple has a bad habit of completely ignoring inquiries from journalists outside this circle of trust."[21] (Targeting top reporters is Media Relations 101.)

And of course many hated the nagging thought that Apple's approach — although it infuriated them — worked.

Key points
- Steve Jobs was arguably the best CEO of the 2000s, and Apple the most successful large company.
- Jobs and Apple were widely acclaimed for marketing genius but not for public relations.
- Jobs and Apple had a love-hate relationship with the media but their approach produced results.

Portrait of the Genius as a Young Man

So what exactly was Apple's approach to communications? How did it develop? And has Apple's communication fallen below acceptable standards?

Or could it be that Apple's communication strategy is one of the things that made Apple great?

Apple in the 1980s was a very different company from the one it became. Witnesses agree that young Steve Jobs was interested in business but lacked knowledge and experience. In particular, the prospective marketing genius "knew nothing about marketing."[22] The genius was not born but made, learning as he went along, including how best to communicate with customers and others.

As one of many struggling businesses in Silicon Valley, Apple needed publicity to sell computers. Marketing communication was not sophisticated, a question of bringing its innovative products to public attention. Apple received a lot of positive press coverage thanks to the innate quality of the product rather than the company's public relations.[23] To customers' surprise Apple computers "worked right out of the box!" Apple's marketing was viral — accidentally viral — before viral marketing was supposed to have been invented.[24]

Even after its initial public offering, the largest one of 1980, Apple was run in a somewhat amateurish way. Naïve young CEO Jobs was inclined to "blurt out" to journalists confidential information about what Apple was planning.[25] The culture was freewheeling and that extended to a free-for-all when it came to speaking to the press. Some Apple staffers allegedly thought, "Don't like that the CEO is going to chop off your project? Slip some confidential details to that pal who's been cultivating you."[26]

Apple gradually developed a distinctive approach to communication, beginning with a more aggressive attitude. On the receiving end were many of those who might be termed stakeholders, including other software companies, employees who wanted to pursue their own ideas, distribution channels, and the press. Jobs was known to call an editor several times when a plan leaked, say the story was inaccurate, denounce the reporter, and offer advertising as an inducement to drop the story.[27]

Learning from communication mistakes

Before Steve Jobs became a colossus on the world stage, he experienced three kinds of communication breakdown that may have played a part in the transformation of communication strategy:

- Product debacles magnified by premature publicity.
- Incontinent communication with the media leading to unwelcome revelations.
- Squabbles that embarrassed because they were conducted in public.

(1) Premature publicity costs credibility

Many software companies release new programs in beta versions, inviting users to test the new software and help the manufacturer to debug it. But Apple could not afford to market computers that did not work. The Apple II computer made the company's initial fortune but the Apple III was a disappointment. It had to be revised and relaunched.

The big launch that later became an Apple trademark sometimes disappointed in the early years. The launch of Jobs' NeXT computer, on October 12, 1988, outdid all previous launches for size and theatricality, with three thousand people waiting in the audience two hours before it began. But the product was expensive and neither hardware nor software was fully ready. It did not go on sale until the middle of the next year and sold only 400 a month, compared with a production target of 10,000 a month.[28]

Apple also under-delivered with its proto-iPad, the Newton. One of the few substantive references to Apple in public relations textbooks is to this instructive fiasco.[29] The company "pulled out all the PR stops," announcing it at a "grandiose" press conference before even a prototype had been built. It was a full year before Newton went on sale and it had severe shortcomings. It was heavy, its battery ran out quickly and little software was available for it. Its erratic handwriting recognition was lampooned in the "Doonesbury" cartoon strip. "Even Apple seemed unclear about the function of the product and ran adverts with the strap-line 'what is it?'"[30]

The lessons learned (as well as the need to make a better product) were not to release an important product to the public that had not been rigorously tested, in private,[31] to plan the launch more carefully and not to over-promise.

(2) Lack of control makes private life public

A number of bruises caused Jobs' early passion for the media to evolve into a more guarded, calculated approach. Although Jobs appeared on the cover of *Time* magazine in 1982, an article for the year-end issue revealed less than flattering personal information. The bruise was deepened by Jobs' expectation that he would be anointed "Man of the Year," whereas *Time*'s main story turned about to be about the computer itself, with the "Machine of the Year" on the cover. Jobs later said it had made him cry.[32]

Henceforward, Jobs avoided coverage of his personal life, whether in books or the press,[33] until, with death looming, he worked with Walter Isaacson on an authorized biography.

(3) Internecine quarrels make awkward headlines

The first incarnation of Apple was undisciplined, a business in flux, with teams and individuals jockeying for power and resources. It was noisy and, once Apple reached a certain size, attracted media attention. Co-founder Steve Wozniak decided to leave in 1985 and innocently answered questions about his departure from a reporter. He was quoted as saying that Apple had been going in the wrong direction for five years.[34] The *Wall Street Journal* pursued the story that Jobs then sought to prevent Wozniak continuing to use an Apple supplier.[35]

In the mid-1980s, Jobs lost control of Apple and left to found NeXT. The situation was unclear for a time, there was a media scrum outside Jobs' house, and newspapers suggested Apple was thinking about firing him as chairman.[36] There were lawsuits.[37] The adversaries told their sides of the story to *Newsweek*, the *San Francisco Chronicle* and others.[38] Coverage died down but this struggle for supremacy vied with its technological achievement as the most memorable thing about Apple in the late 1980s.

Reinventing communication strategy

Apple floundered. Its personal computer market share fell to only 4%. One year it lost $1 billion. Management seemed to be stuck in a revolving door. "Apple's dying today. Apple's dying a very painful death... I don't really think it's reversible at this point in time," said Jobs in 1995.[39] But when Apple bought NeXT to secure its supply of operating system software, he returned to Apple as an adviser.[40] In a short time, he took effective charge once again. He had used his time in the wilderness well, returning to Apple older, wiser and more focused.

Jobs created Apple 2.0, turning the business around while preparing for "the next big thing."[41] The next big thing would be the opportunity for Apple to devise and bring to market a new product that was clearly superior to anything that had gone before.

A new communication strategy flowed directly from the business strategy. Surprise played a vital part. The strategy was to maintain secrecy about the product pipeline, while cultivating an air of mystery, and then launch with a big bang. It focused on consumers and, to a much lesser extent, investors.

It was not necessary to have good relations with all stakeholders, to be a generally admired company, or to have two-way symmetric communication. It was necessary that customers and investors (and employees) should be managed in a way that enabled the company to achieve its objectives.

Key points
- The roots of Steve Jobs' distinctive approach to communication lay in his history, running a start-up and then finding himself in the wilderness for several years.
- Mistakes were made, notably premature product launches, media intrusions into private life, and internal power struggles.
- When Jobs returned to Apple in the late 1990s, one of his innovations was a communication strategy built on control, surprise and focus.

Making technology pay

Apple's position as a technology leader can only be maintained through innovation and vigilance. The recent history of technological advances has been of one after another innovative business being overtaken by one of two fates. Either competitors copy the innovative products and sell them more cheaply. Or competitors innovate more successfully and turn the original innovator into a has-been. Apple achieved major breakthroughs with the iPod, the iPhone, and the iPad (and continues to innovate successfully, see fig. 8.1) but there is no guarantee that this will continue.

Apple is candid about the competitive environment, stating in its annual report: "The markets for the Company's products and services are highly competitive and the Company is confronted by aggressive competition in all areas of its business."[42] It referred to the pace of change in the industry, with new products constantly coming on to the market and new technology quickly changing what products could do. Competitors were known for seeking market share through price-cutting, at the expense of margins. And they were expected to try to copy Apple's innovations. When Apple disclosed among court papers an email from Jobs to the company's top managers on strategy, the leitmotif was leaping ahead of the competition.[43] Later in the annual report, Apple listed the many risk factors affecting it, notably the creation, use and preservation of intellectual property.

Fig. 8.1 Selected Triumphs of Apple 2.0

New categories entered – and dominated:
Media playing software – iTunes – January 2001
Portable media players – iPod – October 2001
Smartphones – iPhone – January 2007
Third party apps – App Store – July 2008
Tablets – iPad – January 2010
Mobile payments – Apple Pay – September 2014 *
Smartwatches – Apple Watch – September 2014 *
Music streaming – Apple Music – June 2015 *

* OK, the jury is still out...

Knowledge about the inner workings and plans of a business helps competitors. For technology businesses, keeping product plans confidential is particularly important. The story of the iPad vividly illustrates the point (see Introduction). Apple kept its new product a secret and gave it the best possible start. Competitors had to be prevented from copying it and selling copies at a lower price. To maximize profits, Apple needed to extend the period during which the iPad was the only product of its kind on the market.

Sandy Nairn, the leading investment manager, made a study of the history of financing technology-based industries which is instructive for anyone interested in the operation of a company like Apple. He concluded that new technologies, whether they are industrial infrastructure such as canals and railways or modern electronics such as phones and computers, need time with the market more or less to themselves to earn sufficient return for investors. When an existing technology is overtaken by a new one, returns for the old technology decline. And "in the long run, manufactured items all look like toasters."[44]

The pattern goes back to the canals, the innovation in transportation that enabled bulk goods to be moved cheaply over long distances for the first time. The development of this infrastructure in the 18th century was one reason why Britain became the first industrial state. The canals' position was still unchallenged in 1824-25. Nairn calculated that in that year investment in canals was the equivalent of peak annual global capital expenditure on telecommunications in the 20th century. Alas for investors, that was also the high point for canal stock prices. Their heyday ended with the advent of the railways in the mid-1830s. It was a similar story in America.[45] And each technology developed according to a similar pattern.

The rate of innovation for consumer electronics has accelerated. The shelf life of the latest, greatest product is now very short, as with the example of tablet computers from 2010 to 2012. The first iPad went on sale on April 3, 2010, iPad 2 went on sale on March 11, 2011, the new iPad (iPad 3) went on sale on March 16, 2012, and the fourth generation iPad (iPad 4) went on sale on November 2, 2012.[46] The fourth generation iPad was announced alongside the iPad mini, introduced to meet the competitive threat from the smaller, cheaper tablets. Each new version was added to stay ahead of approaching competitors. The average period of time as the lead product was less than a year. The faster the rate of innovation and the greater the competitive pressure, the greater the importance of prolonging and exploiting the time at the top.

One way of helping to ensure a period of market leadership for new technology is to keep it a secret until launch. In the case of the iPad, Apple secured this by delaying competitors' ability to start work on iPad imitations until they could buy one and take it apart (as Apple itself had back in 1981 with the IBM PC).[47]

Another way is to use intellectual property law. The value of intellectual property is greater than it has ever been. Increasing financial resources have been spent on acquiring it and protecting it, through patent wars, in which businesses are disputing in court competitors' access to technology while defending their own right to use it. One example was Google's acquisition of Motorola Mobility for $12.5 billion that reportedly gave Google access to more than 17,000 patents and 7,500 pending patents. More than 500,000 applications a year are filed with the US Patent and Trademark Office, and the number of new patent cases doubled between 2008 and 2012.[48]

Apple has been involved in patent wars, filing lawsuits in attempts to prevent other companies stealing its intellectual property. For example, in April 2011, Apple filed a lawsuit against Samsung over the iPhone and iPad, saying: "Instead of pursuing independent product development, Samsung has chosen to slavishly copy Apple's innovative technology, distinctive user interfaces, and elegant and distinctive product and packaging design, in violation of Apple's valuable intellectual property rights."[49]

It turned into "a vast legal quagmire"[50] and the quagmire remains deeply quaggy.

What is beyond reasonable doubt is the value of the intellectual property at stake. And patented intellectual property could be the tip of the iceberg. There is no register of intellectual property other than patents and sound reasons for shrouding the whole subject in mystery.[51] The lesson for communication strategy is that the one sure way to stop competitors copying innovations is to keep them secret and protect the secret.

Controlling who communicates

The most debated aspect of Apple's communication strategy under Jobs was control, taking steps this book advocates any company should consider:

- One of Jobs' first steps on his return to Apple in the late 1990s was to tighten control of communications and culture. He allegedly imposed "an absolute ban on talking to anyone outside the company who uses words as a tool of his trade" unless chaperoned by a public relations officer.[52] "Whispering into the ear of a friendly reporter became grounds for being escorted out of the building by an armed guard, never to return." It may have been draconian but far too much information had been escaping into the public domain where it was readily available to competitors and critics. Before Jobs' return, Apple employees did their own PR, in part by leaking information.[53]

- Apple allowed only selected managers to speak to the media on each subject. For example, only five people were permitted to speak to the media when Apple launched the iPhone in 2007. This did not include even the most senior people who built the product. As one of the five explained: "They're likely to get asked questions that they know the answers to but that they haven't learned how to gracefully avoid answering."[54]

- While keeping most journalists at a distance, Apple singled out certain key journalists for special treatment. They were those like Walt Mossberg, then at the *Wall Street Journal*, and David Pogue, then at the *New York Times*, who were the most influential in forming positive or negative opinions about new products, and those in a position to grant occasional headline or front cover publicity.

The what, when and how of communication

The release of information outside the company was severely restricted. Apple decided, as far as possible, who received what information and when. All information was controlled but above all it aimed to prevent information reaching competitors that would help them develop products to compete with or move ahead of Apple products.

Analysis suggests that it focused on *controlled disclosure* of three strands of information:

- By far the largest category by volume, the information about products and services, once they have been launched, required to market those products and services effectively.

- Financial and corporate information to the extent required by laws and accounting standards or that would be to the company's competitive advantage in some way.

- Once again for competitive advantage, carefully selected statistics, such as numbers of products sold.

Most other categories of information were off limits. As Jobs said on one of Apple's quarterly earnings calls, "We don't talk about unannounced products."[55]

Other information Apple did not disclose included research and development, details of planned events, suppliers, personnel, and what went on inside the company.[56] However, there are reports of carefully controlled leaks about forthcoming products to help stoke customer eagerness, while commenting neither on individual stories nor on the alleged policy. "Their strategy is to say nothing; it keeps everyone guessing what Apple is up to, generates free publicity, and keeps them out of the trouble everyone gets into," one journalist told Mark Gurman. Among the common media relations techniques allegedly used were steering journalists by saying something like, "if you were totally off-base I would tell you," by drawing attention to writers' record with Apple information, and by warning of potential relationship· problems if the story went the wrong way.[57]

Apple was disciplined enough to resist the temptation to make impromptu revelations. Jobs spoke in public, on carefully selected occasions, without divulging information prematurely. At one 2004 industry conference, a Palm Treo PDA user asked him if Apple would please produce a smartphone. Apple was already developing the iPhone it would launch three years later.[58] Many executives would have thought: "We're developing a smartphone. Here is a competitor's customer offering to switch to our product. Surely I should give him — and other potential customers — some encouragement." The average executive might have said: "You'll have to wait and see but we never rule anything out." Some CEOs would have said, "I'm sure we'll be able to make your dreams come true very soon." Not Steve Jobs. He remembered the big picture, stuck to the communication strategy, and told the Palm customer it would be best to stay happy with his Treo.[59]

Apple became known for huge, set-piece events to launch new products, the famous "big bang" launch. The paucity of information ahead of each event was key to its success. Apple was never telling the world what it already knew. Gurman's account gave an idea of the meticulous organization and behind-the-scenes work with the media that went into these events.

Apple conducted a dialog with analysts and investors without revealing the information it wanted to remain secret. The results could be seen in analysts' reports. Apple did not hold investor days, that is, long, in-depth presentations to investors and analysts about the company. Given its policy of not discussing its product pipeline, this is scarcely surprising. Guidance was conservative. And it ensured that expectations of new products and services were modest. Even those who followed the company closely could be surprised. For example, on the launch of the iPhone, "In our wildest dreams, we could not have conceived of a product with so many next-generation features, highlighted by Apple's incomparable focus on ease of use."[60]

Actions, not words

Apple continues to economize on words and be generous with action. In January 2014, a *Wall Street Journal* article speculated that Apple planned a large-scale mobile payments service, exploiting its access to information about hundreds of millions of customers, especially of the iTunes Store. Apple refused to comment or make anyone available for interview.[61] Through the summer of 2014 expectations mounted of Apple's most important product launch since Tim Cook succeeded Jobs. It was no surprise when Apple announced larger iPhones, Apple Pay, the new mobile payment system, and Apple Watch, a new product category. Yet, as before, the nature of Apple Pay and what the new watch would be like were secret. Everything went according to plan and Cook concluded "Anybody coming out of there yesterday knows that innovation is alive and well in Cupertino."[62]

Otherwise, Cook joked that he would "like to find a way to be more secretive but unfortunately the rumor mill goes a little beyond me."[63]

Despite its robust finances, technological strength and huge customer base, its competitive position is precarious. Apple could not afford to relax without risking the fate of former technology giants such as Nokia, Burroughs or Compaq. According to one investor, its future was so uncertain ahead of the September 2014 multiple product launch that it might become obsolete in two or three years.[64]

The future of technology is always unclear. It only seems obvious in hindsight. Investing in technology and piloting a technology business are intrinsically haphazard and hazardous. It could be less so if Apple is able to shift from a company that relies entirely on its ability to find and deliver the next big thing to a business model more reliant on the services supplied through its ecosystem.

Focused communications

How should Apple be seen in relation to public relations theory? In its early years, Apple fitted the most primitive of Grunig and Hunt's four PR models, the press agentry/publicity model. This was similar to the way public relations worked in the 19th century, as businesses, press agents and people like P. T. Barnum, promoter of the Barnum & Bailey Circus, sought maximum publicity, chiefly in newspapers, using any available means.

After 1997, Jobs introduced the focused strategy that has become familiar if not always well understood. Instead of the one-size-fits-all approach to stakeholder relations, it focused on the stakeholders that really matter (see chapter 12). Above all, this meant customers, with whom it developed a strong bond. Apple described one of its Mac computers as "insanely great." Many fans, comparing its products with badly designed and hard-to-use products from other technology companies, regarded that description as accurate, not hyperbole. Its marketing chief, Phil Schiller, was on record as saying that he received 300 emails a day, some of them from people who are swearing and angry. "You have to deal with their rage and accept it and be proud that the reason you're getting this hate mail with screaming and swearing is because they love your product, they love your brand."[65]

However, Apple did not treat its customers as equals, as symmetry-excellence theory suggests. Jobs scoffed at the idea that Alexander Graham Bell would have done market research before inventing the telephone. Not for him the classic approach of finding out what customers want and giving it to them. "People don't know what they want until you show it to them."[66]

Key points
- Apple's market leadership depends on continuous innovation, vigilance and hence control of information.
- The story of Apple under Steve Jobs showed the benefits of controlled disclosure, focused on the strategy.
- What does the experience of the world's most valuable company mean for public relations?

Was Jobs' Apple good or bad at public relations?

Was Apple under Steve Jobs, as the specialist public relations literature implies, extraordinarily good at marketing yet extraordinarily poor at PR? If its communications were judged by their effectiveness, Apple would be considered extraordinarily good. Yet it has not been praised in the PR literature.

So was Apple just an exceptional case? Maybe only Jobs' Apple could behave as it did and get away with it?

Critics might argue that Apple succeeded because of its dominant position in its market and in spite of its public relations. Yet its distinctive communication strategy only began when Apple nearly went out of business, when the idea that Apple might ever achieve market dominance would have seemed ridiculous to most people. And the element of surprise became more difficult to achieve as the company grew. It is surely intriguing that the same unorthodox communication strategy was effective both for the struggling Apple of the late 1990s and for the world leader of 2010.

If the world's best large business breaks the communications mold, maybe we need a new mold?

And Apple is far from being alone among leading companies in its reluctance to reveal its plans. Three other giants of the digital age control their communications with great care: Alphabet (Google), Facebook and Amazon.

- ALPHABET invests in many different projects but does not disclose them all or reveal which are strategically important. It is known for investing in big things, "moon shots," such as driverless vehicles or anti-aging biotech, but nobody outside the firm knows what it fully intends. Alphabet says it defaults to open but wisely keeps strategic knowledge to itself. The algorithms that make its core Google business work are secret. It emerged through an apparent leak in 2014 that the company had paid a research firm to examine the potential for it to enter the fund management business, possibly as a distributor. Will Alphabet go into fund management? Probably the world outside Alphabet will find out only when it launches such a business — or not. And it is in Alphabet's interest that competitors should be able to do no more than guess. The firm spent $8 billion on research and development in 2013 and 18,593 people, nearly half its workforce, were in R&D. But it gave no further details.[67] Breaking out the results of Google has underlined the value of Alphabet's core business without shedding much light on its new businesses.

- FACEBOOK claims that its "mission is to give people the power to share and make the world more open and connected."[68] That desire does not, of course, extend to strategic information about Facebook. Quarterly results announcements look back at the events of the past quarter and contain only the vaguest information about the future. For example: "People who use our mobile products are more engaged, and we believe we can increase engagement even further... At the same time, we are deeply integrating monetization into our product teams in order to build a stronger, more valuable company."[69] For further details, wait and see, seems to be Facebook's approach.

- AMAZON "If there were a prize for corporate secrecy, Amazon would have an excellent chance of winning," according to *The Economist*.[70] It took Amazon ten years to disclose even basic information about its extraordinarily successful Amazon Web Services (AWS) cloud-computing business at its April 2015 quarterly results. By then, analysts valued AWS, the world market leader for cloud services, at $44 billion, with confirmed annual sales of $5 billion in 2014. A prize for corporate secrecy then, and also one for communication strategy.

In Summary

- Apple's success demands a rethink of some of the standard assumptions of public relations.
- Instead of trying to be open and transparent, Apple in the Steve Jobs era controlled the flow of information in the interests of its business strategy, developing products in secret then launching them with a "big bang."
- For other digital giants including Amazon, Facebook and Alphabet (Google), control is a key element of their successful communication strategies. This requires attention to the detail of communication, while always keeping in mind the big picture.

References

[1] John Locke, *An Essay Concerning Human Understanding*, 1690, (London: Thomas Tegg, 1825), Book II, 255.

[2] Apple Inc. financial statements. Robert Hum & Giovanny Moreno, 'New King of the S&P 500,' CNBC.com, August 9, 2011, citing Standard & Poor's Howard Silverblatt.

[3] "The λόγος of logos," *The Economist*, September 4, 2014.

[4] Morton T. Hansen, Herminia Ibarra & Urs Peyer, 'The Best Performing CEOs in the World,' *Harvard Business Review*, January 2010.

[5] Adam Lashinsky, 'The Decade of Steve,' *Fortune*, November 5, 2009. Adam Hartley, 'Steve Jobs Named as Man of the Noughties,' *TechRadar*, December 21, 2009, <http://www.techradar.com/news/computing/apple/steve-jobs-named-as-man-of-the-noughties-660693>.

[6] According to General Sentiment - Gregg Keizer, 'Apple Reclaims top Brand Spot after iPhone 4S Launch, Jobs' Death,' *Computerworld*, January 27, 2012.

[7] Apple Inc. news release, October 5, 2011.

[8] Robert Crampton, 'Bullying, Belittling and Swearing at People. So Why Does Steve Jobs Deserve to be Deified?' *The Times*, October 25, 2011.

[9] Schlender & Tetzeli, *Becoming Steve Jobs*, 109.

[10] See Yukari Iwatane Kane, *Haunted Empire: Apple after Steve Jobs*, (London: William Collins, 2014).

[11] Popular store: 'iTunes Store Tops 10 Billion Songs Sold,' Apple Inc. news release, February 25, 2010. 1m iPhone 4Ss: 'iPhone 4S Pre-Orders Top One Million in First 24 Hours,' Apple Inc. news release, October 10, 2011. 'Apple's App Store Downloads Top 25 Billion,' Apple Inc. news release, March 5, 2012. Word of the year: 'App 2010 Word of the Year, as Voted by American Dialect Society,' American Dialect Society news release, January 7, 2011. 315m devices: 'Apple's App Store Downloads Top 25 Billion,' Apple Inc. news release, March 5, 2012. 1st quarter sales: 'Apple Reports First Quarter Results,' Apple Inc. news release, January 24, 2012.

[12] Kevin Maney, 'Apple's 1984 Super Bowl Commercial Still Stands as Watershed Event,' *USA Today*, January 20, 2004. Narrative: Micael Dahlen, Fredrik Lange & Terry Smith, *Marketing Communications: A Brand Narrative Approach*, (Chichester, UK: John Wiley & Sons Ltd, 2010), 23. Beth Snyder Bulik, 'Marketer of the Decade: Apple,' *Advertising Age*, October 18, 2010.

[13] Exemplifies the marketing concept: Louis E. Boone and David L. Kurtz, *Contemporary Marketing*, (Mason, OH: South-Western Cengage Learning, 2012), 11. See also: Roger A. Kerin, Steven W. Hartley & William Rudelius, *Marketing: The Core*, (New York: McGraw-Hill/Irwin, 2010). Carl McDaniel, Charles W. Lamb & Joseph F. Hair, *Essentials of Marketing*, (Mason, OH: South-Western Cengage Learning, 2011). William M. Pride & O. C. Ferrell, *Foundations of Marketing*, (Boston, MA: Houghton Mifflin Company, 2009). Gary Armstrong, Philip Kotler, Michael Harker & Ross Brennan, *Marketing: An Introduction*, (Harlow, UK: Financial Times/Prentice Hall, 2009), 268.

[14] Thompson et al, *Crafting and Executing Strategy*, 3. Richard P. Rumelt, *Good Strategy/Bad Strategy: The Difference and Why it Matters*, (New York: Crown Business, 2011).

[15] Seitel, *The Practice of Public Relations*, 12th edn., 230, 302 & 365-366.

[16] E.g.: Craig E. Carroll, (ed.), *The Handbook of Communication and Corporate Reputation*, (Chichester, UK: John Wiley & Sons, Inc., 2013); Robert L. Heath, (ed.), *Sage Handbook of Public Relations*, (Thousand Oaks, CA: Sage Publications, Inc., 2010); Holtzhausen & Zerfass, (eds., *The Routledge Handbook of Strategic Communication*; Sriramesh, Zerfass, & Kim, *Public Relations and Communication Management*; Toth, (ed.), *The Future of Excellence...*

[17] Joseph Campbell, *The Hero With a Thousand Faces*, (Princeton University Press, 1949).

[18] Christopher Brennan, 'Apple Secrecy and How the PR is Arse over Tit but Works Just Fine Thank You Very Much,' *All Points North*, July 14, 2008.

[19] Christian Zibreg, 'Opinion: Why Apple PR Sucks,' *Geek.com*, August 18, 2009.

[20] Rex Hammock, 'The Real News: The Apple PR Machine Attenuates,' *Rexblog.com*, July 14, 2010.

[21] Zibreg, 'Why Apple PR Sucks.'

[22] Isaacson, *Steve Jobs*, 75.

[23] Michael Moritz, *Return to the Little Kingdom: Steve Jobs, the Creation of Apple, and How it Changed the World*, (London: Duckworth Overlook, 2009), 238.

[24] Jeffrey Rayport, 'The Virus of Marketing,' *Fast Company*, December 31, 1996.

[25] Moritz, *Return to the Little Kingdom*, 282, 285-6 & 236.

[26] Jeffrey S. Young & William L. Simon, *Icon Steve Jobs: The Greatest Second Act in the History of Business*, (Hoboken, NJ: John Wiley & Sons, 2005), 235.

[27] Moritz, *Return to the Little Kingdom*, 314.

[28] Isaacson, *Steve Jobs*, 232-7.

[29] Thomas L. Harris, 'Integrated Marketing Public Relations,' in *The Handbook of Strategic Public Relations...*, ed. Caywood, 97.

[30] Matt Haig, *Brand Royalty: How the World's Top 100 Brands Thrive & Survive*, (Philadelphia, PA: Kogan Page, 2004), 199.

[31] Moritz, *Return to the Little Kingdom*, 310.

[32] Isaacson, *Steve Jobs*, 106, 139-141.

[33] Alan Deutschman, *The Second Coming of Steve Jobs*, (New York: Broadway Books, 2000), 226.

[34] Luke Dormehl, *The Apple Revolution: Steve Jobs, the Counter Culture and How the Crazy Ones Took Over the World*, (London: Virgin Books, 2012), 282.

[35] Isaacson, *Steve Jobs*, 193.

[36] Isaacson, *Steve Jobs*, 216.

[37] Frank Rose, *West of Eden: The End of Innocence at Apple Computer*, (London: Arrow Books, 1989), 320.

[38] Isaacson, *Steve Jobs*, 215-8.

[39] Steve Jobs, *Steve Jobs: The Lost Interview*, Paul Sen, Robert X. Cringely, 2012, originally recorded 1995.

[40] 'Apple Computer, Inc. Finalizes Acquisition of NeXT Software Inc.,' Apple Inc. news release, February 7, 1997.

[41] Rumelt, *Good Strategy/Bad Strategy*, 14-15.

[42] Apple Inc., Form 10-K for Period Ending September 28, 2013, 6 & 9-20.

[43] Zachary M. Seward, 'The Steve Jobs Email that Outlined Apple's Strategy a Year Before His Death,' *Quartz*, April 5, 2014.

[44] Bruce C. N. Greenwald & Judd Kahn, *Value Investing: from Graham to Buffett and Beyond*, (Hoboken, NJ: John Wiley & Sons, Inc., 2001), 82.

[45] Nairn, *Engines That Move Markets*, 4-5 & 29.

[46] 'Apple Launches iPad 2,' 'Apple Launches New iPad,' 'Apple Introduces iPad Mini,' Apple Inc. news releases March 2, 2011, March 7, 2012 and October 23, 2012.

[47] Isaacson, *Steve Jobs*, 135. Don Clark, 'Familiar Names Lie Inside the Apple iPad,' *Wall Street Journal*, April 6, 2010.

[48] Ian Sherr & Brett Kendall, 'Veto of Apple Ruling Likely to Upend Big Patent Battles,' *Wall Street Journal*, August 5, 2013.

[49] Apple Inc., Apple's filing in Apple v. Samsung, April 15, 2011.

[50] Marissa Oberlander, Martin Stabe & Steve Bernard, 'The Smartphone Patent Wars,' *Financial Times*, October 17, 2011.

[51] 'Can You Keep a Secret?' *The Economist*, March 16, 2013.

[52] Young & Simon, *Icon Steve Jobs*, 235.

[53] Deutschman, *The Second Coming*, 255.

[54] Adam Lashinsky, *Inside Apple*, (New York: Business Plus, 2012), 129.

[55] Steve Jobs, Apple Inc. 4th Quarter 2010 Earnings Call, October 18, 2010, Morningstar transcript.

[56] Lashinsky, *Inside Apple*, 130.

[57] Mark Gurman, 'Seeing Through the Illusion: Understanding Apple's Mastery of the Media,' *9TO5Mac*, August 29, 2014.

[58] Dan Rowinski, '4 Real Secrets We've Learned So Far About Apple,' *readwrite.com*, August 7, 2012.

[59] Kasper Jade, 'Jobs: Apple Developed, but Did Not Ship Apple PDA,' *AppleInsider*, June 7, 2004.

[60] Charlie Wolf & John Lynch, *Apple Computer, Inc. (AAPL) – Buy*, Needham & Co, LLC, January 10, 2007.

[61] Douglas MacMillan & Daisaku Wakabayashi, 'Apple Pushes Deeper into Mobile Payments,' *Wall Street Journal*, January 24, 2014.

[62] Brad Stone & Adam Satariano, 'Tim Cook's Apple: The Exclusive Story Behind the Making of the Apple Watch and the Revolution in the Company's Culture,' *Bloomberg BusinessWeek*, September 22, 2014.

[63] Stone & Satariano, 'Tim Cook's Apple.'

[64] Andrew Trotman, 'Apple Could be Obsolete in Two Years,' *Daily Telegraph*, July 24, 2014, quoting Pedro de Noronha of Noster Capital on CNBC.

[65] Haig, *Brand Royalty*, 200.

[66] Isaacson, *Steve Jobs*, 170 & 567.

[67] Algorithms: Eric Schmidt & Jonathan Rosenberg, *How Google Works*, (New York: Grand Central Publishing, 2014), 143. Guess: Madison Marriage, 'Google Study Heightens Fund Industry Fears,' *Financial Times*, September 29, 2014. R&D: Google Inc., Form 10-K for Year Ending December 31, 2013.

[68] Facebook, Inc., *About Facebook*, <https://www.facebook.com/facebook/info?tab=page_info>.

[69] 'Facebook Reports Third Quarter 2012 Results,' Facebook, Inc. news release, October 23, 2012.

[70] 'The Cheap, Convenient Cloud,' *The Economist*, April 18, 2015.

CHAPTER 9

From Truth to Narrative

"'Did not our fathers resist the Medes [Persians] not only with resources far different from ours, but even when those resources had been abandoned? And, more by wisdom than by fortune, more by daring than by strength, did not they beat off the barbarian and advance their affairs to their present height? We must not fall behind them, but must resist our enemies in any way and in every way, and attempt to hand down our power to our posterity unimpaired.' Such were the words of Pericles. The Athenians, persuaded of the wisdom of his advice, voted as he desired."
— Thucydides, "History of the Peloponnesian War."[1]

Pericles led democratic Athens through his supreme mastery of strategic narrative. He could lay before the Athenians a picture of the future that awaited them if they agreed to what he proposed.[2] All organizations need such an outcome to be thought-through and painted, in the form of a strategic narrative.

Truth and narrative

Telling the truth is usually contrasted with telling lies but there is rarely a straightforward choice between telling the whole truth and telling a pack of lies (Chapter 5). To recapitulate the issue discussed in chapter 6 (Optimism and the Strategy of Truth), anyone constructing a narrative position makes a choice between realism and optimism. The facts as we believe them to be or the facts as we would like them to be. Optimism is probably the most pervasive distortion of the facts in the construction of a story.

These choices are made at the level of the simplest message or text. But texts are complex. A written text may be read in many different ways. A spoken text may be heard in many different ways. Even a simple message is subject to interpretation. What is the message? Is it the message intended by the speaker? Is it the message actually spoken or sent? Is it the message as heard or received? Or is it the message as perceived by the hearer or receiver.[3] And which one of these and other possibilities is "the truth"? Through deconstruction, Jacques Derrida and other semioticians brought new attention to this idea. They achieved such influence that it is notably surprising to be presented, decades into the post-structuralist era, with such a slogan as "Tell the truth".

Life as a confessional, in which everyone routinely tells the truth, the whole truth, and nothing but the truth, is a social and psychological delusion.

Narrative theory emphasizes the subjective nature of knowledge about society because of the almost infinite possible number of different points of view. When constructing a position or narrative, the aim should be to combine a subjective point of view with consideration of the known facts. What does that mean in practice?

Narrative in practice

The practical effect of narrative in daily life is easy to understand in the context of the resumé or curriculum vitae, a real life text that is familiar to anyone who has been in the executive job market. Woe to the executive who tells barefaced lies. It would be both wrong and dangerous to claim a qualification the executive does not hold, or a position the executive did not occupy.

But for any resumé to be the absolute truth would be impossible because the resumé is subjective. It must be factual but cannot be "the truth." It is an autobiographical narrative, in which the author selects and highlights desirable events, experiences and characteristics but omits or makes light of the undesirable. The typical resumé imposes order on the chaos of real life, replacing its everyday messiness with a neat catalog of events and achievements.

It is definitely not the whole truth: "If you must include a negative event, such as failing an examination or being dismissed from a post, you are advised to make as little of it as possible without being dishonest."[4] When it comes to narrating our careers, we are all propagandists. We all apply deliberately what jaundiced journalists like to call "spin." Water Lippmann said: "Great men, even during their lifetime, are usually known to the public only through a fictitious personality." Perhaps not just great men?

The resumé is but a formulaic example of what people and organizations do all the time. Before resumés, people of relatively high status such as a noble or merchant might commission portrait paintings in a particular style, in appropriate dress, with significant objects and against a significant background in order to tell the desired story about themselves. After resumés, indigenes of the internet might carefully select events, photos and recommendations on Facebook pages or Pinterest pinboards to tell the desired story about themselves.

Not many people go into the witness box and claim to be unable to tell the truth, the whole truth and nothing but the truth "on the grounds that they don't know what truth is or how to tell it."[5] That may be the case. But even people who go into the witness box thinking they know what the truth is and how to tell it, are in fact unable to tell the truth, the whole truth and nothing but the truth. What they actually tell is not the absolute, objective truth but a version of it that could more fairly be described as a narrative. James Joyce showed in the "Ithaca" episode of "Ulysses" how a long interrogation, superficially designed to organize facts, could be transformed into a narrative that lends his characters cosmic or comic significance.

Putting together a resumé (or perhaps a LinkedIn profile) may be the most purposeful narrative someone in business ever constructs. Yet we go through a less conscious but similar process every time we tell a story. And we tell stories all the time because we are built that way. Psychologists believe that much of what we say to others and even much of what we think naturally takes the form of a story.

Roland Barthes pointed out in the 1960s that narrative is and always has been everywhere.[6] People are not telling any more stories today than they were before Barthes. But most of the time we do so unconsciously, without thinking to ourselves, "Now I'm going to tell a story." Barthes helped inspire the interest of social scientists in narrative. And this led to the conscious use of narrative beyond the literary sphere. In time, the narrative tool was taken up outside academe by people in different walks of life, including professional communicators. For example, in advertising, "Before we write anything about advertising... we have to understand that at its core, it's storytelling."[7] And see chapter 10 on framing.

(Storytelling may have become a management fad that is almost a cult but that does not detract from the value of the idea, especially and naturally in communication.)

The narrative model

Appreciation of the significance of narrative plays havoc with conventional thinking about communication, captured in the simplest model of a speaker addressing a hearer (audience). Although this model only describes a single, solo communication, Aristotle and his modern followers (see chapter 4) all simplified drastically. They omitted any reference to context, code (the shared system of meaning on which a message relies), or attitudes, among other factors. Semantic problems and problems of effectiveness were ignored.

But persuasive communications including advertising and public relations could be seen as orchestrated communication between the source and the receiver, using research to evaluate attitudes and provide feedback, in order to persuade audiences and sell products.[8]

These now standard formulae may be helpful tactically, for analysis of a single communication. But, as seen in chapter 7, even when augmented by multiple senders and receivers, message channels, noise, feedback, and other factors,[9] these kinds of formulae are not adequate for the purposes of communication strategy. A more strategic model is the one set out at the very start of this book:

- What is our position (our story)?
- When do we need to tell it? (And when do we need to keep shtum?)
- To whom?
- How? And how do we stop other people spoiling it?

Rather than modeling only a single incident of communication, this allows for a stream of communication over an indefinite period that could last for years. And it does not assume that there will be a communication, in the conventional sense of a message sent from a speaker to an audience. There could even be silence.

Key points
- Texts are complex and subjective — they may be understood in different ways.
- In selecting the stories we tell, we are strategic rather than truthful.
- Strategic communication fits a narrative model better than the simple speaker-subject-hearer (source-message-receiver) model.

The power of narrative in communication strategy

The summer of 1805 saw Napoleon's Grande Armée encamped along the English Channel coast, waiting for the chance to invade England. But Napoleon secretly decided on a new strategy. Its aim was to defeat and bring to an end the third coalition of powers against France, and thereby provide security for France and for his regime. Its immediate objective was to encircle and destroy the Austrian army at Ulm in Bavaria.

For the strategy to succeed required that the enemy should fail to recognize Napoleon's real intentions. In late August, he confided in two close associates, Berthier, chief of staff, and Daru, lieutenant-general. (His secrecy contrasted with "the total lack of secrecy" of the Coalition.)[10] Napoleon dictated to Daru in a six-hour torrent the detailed orders that broke camp and marched the army across France, and what is now Germany, Austria and the Czech Republic, a total distance of around 1,000 miles.

Fig. 9.1 Napoleon's Narrative: Austerlitz 1805

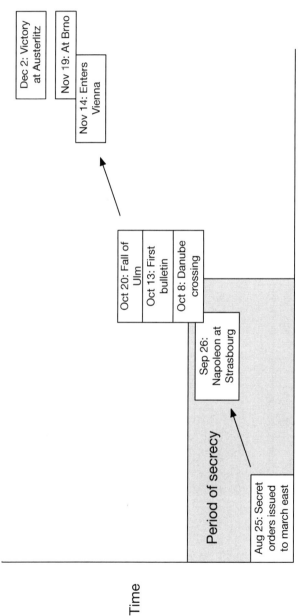

Napoleon issued the orders on August 25, 1805, in a news blackout. "Rigorous censorship was applied, with post offices occupied and newspapers muzzled." He deployed his troops stealthily and also took measures to deceive the enemy. He aimed to dupe the enemy into believing that the Grande Armée remained at Boulogne. And he made the substantial French forces in Italy look as though their intentions were aggressive — in other words, to lead the Allies to expect a French thrust through Italy. Although the Grande Armée crossed the Rhine at the end of September, the Austrians believed, until it was too late, that the subsidiary army in Italy was Napoleon's main force and that the principal French initiative would be there, as it had been in 1796 and 1800. The leading French corps crossed the Danube below Ulm on October 8. "Never was astonishment equal to that which filled all Europe on the unexpected arrival of this army."[11]

Once the need for total secrecy had passed, as his plans came together and the trap was sprung, Napoleon began to tell his strategic story. It helped to motivate his supporters and dishearten his enemies. He wrote the first of 37 bulletins that were "exciting to read, even as fiction."[12] This was dated October 13. The strategy was secret; the strategic narrative was timely and compelling. After surrounding and capturing the Austrian army at Ulm on October 20, Napoleon moved on to Vienna and Brno, and finally defeated the combined Austrian and Russian armies at Austerlitz on December 2.

In British mythology, Nelson's decisive victory at Trafalgar (October 21, 1805) saved the country from French invasion and was the turning point of the Napoleonic wars. This is not to diminish the achievement of Trafalgar, which made an invasion of England impossible for the rest of the war but, by the day of the battle, Napoleon had long moved on.

Modern strategic narrative

What should a strategic narrative consist of? The limitations of generic communication strategies have already been mentioned. And the study of rhetoric in public relations has concentrated on crises. A number of typologies have been put forward for crisis communication, notably Benoit's comprehensive "image repair theory," discussed in chapter 13. A crisis creates a need for a rhetorical solution that is specific. It is easiest to generalize when the need is for a response to an existing rhetorical situation[13] than under ordinary conditions, when situations and objectives are disparate. However, the best guidance is that there are four strands that need to be woven into any company's strategic narrative:

(1) Selling the strategy

The most obvious job of the strategic narrative is to sell the strategy itself. This was the role performed by Napoleon's communications once his surprise had succeeded. Chapter 17 integrates this task into the creation of a communication strategy.

(2) The creation myth

Any community or organization needs to share a story about where they come from. Human beings are naturally curious about causation. Anyone interested in a business is likely to want to know: how did it start, and how did it end up like this? "Consumers tend to think of long-lived companies as trustworthy. By communicating their past imaginatively, businesses capitalize on an asset."[14]

It is in the organization's interest to answer the question by writing its own story. This is the creation myth or foundation narrative. Apple's foundation narrative started with two guys experimenting in a garage. MyTravel's foundation narrative involved an entrepreneur buying a small shop in a small town in the boondocks. BAA's foundation myth was a version of the story of flight (see chapter 16).

To see how important corporate heritage can be, look at the efforts made by people associated with Apple to boost the biography of Steve Jobs by Brett Schlender and Rick Tetzeli, published in 2015, in preference to the 2011 biography by Walter

Isaacson published just after Jobs' death.[15] And by the standards of business biographies, the earlier author did a fine job. However, it would be understandable if, in a culture where standards are so high, fine might not be considered good enough.

(3) Making the world a better place

The strategic narrative must include the business strategy, it should include a foundation story, and the third strand should be a social purpose narrative — the story of how the firm is making the world a better place. Øyvind Ihlen noted that the three companies most admired in America (2007), according to *Fortune*, were GE, Toyota and Starbucks, and gave the examples of GE's commitment to invest in innovative solutions, Toyota's production of hybrid vehicles, and Starbucks' leadership role in the community.[16]

Businesses contribute to society by employing and training people, by funding pensions, by rewarding shareholders, by paying taxes, and more broadly by development and investment. This is all important and should form part of the social purpose narrative. But it is not the most important part.

How is your business making the world a better place by what it does for a living? This is most likely to be by offering a product or service. If you don't think your employer is doing anything to make the world a better place, maybe you shouldn't be working there. Remember that even Al Capone had a social purpose narrative (chapter 2).

Critics accuse business of making the world a worse place by exploiting labor, exploiting consumers, exploiting resources and despoiling the environment. You might respond to them by:

- Ignoring them.
- Engaging on their terms.
- Or, preferably, by telling your own story.

Telling your story may involve overt corporate social responsibility-type activity but it is better to explain how you are making the world a better place through the organic operation of the business.

The "better place" narrative feels modern but is not new. In the advertisements created by Bruce Barton in the 1920s, General Motors said it was "Making the nation a neighborhood."[17] And InterNorth, Inc., Enron's predecessor, said, "We work for America," at the beginning of the 1980s.[18] Perhaps Enron did indeed work for America before it turned to the dark side.

One of the strongest "better place" narratives belongs to the pharmaceutical industry. Jim Collins and Jerry Porras made a study of large capitalization visionary ("built to last") companies. These were companies whose long-term performance had been outstanding and that were likely to be the envy of their peers. It was no accident that these companies were all inspired by a set of ideals. The first, obvious example Collins and Porras gave was Merck & Company, inspired by the fight against disease.[19]

During the Ebola epidemic in West Africa, GSK gave prominence in its communications to "Our fight against Ebola."[20] GSK's Ebola vaccine is likely to play only a small part in its business but could be a major weapon against Ebola. And the story of GSK's work on Ebola helped the company in a number of ways. It highlighted the fact that the company's restructuring was making vaccines one of its core businesses, picked up on a major international news story, and helped to make people feel good about GSK. Johnson & Johnson and Merck were also developing Ebola vaccines but appeared to give the Ebola story less prominence. GSK also highlights its work over many years on a vaccine against malaria. It is likely to be first to market with such a vaccine. Malaria kills half a million Africans every year but is of less interest to television news than Ebola.[21]

In fact, the majority of the companies discussed in this book, and the companies with which I have been associated, have used this "better place" narrative at some point. Each of Apple's revolutionary new products promised an impact on the daily life of its users and the Apple Watch even holds out extensive health benefits. BP's "Beyond Petroleum" narrative positioned the company in a greener future in which fossil fuels would play a smaller part. BAA's corporate narrative told how airports were at the heart of cities' prosperity and growth (see chapter 16). MyTravel made the world a better place by enabling millions of ordinary people to enjoy a break in the sun — fun but with health benefits.[22]

(4) Safety First

At BAA, the world's leading airport company in the 1990s and early 2000s, the first priority was safety.

For a company that provided the facilities for millions of people to arrive and depart by air — in safety — this was perhaps not surprising. But the idea can be taken further. For any firm that makes products or provides services to consumers, the safety of these consumers must be paramount. It may be argued that other things are more important — shareholder return, perhaps, or satisfying customers. The trouble is that a failure of safety impairs the ability to achieve all other objectives. Safety is a most basic need.

This is easily illustrated in the case of a leisure travel company. The punctuality of the flight, the quality of the accommodation, the breadth of the menu, the interesting sights, the opportunities to party, and so on, all become irrelevant if the customer suffers death, injury or serious illness.

But is such an objective appropriate for businesses that are less directly responsible for customers' welfare? Even where there is no consumer involvement, safety is still the consideration that trumps all others because, when there is a question mark over safety, this can color all subsequent events. In the Gulf of Mexico accident (2010), and in many other crises, the fundamental issue was safety (see chapter 14).

Giving priority to safety puts you in an unassailable rhetorical position. Whenever questions arose, BAA was able to point to its absolute commitment to safety. I lost count of the number of statements I wrote in my time at BAA that began with some variation of "safety is our top priority." This was the smartest move BAA's management ever made.

In Summary

- In everyday life, people pick and choose among facts and feelings to tell stories. This behavior may be regarded as manipulative, strategic, or simply human, depending on your perspective.
- Strategic communication means more than sending messages. It answers questions such as: What is our story? When, how and to whom should we tell it? And when is it better to say less or nothing?
- Any organization's communication strategies should incorporate strategic narratives covering selling the strategy, its own history, its social purpose (making the world a better place), and putting safety first.

_____

References

[1] Thucydides, *History of the Pelopennesian War*, translated by Richard Crawley, 1876, (London: J. M. Dent & Sons Ltd., 1910), Book I, 97.

[2] Freedman, *Strategy*, 37.

[3] Sven Windahl, Benno H. Signitzer & Jean T. Olson, *Using Communication Theory*, (London: Sage, 2009), 172.

[4] Brian Alleyne, *Narrative Networks: Storied Approaches in a Digital Age*, (London: Sage Publications Ltd, 2015), 106.

[5] D. H. Mellor, *Mind, Meaning, and Reality: Essays in Philosophy*, (Oxford University Press, 2012), 47.

[6] Roland Barthes, 'Introduction to the Structural Analysis of Narratives' in *The Narrative Reader*, ed. by Martin McQuillan, (London: Routledge, 2000), 109-114.

[7] Hegarty, 'Who's Lighting the Campfire.'

[8] Brown, 'Symmetry and Its Critics.'

[9] David S. Waller & Michael J. Polonsky, 'Multiple Senders and Receivers: A Business Communication Model,' *Corporate Communications: An International Journal*, Vol. 3, No. 3, (1998), 83-91.

[10] Alistair Horne, *How Far From Austerlitz: Napoleon 1805-1815*, (London: Papermac, 1997), 77-79.

[11] Horne, *How Far From Austerlitz*, Blackout: 81. Astonishment: 112.

[12] Andrew Roberts, *Napoleon the Great*, (London: Penguin Books Ltd, 2014), 370-372.

[13] George Cheney, Lars Thoger Christensen, Charles Conrad & Daniel J. Lair, 'Corporate Rhetoric as Organizational Discourse,' in *The Sage Handbook of Organizational Discourse*, (London: Sage, 2004), 87.

[14] Michael Rowlinson, quoted in Alicia Clegg, 'A Rummage in the Corporate Attic,' *Financial Times*, July 24, 2008.

[15] Peter Burrows, 'Why Apple Feels the Need to Defend Steve Jobs,' *BloombergBusiness*, March 27, 2015.

[16] Øyvind Ihlen, 'Good Environmental Citizens? The Green Rhetoric of Corporate Social Responsibility,' in *Rhetorical and Critical Approaches to Public Relations II*, ed. Heath, Toth & Waymer, 360-374.

[17] Roland Marchand, *Creating the Corporate Soul: The Rise of Public Relations and Corporate Imagery in American Big Business*, (Berkeley: University of California Press, 1998), 138-139.

[18] Vernon E. Dalton, 'We Work for America,' *Public Relations Journal*, (November 1983), 23-24.

[19] Jim C. Collins and Jerry I. Porras, *Built to Last: Successful Habits of Visionary Companies*, (London: Random House Business Books, 2005), 47.

[20] <http:www.gsk.com> home page, accessed March 10, 2015.

[21] Andrew Ward, 'Researchers Hunt Malaria Vaccines for People and Mosquitoes,' *Financial Times*, April 24, 2015.

[22] Daniel J. Levitin, 'Hit the Reset Button in Your Brain,' *New York Times*, August 9, 2014.

CHAPTER 10

Profile: Mobil and the high profile advocacy strategy

"There is a whole race of beings to-day whose passion is to keep their names in the newspapers."
— William James, "Principles of Psychology"[1]

"Sufficient for the day is the newspaper thereof."
— James Joyce, "Ulysses"[2]

New York City in the 1980s was a mecca for the world's largest corporations, even more than it is today. Two of the biggest oil companies, Exxon and Mobil, had trophy headquarters at 1251 Sixth Avenue (54 floors) and 150 42nd Street (42 floors), respectively (both designed by Harrison & Abramovitz). Mobil was the second largest American oil company; Exxon was the largest, twice the size of Mobil. The two companies took radically different approaches to communication. Which was the better approach, high profile or low profile? Mobil or Exxon?

Sent to New York by my oil company employer to work in public affairs, it was my job to observe the scene from a much smaller building, opposite Saks on Fifth Avenue. There was no question which of the two companies was more interesting: Mobil was mesmerizing, whereas Exxon was scarcely visible to outsiders beyond its chain of gas stations. Mobil was consistently in your face. It was in the face of the media, in the face of the government and in the face of the many vocal opponents of Big Oil. And Mobil's high profile advocacy strategy did not have to be deduced: the strategy was proclaimed.

Energy crisis

Mobil did not always have such a strategy or such a high profile. It began life as the Standard Oil Company of New York (Socony), one of the baby oil companies brought into being early in the 20th century by the dissolution of the Standard Oil trust. Later it became one of the companies, sometimes known as the "Seven Sisters," that dominated the world oil industry in the post-war period. Whether measured by sales, profit or market value, they were enormous, wealthier than many sovereign states. They were global and vertically integrated, handling every stage from finding and extracting crude oil from the ground to selling refined products to businesses and consumers. Their style and spread contributed to paranoia about multinational corporations although their political vulnerability was revealed at the end of the 1960s.

At home, in the West, oil companies came under increasing scrutiny for a number of reasons. Criticism of institutions increased and concern for the natural environment became a major political issue. Accidents involving the new supertankers and offshore oil wells hit the headlines. When *Torrey Canyon* hit rocks off southwest England in 1967, with 120,000 tons of crude oil on board, it was the world's largest ever shipwreck and the most polluting. When a drilling rig suffered a blow-out in 1969, six miles off the coast of Santa Barbara, California, it caused an oil spill in a most sensitive spot: "The ooze on the beaches — and on oil-soaked birds — became one of the emblematic images in the nation's new environmental consciousness."[3] The Santa Barbara oil spill may even have been the catalyst for the emergence of corporate social responsibility in trend-setting California.[4]

Somewhere around 1970, the world oil market changed from a calm buyer's market to a seller's market, that favored the oil-exporting countries. Demand for oil was rising while new sources were harder to find. By 1970, American oil production had peaked and the US imported 28% of its oil. Western economy and society were heavily dependent on the fuel they could no longer control. Over the next three years, slowly at first but eventually in a rush precipitated by the Yom Kippur War, the producing countries demanded and obtained part or full ownership of the oil companies' concessions and raised the price of their oil. In the space of a few weeks at the end of 1973, the price quadrupled, triggering the 1974-75 recession. OPEC imposed an embargo on the USA and, amid the resulting shortages, its gasoline consumption fell 8% in the first quarter of 1974.

Opinion polls said Americans were inclined to blame the oil companies, whose profits were increasing, more than the Arabs. "As motorists waited in their cars, listening to the radio describing new shortages, they looked up angrily at the giant sign at the head of the line proclaiming Mobil, Texaco or Exxon: the symbols no longer of plenty but of an infuriating and ill-organized shortage."[5] Mobil and the others were the scapegoat for economic crisis. A national poll in 1975 showed that 67% had "low approval" of big companies, up from 47% a decade before, and when it came to oil companies, three-quarters thought they made too much profit.[6]

The crisis had numerous repercussions, including approval for the Trans Alaska Pipeline to bring oil from Alaska's North Slope to market and a 55 miles per hour speed limit on American roads for several years. Oil companies faced unwelcome regulations and the threat of antitrust action. And around the same time, as Mobil itself later said: "Watergate ushered in a new era of investigative journalism, and crusading reporters quickly turned their sights on business."[7] These were the years when suspicion of big business ceased to be only a concern of the political left in America and joined the mainstream.[8]

Oil company seeks high profile

Mobil (Socony) changed direction after 1965, when "brash" Rawleigh Warner Jr became its president.[9] For much of its life, the company had been associated with Exxon, notably in the Stanvac joint venture responsible for sales in many countries. Stanvac was dismantled on antitrust grounds in 1960 and after that the companies diverged. Warner affirmed the company's independence, rebranding it Mobil, one of its existing trade names. Chermayeff & Geismar's superb design was a stylish, streamlined, timeless logo incorporating the new name in blue with a bright red "o," and a new alphabet to match. It was rolled out to print, packaging, signage and vehicles throughout the world.[10] The new branding somehow encapsulated the spirit of the road and turned the highways into a showroom for Mobil. It is one of the few corporate identities of that era which looks as though it could have been designed yesterday.

In 1969, Warner moved up to chairman and chief executive, with William P. Tavoulareas succeeding him as president. Tavoulareas was a shrewd accountant and lawyer who handled Mobil's negotiations in the Middle East. He believed in straight talking and talked tough: "I never became afraid of speaking my mind… My father came from a poor village in the mountains of Greece. It wasn't much of a place but in the 400 years of Turkish occupation of Greece that village was never conquered."[11] The new team, alone among the major oil companies, felt driven to make a loud and clear rhetorical response to these treacherous times for Big Oil.[12] It decided to seek a high profile for the company and its views, and confront those with whom it disagreed. Warner said: "I think it's wrong for business to hunker down and wait for the storm to blow over."[13]

The new communication strategy could be termed "high profile advocacy." In one sentence, it was to lecture, charm, argue and bully the American body politic into seeing every public issue from Mobil's point of view.

Mobil reinvents media relations

Mobil found the ideal instrument for its new policy in Herb Schmertz, vice-president for public affairs. "Herb calls a spade a spade," said one of his colleagues. Schmertz himself said that he was not averse to confrontation. (He later urged: "Speak out, continually and consistently, and do not be afraid of confrontation.")[14] Schmertz was a member of Mobil's board of directors and became: "The most powerful and successful corporate-public-relations man in the world."[15]

Schmertz made Mobil's voice heard by articulating views on important issues when the opportunity arose, writing signed material for the press including letters to the editor, and making public speeches. But Mobil believed that the media was biased against the oil industry. (Thomas Jefferson was not impressed either. "The man who never looks into a newspaper is better informed," suggesting that a paper might be divided into four chapters headed Truths, Probabilities, Possibilities and Lies. "The first chapter would be very short...")[16]

Media bias is almost unavoidable. First, what is news? Editors decide what stories to cover, how much and how prominently, taking into account news values and news factors. This remains the case in the age of social media. Social media coverage is merely another factor for the editor to take into account when deciding what is newsworthy.[17] Second, stories are necessarily subject to framing, the process of organizing narrative. Any narrative has to be framed because it must have boundaries, including a beginning and an end. Journalists (and now citizens, in the case of social media) frame stories by selecting which facts to report and then selecting the context in which they report those facts. The chosen frames shape and limit audience perceptions of stories. Frame analysis, asking questions such as why a journalist told a story in a particular way and what alternative frames could have been chosen, is a major component of yet another academic discipline, media studies.[18]

"Talking back" to the media, unusual in the 1970s and 1980s, has become more common, especially in the political arena. We have become used to news management, the concerted effort to influence consistently the content and direction of television news in particular by political operatives, as recounted in numerous memoirs.[19] Politicians who actively attempt to manage the media are believed to have obtained an advantage, however, the political debate is by its nature high profile. The considerations for businesses and others in public life are not the same as for politicians.

For example, the pharmaceutical industry has been accused of using propaganda to sell more drugs.[20] But public understanding of the issues is equally likely to be influenced by media framing. For example, certain media outlets frame stories about new drugs and medical devices by choosing to exclude the involvement of businesses and attribute advances to individual researchers, universities or charities. But when they report any problems such as drugs' adverse effects or high prices, they name any businesses involved in the shenanigans. This framing promotes their view that the pharmaceutical industry is interested only in profit at all costs and operates against the public interest. Yet pharmaceutical companies have generally refrained from attempting to strong-arm the media in the manner of political "spin doctors," for reasons that should be clearer by the end of this chapter.

Nevertheless, Mobil was determined to act.

There was insufficient scope, in the prevailing media conditions, to be heard as it should be, no matter how actively the company's executives spoke out.[21] This situation both harmed the company's image and made it more difficult to do business.

In this situation, Mobil's most important weapon was advertising. Frustrated by newspapers it saw as unsympathetic, and by television networks that were equally unsympathetic and averse to businesses editorializing, Mobil resorted to advertising on a large scale. It used the corporate checkbook to buy the space it believed it was being unfairly denied. In the 1970s and 1980s, the Mobil experiment found out what happened when one very wealthy corporation used that weapon vigorously. "Although other corporations produced advocacy messages... none spoke so regularly on so many issues of public policy as Mobil did."[22]

And Mobil linked its advocacy to the idea that first amendment rights should not only be for people but for corporations too.

Mobil reinvents issue advertising

The history of corporate advertising can be divided into two eras: Before Mobil and After Mobil. Before Mobil, even more than today, advertising was mostly about products and services. Such corporate advertising as there was tended to be pompous, bland and vacuous image advertising. Bland would not have suited Mobil's purpose, which was to acquire the editorial coverage it believed that it deserved, as a major player, but was being denied. And it aimed to tell a different story, in which oil companies would be heroes rather than the villains of the energy crisis.

Mobil's stroke of genius was to use the space it bought creatively. Though the media of the 1970s were limited in range by the standards of the internet age, they did offer at least one outlet for audience participation: the op-ed page. The typical op-ed page published a curated cocktail of editorial, letters to the editor, syndicated columnists and comment from people not employed by the paper. But contributions to the op-ed page were still subject to editorial control. The opportunity to outflank the editor arose when the *New York Times* added an extra page with space on it for advertising.

This was the catalyst for Mobil to design its first advertorial, published on October 19, 1970, which made the case, surprisingly for an oil company, for investment in mass transit[23] — "America has the world's best highways. And the world's worst mass transit. We hope this ad moves people..."

Mobil constructed and deployed narrative to great effect, as in these brief extracts from its advertisements, most of which took several hundred words to tell a story with panache:[24]

- "If we tell you oil companies don't make enough profit, you'll have a fit. Oil companies don't make enough profit. Sorry..."
- "43,141 companies have a monopoly on the U.S. oil business..."
- "There once was a squirrel who collected nuts and stored them. In this way, he was able to see himself safely through the long, hard, cold winters..."

Mobil was a pioneer in its use of narrative, as in other communication techniques. Herb Schmertz was one of the greatest business storytellers of all time.

From the outset, Mobil's advertising was designed to sit comfortably among the editorial content so the standard of writing was as high. Mobil's advertising was notable for its "rhetorical artistry," usually epideictic — rhetoric that praises and exploits values and beliefs that are shared by the speaker and the audience. When appropriate, it also used the rhetorical device of antithesis, suggesting that the company and its audience shared a common enemy. And it set out to put forward a corporate personality with authority but also character, argumentative but likable, not unlike Schmertz himself.[25]

From 1970 onwards, the company paid for op-ed pieces to appear each week in six major American newspapers: the *Boston Globe*, *Chicago Sun-Times*, *Los Angeles Times*, *New York Times*, *Wall Street Journal* and *Washington Post*. Sometimes the pieces appeared in up to eighty papers at a time. Mobil's annual budget for issue advertising was about $2.5 million in the 1970s, a colossal amount in those days for a sort of public relations campaign. It was not entirely alone. When the oil crisis broke at the end of 1973, the majors advertised to defend their rising profits. But Mobil was by far the most prolific and consistent advertiser.

From 1975, the company launched a different style of column, "Observations," that it believed would be more suitable for magazines such as *Parade*, *Reader's Digest* and the Sunday supplements. At the peak of its campaign, "Observations" appeared in around 500 magazines. In addition, Mobil took 60 second spots on 80 TV stations, synchronized with the op-eds.[26]

After Mobil, much corporate advertising was still pompous, bland and vacuous. David Ogilvy said in the 1980s that 81 of the top 100 American corporations were doing corporate advertising and most of them were making a hash of it.[27] But some of it was more interesting — the issue ads that Mobil pioneered, and a few others (like United Technologies, with great lines like: "The punks who killed heavy metal").

Mobil reinvents sponsorship

Mobil's next move was to buy space on television and in the arts, and to produce its own television reports. On January 10, 1971, it sponsored its first "Masterpiece Theatre" show with WGBH in Boston, initially paying only $10,000 per hour. It was the start of a series that brought critically acclaimed drama and documentaries to American public television over the course of decades, from "Upstairs, Downstairs," to "Life on Earth." This was the largest sponsorship deal for public TV. Mobil went on to pay for many other high profile cultural projects, on and off TV, such as "Tuesday Night at the Museums." It not only provided direct grants but also spent on a large scale to publicize what it was doing, e.g., through the Mobil Season on TV.[28] By 1980,

"Masterpiece Theatre" alone was costing Mobil $4 million in funding plus $2.5 million for associated promotion.[29]

Mobil claimed that certain groups would identify with the projects and causes the company supported. It believed that company-supported cultural excellence suggested corporate excellence. And it believed that its sponsorship program provided "credibility for its larger agenda."[30] It described the sponsorship program as "affinity-of-purpose marketing," and hoped that this "affinity-of-purpose" would translate into a preference for doing business with Mobil. Schmertz listed eight additional benefits of the sponsorship program: fulfilling an obligation to support non-profit institutions, making top management look good, making employees feel proud, providing an opportunity for civic leadership, providing entertainment opportunities, making connections with like-minded politicians, and helping recruitment.[31] All of these were worthy but were any of them critical to the success of Mobil's business strategy? Or were they strategically peripheral?

Key points
- New leadership at Mobil, the giant oil company, responded to political, social and economic change with a bold new communication strategy, led by Herb Schmertz, a virtuoso of rhetoric.
- From 1970, Mobil set out to lecture, charm, argue and bully the American body politic into seeing every public issue from its point of view. Its refreshingly direct approach revolutionized relations with the media, issue advertising, and sponsorship.

"Why do we buy this space?"

Businesses rarely reveal their communication strategies, let alone explain them, but Mobil was exceptionally forthcoming. "Why do we buy this space?" — Mobil asked rhetorically in one of its 1982 op-ed slots.[32]

The answer was political — for the good of business and for the good of society. Schmertz had sourced his techniques of creative confrontation, issue advertising, and fighting back against what he saw as unfairness, in the political world, where he was actively involved in the presidential campaigns of the Kennedys.

As well as directing what Mobil said about itself, Schmertz set down his thinking in a book, written near the end of his time there, "Goodbye to the Low Profile: The Art of Creative Confrontation," and in a chapter he contributed to a book on "Strategic Issues Management."[33]

Mobil embarked upon its communication program with three broad themes in mind:

- The vulnerability of the free world to political control of oil.
- The need for realism on the environment.
- Rebutting criticism of business.

Its ads attacked allegations that oil companies were making outrageously high profits — these were needed to finance oil exploration — or that they were hoarding oil to inflate prices. They opposed excessive regulation, opposed price controls and debated the balance between economic growth and protecting the environment. And they expressed Mobil's view on whatever issue was top of its agenda or current at the time. It was "a ground breaking advocacy strategy to promote interests that went far beyond its immediate business objectives."[34]

Mobil said that both business as a whole and the country benefited when business voices were heard in the media. "Our nation functions best when economic and other concerns of the people are subjected to rigorous debate." It wanted to tell the public about the contribution of business. It was pleased above all to have stirred things up: "We've been reviled, revered, held up as a model and put down as a sorry example."

Controversies

Through the 1970s and 1980s, in line with its philosophy, Mobil courted controversy. Its advertorials tackled an ever-widening range of subjects about which Mobil had an opinion. The controversies multiplied. One squall occurred when Schmertz accused American TV of exporting "trash" like "Dallas" and "Dynasty." More seriously, there was an "angry colloquy" between long-serving anchor Dan Rather and Schmertz on air in a CBS seminar on news management.[35]

Mobil's issues sometimes became personal. When *Harper's* described Mobil's president as "red-faced," "choleric," and a "representative of the merchant class," Tavoulareas sued for libel — but lost.[36] No lesson was learned from this because a more serious storm blew up in 1979, when the *Washington Post* claimed that Tavoulareas was involved in a shipping business that gained from its connection with Mobil. He again sued for libel. "This libel game, like most, pinged and ponged, passed go several times, and cost both sides a fortune." The Supreme Court settled the battle, in favor of the newspaper, after more than eight years of litigation[37] — and adverse media coverage.

The episode highlighted the difficulties inherent in Mobil's communication strategy:

- First, there was no retreat. Mobil launched frontal attacks and held its ground. But the decision to run a libel lawsuit all the way to the Supreme Court gave the original allegations a lot of publicity over a long period. It is possible that a simple denial with no further action back in 1979 would have brought the matter to an end with a whimper — or a whisper — rather than a bang.

- Second, Mobil's high profile strategy turned it into a prime target. The media covered the libel story even more avidly than they would have in the case of another company because Mobil had made itself a bellicose household name. Mobil even stoked the controversy indirectly by placing advertisements to generate publicity for an initial verdict that was in Tavoulareas' favor.[38]

- Third, arguably Mobil did not focus enough on issues that were really important for its business — the big picture. It did of course speak out about these issues but it also made a point of speaking out about whatever caught its eye.

Going ballistic

The *Washington Post* libel case led indirectly to a confrontation with the *Wall Street Journal*. Deteriorating relations, resulting partly from muscular investigative reporting of the libel story by the *Journal*, culminated in a new article. Writing up the company's plans to build a new office building in Chicago, the newspaper focused on an (undisputed) link between one of the leasing agents for the building and Warner. And the report about Chicago referred back to the Tavoulareas case.[39] Mobil went ballistic.

It terminated relations with the newspaper, not merely freezing the *Journal* out but calling journalists to tell them it would no longer speak to them. The company said it would cease to supply the newspaper with any information. (This was before the doctrine of fair disclosure, see chapter 3.) And of course Mobil stopped advertising.

As Schmertz told the tale of this quarrel, the company believed that its coverage could not be any worse and therefore saw no point in having a relationship. Mobil had a heroic new storyline of company battles newspaper. It was seemingly worthwhile to gain maximum attention for the company's view that the leading American business paper was more interested in gossip and innuendo than business.[40]

This was a tactical, personality-driven issue, whereas on the important strategic issue of oil industry profits and prices, the *Journal* had been on the side of business, arguing in editorials that profits were necessary to fund exploration and that prices should be set by the market in order to reduce demand and stimulate supply.

And boycotting or freezing out media groups, reporters or analysts is a great way to make enemies. (When the Labour Party's governing body decided to boycott Murdoch newspapers, Peter Mandelson, who was in charge of its communications, briefed Murdoch journalists privately because he was sure the ban was against the party's interests.)[41]

The broader question of how to handle different types of criticism is addressed in chapter 17.

Confrontation

Schmertz subtitled his book "The Art of Creative Confrontation," and there was a chapter dedicated to "The Art of Creative Confrontation." And Warner believed that businesses shied away from confrontation when it should be part of the everyday communications toolkit.

Was it partly a question of personality? Schmertz jokingly admitted to shouting at people who annoyed him behind the wheel of his car. "It doesn't always work, but I feel better after the cathartic purge."[42]

From time to time, confrontation is necessary and unavoidable. I have involved lawyers to prevent TV news from broadcasting unfair, unjustified and irresponsible allegations that would have damaged companies I represented. Once normal media relations had fallen short, confrontation was necessary in extreme cases like these to stop damaging media coverage. I have also threatened in extreme circumstances to cancel advertising to persuade editors to stop unwarranted criticism. Using advertising to influence editorial is controversial but not unethical. The tactic may look unethical if it is framed as a question of the freedom of the press. It no longer looks unethical if it is framed as a question of self-defense — if another business, in this case a newspaper, tries to damage my business, I must have the right to take action, within the law, to prevent it. Feeding the mouth that bites you is not ethical but stupid.

But I have never advocated an editorial boycott because depriving journalists of company comment would not have meant an end to negative reports about my firm or client. It would simply have meant that the stories would be sourced from elsewhere.

And if a business decides to respond to an adversary, the response needs to be proportionate. As in the military sphere, a response that is perceived as disproportionate is likely to supersede the original grievance as the public issue. By turning confrontation into its normal modus operandi and, arguably, allowing itself to be distracted from the big picture (see chapter 18), Mobil sometimes did not quash damaging stories but amplified and multiplied them.

Political consequences?

Mobil was clear that its communication strategy was driven by domestic politics, and its communications focused on the American media and public.

Everyone in public life faces the same basic choice as Mobil, between making the case softly, speaking directly to those whose support it needed, and making the case loudly, to the world at large. To Warner and his team, the answer was obvious: Stop being pushed around and stand up for yourself. When the oil companies found themselves suddenly unpopular after Santa Barbara and the oil crisis, the case for the defense initially went by default. Mobil stepped in, made the case with flair, and stood up for business as a whole.

It is hard to assess how far it achieved political results. A study of 149 Mobil op-ed columns between 1976 and 1980 found it hard to distinguish the effects of Mobil's campaign on the political climate for business from broader developments. The deregulating Reagan administration surely made a larger contribution to improving the business climate than Mobil's communication programs. And public opinion did not warm to the oil industry, which was "public enemy number one" in the oil crises of both 1974 and 1979.[43]

This was despite Mobil's efforts, which were viewed with a degree of skepticism. One oilman commented at the time: "When people see one of their ads their first question is, 'Why aren't they using the ad costs to find more oil?' Their second thought is that, if the oil companies are trying to convince us of something, the opposite must be true." On the other hand, Schmertz cited differences in public views on energy issues between cities where it had advertised and cities where it had not.[44] And perhaps without Mobil public opinion would have been even more hostile?

The question is not only whether the arguments needed to be made, and whether the story needed to told, but by whom. Could the job be done only by Mobil? Was the job best done by Mobil? An alternative would have been for the public to be informed, as often happens, by politicians, by pro-business interest groups and by business lobby groups. As an example from the same period, when the issue of dioxin contamination in paper mills threatened the paper industry, the American Paper Institute developed a "Dioxin Public Affairs Plan" to manage the issue and communicate the facts while minimizing health concerns. Individual paper companies were largely spared an unwelcome spotlight.[45] A similar question arises in connection with broad business issues today. For example, there is said to have been a decline in public trust in business. This is a concern for business but is unlikely to be a sufficient concern for an individual business to be worth devoting much resource (see chapter 18).

At the level of the particular issues Mobil tackled, creative confrontation was by its nature controversial and could be counter-productive, as in its disputes with the *Washington Post* and the *Wall Street Journal*.

And an extra problem for a company like Mobil taking a high profile on all kinds of issues is that, "by taking a stand on a particular issue, the company is automatically creating a negative image with one or several constituencies." It risked alienating some of those who should have been its allies, like the *Journal* and the US government. Mobil stood to benefit from the government's goodwill or suffer from its hostility. At one point, President Jimmy Carter singled out Mobil as "perhaps the most irresponsible company in America."[46]

Corporate consequences

Mobil's role as the outspoken warrior automatically meant raising its profile. It welcomed this — "Goodbye to the low profile." And its communications were also designed to burnish its image and show off different aspects of its corporate personality.[47] Its activities could be seen as an example of reputation management before that term became current. (See chapter 12.)

The high profile suited its feisty temperament and impressed people in PR and entertainment but did it do the company any good?

Richard Crable and Steven Vibbert referred to the axiom that a company benefits from differentiating itself from business in general and others in its industry. They were impressed that Mobil established itself as the loudest voice in the oil industry although they noted that others were "content to remain in the background."[48]

Both advertising and PR agencies tend to rely on another axiom: familiarity fosters favorability. It is widely believed that the higher the percentage of consumers who are familiar with a product, service or brand, the higher the percentage who like it. One survey of 45 American companies in the late 1980s suggested that the best liked spent more than twice as much on corporate advertising as the least liked. And companies that become well-known, as a result of corporate advertising, are claimed to benefit from a better chance that people will recommend their products, invest in them or seek information from them.[49] These studies are favorites with agencies for obvious reasons.

One reason for the apparent correlation of familiarity and favorability, depending on how a study is constructed, may be that it is impossible to recommend (or condemn) a company you have never heard of. (See chapter 5 for businesses that choose not to be well-known.)

But there is also survey evidence that appears to conflict with the axiom. For example, a 1990 study tested the hypothesis that, "the greater a firm's current media visibility, the better its reputation," and refuted it.[50] And in 2000, a random population was asked to nominate companies with the best and worst reputations. Those with most nominations for best reputation were very well-known but were not the companies with most nominations. In the case of the company with the highest total nominations, 99% were for the worst reputation.[51]

It seems more likely that familiarity is neutral. Prominence is an obvious prerequisite for large-scale favorability. But favorability is an independent variable. You are as likely to be disliked as to be liked, depending on a number of other factors such as behavior, relationships, characteristics, and qualities.

In the case of Mobil, Schmertz cited research by Harris into public attitudes to 40 corporations. Respondents had a low opinion of oil companies but Mobil was seen as the best of a bad bunch, leading the industry on 19 out of 21 public issues mentioned, and with the best quality products. He cited some 1982 market research that suggested a preference among college graduates in Boston for Mobil's gasoline. The respondents also identified Mobil strongly with issue advertising and quality TV. But it was not clear how far this possible edge over poorly regarded competitors was a tangible benefit. The veteran PR journalist, Jack O'Dwyer, believed that the connection was too tenuous: "The public's opinion of Mobil is based on the local gas station, not on anything Herb Schmertz does." And research with politicians in the 1970s said most of them had read Mobil ads about energy but the majority did not believe they were helpful or influential.[52] And, finally, *Fortune*'s most admired companies survey began in the mid-1980s. In January 1985, with Warner in his prime, Mobil came sixth in the list of most admired petroleum refiners.[53] (Low profile Exxon came third, and see chapter 12 on the value of such rankings.)

Mobil's media coverage was in question. After all, it was negative media coverage that stimulated Mobil to formulate its new strategy. Alienating and then boycotting the most important American newspaper for business was not exactly a triumph. As Michael Kinsley said a couple of years later: "It would not surprise me if the Journal has been out to get Mobil... If Mobil seems particularly tempting, this is just a natural result of the contentious image [it] has worked so hard to cultivate."[54]

Key points
- Mobil explained that its communication strategy aimed partly to influence issues and partly to redress an anti-business imbalance in the public arena.
- Eagerly embracing controversy and confrontation, Mobil lost focus on the most important issues and made itself a tempting target for critics. Falling out with the Wall Street Journal was especially questionable.
- There is limited evidence that Mobil's exertions helped it to achieve strategic objectives, either through a more favorable political and media climate or being regarded more favorably by significant interests.

Impact on business communication

Putting these doubts aside, Mobil made a big impression on the field of public communication. Works on public relations written in the 1980s cited Mobil frequently. Respected textbooks used Mobil advertisements as illustrations. The 1989 edition of "Seitel" featured thirteen index references to either Mobil or Schmertz and a section on issues advertising in the oil industry. Schmertz was widely quoted. In 1982, he was named "Public Relations Professional of the Year." Harold Burson, founder of the Burson-Marsteller agency, described Schmertz as "a major positive force." Jarol Manheim said, "Schmertz was a force not merely in American politics, but in American society." And Lee Iacocca mischievously suggested that more people knew Schmertz than knew who ran Mobil.[55]

Other companies followed Mobil's lead to some extent. Oil companies became the main funders of PBS programs. At the high profile extreme, when the networks rejected advertising from McDonnell Douglas in support of the space program as too controversial in 1989, it resorted to an occasional network to air the ads. Industry bodies have run issue campaigns, such as The Health Insurance Association of America's year long campaign against the Clinton administration's healthcare plans, "Harry and Louise."

Less controversially, many companies have engaged in advertising with a more subtle political purpose. In the early 1980s, BP's campaign, "BP: Britain at its best," sought to align the company with the national interest in its home market. Philip Morris celebrated the bicentennial with ads highlighting accomplished Americans. GE identified itself with ecomagination, an initiative to find innovative, economy-friendly solutions to environmental problems. But most issue advertising was on a much smaller scale than Mobil's and did not court the same degree of controversy.

Advocates of corporate advertising say that it can increase sales, although less directly than product advertising, enhance reputation by increasing understanding of the organization, and recruit and keep staff. However, it probably has less credibility with the audience than non-commercial op-ed. It is extremely expensive. And there may be something in the traditional public relations view that: "Publicity, through news releases and other methods, is eminently more powerful than advertising"[56] — because, in ideal conditions, it is a form of third party endorsement. A more subtle form of op-ed may be more credible, as in ADP's use of the "BrandVoice" space in *Forbes* magazine to present an infographic about upgrading human capital management.[57]

The impression made by Mobil has faded with time. The 2013 edition of "Seitel" no longer mentions Mobil and Schmertz, although "Cutlip" still allots a full page to reproducing one of their classic ads from 1983.

Nevertheless, it is hard to disagree that: "Schmertz revolutionized the field [of PR] by solving communication problems with strategies that no-one had thought of before."[58]

The case for a high profile strategy has never been made more cogently. In a way, Schmertz was ahead of his time. He liked to imagine the author of a Mobil ad "at the typewriter, banging away in righteous indignation,"[59] and it is easy to imagine that if a doppelgänger were there now in some parallel universe, he would be furiously tweeting, blogging, and buying advertising space on news websites and social media.

However, the high profile advocacy strategy used by Mobil in the 1970s and 1980s, before the internet, would involve much greater risk if used today. Mobil complained of limited access to the media but used its vast resources to find ways round the limits. It could outspend virtually any opponent. In the fights it picked, the role of the mass audience was largely as spectator. Now, in any fight picked by an oil company, it is much easier for the formerly quiescent mass audience to join in. The more loudly the company shouts, the more likely it is to provoke those who are potentially hostile to make their own voices heard and shout it down. (See chapter 4 on the analogy with military action stirring greater unrest.)

From its earliest days, Mobil's communication program lacked sufficient focus on its key issues and key audiences. Rather than focusing like a laser on the most important issues, it roamed freely over the whole arena, flitting from subject to subject. Rather than selecting target audiences who would influence important decisions, its audience was the population of the United States. Segmenting audiences was more difficult before the internet but there were ways and means even then.

Now Mobil, the highest profile oil company, is no more, and Warner's epitaph in the *Wall Street Journal* neglected his impact on the business in favor of the headline: "Mobil Chief Mastered Public Relations."[60]

All change

By 1972, Mobil was the world's eighth largest non-financial business by sales. (Exxon was second largest, just over twice the size of Mobil.) Through the 1970s, Mobil claimed earnings growth of 16% a year, highest of the American majors. This was a period when big oil companies could hardly fail to make money since the price of crude oil (West Texas Intermediate), that had been relatively stable, took off from $3.30 at the beginning of 1970 to $39.50 in mid-1980. Mobil was aggressive and sophisticated but sprawling.[61] By 1980, it employed 213,000 people in over 100 countries.

In 1976, Mobil diversified away from energy, buying Marcor Corporation, owner of the Montgomery Ward department stores and Container Corporation (paperboard and packaging). Mobil Oil then became a subsidiary of Mobil Corporation, incorporated in Delaware. Tavoulareas explained that: "As a result of our concerns about governmental attitude toward the oil industry and the potential for the private sector to go forward in energy investment in this country, we developed a diversification policy aimed at giving our shareholders additional sources of US earnings in relatively unregulated industries."[62] Other oil companies also diversified into other sectors including copper, office products, and even circuses.

This came to be seen as a major strategic error. Not only did diversification distract management from the core energy business but it undercut the vital policy argument that profits were required to finance exploration for new oil supplies. Buying retailers looked like using profits from high oil prices to move out of the oil business. And investors turned against conglomerates.

Mobil explored widely for oil and gas to replace its Middle East reserves, especially in the Gulf of Mexico and the North Sea.

It sought to buy a middle-size oil company, tilting against first Conoco in 1981, then Marathon in 1981-82. In 1984, it won Superior, then the largest remaining American independent oil producer, for $5.7 billion. But it was criticized for apparently being more enthusiastic about diversifying away from oil or, failing that, buying other oil companies, than looking for its own oil.[63] And Mobil's aggressive image hurt its acceptability as an acquirer both politically and with the target companies.

The price of oil turned down with the early 1980s recession. Mobil was locked into expensive contracts and indebted as a result of its Superior acquisition, with declining oil reserves and falling sales. Its new non-energy businesses were taking its focus away from the core and they performed poorly.

Once Warner retired and Schmertz moved on, in the late 1980s, Mobil altered course. Warner's successor, Allen Murray, changed the business strategy, refocusing the company on oil, disposing of non-core businesses and slimming down. By the mid-1990s, the company's workforce was three-quarters smaller. Murray also changed the communication strategy, toning it down and focusing on strategic (priority) stakeholders (see chapter 12). "The only reason I want to see my name in print," he said, "is if it helps the stock."[64]

And the former Standard Oil Company of New York vacated its 150 East 42nd Street skyscraper and moved to suburban Virginia.[65]

By the mid-1990s, there was a view that the downsized Mobil was on the small side for an oil major in the 1990s. The company contemplated a merger with BP, from which it withdrew. Then, in 1998, it agreed to merge with Exxon In effect, it was a takeover.[66]

Chapter 13 takes up the story, with a comparison between Mobil and Exxon communication strategies and an assessment of the merged company.

In Summary

- For most of the 1970s and 1980s, Mobil adopted a high profile advocacy strategy that involved "creative confrontation."
- Mobil's novel approach was influential on advertising and public relations. It led indirectly to the rise of reputation management in the 1990s.
- Mobil made an eloquent case for high advocacy. But a communication strategy that was more targeted at its strategic stakeholders would arguably have been more effective and less risky.

References

[1] James, *The Principles of Psychology*, 308.

[2] James Joyce, *Ulysses*, 2nd edn., 1926, (The Folio Society, 1998), 133.

[3] Daniel Yergin, *The Quest: Energy, Security, and the Remaking of the Modern World*, (New York: The Penguin Press, 2011), 469.

[4] Robert E. Brown, 'Sea Change: Santa Barbara and the Eruption of Corporate Social Responsibility,' *Public Relations Review*, Vol. 34 (2008) 1-8.

[5] Anthony Sampson, *The Seven Sisters: The Great Oil Companies & the World They Shaped*, (London: Bantam Books, 1974), 318.

[6] Michael J. Connor, 'Mobil's Advocacy Ads Lead a Growing Trend, Draw Praise, Criticism,' *Wall Street Journal*, May 14, 1975.

[7] Mobil Corporation advertisement, 'The Myth of the Crusading Reporter,' *Wall Street Journal*, November 1, 1983.

[8] Michael B. Goodman & Peter B. Hirsch, *Corporate Communication: Strategic Adaptation for Global Practice*, (New York: Peter Lang Publishing, Inc., 2010), 105.

[9] Douglas Martin, 'Rawleigh Warner Jr., Brash Chairman of Mobil, Dies at 92,' *New York Times*, July 2, 2013.

[10] Chermayeff & Geismar, <http://www.cgstudionyc.com/identities/mobil>.

[11] William D. Smith, 'Brooklyn Accent In Mobil Executive Suite,' *New York Times*, January 17, 1971.

[12] Richard L. Crable & Steven L. Vibbert, 'Mobil's Epideictic Advocacy: Observations of Prometheus-bound,' in *Public Relations Inquiry as Rhetorical Criticism: Case Studies of Corporate Discourse and Social Influence*, ed. by William L. Elwood, (Westport, CT: Praeger, 1995), 29-30, reprinted from *Communications Monographs* 380-394 (December 1983).

[13] Told to *Newsweek* in 1976: Laurence Arnold, 'Rawleigh Warner, Mobil CEO Who Shaped Company Image Dies at 92,' *Bloomberg*, July 1, 2013.

[14] Herb Schmertz, 'Reaching the Opinion Makers,' in *Strategic Issues Management: How Organizations Influence and Respond to Public Interests and Policies*, ed. by Robert L. Heath, (San Francisco, CA: Jossey-Bass Publishers, 1988), 199-237.

[15] Spade: William D. Smith, 'Mobil Finds Speaking Out Pays,' *New York Times*, August 22, 1975. Confrontations: Schmertz & Novak, *Goodbye to the Low Profile*, 60. Street fighter: Michael Kinsley, 'Mobil's Media Master Offers a Corporate Lesson Plan,' *Wall Street Journal*, April 24, 1986. Bernice Kanner, 'Oil Slick: Mobil's Herb Schmertz is the Lord of P.R.,' *New York Magazine*, March 31, 1986, 46-51.

[16] Thomas Jefferson, 'Letter to John Norvell, June 14, 1807,' in Joyce Appleby & Terence Ball, *Thomas Jefferson: Political Writings*, (Cambridge University Press, 1999), 275.

[17] Johann Galtung & Mari Ruge, 'The Structure of Foreign News: The Presentation of the Congo, Cuba and Cyprus Crises in Four Foreign Newspapers,' in Stan Cohen & Jock Young, (eds.), *The Manufacture of News*, (London: Constable, 1981), originally published 1965. Gill Branston with Roy Stafford, *The Media Student's Book*, (London: Routledge, 2010), 5th edn., 334-357. Pamela J. Shoemaker, Jong Hyuk Lee, Gang (Kevin) Han & Akiba A. Cohen, 'Proximity and Scope as News Values,' in Eoin Devereux, *Media Studies: Key Issues and Debates*, London: Sage, 2007, 231-248.

[18] Jenny Kitzinger, 'Frame and Frame Analysis, in *Media Studies: Key Issues and Debates*, ed. by Eoin Devereux, (London: Sage, 2007), 134-161. See also C. E. Carroll & M. E. McCombs, 'Agenda-Setting Effects of Business News on the Public's Images and Opinions about Major Corporations,' *Corporate Reputation Review*, Vol. 6, No. 1, (2003), 36-46.

[19] See, for example, *Nicholas Jones, Soundbites and Spin Doctors: How Politicians Manipulate the Media – and Vice Versa*, (London: Indigo, 1996).

[20] E.g. Marcia Angell, *The Truth About Drug Companies: How They Deceive Us and What to Do About It*, (New York: Random House, Inc., 2005).

[21] Schmertz & Novak, *Goodbye to the Low Profile*, 114-153.

[22] Robert L. Kerr, *The Rights of Corporate Speech: Mobil Oil and the Legal Development of the Voice of Big Business*, (New York: LFB Scholarly Publishing, 2005), 1.

[23] Gary C. Woodward & Robert E. Denton, *Persuasion and Influence in American Life*, (Long Grove, IL: Waveland Press, Inc., 2014), 242.

[24] Schmertz & Novak, *Goodbye to the Low Profile*, 129-139.

[25] Artistry: Crable & Vibbert, 'Mobil's Epideictic Advocacy,' 44. Curmudgeon: Burton St John III, 'Conveying the Sense-Making Corporate Persona: The Mobil Oil "Observations" Columns, 1975-1980,' *Public Relations Review*, Vol. 40, No. 4, (2014), 692-699.

[26] Leading advertiser: Otis Baskin, Craig Aronoff & Dan Lattimore, *Public Relations: The Profession and the Practice*, 4th edn., (New York: McGraw-Hill, 1997), 355. Synchronized: Otto Lerbinger, *Corporate Public Affairs: Interacting with Interest Groups, Media, and Government*, (Mahwah, NJ: Lawrence Erlbaum Associates, Inc., 2006), 158.

[27] *Ogilvy on Advertising*, (New York: Vintage Books, 1985), 117.

[28] Next move: Edward Herman & Noam Chomsky, 'A Propaganda Model,' in *Media and Cultural Studies: Keyworks*, ed. by Meenakshi Gigi Durham & Douglas M. Kellner, (Oxford: Blackwell, 2006), 272. Masterpiece Theatre: 'Mobil Oil Backs Public TV Series,' *New York Times*, July 14, 1971. Sponsorship: Schmertz & Novak, *Goodbye to the Low Profile*, 192 & 195. Season: John J. O'Connor, 'Can Public Television Be Bought?' *New York Times*, October 13, 1974.

[29] Idea by Schmertz: Martha Bayles, 'A Little Froth on Masterpiece Theatre,' *Wall Street Journal*, October 19, 1987. Created: John J. O'Connor, 'Capturing the Drama of History,' *New York Times*, April 2, 1978. 1980: Nancy Pomerene McMillan, 'A 10th Birthday For Masterpiece Theater,' *New York Times*, September 21, 1980.

[30] James Ledbetter, *Made Possible By…. The Death of Public Broadcasting in the United States*, (London: Verso, 1987), 144-145.

[31] Schmertz & Novak, *Goodbye to the Low Profile*, 181-183.

[32] Quoted in Edward C. MacEwen, 'Corporate Advertising and Its Role in Public Relations,' in *Experts in Action: Inside Public Relations*, ed. by Bill Cantor & Chester Burger, (New York: Longman, 1989), 189.

[33] Schmertz, 'Reaching the Opinion Makers.'

[34] Kerr, *The Rights of Corporate Speech*, 1.

[35] Dynasty: '2 TV Series Scorned,' *New York Times*, July 14, 1984. CBS: Ralph Engelman, *Friendlyvision: Fred Friendly and the Rise and Fall of Television Journalism*, (New York: Columbia University Press, 2009), 317.

[36] John R. MacArthur, 'The Publisher's Role: Crusading Defender of the First Amendment or Advertising Salesman?' in *The Art of Making Magazines: On Being an Editor and Other Views from the Industry*, ed. by Victor S. Navasky & Evan Cornog, (New York: Columbia University Press, 2012), 148.

[37] Libel game: Donald W. Blohowiak, *No Comment! An Executive's Essential Guide to the News Media*, (New York: Praeger, 1987), 191. Supreme Court: Agis Salpukas, 'William P. Tavoulareas, 75, Former Mobil President, Dies,' *New York Times*, January 16, 1996.

[38] Seitel, *The Practice of Public Relations*, 4th edn., 1989, 558.

[39] James B. Stewart & Richard B. Schmitt, 'Mobil Set to Start $300 Million Tower in Chicago Venture,' *Wall Street Journal*, November 16, 1984.

[40] Schmertz & Novak, *Goodbye to the Low Profile*, 60-65.

[41] Publicity: Peter Spence, 'Sainsbury's Offer Value Alternative to Journo Barred From Tesco Dinner,' *City A. M.*, April 10, 2014. Boycott: Lerbinger, *Corporate Public Affairs*, 112-114. Peter Mandelson, *The Third Man: Life at the Heart of New Labour*, (London: HarperPress 2010), 90.

[42] Kanner, 'Oil Slick,' 50.

[43] 149 columns: Crable & Vibbert, 'Mobil's Epideictic Advocacy.' Public enemy: Daniel Yergin, *The Prize: The Epic Quest for Oil, Money, and Power*, (New York: Simon & Schuster, 1991), 692.

[44] Oilman: Smith, 'Mobil Finds Speaking Out Pays.' Schmertz: Schmertz, 'Reaching the Opinion Makers.'

[45] Jarol B. Manheim, *All of the People, All the Time: Strategic Communication and American Politics*, (Armonk, NY: M. E. Sharpe, Inc., 1991), 113.

[46] Negative image: Paul A. Argenti, *Corporate Communication*, 4th edn., (New York: McGraw-Hill/Irwin, 2007), 52. Carter: Martin Tolchin, 'Carter Castigates Mobil on Decontrol,' *New York Times*, June 1, 1979.

[47] Gerri L. Smith & Robert L. Heath, 'Moral Appeals in Mobil Oil's Op-ed Campaign,' *Public Relations Review*, Vol. 16, No. 4, (Winter 1990), 48-54.

[48] Crable & Vibbert, 'Mobil's Epideictic Advocacy.'

[49] Joan Reisman, 'Public Relations in Disguise?' *Public Relations Journal*, Vol. 45, No. 9, (September 1989).

[50] Charles Fombrun & Mark Shanley, 'What's in a Name? Reputation Building and Corporate Strategy,' *The Academy of Management Journal*, Vol. 33, No. 2 (June 1990), 233-258.

[51] Naomi A. Gardberg & Charles J. Fombrun, 'For Better or Worse — USA The Most Visible American Corporate Reputations,' *Corporate Reputation Review*, Vol. 4, No. 4, (January 2002), 385-391.

[52] Boston: Schmertz & Novak, *Goodbye to the Low Profile*, 123 & 189-190. O'Dwyer: Kanner, 'Oil Slick,' 51. Politicians: Research by Yankelovich, Skelly & White, quoted in Lerbinger, *Corporate Public Affairs*, 163.

[53] Patricia Sellers, 'America's Most Admired Corporations,' *Fortune*, January 7, 1985.

[54] Michael Kinsley, 'Mobil's Media Master Offers a Corporate Lesson Plan,' *Wall Street Journal*, April 24, 1986.

[55] Respected textbooks: Seitel, *The Practice of Public Relations*, 4th edn., 1989. Baskin et al, *Public Relations*, 357. Cantor & Burger, *Experts in Action*, 189 & 201. PR of the year: Blohowiak, *No Comment!* 179. Burson: Kanner, 'Oil Slick,' 51. Manheim: Manheim, *All of the People, All the Time*, 100. Iacocca: Lee Iacocca & Sonny Kleinfield, *Lee Iacocca's Talking Straight*, (New York: Bantam Books, 1989), 118.

[56] Advocates: Argenti, *Corporate Communication*, 87-101. Op-ed: Michael Ryan, 'Op-Ed,' in *Encyclopedia of Public Relations*, ed. Heath, Vol. 2, 592. Publicity: Seitel, *The Practice of Public Relations*, 8th edn., 334.

[57] 'The HR Guide to the Galaxy,' *Forbes*, May 25, 2015.

[58] Textbooks: Seitel, *The Practice of Public Relations*, 12th edn., 2013. Broom & Sha, *Cutlip and Center*, 251. Revolutionized: Argenti, *Corporate Communication*, 43.

[59] Schmertz & Novak, *Goodbye to the Low Profile*, 134.

[60] Stephen Miller, 'Mobil Chief Mastered Public Relations,' *Wall Street Journal*, July 2, 2013.

[61] Sampson, *The Seven Sisters*.

[62] John J. Clark & William P. Tavoulareas, 'The Mobil Corporation: Perspectives by William P. Tavoulareas,' *Financial Management*, Vol. 9, No. 3 (Autumn, 1980), 7-14.

[63] Robert J. Cole, 'Marathon in Search of Merger Partner,' *New York Times*, November 12, 1981.

[64] David Kirkpatrick, 'Allen Murray Mobil Oil King from Queens,' *Fortune*, August 3, 1987.

[65] Sam Roberts, 'Metro Matters; Parting Shots by a Molder of Public Images,' *New York Times*, May 2, 1988.

[66] Allen R. Myerson & Agis Salpukas, 'Behind Exxon-Mobil Talks Lies a Humbled Oil Industry,' *New York Times*, November 27, 1998. 'The New Oil Behemoth,' *New York Times*, December 2, 1998.

CHAPTER 11

Friction: Troubleshooting issues and crises

"His hands were sticky with blood. He dropped the axe with the blade in the water, snatched a piece of soap that lay in a broken saucer on the window, and began washing his hands in the bucket. When they were clean, he took out the axe, washed the blade and spent a long time, about three minutes, washing the wood where there were spots of blood rubbing them with soap. Then he wiped it all with some linen that was hanging to dry on a line in the kitchen and then he was a long while attentively examining the axe at the window. There was no trace left on it, only the wood was still damp."[1]

In Doestoevsky's "Crime and Punishment," Raskolnikov cleans his murder weapon in a daze. More recent fictional accounts of crime have often included the stock character of the cleaner, of whom the most memorable was probably Winston Wolfe (Harvey Keitel) in the movie "Pulp Fiction" — "I'm Winston Wolfe. I solve problems."[2]

Sometimes it's only the cleaner who both appreciates the urgency of the situation and has a cool enough head to do something sensible about it.

A favorite post-war plot device, especially in movies, involves unpleasant incidents eventually being uncovered to be the criminal conspiracy of a multinational corporation. The device was taken to extremes in "Thunderball,"[3] the first James Bond novel to feature SPECTRE (1961), and "The Parallax View,"[4] (1974) whose premise was a corporation whose business was assassination. These were not just fiction but fantasy. Instances of deliberate law-breaking by major listed companies are rare. My experience of working at a senior level in a number of such companies is that both board directors and executives go to the utmost lengths to avoid infringing any law in any jurisdiction. When a business is at fault in a crisis, the fault is almost always negligence.

Cleaning

"Cleaning" or troubleshooting has sometimes seemed to be a full-time job. Customers' lives and the firm's business were often at risk, though not usually from crooks. I learned to be a "cleaner" not from textbooks, courses or seminars (or crime) but by seeing and doing over many years.

Crisis management? Not for the most part. Putting melodrama to one side, the problems that had to be solved, the messes that had to be cleaned up, were not crises but issues. They were often difficult issues but they were still part of business as usual. In all that time, there was only one full-blown crisis that really deserved the term. That was when a firm I worked for came close to collapse.

There is a danger of neglecting issues that are developing potentially dangerous narratives until it is almost too late. In a crisis, you are likely to be confronted with some variation of the following story: "Something terrible has happened. They are to blame. We have to make sure they pay." Before this point is reached, the organization targeted by critics needs an alternative narrative that can be put forward in the right way and at the right time. It is much easier to do this by building on existing stories, developed as part of a communication strategy, than starting with an empty space.

"What are we going to do in a crisis?"

CEOs and their boards are nervous. There but for the Grace of God... The best-laid plans are liable to be confounded by what seems like the modern equivalent of the Furies. One of the most worrying questions posed today by CEOs and their teams, including chief communication officers, is: "What are we going to do when we face a crisis?" (For the short answer, see key points of crisis communication strategy at the end of chapter 13.) Experts claim that it is not a question of "if" but "when." More and more effort is being expected to assuage crisis anxiety.

Some believe that the world is experiencing more and larger crises, noting "the sheer number and magnitude of corporate falls from grace since 2002," with "corporate disasters seemingly everywhere."[5] "Crises have become the normal state of nature."[6] "Seitel" spoke about the "ever-increasing magnitude" of crises and said that we are "always one step away from crisis."[7]

It is easy to list a catalog of recent dramas, including:

- The explosion of the *Deepwater Horizon* platform in the Gulf of Mexico, followed by leaking oil and retribution (see chapter 14).
- The cruise liner *Costa Concordia* running aground off the Italian coast, failing to evacuate passengers and crew safely, and losing 32 lives.
- The Japanese tsunami that caused meltdowns at nuclear plants.
- And, after 2007-08, the banking industry seemed to some observers to be in a state of permanent crisis.

It may seem that the 21st century is uniquely subject to crises but now recall that the 1970s and 1980s saw dramas including:

- *Amoco Cadiz* (largest oil spill to date, off the coast of Brittany, France);
- Love Canal (toxic waste in Niagara Falls, New York);
- Three Mile Island (nuclear accident in Harrisburg, Pennsylvania);
- Union Carbide (chemical leak in Bhopal, India, which killed thousands of people);
- Chernobyl (nuclear accident in Ukraine);
- Pan Am Flight 103 (in-flight bomb, Lockerbie, UK); and
- *Exxon Valdez* oil spill in Alaska (see chapter 13); among others.

Crisis management has become an established business specialism: "The lessons of now-infamous events… helped develop a distinct practice supported by consultants, scholarship and specially tasked managers inside vulnerable organizations."[8] A whole industry has arisen to answer the crisis management question — "What are we going to do when we face a crisis?" — and feed on the fears that trouble the executive suite. The crisis industry has a vested interest in stoking anxiety about the difficulty of coping without professional help and the allocation of resources. Fear has further stimulated professional interest in crisis communications, the nexus between crisis management and public relations. It has soared in line with the perceived boom in crises, exploited by consultants and pundits.

There has been a corresponding change in specialist literature from issues to crises. Crisis management books are legion and a large body of academic work has accumulated. Most scholars mining public relations have behaved for two decades as though the issues management seam has been worked out. However, Robert Heath has produced three volumes in two decades of "Strategic Issues Management."[9] In 1988, Heath suggested that issues management might be "maturing into a discipline," when it was actually fizzling out.[10] Scholars have generally migrated to crisis management. Most current public relations textbooks apportion a whole chapter or section to crisis communications, whereas for decades textbooks did not even have an entry for "crisis" in the index. Early editions of "Seitel" had a serviceable chapter on "Managing Public Issues," which has now been replaced by one on "Crisis Management."[11]

Glamorous crisis management sells more books than dowdy issues management.

Distinguishing crises from issues

How to recognize a crisis is made more difficult by the lack of any universally accepted definition. There are almost as many definitions of a crisis as there are books on crisis management. One review examined twenty competing definitions.[12]

"Cutlip," the doyen of public relations textbooks, said crisis management helps organizations "strategically respond to negative situations."[13] But if every "negative situation" were to be regarded a crisis, then dealing with crises would be an everyday activity, and that flies in the face of common sense. Commonplace incidents such as bad weather, machinery breakdowns, product recalls, and cyber security breaches do not normally qualify as crises unless they are catastrophic. These are issues.

The International Association of Business Communicators suggested that a crisis threatens "integrity, reputation, or survival."[14] The crucial difference between the issues that arise in business as usual, however negative, and a crisis, must be one of scale. Is the impact strategic? But impact (severity) is not enough. To be a crisis, the impact must also be sudden (acute). Borrowing medical terminology, only a severe, acute condition should be regarded as a crisis. Chronic conditions are not crises but issues, although they may have the potential to develop into crises.

"Cutlip" also referred unhelpfully to a category of "emerging crises."[15] If you can see it coming a long way off and if it can be avoided, it is not a crisis but an issue. And a so-called paracrisis, in which an entity is subject to a barrage of criticism on social media but has done nothing wrong, is also not a crisis but an issue.[16]

Crisis was described as "a much over-used term" as long ago as 1978. Since then, crisis anxiety has escalated to its current all-time high. In fact, how likely it is that there will be a crisis, and how serious it will be, varies by industry and by organization.[17]

Risk

The Age of Crisis Management is also the Age of Risk Management. Risk management, the idea that risks should be identified and assessed, and then action taken to mitigate them, is an activity that logically precedes crisis management. But it does not obviate the need for crisis management. Risk identification and assessment can never capture all risks. There are always unknown unknowns. Thorough risk assessment in the aviation industry failed to anticipate the large-scale business interruption that was caused in 2010 by volcanic ash from an Icelandic volcano. Some risks cannot practically be mitigated and so many risks can be identified that it would it would not be a sensible use of resources to try to mitigate them all completely.

Giant risks, like secrets, sometimes hide in plain sight. On a much larger scale, the risk that terrorists would attack the World Trade Center, as they did on September 11, 2001, and the risk that the credit bubble would burst to cause the global financial crisis, were both foreseen as possibilities by some. But they were not prioritized and no mitigation was put in place.

If risk management leads people to think that the risks have all somehow been wrangled under control, it can lead to a false sense of security in the boardroom and the executive suite. There will always be unknown unknowns. Risk management may provide a good night's sleep but it is an illusion. The Furies can strike at any time, without warning.

There is a balance to be struck. One the one hand, "No organization is immune from a crisis anywhere in the world even if that organization is vigilant and actively seeks to prevent crises."[18] Although much can be done to accident-proof an organization, directors and executives know that it is impossible to prepare for all eventualities and be sure there will never be a crisis. On the other hand, what most need to deal with most of the time is issues, not crises. But issues can go out of control if they are not managed well...

Key points
- A crisis is an incident that is unexpected, negative and overwhelming.
- Fear of crises is at an all-time high, leading to a boom in crisis management.
- Crisis anxiety has also led to a boom in risk management, which is a useful technique but not a panacea.

Friction

The concept of *friction* from military strategy, that was introduced in chapter 1, is a useful analogy.

"If Clausewitz had written only about friction in war, his place among the heroes in the Valhalla of strategic theory would be secure for all time."[19]

This is how he introduced the concept in "On War":

"Unless you have experienced it yourself, it is impossible for you to understand the difficulties that are inherent in war. You will not see why being a commander should require outstanding ability. Compared with a problem in mathematics, everything looks straightforward. It does not seem to demand an extraordinary amount of knowledge. But as soon as you have witnessed it, the reality of war becomes clear... Everything about war is simple but the simplest thing is very difficult. These difficulties multiply to produce a *friction* that is hard to comprehend unless you have seen the difficulties for yourself."[20]

It is like someone planning to make a short journey one evening. It should be an easy trip. But once the journey has begun, mechanical problems develop, the weather deteriorates, the traffic is suddenly congested, the traveler is diverted for miles down country lanes, and the diversion seems to go round in circles. What was intended as a short trip now has no end in sight, and the traveler is eventually grateful for the chance to stay the night in a shabby motel. (Updated from Clausewitz.)

Clausewitz summed up as friction the numerous difficulties that are encountered in warfare, from the activities of the enemy to logistical problems, hostile physical surroundings, and the difficulty of assessing what is happening on the ground. He said that friction was what distinguished real warfare from warfare on paper. And he argued that friction was inevitable. Modern strategy theorists, following Clausewitz, have stressed that technological and other advances may reduce friction but can never eliminate it. Friction is intrinsic to warfare.[21]

The idea of friction has not been much borrowed.[22] Yet there is a parallel between the difficulties faced in implementing a military strategy and those faced in implementing a strategy in business. In communication strategy, one source of friction is the variable, unpredictable performance of those who communicate (speakers). But the main source of friction is the public issues that face the organization. As in warfare, there are too many unpredictable and even unknowable independent variables for certainty in managing these issues ever to be achieved.

If the problem is friction, what is the solution? One solution adopted by military planners is ever more intensive use of systems and ever more detailed planning. Clausewitz believed that this was futile and, instead, he advocated simplicity and humility. He recommended reining in complexity and proceeding simply and modestly, in the recognition that a grand scheme might hold out the promise of a more impressive result but would also be more likely to fail.[23] This recommendation has been augmented by modern strategists with a call for flexibility and contingency planning.[24]

The message for those managing issues and preparing for possible crises is not to become too bogged down in highly detailed risk management but to aim instead for flexibility and simplicity.

Issues management can prevent crises

The convergence and overlap of crisis management and issues management has deposited "quicksand in the definitional landscape."[25]

The term "issues management" is used in two different but related senses. First, a technique, half way between planning and corporate communications, that involves scanning the business environment for signs of trouble and taking remedial action. After enjoying a period in vogue, it became much less popular and has been largely superseded in corporate popularity by risk management. Second, it can mean simply managing issues. Here, the emphasis is less on trying to spot potential disasters on the horizon and more on handling pesky problems that don't go away.

Many people have proposed a process for issues management. This is mine:

Fig. 11.1 Issues Management Process

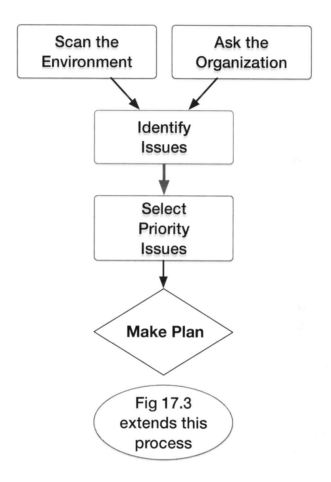

The first step is to find all the issues that could reasonably affect the organization, by scanning the environment and asking people inside for their suggestions.

The second step is to decide which of all these issues should be given priority. The decision to be made is primarily which issues could affect achievement of the objectives set by the overall business strategy. This is a strategic decision, discussed in chapter 17 (see section 3.1, Select Issues), which looks at the resulting plan.

These issues can be extremely long-lived. For example, the issue of how to develop metropolitan airports in a democratic society has been troublesome since the second world war.

To take a different example, oil companies have long faced popular concern, when energy prices were rising, that they might be profiteering. This arose when OPEC triggered a sharp rise in oil prices in the early 1970s. Until then, gasoline prices were low, stable, and therefore of little concern. The question that came to the fore was: were oil companies simply passing on the higher cost of raw material to consumers or were they taking extra profits along the way? (Gas and electric utilities face a variation of this issue when their input costs are rising.) This public concern was one of the early targets for Mobil's issue advertising, discussed in chapter 10. This issues's longevity is such that, four decades later, ExxonMobil's "Perspectives" blog was still working to clarify it for the public.[26]

The issues management process works well for slow burning issues. But what about the unexpected?

Put out the fire (without fireworks)

When you softly collide with another pedestrian in the street, do you:

a) Stop all the passers-by to witness the scene, apologize loudly and lengthily, solemnly undertake never to bump into anyone again, and offer the victim generous compensation.

b) Threaten to complain to the media or sue the other party for assault.

c) Say excuse me or sorry, smile, and walk on.

And which of these do you expect from the other party?

There is a widespread view that when an organization meets a crisis, the best course of action is to highlight it — to get out in front of the problem and over-react to it. To upturn and mangle the Chinese character for crisis beyond recognition, this is the view that a threat is the opportunity to launch a crisis. Some critics don't want to smooth over minor problems because, to them, all problems are useful evidence for demonstrating that the system is evil.

Downplaying a crisis is considered in some quarters to be tantamount to dismissing the suffering of the victims. No matter what the offense, option (a) — overreaction — is what they expect from institutions. And option (b) — another kind of overreaction — is what they would urge injured parties to do.

This chapter opened by drawing an analogy between issues management and cleaning. The oft-quoted analogy with firefighting is also helpful. All agree that the fire needs to be put out but the orthodox crisis communication view is that not only should the fire be put out, it should be seen to be put out, with a flourish. According to this view, the media should be invited to witness it. Webcams should be set up. The CEO should give interviews. "Stakeholders" should be invited to dialog. The organization should apologize for the fire and take full responsibility for it. A fire is not only a crisis but also a drama that must play out according to fixed conventions. See option (a) above.

Yet people put fires out without fuss all the time, usually with an apology, often with no or minimal compensation, including people in organizations. The waiter who brings the wrong drink. The online retailer who delivers the wrong product. The airline when the flight is delayed. The guy who bumps into you in the street. All of these issues involve an apology en passant. All of these issues are routinely put right in moments. These issues only become serious when either a major incident occurs or the usual low level apology mechanism breaks down. Otherwise, none of these issues have consequences for the organization that is the culprit — *unless* it overreacts. In the case of the street collision, the only sensible option is option (c), the passing excuse me.

A fire's main feature is its potential to cause damage. If the fire can be put out without coming to public attention, it should be. Unless a fire is a raging conflagration, it is probably not a crisis but just an issue. Only if it is clear that putting the fire out quietly is impossible should it be declared a crisis.

My own fire fighting experience includes bombings, hurricanes, crashes, changes of management, business closures, large-scale redundancies, and actual as well as metaphorical fires. Among these issues, there were many "negative situations" but only one became a real crisis. The others were the sorts of problems that often feature on lists of crises but were really issues, which it was possible to prevent from turning into full-blown crises. It was my job to help troubleshoot those issues.

Key points
- Friction is intrinsic to business as it is to warfare.
- Effective issues management and troubleshooting can prevent crises developing.
- If possible, fires (i.e., troublesome issues) should be quietly extinguished. This may seem obvious but it is not universally accepted.

Containment

When you cause a serious incident, the best course of action is to apologize, make restitution, investigate what went wrong, take steps to make sure it can't happen again, and cooperate with investigation by the authorities. As much as possible of this action should be taken immediately; all of it should be taken quickly. (Chapter 13 looks at the thorny question of when and how to apologize.)

This does not mean overreaction. But if the incident involved deaths or serious injuries, or has a significant consumer dimension, it will be necessary to communicate with those affected both through the media and directly.

In 2012, HSBC, the world's second largest bank by assets, showed how an extremely serious issue could be managed and prevented from turning into a crisis. The bank was investigated for allegedly breaking American money laundering and sanctions laws. In July 2012, a Senate committee reported that HSBC had exposed the country to "money laundering, drug trafficking and terrorist financing." HSBC paid US authorities $1.9 billion to settle.[27] This was the largest ever payment made up to that time in connection with such alleged offenses. It was serious, both a major legal issue and a threat to the bank's status.

HSBC had changed management since the alleged offenses. It issued brief statements in which it apologized, accepted responsibility, and said it was now a fundamentally different organization.[28] HSBC did not follow crisis management convention into overkill. It did not get out in front of the problem and overreact to it. No doubt it did also communicate in private and as appropriate with its strategic (priority) stakeholders. And it has taken measures to improve compliance. This was one of a number of problems dating back to a period when the bank had a decentralized system of governance. A series of issues then "painfully exposed [that system] as no longer fit for purpose."[29]

Whatever may have happened in years gone by, the handling of this issue by its current management charted an exemplary course between the two extremes of saying too little and saying too much.

(Not) Overreaction

The standard advice of media pundits and public relations textbooks would have been that its communications should match the scale of the problem: gigantic. All of these actions have been taken by large businesses facing perceived crises and could have been taken by the bank in 2012:

- It could have taken out full-page advertisements to say: "We're sorry. This is what we have done to put things right. It will never happen again." (But see the more salient Swiss issue discussed below.)
- It could have accepted and sought invitations to give press and television interviews, and it could have appeared on talk shows to apologize and explain.
- It could have hosted a question and answer session on Twitter, (like the disastrous session hosted, and aborted, by another major bank).[30]
- It could have arranged media profiles of its CEO, appointed since the alleged wrongdoing.
- It could have "reached out," in crisis-social worker terminology, to anyone who might have been affected.
- Its CEO could have visited the families of victims of drug abuse or terrorists and shed tears.

- It could have made donations with several zeroes in front of television cameras to charities handling the fall-out from drug abuse.
- It could have launched an industry campaign to make the world's banks and their millions of employees more aware of the problem of money-laundering and how to avoid it.

We can never know exactly what the outcome of such a high profile campaign would have been but we can be sure it would have made matters much worse. The story would have gathered a great deal more traditional and social media coverage. Many people who are unaware of what happened would have learned about it. Many people who don't know HSBC would have become familiar with it, and not in a good way. Journalists would have looked through their electronic press clippings and revisited any other stories they could find suggesting that HSBC had been less than saintly. Other recent banking scandals, such as the manipulation of Libor, taxpayer bail-outs and bankers' pay, would have been connected to the HSBC story, whether or not HSBC was involved in those. Politicians would have felt compelled to castigate bankers and called for more inquiries. Pension funds and ethical investment groups would have debated whether HSBC was an acceptable investment. Having avoided a hearing in a court of law, HSBC would have undergone a trial in the kangaroo court of public opinion. The stain on the bank's good name would have been larger, longer lasting and more indelible.

As a result of HSBC's cautious approach, there were two brief showers of headlines. The first was when the investigation became public in July 2012. The second was when it ended in December 2012. Since then, there have been only sporadic follow-ups.[31] The storm passed. Within a week of the settlement's being announced, Deutsche Bank upgraded HSBC stock to "Buy." Deutsche Bank noted that the bank serves as a "safe haven."[32] A safe haven, that is, from the vicissitudes of financial markets, rather than from law enforcement. Finally, HSBC attended a hearing at the UK Parliamentary Commission on Banking Standards on February 6, 2013, at which this issue accounted for about 15 minutes of a 2¼-hour session.[33]

Money laundering remains an issue that will not entirely go away for HSBC. It admits there is still work to do. But it is now an issue the bank is managing rather than a looming crisis.[34]

HSBC had nothing to gain from a public inquisition into the past. Yet, strangely, HSBC's near-silence flouts much of the conventional wisdom, from the crude "Any publicity is good publicity," to the most respected academic authorities on public relations and crisis management.

Another reason for HSBC to select a low media profile strategy was the context. There are no absolute rules about issues communication. It all depends on the context.

In this case, part of the context was the barrage of "conduct" issues facing banks. At one point, analysts estimated that HSBC might face a total of $12.4 billion in costs related to these issues between 2011 and 2016, with half yet to come.[35] Of this figure, $1.9 billion was in connection with anti-money laundering action while the rest was for a number of other issues, of which the most important were compensation for payment protection insurance, American mortgages, LIBOR and interest rate swaps. Perhaps even more significant were the barrages of conduct issues facing other banks. In 2014, it was the turn of BNP Paribas to be in the spotlight.[36] Eventually, it agreed to a $8.97 billion settlement for alleged American sanctions violations, dwarfing HSBC's settlement. Both in the context of HSBC's conduct issues and in the context of the conduct issues facing large banks, the original issue has become less prominent.

And another aspect of the context was the fact that HSBC is a bank of global importance that until recently had its headquarters in Hong Kong. HSBC always has the option of moving somewhere more congenial if the political and regulatory climate in the UK becomes too sour.

Swiss postscript

Another banking conduct issue hit the headlines in early 2015, particularly in Britain. This was the long-running investigation by several countries of private banking units based in Switzerland for alleged involvement in aiding tax evasion. The timing was unfortunate. It became a political issue in the lead-up to the British general election when questions were raised about accusations that prominent people were involved in tax schemes and about whether the authorities had been rigorous enough.

As before, HSBC kept out of the political argument and kept a sensibly low profile. It published an open letter explaining what it had done to reform its Swiss private bank, that stated: "The media focus has been on historical events that show the standards to which we operate today were not universally in place in our Swiss operations eight years ago. We must show we understand that the societies we serve expect more from us. We therefore offer our sincerest apologies."[37] HSBC's chairman added in the annual report: "We deeply regret and apologize for the conduct and compliance failures highlighted which were in contravention of our own policies as well as expectations of us."[38]

The *FT*'s Lex commented: "Moralists and politicians won't want to hear this. But the impact of HSBC's Swiss private banking scandal on the stock's investment case can be summarized in a word — zip."[39] And HSBC still has nothing to gain from a public hearing for past sins. The 2015 Swiss issue loomed larger in the media than the 2012 issue but, even so, by the time the UK election was over, in mid-year, it had receded.

Part III looks more deeply into issues and crisis management through the examples of Exxon, BP, Carnival and BAA. And chapter 17 integrates issues management into communication strategy.

In Summary

- The prospect of a full-blown crisis is daunting. But only only sudden, severe incidents count as crises. The rest are issues and can be managed.
- Friction — in the shape of issues — is an unavoidable part of doing business.
- If issues can be wrangled discreetly, without becoming full-blown crises, the outcome is likely to be more satisfactory, as shown by the case of HSBC.

References

[1] Fyodor Doestoyevsky, *Crime and Punishment*, translated by Constance Garnett, (New York: P. F. Collier and Son Company, 1917), 81.

[2] *Pulp Fiction*, directed by Quentin Tarantino, Miramax Films, 1994.

[3] Ian Fleming, *Thunderball*, (London: Jonathan Cape, 1961).

[4] *The Parallax View*, directed by Alan J. Pakula, Paramount Pictures, 1974.

[5] Leslie Gaines-Ross, *Corporate Reputation: 12 Steps to Safeguarding and Recovering Reputation*, (Hoboken, NJ: John Wiley & Sons, 2008), xvi.

[6] Christopher Lehane, Mark Fabiani & Bill Guttentag, *Masters of Disaster: The Ten Commandments of Damage Control*, (New York: Palgrave Macmillan, 2012).

[7] Seitel, *The Practice of Public Relations*, 8th edn., 201-2; Seitel, *The Practice of Public Relations*, 12th edn., 349.

[8] Simon Moore & Mike Seymour, *Global Technology and Corporate Crisis: Strategies, Planning and Communication in the Information Age*, (New York: Routledge, 2005), 30.

[9] Robert L. Heath (ed.), *Strategic Issues Management: How Organizations Influence and Respond to Public Interests and Policies*, (San Francisco, CA: Jossey-Bass Publishers, 1988); Robert L. Heath (ed.), *Strategic Issues Management: Organizations and Public Policy Challenges*, (Thousand Oaks, CA: SAGE Publications, Inc., 1997); Robert L. Heath & Michael J. Palenchar, (eds.), *Strategic Issues Management: Organizations and Public Policy Challenges*, (Thousand Oaks, CA: SAGE Publications, Inc., 2009).

[10] Heath (ed.), *Strategic Issues Management*, (1988), 333.

[11] No index ref. in e.g.: Bernays, *Public Relations*, 1952; Cutlip & Center, *Effective Public Relations*, 1st edn., 1952; Grunig & Hunt, *Managing Public Relations*, 1984; Cutlip, Center & Broom, *Effective Public Relations*, 6th edn., 1985. But Seitel: *The Practice of Public Relations*, 4th edn., 525-543.

[12] Robert L. Heath & Dan Pyle Millar, 'A Rhetorical Approach to Crisis Communication: Management, Communication Processes, and Strategic responses,' in *Responding to Crisis*, ed. Millar & Heath, 1-17.

[13] Broom & Sha, *Cutlip and Center*, 11th edn., 40.

[14] Caroline Sapriel, 'Effective Crisis Management: Tools and Best Practice for the New Millennium,' *Journal of Communication Management*, Vol. 7, No. 4, (2003), 348.

[15] Broom & Sha, *Cutlip & Center*, 11th edn., 305.

[16] W. Timothy Coombs & J. Sherry Holladay, 'The Paracrisis: The Challenges Created by Publicly Managing Crisis Prevention,' *Public Relations Review*, Vol. 38, (2012), 408-415.

[17] Over-used: Holsti, O. R., 'Limitations of Cognitive Abilities in the Face of Crisis,' in *Studies on Crisis Management*, ed. by Carolyne F. Smart & W. T. Stanbury, (Toronto: Butterworth, 1978), 41. Varies: John J. Burnett, 'A Strategic Approach To Managing Crises,' *Public Relations Review*, Vol. 24, No. 4, (1998), 477.

[18] W. Timothy Coombs, 'Parameters for Crisis Communication,' in *The Handbook of Crisis Communication*, ed. by W. Timothy Coombs & Sherry J. Holladay, (Oxford, UK: Blackwell Publishing Ltd, 2010), 17.

[19] Gray, *Modern Strategy*, 94.

[20] Clausewitz, *On War*, chapter VII, my free translation.

[21] Thomas G. Mahnken, 'Strategic Theory,' in *Strategy in the Contemporary World*, Baylis, Wirtz & Gray (eds.), 69.

[22] Howard Nothhaft and Hagen Schölzel wrote a rare piece connecting strategy in communication with military strategy - '(Re-) Reading Clausewitz' in Holtzhausen & Zerfass, *The Routledge Handbook of Strategic Communication*.

[23] Peter Paret, 'The Genesis of On War,' in *On War*, Howard & Paret (eds.), 1989, 17.

[24] Gray & Johnson, 'The Practice of Strategy,' 369.

[25] Tony Jaques, 'Issue and Crisis Management: Quicksand in the Definitional Landscape,' *Public Relations Review*, Vol. 35 (2009), 280.

[26] Ken Cohen, 'Gas Prices and Industry Earnings: A Few Things to Think About the Next Time You Fill Up,' ExxonMobil Perspectives, April 27, 2011 - <http://www.exxonmobilperspectives.com/2011/04/27/gas-prices-and-industry-earnings-a-few-things-to-think-about/>.

[27] The investigation was initially disclosed by HSBC in SEC filings and its Interim Report 2010, 187. Senate committee: HSBC Exposed U. S. Financial System to Money Laundering, Drug, Terrorist Financing Risks: Senate Subcommittee Holds Hearing and Releases Report, US Senate Permanent Subcommittee on Investigations news release, July 16, 2012. Settlement: Christian Berthelsen, Matthias Rieker & Brett Philbin, 'HSBC to Pay Record $1.9 Billion Settlement,' *Wall Street Journal*, December 11, 2012.

[28] 'HSBC Announces Settlements with Authorities,' HSBC Holdings plc news release, December 11, 2012; 'Message from HSBC Group Chief Executive Stuart Gulliver,' HSBC Holdings plc news release, July 30, 2012; 'HSBC statement on testimony before the United States Senate Permanent Subcommittee on Investigations,' HSBC Holdings plc news release, July 16, 2012.

[29] David Kynaston & Richard Roberts, *The Lion Wakes: A Modern History of HSBC*, (London: Profile Books Ltd, 2015) 629.

[30] Walter Hamilton, 'Latest Debacle for JPMorgan Chase: PR Nightmare on Twitter,' *Los Angeles Times*, November 13, 2013.

[31] E.g.: Matt Taibbi, 'Gangster Bankers: Too Big to Jail - How HSBC Hooked Up With Drug Traffickers and Terrorists. And Got Away With It,' *Rolling Stone*, February 14, 2013.

[32] Peter Nurse, 'Broker Note Briefing: Thursday,' *Wall Street Journal*, December 13, 2012.

[33] Denise Roland, 'HSBC Chiefs Grilled On Banking Standards - As It Happened,' *Daily Telegraph*, February 6, 2013, <http://www.telegraph.co.uk/finance/newsbysector/banksandfinance/9851978/HSBC-chiefs-grilled-on-banking-standards-as-it-happened-Feb-6-2013.html>.

[34] Brett Wolf & Aruna Viswanatha, 'Exclusive: HSBC Still In Regulators' Crosshairs Over Money-Laundering,' *Reuters*, January 17, 2014.

[35] Chris Manners, Fiona Simpson, Anil Agarwal & Silvia Fun, *HSBC*, Morgan Stanley Research Europe, April 25, 2014.

[36] Devlin Barrett, Christopher M. Matthews & Andrew R. Johnson, 'BNP Paribas Draws Record Fine for Tour de Fraud,' *Wall Street Journal*, June 30, 2014.

[37] The open letter was published as an advertisement in UK newspapers on February 15, 2015, and was addressed to "all HSBC customers, shareholders and colleagues." HSBC also provided background information, 'Update on the Swiss Private Bank,' at <www.hsbcprivatebank.com/swiss_bank_update>.

[38] 'HSBC Holdings plc Annual Report and Accounts 2014,' HSBC Holdings plc, 5.

[39] Lex, 'HSBC: Current Accountability,' *Financial Times*, February 17, 2015.

CHAPTER 12

Allies: Reputation and stakeholders

"You don't have to know what everyone knows but it is important to know what not everyone knows."
— attributed to Mikhail Botvinnik

In "The Great Gatsby," F. Scott Fitzgerald touched on one of the central problems of public communication. Gatsby the tycoon loved and lost a girl called Daisy. He hoped to win her back and he had a strategy.

Gatsby's solution was to buy a mansion across the bay from Daisy. There he lived in style, threw lavish parties, and hoped that something would turn up. In the end, Gatsby appealed to his neighbor, who happened to be Daisy's cousin. "'He wants to know ... if you'll invite Daisy to your house some afternoon and then let him come over.' ...He had waited five years and bought a mansion where he dispensed starlight to casual moths so that he could 'come over' some afternoon to a stranger's garden."[1]

Gatsby had no interest in the "casual moths" attending the parties. His only interest was in Daisy. Gatsby hoped that she would come to one of his parties or that she would at least hear of him by reputation. The whole artillery of his entertainment program was aimed, but subtly and indirectly, at one target. He hoped to reach her by reputation before being forced to try a more direct method.

Gatsby's conundrum is a microcosm of one of the communication questions we all face: how best to reach our targets.

This chapter addresses the fundamental questions "To whom?" (who are our targets) and "How?" (how best to reach them), looking at three different approaches:

1. Reputation management.
2. Stakeholder theory.
3. Communication strategy.

Reputation, ancient and modern

Businesses are increasingly worried about their reputations, so much so that a survey by Deloitte reported that executives think reputation is their number one strategic risk.[2] This chapter examines how reputation came to be seen as that important and asks whether they are right to be so concerned. And is reputation management the best response to the perceived problem?

Chapter 1 asserted that gaffes threaten a reputation but it is a curious fact that, until recently, the word "reputation" was nowhere to be found in most texts on communication. There was nothing significant on reputation in early editions of leading public relations textbooks. Nor did reputation feature in standard texts on communication theory.[3] (See note for a rare example to the contrary.)[4]

Chapter 4 showed that public communication is as old as the hills — as old as the tels of the Fertile Crescent, anyway. Chapter 6 referred to Aristotle's belief that the effect of a communication depends not only on what is said but on the character of the speaker.

A good reputation was prized down the ages but it is one of a cluster of related desirable attributes that have been more or less taken for granted, such as honor, integrity, trust, credibility, authority, reliability, dependability, status, gravitas, dignity, soundness, standing, acceptability, character, good name, prestige, renown and esteem. Thus the 24-volume "Encyclopaedia Britannica," the most comprehensive encyclopedia before the digital age, had no entry or index reference for reputation. Nor did the 4-volume "International Encyclopedia of Communications," published in 1989.[5] Brand, identity and image were discussed but reputation, credibility, esteem and the others were not, probably because they were thought to flow naturally from a person's qualities and behavior.

The family: brand, image, identity, reputation

The modern concept of reputation had three close relatives: brand, identity and image. Taking each of the four in turn:

(1) Brand

A brand is "a name, term, design, symbol or any other feature that identifies the seller's good or service as distinct from those of other sellers."[6] Brands came into widespread use in the 19th century for consumer goods. They were a useful way for consumers to distinguish the products they preferred and a useful way for businesses to promote their products to consumers. Eventually brands were applied not only to products but to families of related products from the same business and to the business itself. So brands are used in marketing to identify, distinguish and endorse products and services but can also identify and distinguish an organization or even a person. Coca-Cola is both a product and the company that makes it. George Clooney, Barack Obama and Pope Francis are examples of human beings who have also become global brands (without implying that they are trying to sell products or services). Through the 20th century brands became more and more important. Even those opposed to the entire existing world order (e.g., ISIL/Daesh) are brands. And awareness that brands could be extremely valuable assets has increased, with the biggest tech brands thought to be worth over $100 billion.

(2) Identity

"Identity" has been defined as "those organizational characteristics that are most central, enduring, and distinctive," and the organization's identity as: "who/what do we believe we are."[7] Wally Olins argued that identity is at the heart of business and other institutions, provocatively taking as an example the origination of a new identity by the Confederate States of America.[8] He posited that every organization needs a sense of purpose and a sense of belonging for its people. Thus identity comes from within. It is above all about the people who make the organization what it is. Everyone outside follows on. Olins said that identity tends to be reduced to its simplest manifestation, the logo, when it should be "visible, tangible and all-embracing," including not only the look of the firm but its products, locations, communications and even its behavior toward others. Still, the emphasis remained on "how the visual style of an organization affects its positioning in the market."

In the 2000s, this visual emphasis was beginning to look dated. It was increasingly argued that the answer was a corporate or brand narrative: "Companies that do not tell a compelling and consistent brand story that speaks to both the rational and the emotional needs of audiences risk creating a shallow, short-term 'brand' that is easily destroyed by external factors."[9] (See chapter 9.)

Fig. 12.1 Presentation and Outcome

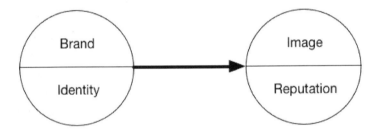

Both the brand and identity are created by the organization and presented to the outside world. Consumers, investors, governments, and other outsiders may have opinions and feelings about a brand or identity they encounter but these reactions do not alter it. What they think and feel about it is something separate, an outcome. Until recently, this outcome was most likely to be described as the image.

(3) Image

An "image" in science or the arts is simply a picture, a visual representation of a real or imaginary object. In public communication, image has a more specific meaning. The image of an organization (or a person) is the way others see it. In terms of the most basic speaker-subject-hearer communication model — sender speaks or transmits message to receiver — identity is what speakers say about themselves (though sometimes unconsciously) whereas image is what receivers perceive. "A corporate image is any singular piece of knowledge, attitude or behavior that an individual possesses towards an organization."[10] Much of what Mobil, for example, was trying to achieve in its communication program was to boost its image.

Image was a term beloved of people in advertising, corporate communications, marketing and design in the 1970s and 1980s that has gone out of fashion. In the 2010s, it is no longer much talked about. It has become more polite, respectful, politically correct and with-it to talk about reputation. This happened because image has also been used, confusingly, to mean not how others see the entity but how the entity would like to be seen. The trouble with the second meaning, the desired image, is that, as a fabrication by the sender of a message, it "implies a degree of falseness." This is the sense in which "we talk about the image of a consumer product or of a politician."[11] It was this implication of falseness, encouraged by Daniel Boorstin's "The Image: A Guide to Pseudo-Events in America,"[12] that contributed to image coming to be seen as a pejorative term like propaganda. Image came to be contrasted with grubby reality.[13]

Although image continued in widespread use until the 1990s, its fall from grace produced conditions that were ripe for a change of terminology, if not a paradigm shift.

(4) Reputation

Conditions were ripe for *reputation*. As a prescient few perceived, reputation, a much older idea than brand, image and identity, was ripe for rejuvenation and repackaging.

Reputation Management

It is hard to say exactly when professional communicators began to pay serious attention to the concept of reputation. In the 1970s and 1980s, public relations and corporate communications managers were often responsible for the corporate brand or identity, while marketing managers looked after product brands. But Warren Newman, president of Britain's Institute of Public Relations, spoke about "the management of reputation" back in 1987.[14] And an offshoot of Olins' agency, Wolff Olins/Smythe, extended its reach into public relations by making the leap of re-inventing the images that businesses were trying to engineer for themselves as reputation. They argued that reputation, like identity, came from within, in the sense that it was the way the organization behaved. Like identity, it could be managed. They contrasted managing reputation with conventional public relations, which they said in 1992 was "associated with the unthinking passing on of corporate propaganda."[15] The plan was for reputation to be more honest.

The value of reputation has long been well understood. For example, within days of *RMS Titanic* striking an iceberg in 1912, the *New York Times* said that the owner had not merely lost the ship but its reputation, and that its reputation was worth many ships,[16] a verdict that reads as though it could have been written yesterday. But now the concept of reputation was being refurbished and redeveloped for a contemporary market. It was later argued that the best results come when a firm is able to synchronize employee and customer views of what was sometimes called the corporate personality.[17] And some public relations and corporate communication professionals would say that what they were doing all along was managing reputation.

It seemed obvious that a firm's reputation influenced decisions such as those by investors or by consumers choosing products[18] but, at first, there was little hard information about what factors governed reputations.[19] Reputation was something about which an experienced communication professional might have an intuition but the evidence had not been gathered and studied to make possible a rational debate.

Scholarly works on reputation began to appear. When business school professor Charles Fombrun published "Reputation: Realizing Value from the Corporate Image" in the mid-1990s, it was the catalyst for the development of a new field of Reputation Management.[20] Fombrun and his colleagues inaugurated an annual conference at New York University's Stern School of Business in 1997, launching a new business specialism and academic discipline. Later that year, they launched a scholarly journal, *Corporate Reputation Review*. The maiden double issue surveyed what it called the "reputational landscape."[21] The editorial board included not only leaders of the new school of thought but figures from public relations, such as James Grunig, and from branding, such as Olins. Also in 1997, Fombrun and Cees Van Riel founded a reputation management consultancy, the Reputation Institute, Inc., that devised a proprietary framework for analysis of the views of stakeholders.

While regiments of public relations scholars were refining and elaborating the symmetry-excellence theory, and much smaller numbers were critiquing it, and reviving interest in rhetoric, a new body of theory was thus emerging that would circumvent the symmetry-excellence paradigm. It has even been called the "reputation paradigm."[22] Since then, reputation management has made considerable headway with managers but much less progress in academe. Of the four leading public relations textbooks, only "Seitel" has so far paid significant attention to reputation.[23] PR and reputation management have proceeded down parallel lines of development, rather than engaging with each other.

Reputation management aligned with common sense in saying that a firm with a good reputation is more likely to succeed than a firm with a poor reputation. In particular, the more reputable firm would be more likely to sell products or services. Reputation management is touted as the science of making this happen. It is Corporate Communication Made Simple. And reputation management did not have the dubious associations of PR.[24]

A study of Fortune 500 companies at the turn of the century already showed that reputation management was "gaining ground as the driving philosophy" for communications in large businesses.[25] In the field of risk management, reputation has been widely accepted as at risk and it is even possible for a firm to insure its reputation.

For, To and With Whom?

Reputation management experts advised companies to develop a reputation actively by shaping a unique identity, to distinguish themselves from competitors, and "projecting a coherent, consistent set of images."[26]

This immediately prompts the question: *Projecting to whom?*

Fig. 12.2 Image or Reputation With Whom?

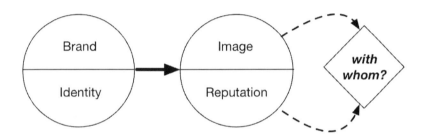

The assumed answer was: more or less everyone. According to Fombrun, "Reputation embodies the general estimation in which a company is held by employees, customers, suppliers, distributors, competitors and the public." He continued: "a company must establish strong relationships not only with customers but with other key constituencies."[27]

The failure to differentiate between those whose views made up a reputation was a serious flaw. Reputation management tended to address the mass of the general public, in the same scattershot or broadcast approach that had been employed by Mobil in the days of Herb Schmertz. The targets were numerous, distant and obscured in a haze.

Admittedly, it is possible for a scattershot communication to have a hidden target. It is open to the communicator to address millions, while really hoping to reach the ears of a handful, like Gatsby throwing parties with no interest in the guests except the one girl he hoped would come. David Ogilvy said that the hidden agenda for most corporate advertising is a pitch to investors.[28] However, scattershot communication is wasteful and prone to side effects, in the form of reactions from those for whom the message is not intended. (See chapter 10.) In the case of Mobil, the company's decision to take a high profile probably came first and the high profile drove its approach to the audience, rather than sophisticated analysis of its audience driving the choice of communication channels. Instead of focusing on those that were really important to the firm it used a loud hailer to communicate with the entire population of the United States.

The only demonstrable outcome of such a campaign was likely to be a vague improvement in ratings by the general public or by those contributing to *reputation rankings*.

Keeping score

These reputation rankings, which may be either published or compiled for private use, are subject to a number of shortcomings:

- The most widely publicized figure is usually the total score. This may be the average of a number of aspects of perceived performance or character, such as how a business treats employees, its profitability and the quality of its products. And it may be a composite of ratings from different groups.[29] It is a snapshot of the popularity of a business. It is interesting to see how popularity varies over time and relative to other businesses but not very important. Oil companies are less popular than tech companies and that is unlikely to change.

- The results vary in bizarre ways. It might be supposed that the ratings of Apple, as the world's most valuable company and one of the best known, would be fairly consistent. Indeed, in June 2014, institutional investors voted Apple "World's Most Respected Company" for the fourth time in five years (*Barron's*). And over at *Fortune*,

Apple was anointed "World's Most Admired Company" for the eighth year running in 2015.[30] The *Fortune* survey is probably the best known and most widely quoted of all reputation surveys. For this, the Hay Group surveys senior business people about their perceptions of nine attributes: innovation, people management, use of corporate assets, social responsibility, quality of management, financial soundness, long-term investment value, quality of products and services, and global competitiveness. Apple came top on all nine in 2015. Contrast these results with the Reputation Institute (RI), linked to *Forbes*, where Amazon was named "America's Most Reputable Company" for 2015 but Apple was down at number 198. This was the outcome of a consumer survey and *Forbes* commented that, "When it comes to overall reputation, consumers don't care about innovation as much as other issues like whether the company seems fair and ethical and whether it's making some sort of positive impact on society."[31] It could be that Apple is liked by business people and disliked by consumers. But that does not seem at all likely when Apple is able to sell each of its innovative new iPhones to tens of millions of consumers (and see chapter 8).

- Some surveys highlight special interests or are carried out as lobbying activities by special interests, aiming to draw attention what they judged to be the best and worst firms. It may be worth avoiding the lowest positions. Otherwise, clawing up such rankings seems fruitless. There are even scam surveys that charge businesses for participation, so that the "results" are skewed in favor of those who pay the bribe. Propaganda, anyone?

What is it worth?

Reputation management had the benefit of focusing attention on outcomes. But, as in the case of these popularity charts, the outcomes were often facile. For several years, I served as "chief reputation officer" of a major company that enjoyed an excellent reputation as measured by reputation surveys. My official job title was the more traditional "director of corporate affairs." My firm consistently came top of its sector. The high rating felt good and encouraged management. It was easy to sell the concept of reputation management to colleagues. It looked good on my resumé. This was in the days before Twitter but, if such a thing had been possible, I would probably have tweeted every time the company did well in the ratings. But did the firm's position in reputation rankings give it any real advantage? And can I honestly claim, looking back on it, that the company's high rating was the result of my endeavors?

Reputation management advocates sometimes credit the halo effect of a good reputation with an impact on behavior. For example, it was suggested that, "The high degree of generalized favorability" enjoyed by Apple might cause a halo effect that would lead consumers to overlook product flaws. Or perhaps it might lead investors to accept irregularities in the treatment of stock options.[32] It is difficult to prove cause and effect in these cases but it is at least as likely that these behaviors would be encouraged by Apple's effective communications with customers and investors (chapter 8).

Putting halo effects aside, how beneficial is it to achieve a good reputation among people who have no connection with you, or only a tenuous connection? How beneficial is it if you have no relationship and do not even know who they are? If you are running a firm that sells hamburgers, how much do you care what managers in the oil industry think about your company? And vice versa? That is often what reputation management measures — the impressions of people who have little connection with you.

The opinions you should care about are those of people who have relevant decision-making power. These decision-makers are the consumers who buy a technology company's gadgets or software, the governments who award licenses to companies exploring for oil or minerals, the investors who own the company and ultimately reward or replace management, and so on.

Key points
- Reputation management has largely superseded the concept of image in corporate communication.
- But the obvious question is: "Reputation with whom?" It often goes unasked and unanswered. Reputation rankings have a number of shortcomings both as a measure of performance and a guide to policy.

Audiences, targets, publics and stakeholders

If it is obvious that an organization's reputation influences decisions that affect it, then it should also be obvious that the organization (or someone in public life) should focus its reputation management or communication efforts on those who have relevant decision-making power.

Yet this proposition is controversial. It raises the question of what is the appropriate relationship between an organization and those outside. A number of competing terms have been put forward to describe them, each with different connotations — notably publics, audiences, and stakeholders. Viewing the outsiders as the receivers in a source-message-receiver model is an over-simplification. And although "constituency" is a term used by some in reputation management and corporate communications, it is confusing because it usually implies representative democracy.

Once again, taking each of the principal three concepts in turn:

(1) Audience and target audience

"Audience" is the oldest and most widely used word. It denotes all kinds of groups of recipients of communication, from the populace assembled in the Greek theater to the dispersed mass audience of radio and television, and the global audience of users of the internet. The term is used in marketing, advertising and, to some extent, in public relations. Audiences, target audiences and targets are more or less interchangeable, although the audience is dynamic: "We communicate with an audience because we expect, demand or fear feedback."[33] The problem with the word is the implication that an audience is marooned on the receiving end of communication. This implication is not objectionable to those who aim to persuade but it is objectionable to those who insist on mutuality and subscribe to the two-way symmetric model of public relations.

(2) Public

"Public" is the term preferred by public relations scholars. The term has a long history in politics that evolved into the modern idea of a public, in contrast with the general public, as a group brought into being by an issue.[34] There is obvious potential for confusion between "the public" in the sense of the general public, i.e., everyone, or all citizens, and "a public," in the more specialized sense of a group which has a strong interest in or link to a subject or issue, such as the residents of a particular neighborhood or the users of a particular service. A more current term for this might be "special interest group." Nevertheless, scholars including Scott Cutlip, Allen Center, James Grunig and Todd Hunt all used the term. Symmetry-excellence theory called for two-way symmetric communication with publics.

But how should these publics be recognized? Grunig developed a situational theory of publics to explain "when and how people communicate and when communications aimed at people are most likely to be effective."[35] Grunig suggested that a public arises when an organization makes a decision that affects that public. It disappears again if it ceases to be affected. As the situation changes, so the publics change. (One application of this theory is to communication in a crisis — see chapter 13.) He differentiated between publics that communicate actively, passively or not at all. He also differentiated between publics and stakeholders. Publics choose themselves. But stakeholders, like audiences, are chosen by the organization (although stakeholder theorists who take a normative view would probably demur — see below). The situational theory of publics in communications resembles segmentation in marketing. In the same way as the market as a whole is broken down into segments that have a differential response to marketing approaches, the situational theory aimed to break down the general public, into publics that communicate differently — two-way, naturally.[36]

(3) Stakeholder

"Stakeholder" is the vogue term of the 2010s. No sooner had symmetry-excellence become the dominant theory of public relations, than management and communication alike were strongly influenced by the new field of stakeholder theory. The word emerged from the idea that some groups should be entitled to rights over organizations, in addition to any legal rights they might have. Apart from being a "horrible" word, according to *The Economist*, stakeholder is an awkward term because its definition is contested[37] and because it tends to be a term that serves critics rather than institutions. Arguably many so-called "stakeholders" are really stake*scroungers* (also known as stakeseekers)[38] with a claim that is more or less dubious. However, it has become so ubiquitous that making a point of avoiding it here would require too much circumlocution.

Stakeholders versus shareholders

The origins of stakeholder theory are hard to trace and the large and growing body of literature uses concepts in different ways, involving "diverse and often contradictory evidence and arguments."[39] One starting point is a definition of stakeholders by management theorists at Stanford Research Institute (SRI) in the 1960s as "those groups without whose support the organization would cease to exist," such as owners, employees and customers. SRI argued that management needed to understand these stakeholders so that objectives could be set that stakeholders would support.[40] The support of the stakeholders would make the objectives achievable. This idea fitted into the traditional shareholder capitalism approach that saw the firm's primary responsibility as providing profits for shareholders.

The alternative, stakeholder approach, traditionally found in

Europe, makes shareholders one of a number of stakeholders for whom the firm should be creating value. In Germany, for example, the post-war influence of capital markets was much weaker than in America as a result of family ownership, widespread cross-shareholdings, the strong influence of banks, and co-determination law providing for labor representation on supervisory boards. Thus, a public company would typically be responsible to stakeholders including shareholders, banks and organized labor.

Stakeholder theory was taken forward and popularized by Edward Freeman in his 1984 book, "Strategic Management: A Stakeholder Approach."[41] To him, a stakeholder was anyone who could affect or be affected by a company going about its business. He asked whether managers' fiduciary responsibility to the owners could be replaced by a concept of management in which they were obliged to act in the interests of stakeholders.[42] This would mean that owners would no longer be the sole or even necessarily the most important stakeholders. Considering Michael Porter's generic strategies and his theory that five forces shape competitive strategy, (such as the relative power of customers and the threat of new entrants), Freeman suggested adding a sixth force, the relative power of stakeholders.

The new stakeholder theory was taken up and developed in a number of fields, including corporate planning, systems theory, corporate social responsibility, organization theory and, by the 1990s, public relations. Carl Botan and Vincent Hazleton published two major surveys of public relations theory, 17 years apart. The first, in 1989, made no reference at all to stakeholders. In the second, from 2006, the word "stakeholder" occurred 170 times.[43]

At first, the political reality in both shareholder and stakeholder capitalism was often that the firm was autonomous and put its own interests first, paying lip service to its stated objective of serving shareholders or stakeholders. This managerialism came under pressure, particularly in America and Britain, from investors who were inspired by agency theory to demand that management pay closer attention to their interests. Management also faced increasing pressure from groups in society who considered themselves to be stakeholders.

The debate about whose purpose the business should serve continues. Any firm must make its own decision, actively or by default. But surely the purpose of a business is primarily commercial. Commercial purpose is what distinguishes businesses from other types of organization, not necessarily better or worse, but different.

For the sake of our stakeholders

There is another fundamental question at the heart of stakeholder theory. Should the firm should *serve* stakeholders? Or should it *make use* of stakeholders? To use the technical language, should organizations take a *normative* approach to stakeholders, accepting that stakeholders are those groups and individuals with valid claims on it. Or should they take an *instrumental* approach, regarding as genuine stakeholders only those groups and individuals whose interests need to be taken into account by management in seeking to achieve their objectives?

In short, should the organization serve the interests of stakeholders (or owners or whoever) at all times, in everything it does? Or, having decided its ultimate beneficiary, should the firm merely identify as stakeholders those groups that can influence outcomes for the firm and therefore need to be managed by the firm in its own interest (and in the eventual interest of its ultimate beneficiary)?

This echoes the split between symmetric communication and strategy. Those in the business of symmetry would say that equality between the firm and its stakeholders and the development of mutually beneficial relationships between them is the essence of symmetry-excellence. They should therefore reject the notion that the firm should manipulate its stakeholders to achieve its objectives. The normative view would also be that businesses that accommodate their stakeholders tend to perform better,[44] though beware the circular argument (as with symmetry-excellence) that successful companies look after stakeholders and looking after stakeholders is the evidence for their success.

Strategy demands an instrumental view of stakeholders (including shareholders), which says that the firm should put itself first and "take stakeholder opinions into account only inasmuch as they are consistent with" its chosen objectives.[45] The instrumental view enables a business strategy to be made (taking the interests of one or more stakeholders into account) and then executed. Communication strategy is an element in the execution of the business strategy. Stakeholders then become parties who can help or hinder the execution process.

Counting the bubbles

Whether you take a normative view or an instrumental view, you still need some way of determining who the stakeholders are.

Who are the stakeholders? Freeman offered two contrasting diagrams. In the first diagram, which he called the "managerial view," the firm was at the center of a cross. Its four arms were marked owners, customers, employees and suppliers. This corresponded roughly to the original SRI concept of a stakeholder as a necessary supporter. Each of the four arms would be a necessary supporter.

The second diagram, labeled the "stakeholder view," was a circle with the firm in the center and a series of bubbles around the circumference. Each of the bubbles represented a different stakeholder group. Double-headed arrows linked each bubble to the firm, once again implying symmetrical relationships. In this diagram, instead of only four arms, there were eleven bubbles, including the four from diagram number one but also environmentalists, consumer advocates, and even competitors.[46]

Stakeholder theory reflected to some extent public relations thinking and practice about audiences (stakeholders) in reputation management and public relations. David Bernstein included a circular diagram that was strikingly similar to Freeman's in his "Company Image and Reality: A Critique of Corporate Communications," that was first published in the same year as Freeman's book.[47] In Bernstein's diagram there were slightly fewer bubbles and the bubbles were labeled "audiences" rather than "stakeholders." But both authors wanted organizations to keep in mind numerous external groups.

Interest among communicators is of very long standing. In

the early days of public relations pedagogy, the prototypical "Cutlip" textbook included its own diagram that showed relationships including "women's discussion groups," "organized farmers" and "veterans' organizations."[48]

Anyone can try their hand at a stakeholder diagram and it should look something like this:

Fig. 12.3 All the World's a Stakeholder (Stakescrounger)

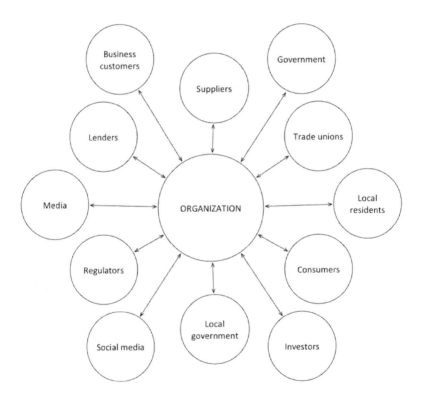

Although they have different connotations, some of the terms that are used can be more or less interchangeable. Stakeholders equals publics equals audiences. Common sense would say that, "Stakeholders are important to public relations professionals because these groups are essentially the 'public' in public relations. Stakeholders, in essence, are the audiences for organizational messages."[49] In this respect, nothing has changed since the 1980s. "Seitel" included a similar diagram depicting twenty of the "most important" publics for a multinational.[50]

Stakeholder theory and diligent public relations people inflated a stream of bubbles. If a stakeholder is anyone who can affect the organization or is affected by it, the list of stakeholders could be very long and very broad. Freeman admitted that identifying stakeholders was the easy part. The task of managing relationships with those stakeholders would be "enormous." And stakeholders may disagree profoundly with each other. But idealists would say that the modern (excellent) organization simply has to shoulder that burden.

"Enormous" does not do justice to the size of the problem. Bernstein told the story of a *Financial Times* survey of business attitudes to corporate advertising. The survey asked firms whether the following were primary or secondary target groups: the entire adult population, the upper social grades, activists/opinion leaders, government and government agencies (national or international), business community, financial community, private investors/shareholders, suppliers, customers, employees (current and potential), students, local communities, the media, and others ("write in").[51] And that was in the 1980s, before stakeholderism became so pervasive in Western business.

For an international firm, the list of stakeholders could run to large numbers of institutions, groups and people in almost every country in the world. The stakeholders could be so numerous and diverse that the effective answer to the question, "Who is my stakeholder," would be "All of mankind." Taking a normative view and considering their businesses' environmental impact, some would need to regard even uncontacted peoples as stakeholders. It has been proposed that organizations should find "undiscovered" or "unknown but important stakeholders" who might be lurking in the undergrowth of social media. It has also been suggested that the non-human environment (trees, for example) should be considered for stakeholder status.[52] The prospect of imagining communication plans for the uncontacted or trees shows the absurd lengths to which descriptive and normative stakeholder theory may ultimately be driven.

In a stakeholder world, the difficulty of seeing the forest for the trees is greater than ever. The solution is communication strategy.

Analyzing stakeholders

Numerous attempts have been made to put forward a method of stakeholder analysis that would enable those unruly bubbles to be arranged in some order of priority. For example:

- Freeman looked at stakeholders potential effects on the corporation, dividing these effects into five categories: economic effects such as higher or lower sales; technological effects; political effects (regulation); social effects ("preconceptions of firm"): and managerial effects.[53]

- In the field of public relations, Grunig developed work on institution building in the third world that included an analysis of the linkages between institutions and their social background and put forward four categories of linkage. He suggested using these linkages as a checklist to plan programs.[54]

- The idea of using the analysis of linkages to find or select stakeholders was taken up, inter alia, by scholars who designed a four-step process for PR campaigns.[55] This process was to identify stakeholders using the linkages model, and then prioritize them according to their attributes, level of interest, and the plan.

- And, amid the competing ways of analyzing stakeholders, Andrew Friedman and Samantha Miles helpfully published a comprehensive survey of the state of the art. They attempted to unravel the many tangled strands of thinking about stakeholders that have developed, which they said was widely recognized to be a muddle.[56]

But it was all unnecessarily complicated because it neglected the imperative to focus on the stakeholders who really matter. The process to identify stakeholders (taking an instrumental view) needed only to be quite simple:

1. Understand how the business works.

2. Make a list of genuine stakeholders. But then...

3. Prioritize by separating the stakeholders into those which are essential and the rest. This can only be done once you understand the strategy, since the strategic (priority) stakeholders are defined the ones likely to affect the strategy for better or worse. If you don't know what your strategy is, it is impossible to pick the strategic stakeholders.

A comprehensive list of stakeholders for most businesses looks much the same — see fig. 12.3. But the strategic stakeholders of different firms are very different from each other.

Take the case of suppliers. For an infrastructure business developing a major project, suppliers could be a strategic stakeholder. Their ability to deliver elements of the project safely, on time, and on budget, could be critical to the success of the whole enterprise. But for a market leading food retailer, suppliers will not be a strategic stakeholder. In current market conditions, the retailer is in a dominant position. When the retailer says "jump," suppliers ask "how high?"

The strategic question is ultimately a relatively simple one: Who can influence whether the strategy can be achieved? Who are therefore the *strategic stakeholders?*

There has been a lot of sound and fury since SRI's original work but, taking an instrumental view, they were close to the mark half a century ago when they said that priority or primary stakeholders are "those groups without whose support the organization would cease to exist." Secondary stakeholders are those which are "not essential for its survival."[57]

Limited resources

Deciding who are the strategic (priority) stakeholders is important because resources, especially management time, are always limited. Given these limited resources, which stakeholders should the organization focus on?

Early in my career, I worked for a multinational giant in its community relations unit. This company had given money to good causes for decades. But instead of managing its donations program strategically, it behaved like an affluent, moderately generous citizen, strolling through a city. Encountering a variety of supplicants — homeless, drug addicts, charity muggers and so on — the mildly embarrassed, well-intentioned wanderer puts a small amount in every hat, tin or outstretched hand. The amount of money at stake at the multinational involved several zeros but was small change in the context of a multi-billion dollar income statement. My controversial proposal was, rather than giving a token sum to almost everyone who could be bothered to send in a begging letter, to try to focus on contributions that would achieve defined objectives in line with the firm's strategy. Even for this giant company, resources were limited, and it was important to use them as effectively as possible.

Much later, I joined BAA, the world's leading airport company, to work for Des Wilson, the virtuoso campaigner (see chapter 16). One of the most important lessons I learned from him was about the importance of focusing on the right target. The target of a campaign should be the people who have the decision-making power, and those who influence them. It sounds obvious, except that campaigners often try to woo everyone to their side, whereas to win you need to persuade the people who make or influence the decision. Money, time and effort spent on bystanders are largely wasted. (I learned the lesson in person but if you can find a copy of Wilson's "Campaigning: The A-Z of Public Advocacy," you can read more very useful tips.)[58]

Focus on the few...

To separate strategic stakeholders from the rest, it is not enough to know the type of business — it is necessary to understand the business strategy. A particular stakeholder could be essential to one strategy but not to another. As strategies change so do stakeholders. I. M. Jawahar and Gary McLaughlin proposed that an organization has different stakeholders at different stages of its life cycle.[59] Although a start-up, for example, will have different stakeholders (on an instrumental view) from a firm in decline, knowing where a firm is in its life cycle is not sufficient to predict its stakeholders. Identifying its stakeholders depends on the strategy, which is unique to each organization (although its strategy will naturally be influenced by where it is in its life cycle).

From an understanding of the overall corporate or business strategy it is possible to decide which stakeholders are in a position of critical power and influence — which are of decisive importance with respect to the desired outcomes. It is not only a question of how much power a stakeholder has but how much power a stakeholder has *in relation to the strategy*.

By considering their strategies, it has been possible to see that companies discussed in these pages have strategic (priority) stakeholders such as governments, regulators, shareholders, lenders and alliance partners. In each case, it is the not the whole class that is a strategic stakeholder but only those members of the class that wield power. In the case of governments, it is those that have the power to make laws, policies and decisions which have a major impact on the organization. In the case of shareholders, it is those large shareholders whose decision to buy, hold or sell ultimately settles who controls the organization.

Managing strategic stakeholders presents different problems depending on the numbers in the category. In most stakeholder categories, relatively small numbers of people have decision-making power. For example, a publicly quoted company may perhaps have a maximum of 20-30 more or less important large shareholders. At each shareholder, decisions about an investment are likely to be made or influenced by a handful of people including a chief investment officer or equivalent, fund managers and an analyst. The important shareholders may also be influenced by a small number of external analysts. Thus the total number of people involved in the shareholder category of strategic stakeholder is sufficiently small for management to know and communicate personally with all the key people.

Companies making and marketing consumer products, and retailers of all shapes and sizes, are examples of businesses for whom personal customers are likely to be strategically important, posing a different problem. A personal relationship is out of the question. What matters is the organization's focus on the consumer. Some, including Apple, have been so successful that consumers may experience the illusion of a personal relationship. (Those whose strategies dictate that local communities should be strategic stakeholders face a comparable problem.)

Consumers are not always strategically important though. For an oil major, the millions of consumers who buy its refined products are engaged in transactions with the corporation but they are not essential for its survival. These consumers' buying decisions are made largely on the basis of price and convenience. Brand loyalty is negligible. Even such a drastic and highly unlikely action by consumers as a boycott across a national market would have relatively little impact on the firm.

...and make them Allies

Having identified the strategic (priority) stakeholders, what should you do with them?

Identifying a strategic stakeholder as a potential ally or strategic partner does not mean that the relationship between organization and stakeholder needs to be one with warm personal feelings in either direction. Nor does it mean that the relationship needs to be equal. Nor does it mean that the parties' interests have to be identical. Nor, finally, does it mean that the organization should be completely open and transparent to the stakeholder.

Investor relations provides one model for this relationship. Providing large shareholders of a public company with inside information would both embarrass them and compromise their ability to trade in the shares, as well as being against the rules. However, there does need to be trust, and it means recognition that the support of the stakeholder is required to achieve the organization's objectives, which means converting the stakeholder into an ally in achieving its objectives. It may well mean persuasion.

The most effective communication strategy is focusing on strategic stakeholders (allies) – the Allies Strategy. This says that, once the organization has determined whose ultimate interest it should serve, it should decide and pursue its own strategy. Stakeholders should then be managed in the interests of the organization. The ones who matter are the strategic stakeholders, who need to be made allies. This is a winning strategy.

Key points
- It is widely accepted that organizations should be responsive to stakeholders but who are legitimate stakeholders and who are merely stakeseekers?
- Normative stakeholder theory provides no satisfactory guide to the allocation of resources between the competing demands of stakeholders.
- A strategic approach to stakeholders would be to focus on the strategic (priority) stakeholders — those whose support is required to achieve strategic objectives — and make them allies.

Alternative communication strategies

There are two alternatives to the Allies Strategy:

(a) Normative Stakeholder Strategy

Organizations still have the option of embracing normative stakeholder theory. This involves taking account of a mountain of scholarly work on stakeholder theory and analysis. You will need to employ specialist consultants who can grapple with this mountain. Your aim will be to work wholeheartedly to engage with all stakeholders with openness and transparency. (Remember to answer the questions they don't even ask — as one textbook advised in chapter 5.) There is no limit to the resources that may need to be devoted to this cause. But then, in normative stakeholder theory, you exist only to serve stakeholders. Good luck.

P.S. Your normative stakeholder strategy will make you an ideal target for activist investors.

(b) Pragmatic Reputation Strategy

A workable communication strategy for a business, following conventional advice, would be to adopt a pragmatic reputation strategy towards stakeholders that looks something like this:

- Set "serving stakeholders" as an objective. Publish the objective. There is no need to specify exactly who the stakeholders are. This can reap a rhetorical reward since at least some stakeholders will believe you are doing the Right Thing.

- Aim to Keep Everybody Happy. Happiness may be measured (very approximately) by a reasonable ranking in published reputation surveys. You will also need to avoid major reputation disasters. A chief reputation officer or vice president, stakeholder relations, could be employed to take care of these matters while the rest of the management team gets on with running the business.

- Engage actively with stakeholders on an issue-by-issue basis. When an issue is salient, you may decide to engage with groups that express interest in that issue.

- Deploy your communication apparatus by function, reporting to the chief reputation officer/VP stakeholder relations. In other words, assign a unit to "manage" each major category of stakeholder. These units may be called investor relations, government affairs, media relations and so on. The functional split is adjustable as pressures rise and fall from different categories of stakeholder.

Even though this communication strategy wastes resources and dissipates focus, it can be effective. It is close to what many successful firms actually do, particularly those who don't want to make waves, and who will not be named here. It is suitable for a CEO who believes in the Allies Strategy but is unwilling to come out of the closet.

In Summary

- Reputation has overtaken identity and image as a paradigm for business communication. Some see protecting and building reputation as the main goal of communication.
- Reputation is often considered and managed on a superficial level. Rankings usually measure popularity, which is almost irrelevant to a firm's standing with its relevant decision-makers.
- The concept of stakeholder is problematic and burdened with a lot of normative theory. The strategic decision is which groups (call them audiences, stakeholders or whatever) have the power to help or hinder the achievement of objectives.
- A winning strategy is to focus on making allies of these strategic stakeholders. A workable alternative is to seem to serve stakeholders while secretly pursuing an Allies Strategy.

References

[1] F. Scott Fitzgerald, *The Great Gatsby*, (London: The Folio Society, 1968), 76. Originally published 1925.

[2] Deloitte, *2014 Global Survey on Reputation Risk*, <http://www.deloitte.com/reputationrisksurvey>.

[3] Including PR textbooks: Cutlip & Center, *Effective Public Relations*, 1952; Cutlip, Center & Broom, *Effective Public Relations*, 1985; Seitel, *The Practice of Public Relations*, 1989; Grunig & Hunt, *Managing Public Relations*, 1984. Examples of communication texts with no index reference to reputation: Bettinghaus & Cody, *Persuasive Communication*, 1994; Denis McQuail, *Mass Communication Theory: An Introduction*, (London: Sage Publications Ltd, 1987); Tim O'Sullivan, John Hartley, Danny Saunders, Martin Montgomery & John Fiske, *Key Concepts in Communication and Cultural Studies*, 2nd edn., (London: Routledge, 1994); Stuart Price, *Communication Studies*, (Harlow, UK: Addison Wesley Longman Ltd, 1996).

[4] John W. Cook, 'Building an International Reputation,' in *Effective Corporate Relations: Applying Public Relations in Business and Industry*, ed. by Norman A. Hart, (London: McGraw-Hill, 1987), 114-124.

[5] *Encyclopaedia Britannica*, 14th edn., 1962. Eric Barnouw, (ed.), *International Encyclopedia of Communications*, (Oxford University Press, 1989).

[6] Sally Dibb, Lyndon Simkin, William M. Pride, & O. C. Ferrell, *Marketing Concepts and Strategies*, 2nd edn., (London: Houghton Mifflin, 1994), 215.

[7] David A. Whetten, 'Theory Development and the Study of Corporate Reputation,' *Corporate Reputation Review*, Vol. 1, No. 1, (1997), 27.

[8] Wally Olins, *Corporate Identity*, (London: Thames & Hudson, 1989), 7.

[9] Stephen Herskovitz & Malcolm Crystal, 'The Essential Brand Persona: Storytelling and Branding,' *Journal of Business Strategy*, Vol. 31, No. 3, (2010), 21-28.

[10] Mary Anne Moffitt, 'Corporate Image,' in *Encyclopedia of Public Relations*, ed. Heath, Vol. 1, 202.

[11] O'Sullivan et al, *Key Concepts in Communication and Cultural Studies*, 144.

[12] Boorstin, *The Image*, especially chapter 5.

[13] David Bernstein, *Company Image and Reality: A Critique of Corporate Communications*, (Eastbourne, UK: Holt, Rinehart and Winston, 1986), 11-14.

[14] Warren Newman, 'New Words for What We Do?' *Institute of Public Relations Journal*, October 1993.

[15] John Smythe, Colette Dorward & Jerome Reback, *Corporate Reputation: Managing the New Strategic Asset*, (London: Century Business, 1992), 6.

[16] 'The Responsibility,' *New York Times*, April 18, 1912.

[17] Gary Davies, Rosa Chun, Rui Vinhas da Silva & Stuart Roper, *Corporate Reputation and Competitiveness*, (London: Routledge, 2002).

[18] Grahame Dowling, 'Managing your Corporate Images,' *Industrial Marketing Management*, Vol. 15, No. 2, (1986), 109-116.

[19] Fombrun & Shanley, 'What's in a Name?'

[20] Charles J. Fombrun, *Reputation: Realizing Value from the Corporate Image*, (Harvard University Press, 1996).

[21] *Corporate Reputation Review*, Vol. 1, Nos. 1 & 2, (Summer/Fall 1997).

[22] Davies, Chun, da Silva & Roper, *Corporate Reputation and Competitiveness*, 58-73.

[23] Broom & Sha, *Cutlip and Center*; Newsom et al, *This is PR*; Seitel, *The Practice of Public Relations*; Wilcox & Cameron, *Public Relations*.

[24] Definition: Amy O'Connor, 'Reputation Management,' in *Encyclopedia of Public Relations*, ed. Heath, Vol. 2, 745-746. Dubious associations: F. E. Campbell, R. A. Herman & D. Noble, 'Con-

tradictions in Reputation Management,' *Journal of Communication Management*, Vol. 10, No. 2, (2006), 191-196.

25 James G. Hutton, Michael B. Goodman, Jill B. Alexander & Christina M. Genest, 'Reputation Management: The New Face of Corporate Public Relations?' *Public Relations Review*, Vol. 27 No. 3, (2001), 247-61.

26 Fombrun, *Reputation*, 6.

27 Fombrun, *Reputation*, 59-60.

28 Ogilvy, *Ogilvy on Advertising*, 117.

29 Charles J. Fombrun, 'Indices of Corporate Reputation: An Analysis of Media Rankings and Social Monitors' Ratings,' *Corporate Reputation Review*, Vol. 1, No. 4, (1998), 327-340.

30 Vito J. Racanelli, 'The World's Most Respected Companies,' *Barron's*, June 28, 2014. 'The World's Most Admired Companies,' *Fortune*, March 1, 2015.

31 Susan Adams, 'America's Most Reputable Companies, 2015,' *Forbes*, May 13, 2015.

32 Donald Lange, Peggy M. Lee & Ye Dai, 'Organizational Reputation: A Review,' *Journal of Management*, Vol. 37 No. 1, (January 2011), 153-184.

33 Martin, 'The Moving Target,' 257.

34 Walter Lippmann, *Public Opinion*, (New Brunswick, NJ: 1991), originally published 1922. John Dewey, *The Public and Its Problems*, (Chicago: Swallow Press, 1927).

35 Grunig & Hunt, *Managing Public Relations*, 148-161.

36 James E. Grunig, 'Situational Theory of Publics,' in *Encyclopedia of Public Relations*, ed. Heath, Vol. 2, 778-780.

37 *The Economist Style Guide*, (London: Profile Books Ltd, 2005), 70. Samantha Miles, 'Stakeholder: Essentially Contested or Just Confused?' *Journal of Business Ethics*, Vol. 108, No. 3, (2012), 285-298.

38 See for example Robert L. Heath, 'Telling a Story: A Narrative Approach to Communication During Crisis,' in *Responding to Crisis: A Rhetorical Approach to Crisis Communication*, ed. by Dan Pyle Millar & Robert L. Heath (Mahwah, NJ: Lawrence Erlbaum Associates, 2004), 167; and Boris Holzer, 'Turning Stakeseekers Into Stakeholders: A Political Coalition Perspective on the Politics of Stakeholder Influence,' *Business & Society*, vol. 47 no. 1, (2008), 50-67; although some even see corporations as stakeseekers: W. Timothy Coombs & Sherry J. Holladay, *Managing Corporate Social Responsibility: A Communication Approach*, (Chichester, UK: John Wiley & Sons Ltd, 2012), 78.

39 Thomas Donaldson & Lee E. Preston, 'The Stakeholder Theory of the Corporation: Concepts, evidence, and implications,' *The Academy of Management Review*, Vol. 20, No. 1 (January 1995), 65-91.

40 R. Edward Freeman, *Strategic Management: A Stakeholder Approach*, (Marshfield, MA: Pitman Publishing Inc., 1984).

41 Andrew L. Friedman & Samantha Miles, *Stakeholders: Theory and Practice*, (Oxford University Press, 2006), 25.

42 Freeman, *Strategic Management*, vi & 249.

43 Carl Botan & Vincent Hazleton (eds.), *Public Relations Theory*, Hillsdale, NJ: Lawrence Erlbaum Associates, 1989. Botan & Hazleton (eds.), *Public Relations Theory II*, 2006.

44 Samuel B. Graves & Sandra A. Waddock, 'Beyond Built to Last...: Stakeholder Relations in Built-to-Last Companies,' *Business and Society Review*, Vol. 105, No. 4, (2000), 393-418.

45 David Campbell & Tom Craig, *Organizations and the Business Environment*, (Oxford, UK: Elsevier Butterworth-Heinemann, 2005), 41.

46 Freeman, *Strategic Management*, 6-25.

47 Bernstein, *Company Image and Reality*, 99.

48 Cutlip & Center, *Effective Public Relations*, 1st edn., 87.

49 Robert R. Ulmer, Matthew W. Seeger & Timothy L. Sellnow, 'Stakeholder Theory,' in *Encyclopedia of Public Relations*, ed. Heath, Vol. 2, 809.

50 Seitel, *The Practice of Public Relations*, 12th edn., 11.

51 Bernstein, *Company Image and Reality*, 95.

52 Kristina Sedereviciute & Chiara Valentini, 'Towards a More Holistic Stakeholder Analysis Approach. Mapping Known and Undiscovered Stakeholders from Social Media,' *International*

Journal of Strategic Communication, Vol. 5, (2011) 221–239. Mark Starik, 'Should Trees Have Managerial Standing? Toward Stakeholder Status for Non-Human Nature,' *Journal of Business Ethics*, Vol. 14, No. 3, (1995) 207-217.

[53] Freeman, *Strategic Management*, 94 & 141-143.

[54] Milton J. Esman, 'The Elements of Institution Building,' in *Institution Building and Development*, ed. by Joseph W. Eaton (Beverly Hills, CA: Sage, 1972), 19-40. David M. Dozier & Larissa A. Grunig, 'The Organization of the Public Relations Function,' in *Excellence in Public Relations...*, ed. Grunig, 399-400.

[55] Brad L. Rawlins, Kenneth D. Plowman & Elizabeth Stohlton, 'A Comprehensive Approach to Prioritizing Stakeholders: A Synthesis of Stakeholder and Public Relations Literature on Identifying and Prioritizing Stakeholders for Strategic Management,' Institute for Public Relations, 2005, <http://hdl.handle.net/123456789/814>. See also Brad L. Rawlins, 'Prioritizing Stakeholders for Public Relations,' Gold Standard paper of the Commission on Public Relations Measurement & Evaluation, Institute for Public Relations, 2006; and Shannon A. Bowen, Brad Rawlins & Thomas Martin, *An Overview of the Public Relations Function*, (New York: Business Expert Press, LLC, 2010). In: Sybille Sachs, Edwin Rühli & Isabelle Kern, *Sustainable Success with Stakeholders: The Untapped Potential*, (Basingstoke, UK: Palgrave Macmillan, 2009), 95, Sachs et al drew a diagram with 16 bubbles and divided stakeholders into four groups: Benefit providers (provide a service to the business, like suppliers); Benefit receivers (receive a benefit from the business, like customers); Risk bearers (most obviously investors, although they give the example of someone living near an airport); and Risk providers (stakeholders who cause risks such as labor unions).

[56] Friedman & Miles, *Stakeholders*, vii.

[57] Max B. E. Clarkson, 'A Stakeholder Framework for Analyzing and Evaluating Corporate Social Performance,' *The Academy of Management Review*, Vol. 20, No. 1 (January, 1995), 92-117.

[58] Des Wilson with Leighton Andrews, *Campaigning: The A to Z of Public Advocacy*, (London: Hawksmere, 1993). See also John Egan & Des Wilson, *Private Business... Public Battleground: The Case for Twenty-First Century Stakeholder Companies*, (Basingstoke, UK: Palgrave, 2002).

[59] I. M. Jawahar & Gary L. McLaughlin, 'Toward a Descriptive Stakeholder Theory: An Organizational Life Cycle Approach,' *The Academy of Management Review*, Vol. 26, no. 3, (2001), 397-414.

PART III

Issues and Crises

In Part III

Communication strategies are plagued by friction (see chapter 11) in the same way as warfare. This friction takes the form of issues and crises. Chapter 12 stressed that the "overreaction" to crises urged by some experts is counter-productive unless there is a real, overwhelming crisis. The aim of part III is to provide anyone who wants an effective communication strategy with the guidance they need to negotiate crises and manage issues:

- Crisis orthodoxy is based to a large extent on the two paradigm cases from the 1980s involving Johnson & Johnson and Exxon. Chapter 13 questions whether, especially in relation to Exxon, the right lessons have been learned, and considers alternative approaches.
- At the end of chapter 13 is a summary of key points for crisis communication strategy.
- Chapters 14 and 15 examine the recent crises involving BP and Carnival, respectively, further developing the arguments of chapters 11 and 13.
- Chapter 16 reviews the development of a single issue over several decades, the provision of airport infrastructure for London. For much of this period, the airports were owned and operated by BAA plc, where the author served as director of corporate affairs.

CHAPTER 13

Crisis Paradigm: the long view

"What in water did Bloom, waterlover, drawer of water, watercarrier, returning to the range, admire?
... its infallibility as paradigm and paragon."
— James Joyce, "Ulysses"[1]

Exxon Valdez, a tanker carrying 55 million gallons of oil, ran aground in Prince William Sound, Alaska. It was March 24, 1989, at 2350. The weather was fine; the sea was calm. Oil started leaking and 11 million US gallons flowed into the sea.[2]

The *Exxon Valdez* accident and the poisoning of Tylenol capsules with cyanide are two cases from the 1980s that feature prominently in studies of crisis communication. They have been called: "Textbook Crises."[3] These cases came to be thought of as paradigms, exemplifying the wrong way and the right way, respectively, to handle a crisis.

The lessons from these paradigm cases form the basis of mainstream beliefs about crisis communication to this day. But some of the key lessons drawn were wrong.

After the *Valdez* accident, experts said Exxon's reputation would never recover. Now Exxon stands as well as a giant oil company possibly can in today's world. How was this achieved?

Tylenol

In September 1982, Extra-Strength Tylenol painkiller capsules on pharmacy shelves in Chicago were found to have been poisoned with cyanide.[4] A small number of unsuspecting victims died and there was widespread panic. Tests showed that the contamination was localized. Federal and local government, retailers, and the manufacturer, Johnson & Johnson, took action to warn consumers and health professionals and to withdraw Tylenol products from the market. Johnson & Johnson was seen to have been the victim of a crime and to have taken decisive action to prevent future problems. The product was re-launched with tamper-resistant packaging.

Johnson & Johnson was not criticized for having left unsealed products vulnerable to interference, standard practice up to that time, but instead gained unprecedented sympathy from the media and the public. *Time* magazine, awarding bouquets and brickbats for the 1980s, described Johnson & Johnson's as: "Most Applauded Corporate Response to a Disaster." It said that the chairman's "frank, decisive response won back customer loyalty, and is now a textbook case in public relations."

Exxon Valdez

The second textbook case was the *Exxon Valdez* oil spill. As in the *Titanic* disaster, it was a case of a ship being steered into a sharp object. The only actors in the event were the crew, the company that owned, operated and had its name on the ship and, peripherally, the US Coast Guard. The company was Exxon Corporation, through its wholly owned subsidiary, Exxon Shipping Company. The incident was quickly identified as "the largest single tanker spill in United States history," although it was still relatively small by world standards.[5] (A Gulf of Mexico spill, from the Ixtoc-1 well in 1979, had already leaked more than 3 million barrels of oil.)

Investigation by the National Transportation Safety Board, published a year and a half after the accident, established that although the proximate cause was incorrect steering while maneuvering to avoid icebergs, there were a number of contributory factors: The ship's captain had been drinking and his "judgment was impaired by alcohol during the critical period." (In March 1990, the captain was acquitted of serious charges but convicted of "negligently discharging oil.")[6] The crew was too small and not sufficiently rested — Exxon Shipping was criticized for failing to provide a competent and alert crew. The Coast Guard was criticized for not monitoring the position of ships moving through the sound using its radars. If the Coast Guard had operated like air traffic control for aircraft, the ship might have been warned that she was heading for disaster.

Damaging media portrayal

At first it was assumed that: "Exxon had enough staff and crisis 'know-how' to handle the spill swiftly and professionally. Such assumptions turned out to be unsound."[7] Cleaning up the spilt oil began badly and proved to be difficult and time-consuming. Critics ran amok:

- Damaging media revelations followed each other in quick succession. That the ship's captain had been drinking. That the man at the wheel was not fully qualified for the task. That clean-up equipment was not readily available. That poor weather made progress difficult. "Each day brought another slap at Exxon's image... By the time another Exxon tanker rendezvoused with the *Valdez* and started pumping out the oil, more than 240,000 barrels had poured into the waters."[8]

- The oil spill became an environmental disaster in the Sound. Many thousands of seabirds and other wildlife perished. Fisheries were badly damaged. Businesses and livelihoods that depended on the sea and coastline were interrupted.

- Exxon did not handle media inquiries corporately but referred them to Exxon Shipping. The parent company had "no comment" for more than a week.[9] Exxon placed an apologetic advertisement in 166 newspapers but not until ten days after the accident, and without accepting responsibility for the damage.[10]

- Exxon's chairman, Lawrence G. Rawl, said nothing for two days and stayed in New York.[11] At first, he "had no time" for media interviews. When he did eventually give a television interview and was asked about the clean-up plan, he said: "It is not the role of the chairman of a large worldwide corporation to read every technical plan." He only visited Alaska two weeks after the accident.[12]

- Exxon Shipping set up a media center in Valdez. Some said that Valdez was too remote and others that the media center should have been at the site of the accident, regardless of the practical difficulties.[13] (I can vouch for the difficulties, having been on a press trip to Valdez that was canceled because of bad weather.) The limited phone lines to Valdez jammed.[14] "Within hours of becoming aware of the nature of the crisis, Mr Rawl should have established a 24-hour crisis-management command center."[15] Other missing elements were a liaison office with government and a news center in New York.

- "Exxon management started... by making excuses."[16] They changed their story, blaming one after another the weather, the Coast Guard charts and the captain's drinking. They fired him.[17]

- When the Coast Guard asked the company for 5,000 workers to be deployed for the summer to clean up the beaches, Exxon refused.[18] (BP's Gulf of Mexico clean-up in 2010 employed ten times as many people. See chapter 14.)

In the court of public opinion, Exxon found itself in the dock. Having accidentally achieved the most disastrous oil spill in American history (at least until 2010), Exxon was accused of the worst public relations disaster, one that became a model for how not to handle crisis communications. "Probably no other company ever got a more damaging portrayal in the mass media."[19] The *Valdez* crisis was analyzed exhaustively and became the raw material for a body of theory and practical advice on crisis management. *Time* awarded its "Least Applauded" epithet for the 1980s to: "Exxon's tar-footed response to its desecration of Alaska's shoreline."[20] It brought Exxon extensive hostile media coverage and a customer boycott of this "polluter without equal."[21] The most stinging sign of public anger was the award by an Anchorage jury of punitive damages against Exxon of $5 billion. Experts examined the *Valdez* and Tylenol cases, contrasted them, and formulated advice on how to deal with a crisis.

Defenses

William Benoit has extensively analyzed the possible responses that could be made to criticism, that is, the "message options," calling his analysis "image restoration" or "image repair." He examined the way organizations respond to crises, taking *Exxon Valdez* as one of his examples. It is the most persuasive analysis of generic rhetorical defensive arguments and has been described as "the definitive work on the strategies used by apologists."[22]

Benoit theorized that there are two elements to the crisis event. First, something happened that was seen as offensive, reprehensible or undesirable. Second, "the accused must be held responsible for the occurrence of that reprehensible act by the relevant audience."[23] In the case of *Exxon Valdez*, the accident was the offensive event and Exxon was widely believed to be responsible for it.

However, it is difficult to generalize from Benoit's message options because the options are narrowed down by the facts of the case. For example, you can only blame someone else if there is a credible fall guy. It only makes sense to use what he called "minimization," which is the argument that the harm has been exaggerated, where the issue is consequences rather than immediate harm. BP used this defense in the Gulf of Mexico oil spill, arguing that the damage to the environment had been exaggerated (see chapter 14). The argument fails when the issue is the immediate impact of an accident.

And whether the communication strategy is likely to be successful does not depend on any intrinsic qualities of the defense but on the circumstances and on how well the argument is made. For example, Benoit said that Exxon used the defense of denial, attempting to shift the blame for the accident to the captain and for delay in cleaning up the oil spill to the public authorities and agencies. The fact that such a defense was not successful in this case does not prove that it is a poor defense. See chapter 15.

Key points
- The Exxon Valdez accident and the Tylenol poisoning became paradigm cases, providing lessons that still form the basis of mainstream crisis communication today.
- William Benoit made an important contribution to crisis thinking through an analysis of possible responses to criticism that he called "image restoration" or "image repair."

Lessons revisited

The basics of crisis communication are broadly agreed and can be consulted in a slew of crisis manuals.[24] There is also a consensus about strategy in the crisis industry, to which theorists, most crisis experts and public relations academics subscribe. This consensus has been summarized in recent works by Kathleen Fearn-Banks and by Timothy Sellnow and Matthew Seeger.[25]

The paradigm cases live on. For years, "Seitel" allocated space to *Exxon Valdez*, including a page of "Lessons of *Valdez*." Other manuals contain similar lessons.[26] Some of these were uncontentious precepts such as obtaining support from independent third parties, keeping employees informed and centralizing communications with a single point person.

However, there is some dissent from this consensus from the practical side of crisis communications — those whose job is getting the situation under control and the organization back on track, rather than researching and commenting. But the hands-on crisis managers have received relatively little attention.[27]

And on five key conclusions drawn from the paradigm cases, the experts drew conclusions that this chapter will now dispute:

- The organization should immediately apologize and take responsibility for what happened. (Benoit's "mortification.")
- The boss should immediately go and take charge on the spot.
- Public relations considerations should come before legal considerations.
- The organization should be open, transparent and, using the slogan discussed in chapter 5, "Tell it all, tell it now."
- By following in the footsteps of Johnson & Johnson, you can not only survive a crisis but even emerge from it stronger than before.

(1) Apologize and take responsibility?

To apologize and take responsibility or not, that is the question. Crisis communication experts believe that apologizing and taking responsibility is both "the right thing to do" for the organization that owns the crisis and an action that takes the sting out of it. But as Eric Dezenhall commented: "All of these PR chestnuts... about apologizing and contrition, there is very, very weak data to show these clichés bear out in reality."[28]

The consensus view dates back at least to *Exxon Valdez*, when its boss was said to have been arrogant. "He showed no emotion over the enormous environmental disaster and offered no apologies."[29] The right response, according to James Lukaszewski, was: "Contrition. The verbalization of regret, empathy, sympathy and even embarrassment."[30] This is said to help the organization because "Apologies and/or expressions of regret... give a human face to the organization and occasionally soften demands."[31]

This is a Big Ask for the embattled CEO and board facing the crisis. In a clear-cut case, where the action of a business caused the crisis, it may be not only the right course but the only course. But often the position is not clear cut.

The Snowden case

Take the case of Edward Snowden. No-one was killed — at least not directly — and the environment was unaffected but, in its way, the Snowden affair was as big a crisis as Tylenol or *Exxon Valdez*. At various times in 2013, confidential information was published about NSA surveillance programs that had been provided by Edward Snowden.

Snowden was employed by the CIA until 2009. After that he was employed by Dell and, for a few months in 2013, by Booz Allen Hamilton. While Snowden was with Dell and Booz Allen he accessed and downloaded NSA files. There is no suggestion in what follows that either firm was in any way to blame. That is precisely the point.

The *New York Times* asked: "Why did Booz Allen assign a 29-year-old with scant experience to a sensitive NSA site in Hawaii, where he was left loosely supervised as he downloaded highly classified documents about the government's monitoring of internet and telephone communications?"[32] But how should Dell and Booz have responded?

Neither company followed the standard crisis communication advice to apologize and take responsibility. Instead, they played it down and said little. Booz Allen, Snowden's employer at the time the leaks came to light, issued a statement on June 11, 2013, that said: "Booz Allen can confirm that Edward Snowden, 29, was an employee of our firm for less than 3 months... Snowden... was terminated June 10, 2013, for violations of the firm's code of ethics and firm policy. News reports that this individual has claimed to have leaked classified information are shocking, and if accurate, this action represents a grave violation of the code of conduct and core values of our firm..."[33] Its 2013 annual report, issued June 21, 2013, made no mention of the issue. Nor did its next results announcement, issued July 31, 2013. Booz Allen had nothing to say to the media. For example, when the *New York Times* profiled Mike McConnell, vice-chairman of Booz Allen and former director of national intelligence, it said that McConnell had declined to be interviewed.

It emerged that most of the time Snowden was obtaining secrets that would be leaked, he was working for Dell rather than

Booz Allen. A Dell spokesman told *Reuters* that he would not comment on any aspect of Snowden's employment. He added that its customer had asked Dell not to talk about him. Dell issued no statement.

Booz Allen and Dell neither apologized nor took the blame. Since the two companies presumably did not believe that the crisis was their fault, why should they apologize and take responsibility for it? By keeping such a low profile in the media, the two companies largely avoided being linked to the Snowden affair. They were not seen to be to blame. Crisis averted without apology.

But are you sorry?

Like Booz Allen and Dell in the Snowden affair, a business (or a citizen) is entitled to ask why, if it does not believe it is at fault, it should take the blame. And why indeed, if it is not at fault, should it be condemned?

Nevertheless, organizations that don't believe they are at fault often face a practical problem. What happens when a journalist asks them if they are sorry? This is particularly awkward in front of TV cameras. Lawyers will advise clients to say nothing that amounts to an admission of guilt. But saying nothing at all looks uncaring and may provoke a hostile popular reaction. (It is not legally necessary to say nothing, though it is advisable to avoid apologizing in terms that admit guilt.)[34] The media know this and often play a cynical role, exploiting the increasing appetite of the mass audience (the mob) for emotion in news (see chapter 1). It is tempting for them to stage a sentimental drama in which a company and its leaders are cast as the villains who have put customers or bystanders in danger (or extreme discomfort in the case of a cruise ship whose facilities have broken down — see chapter 15). When something goes wrong, these villains sometimes fail to show remorse. Thus a business that may not have done anything wrong can find itself demonized.

The best way to handle the "Are you sorry?" problem is by separating this ambiguous question into two parts, blame and sympathy. First, do you accept the blame for this? And second, do you sympathize with the victims? This enables the interviewee to avoid taking the blame but not by backing away or shutting down. Instead, using more emotional language, the question — "Are you sorry" — can be answered with "We are heartbroken" or "We are devastated." The interviewee may go on to talk with feeling about the unbearable sight of so many people suffering or whatever.

The point of this public expression of sympathy is to convince the audience that the speaker shares their feelings. This is not suggested as a cynical approach: in tragic circumstances, the interviewee should genuinely feel the appropriate emotions. This approach is just to give public expression to emotions that, if it were not for the unfortunate turn toward public sentimentality, many of us probably feel would be better expressed person to person.[35]

Expressing sympathy is one aspect of the humane behavior that is required if the organization is not to be seen (or revealed) as brutal. That may need to take the form of action as well as words. Lukaszewski strongly recommends helping any victims, and also people who may be affected indirectly, and communicating with them personally. "Humane words and deeds from the start" are likely to be well received.[36] In a crisis there is likely to be extensive mass and social media attention, in which frenzied, irrational sentimentality often boils over. In such conditions, robotic communication and failure to help are the opposite of what is required. Indeed, they are likely to anger employees, investors and other strategic stakeholders as well as critics. Humane behavior toward vulnerable victims may stave off a crisis altogether.

(2) Where is the boss?

In the *Valdez* case, there appeared to be a leadership vacuum. No one disputes the need for leadership to lead but what exactly should leading mean in a crisis?

Exxon's management was criticized for appearing distant and uncaring. "Seitel" said: "In Exxon's case, from all reports, chairman Lawrence Rawl was involved with the Gulf of Valdez solutions every step of the way. But that's not how it appeared in public."[37] Most argued that Exxon's leader should have been on the spot. "The biggest mistake was that Exxon's chairman... sent a succession of lower-ranking executives to Alaska to deal with the spill instead of going there himself and taking control of the situation in a forceful, highly visible way."[38] "In the aftermath of disaster, no action demonstrates more a company's concern for what has happened than the top man or woman being seen to go to the site, to be seen to take personal charge of the aftermath..." and communicate that concern in person.[39]

Rawl's apparent passivity was compared unfavorably with the intercontinental leap made by Warren Anderson, chairman of Union Carbide, after its Bhopal plant exploded in 1984, killing thousands. "Within days of the disaster, Mr Anderson flew to India to demonstrate his involvement and concern."[40] "His trip at least showed corporate concern. When chairman Rawl explained that he 'had better things to do' than fly to Valdez, Exxon effectively lost the public relations battle."

But there surely needs to be a stronger reason for flying to the site than to be seen to be "doing something."[41] When Anderson arrived in India he was promptly put in jail. He was released but, 25 years later, the Indian authorities were still attempting to extradite him from the US, at the age of 88.[42] It was a farce, which was a great shame because the explosion was a tragedy. The gesture of flying to India may have shown concern but was no substitute for a comprehensive solution to the most egregious business disaster of the last four decades. It destroyed thousands of lives, ruined the company, and continues to fester to this day.

Steven Fink disagreed with other experts: "Mr Anderson's mad dash across the globe was by no means sound crisis management. Instead, it was a foolish, knee-jerk reaction which removed him from his essential management and communications responsibilities for nearly a week and landed him in jail."[43]

This warning that the company was leaderless when it needed leadership the most was prophetic for BP's Gulf of Mexico disaster in 2010, examined in chapter 14. And the question "where is the boss?" came to the fore once again with experts when *Costa Concordia* sank in 2012. This is the subject of chapter 15, which argues against the presumption that the boss must swoop.

(3) Lawyers vs. Reputation

Some public relations people indict lawyers for communication failures in a crisis. "Too many times, the lawyers get in the way with the result that the message 'We care' never gets delivered."[44]

The PR experts claim that protecting reputation is of supreme importance. According to this view, lawyers rarely understand the importance of public relations and try to prevent organizations doing what they ought to do to safeguard their reputations. Instead, those damn lawyers worry about legal issues. For example, Paul Argenti stated that: "the first rule of crisis communication is to admit your mistakes publicly. While this may drive your lawyers crazy, it will build tremendous goodwill in the court of public opinion."[45] Regester and Larkin said that: "whereas we will advocate telling it all, telling it fast and telling it truthfully, lawyers will often advocate saying nothing, doing nothing and admitting nothing."[46] They said that lawyes don't always realize the effect on their clients' reputation.

This effect on reputation is said to be worse than the legal consequences. In the case of *Exxon Valdez*, lawyers allegedly persuaded the company to say as little as possible to avoid compensation payments. And "it has been more or less conclusively proved that the financial damage to Exxon's reputation was worse than any amount of compensation that could ever be imposed."[47] In fact, the opposite has been proved, as shown below.

Legal consequences are not to be dismissed lightly. Apart from financial damage, legal consequences could jeopardize the survival of the organization and the liberty of its executives. And directors considering their fiduciary responsibilities are likely to give more weight to the tangible legal risks than the intangible reputation risks.

Regester and Larkin went on to say that the lawyer's role is to protect the company, specifically against prosecution, against civil liabilities, and against damage to its status with regulators.[48] But what is the job of the communications director if not to protect the company? There should be considerable overlap between what legal counsel is trying to protect and what public relations is trying to protect.

Hostility between lawyers and public relations people is likely to be at its height when they are hired from outside at the moment of crisis. Confrontation between advisers in a crisis is not helpful but new hires may never have met before the crisis and have a short time to make an impact. The client is best served by a team of advisers working together to provide the best solutions. But what the client sometimes gets is a verbal brawl between advisers who are high on testosterone or adrenaline and desperate to impress.

The ideal set-up is a management team that includes a legal counsel and communications director who have developed a good working relationship before a crisis happens. The legal counsel should understand the communication dimension; the communications director should understand the legal dimension. Such an arrangement with my colleague, Greg McMahon, MyTravel's outstandingly able company secretary and legal director, helped the MyTravel Group to focus on the successful resolution of numerous issues.

(4) Tell It All, Tell It Now?

According to experts, "Exxon had been parsimonious and inaccurate with the information it gave out to the media,"[49] whereas they should have told it all, fast.[50] Earlier chapters have expressed misgivings about "tell it all, tell it now." It comes perilously close to advice to make a full confession and plead guilty. (See chapter 5.)

Any time someone bungles a crisis with a response that does not address the issues or give the accused's side of the story, experts condemn them for failing to tell it all, fast. It is basic crisis management to issue a statement without delay (including material on social media). But that is not the same thing as telling it all. Instead of telling it all, there are two essential actions:

- ACHIEVE EMPATHY. When a crisis hits, according to Grunig's situational theory of publics (see chapter 12), it calls into being a public. The new public is composed of those whose interests are affected by it. The organization also needs to remind itself who are its strategic (priority) stakeholders. This may be modified by a crisis to include some or all of those in the new crisis public. If one of the strategic stakeholders is consumers or another public composed of private citizens, there needs to be a populist crisis response, pitched at the level of Facebook Folks. (In the 2010s, "Facebook Folks" seems like a fair replacement for bellwethers such as the anthropologists' Middletown, Peoria, and the man on the Clapham omnibus or the Bondi tram.) This means hitting the right emotional note as well as dealing in facts. It may mean making an appropriate gesture that is commercially irrelevant but will reduce tension.

- TELL THE STORY. This is a situation in which the organization must provide its own narrative. It should include elements of the existing strategic narrative (chapter 9) — history, strategy and social purpose — as well as the immediate problem. And it does not necessarily need to reveal all but it does need to be future-proof as far as possible. Even a relatively small crisis sometimes takes several years to play out. Parties affected by the crisis (or who say they have been affected) may be persuaded by lawyers to make claims long after initial interest has died down. The initial narrative needs to be written with an eye to this scenario.

(5) The cure for crisis?

The belief or assumption that good crisis management can "cure" the problem is pervasive but unrealistic. The myth is that it is possible to have a "good" crisis, if only you follow the example of Johnson & Johnson. Yet Johnson & Johnson's problem was relatively benign since the company did not have to defend itself or take responsibility for any wrongdoing. The company's "canonization" was based on misconceptions about the facts.[51]

It seems clear that the most important factor determining the outcome of a crisis for the organization is who was to blame. Or rather, who was seen to be to blame. "The 'paradigm cases' [Tylenol and *Exxon Valdez*]... had everything to do with the corporation's 'control' of the crisis or lack thereof... Exxon's perceived gross negligence ruled out a victim's stance."[52] "A company's role as either perpetrator or victim in a crisis is the distinction upon which public perception often hinges. The general public's attitude toward the company is more likely to be negative for crises that could have been avoided."[53]

Key points
- This chapter questioned five tenets of crisis communication orthodoxy. Contrary to those tenets:
- Don't automatically apologize and take responsibility.
- The boss should not necessarily rush to take charge on the spot.
- Legal considerations may outweigh public relations considerations.
- Tell your story rather than aiming to reveal all for its own sake.
- Blame is the main determinant of crisis outcomes, not PR.
- See end of chapter 13 for key points of crisis communication strategy.

Irreparable damage?

Was Exxon's reputation really damaged irreparably?

The civil case against Exxon reached a conclusion in 1994, five years after *Valdez*, when a jury awarded punitive damages of $5 billion.[54] This was the second-largest award ever made and the largest in an environmental case. It was the equivalent of a year's profits pre-*Valdez*.

Exxon doggedly fought its way through the courts to overturn the award. Among its arguments was that it was a principle of maritime law that the owner of a ship should not suffer punitive damages for the autonomous actions of the captain.[55] In

2001, an appeals court said that the award was excessive.[56] An appeals panel reduced the award to $2.5 billion in 2006.[57] In the end, in 2008, the Supreme Court reduced the award to $507 million, the same figure as Exxon had paid in compensation to local people for damage caused. Exxon also bore the cost of cleaning up the oil and said it had spent $3.4 billion.[58]

Exxon's management style, including its approach to communication, was very different from Mobil's (see chapter 10). Exxon was confident and assertive in private but relatively quiet in public. It lobbied the US government but modestly and, if possible, under the umbrellas of industry alliances.[59] For example, when Chevron, Mobil and Texaco publicly called for a change in American policy in the Middle East at the height of the oil crisis, Exxon said nothing.[60] Aside from its gas stations, Exxon was largely invisible to the general public, although it also had its name on the ship that seriously contaminated the Exxon brand.

In the immediate aftermath of *Valdez*, some believed that Exxon was doomed. "Exxon's responses have been laced with references to the minimal impact on the bottom line to reassure the financial markets, and with efforts to minimize the company's legal liability. Neither of these strategies has succeeded."[61] Initially, Exxon dropped from 8th to 110th on *Fortune*'s Most Admired Companies list.[62] A review of American corporate reputations carried out in 2002 concluded that its reputation "continues to suffer from the public's long memory of the *Valdez* oil spill in Alaska."[63] And some believed that the company continued to drag around the reputational baggage from the *Valdez* disaster like an immense ball and chain. Looking back in 2003, Ruff and Aziz claimed (erroneously) that its share price never recovered and said: "This happened because the management was thought to be trying to keep a low profile... its public reputation has never fully recovered."[64]

The standard view of crisis communications experts is that reputational damage lasts and that the *Valdez* crisis brought into question Exxon's organizational legitimacy or "right to exist and conduct operations."[65]

This has also been called a license to operate or license to do business. Although such a license may only be a formal requirement in the case of regulated businesses, it can be argued that all businesses have an unwritten license to operate that depends on their alignment with basic norms of acceptable behavior by, say, not completely disregarding safety. (Commitment to safety should be a core element of any company's strategic narrative — see chapter 9.)

Resilience

William Benoit took a longer view of the affair: "There was relatively little that could be done to restore Exxon's image after the *Valdez* oil spill — other than wait until most consumers had forgotten the incident."[66]

And it was not only about consumers. Exxon's ratings in reputation surveys did not tell the whole story. What really mattered was the company's standing with the governments and investors who are its strategic (priority) stakeholders. In fact, the strategy of minimizing financial damage and legal liability, with a low public profile, did succeed for Exxon. Exxon largely shunned the limelight and quietly put its house in order. Once it had finished cleaning up, it concentrated on investing in safety to the point of becoming the industry paragon.[67] Its "Operations Integrity Management System" is considered the gold standard.

The most important development for Exxon since *Valdez* was its merger with Mobil. It was not a merger of equals. Exxon was roughly twice the size of Mobil and acquired the company from its shareholders with no hint of a reverse takeover. There was no suggestion now that Mobil, with its high profile and expensive reputation, needed to rescue a reclusive and reputationally-damaged Exxon. It was Mobil that sought a lifeline, not in any financial difficulty but up something of a strategic blind alley. It was Exxon's senior executives, led by Lee Raymond, president at the time of *Valdez*, who dominated the new management team and board. Two-thirds of the board and three-quarters of the officers came from Exxon.[68]

After the companies merged, judging by its actions, the combined company's communication strategy was more like that of old Exxon than old Mobil. ExxonMobil appointed one of Exxon's corporate lawyers, Ken Cohen, as its new vice-president, public and government affairs. Under Cohen, the company carried out opinion research to establish how various audiences regarded it and what they expected of it.[69] According to Steve Coll in "Private Empire: ExxonMobil and American Power," (winner of the *Financial Times*/Goldman Sachs Business Book of the Year for 2012), this research "sought to map the ways in which ExxonMobil was hated." Half the total audience linked the company primarily with *Valdez*.[70] Its overall reputation was relatively poor. Although the company had greatly improved safety performance, this was not widely appreciated. In short, there was a gap between outside perceptions, which were generally negative, and the internal view that was much more positive.

ExxonMobil took careful steps to close the gap between perceptions and the company's view of reality. This relied mainly on its "issues management" program and low-key campaigns to educated "informed influentials," leading figures in politics and the media, about the energy outlook for the next 25 years. It was consistent, credible communication without expecting either to convert the opposition or to modify its own position.[71] And when Rex Tillerson became CEO in 2006, he reviewed the company's policy stance and did not adopt his predecessor's personal style, said by Coll to have been abrasive.[72]

Cohen inherited a communications function unfairly alleged to have a "media strategy [that] was to say No Comment in fifty different languages."[73] ExxonMobil recognized that a company of its size could not pass unnoticed and cautiously developed its relations with the media but this was still not a company seeking a high media profile, and with good reason. "Exxon knew that for an oil company, the best PR is to receive no attention at all."[74]

Mobil's advertorials were reduced and eventually shelved. Instead, there is a blog on the ExxonMobil website, "Perspectives," under the byline of Ken Cohen. There are three important differences between the advertorials and the blog as ways of expressing the company's views:

- The blog posts are much less strident than Mobil's ads.
- Whereas Mobil's ads dealt with an eclectic range of subjects, the blog is focused on ExxonMobil's core public policy issues.

- And whereas Mobil's ads were an unavoidable presence in the newspaper, no-one sees the blog unless they seek it out. Anyone can read the blog but it has a hidden target, those influential people in government and the media whom the company considers most vital to its interests.[75]

Engagement on the company's terms

ExxonMobil's new communication strategy was more engaged than Exxon's had been but the engagement was still on the company's terms — a targeted profile. Tillerson commented on the company's approach in a speech: "Successful engagement requires a patient, long-term focus... Effective engagement also demands consistency," in the sense of consistently reliable facts, figures and analysis about energy. "Most important, engagement efforts should affirm the guiding principles that lead to the most competitive and effective energy policies..." that is, the principles supported by the company. He also spoke of conveying "the hard truths to policymakers about the costs of ill-informed or ill-advised government interventions."[76]

This engagement was not two-way symmetric communication, the type of dialog that involved business changing to accommodate to society, since "Nothing inside the company has changed."[77] This was ExxonMobil's rhetorical response to the question of organizational legitimacy. And it has a strong "making the world a better place" narrative:

> "We help provide energy that is fundamental to improving the lives of billions of people around the world. Access to energy underpins human comfort, mobility, economic prosperity and social progress. It touches nearly every aspect of modern life."[78]

It was hardly "tell it all." Compared with the old Exxon, ExxonMobil's communications have been much more vigorous, as its capable handling of a relatively minor oil pipeline spill in Montana in 2011 showed. But it was interesting that ExxonMobil still did not send the boss to the scene. Its spokesman was the president of its Pipeline Company. ExxonMobil has been more communicative than Exxon but a lot less high profile than Mobil. Its communications have been research-based, disciplined and organized around issues. Above all, its communications have been focused on what mattered most to ExxonMobil, namely American and foreign government decisions about taxation, regulation, exploration licenses and energy policy, and relations with its strategic stakeholders.

Results

ExxonMobil's patient, low-key communication strategy may be judged by its results. At the time of the accident, Exxon was the world's largest oil company. A quarter-century later, it is still the world's largest oil company.

The shadow of *Valdez* does not seem to have affected the company's long-term performance.[79] In the year ending December 31, 2013, the company's net income was $32.6 billion. (The last financial year before the price of oil plummeted.) It was a relatively poor year but profits were still nearly seven times the year before *Valdez* of $4.8 billion. Dividends per share were increased for the 31st year running and the company said its dividends had increased faster than the S&P 500 index over the same period. It claimed that its total shareholder return was above-average for both the S&P 500 and the industry over ten and twenty years, and that its return on capital employed of 17% led its peer group.[80]

In 1988, Exxon's sales of $76.4 billion made it America's second largest corporation, behind General Motors, according to Fortune.[81] In 2013, ExxonMobil was in second place, with sales of $449.9 billion, now behind Wal-Mart, but it was in first place by profits, ahead of Apple.

ExxonMobil came in at number 25 on *Fortune*'s Most Admired Companies list in 2013. It was the only oil company in the top 50.[82] In June 2014, institutional investors voted ExxonMobil into 14th place in the "World's Most Respected Company" survey, with only 5% saying they "don't respect" the company (*Barron's*.)[83] In some circles at least, ExxonMobil's reputation has recovered quite well from the *Valdez* disaster.

The memory of *Valdez* lingers, and "ExxonMobil is still unlikely to win any popularity contests in the environment community,"[84] along with the rest of Big Oil. However, ExxonMobil's "obsessive attention to safety" has been widely recognized, especially at the time of the 2010 Gulf of Mexico oil spill.[85]

How much does its reputation at large matter anyway? It would matter if one of the company's key performance indicators was its popularity with environmentalists. By the usual success criteria for major oil companies, it does not matter. The key government and financial audiences have a different, much more positive view of the company and that is what matters. Sellnow and Seeger still maintain that ExxonMobil did not fully regain its legitimacy after the crisis, although it continued to prosper. They put its prosperity down to its "global prominence in fulfilling the world's need for oil." Thus it is playing a vital role. It is making the world a better place. They said that Exxon may have defied the "theories' predication" about the dire consequences of a loss of legitimacy but that exceptions are rare.[86] The exceptions are mounting up.

Key points
- Critics said that Exxon was damaged irreparably by the Exxon Valdez crisis and the way it was handled but in fact the company thrived.
- ExxonMobil's communication strategy is quite unlike the high profile advocacy strategy of Mobil, discussed in chapter 10. It has wisely sought a targeted profile and focused on its strategic (priority) stakeholders, with a strong "making the world a better place" narrative.
- Today widely respected and immensely strong, ExxonMobil is a good example of resilience.

Key Points of Crisis Communication Strategy

1. Before going into full-blown crisis response mode, be sure it is really a crisis (a sudden event with an overwhelming impact). If the situation can be calmed down, calm it down. See chapter 11.

2. If it *is* a crisis, respond quickly and vigorously, using your crisis plan as a contingency plan. Follow Clausewitz and be flexible. (Chapter 11).

3. Select someone well-qualified to speak for the organization. Make sure whoever speaks is not only fully briefed but qualified and ready, both mentally and physically. There are good reasons not to pick the CEO. (Chapters 13, 14 and 15).

4. Express sympathy for victims, with feeling, and take responsibility for putting things right as appropriate, but don't take the blame unless the crisis is your fault. (Chapter 13).

5. Don't aim to tell the whole truth as a point of principle. Do give your version of the facts, in the context of your strategic narrative, and explain what is not currently known. (Chapter 13).

6. Don't jeopardize your legal position for the sake of looking good. Ensure legal and communication executives and advisers are working together, not struggling for the upper hand. (Chapters 13 and 14).

7. Even in a crisis, when the media clamor for every ounce and every second of your attention, remember to focus on your strategic (priority) stakeholders (including those directly affected by the crisis). (Chapters 12 and 13).

8. When a crisis hits, it is pandemonium. Doomsayers will predict the End. Many good companies are living proof that, even when a crisis is not handled particularly well, time and sound management heal. The resilient can survive and prosper. (Chapters 13, 14 and 15).

9. Remember that communication can't solve or cure a crisis, although poor communication can make it worse. (Chapters 13 and 14).

10. Although crises are less common than crisis experts sometimes make out, prepare for the possibility that you will face one. As part of your crisis planning:

   • Cover the logistics thoroughly, including emergency communication channels and social media capability.

   • Do risk management but don't let this lull you into complacency, and retain flexibility. Risk management cannot prevent all crises. (Chapter 11).

   • Detoxify your corporate and branding structure to limit the damage to your organization caused by operating incidents. (Chapter 15).

   • Make ready your strategic narrative, including top priority for safety. (Chapter 9).

In Summary

- Contrary to some of the lessons usually drawn from the crisis paradigm cases of Tylenol and *Exxon Valdez* in the 1980s:
  a) It is not always wise to apologize and take responsibility.
  b) The boss should not necessarily go and take charge.
  c) Legal considerations may be more important than PR.
  d) Instead of telling it all, fast, it is important to hit the right note with strategic stakeholders and tell the right story.
  e) While Johnson & Johnson handled its Tylenol crisis well, the main reason it fared better than Exxon was that one was blamed and the other was not.

- Critics prophesied Exxon's doom. But, in the succeeding years, the company patiently focused on its core issues and strategic stakeholders. ExxonMobil today is an immensely strong company in an unpopular but essential industry. It is justly respected by those who matter most to it.

References

[1] Joyce, *Ulysses*, 628-9.

[2] Sheila McNulty, 'Exxon Valdez Fine Cut by US Supreme Court,' *Financial Times*, June 26, 2008.

[3] Kathleen Fearn-Banks, *Crisis Management: A Casebook Approach*, (New York: Routledge, 2011), 90-109.

[4] '5 Die After Taking Tylenol Believed to Contain Cyanide,' *New York Times*, October 1, 1982.

[5] Largest: Richard Golob, publisher of Golob's Oil Pollution Bulletin, quoted in 'Largest U.S. Tanker Spill Spews 270,000 Barrels of Oil Off Alaska,' *New York Times*, March 25, 1989. For league table see: 'The Gulf of Mexico Oil Spill: Black Storm Rising,' *The Economist*, May 6, 2010.

[6] John H. Cushman, Jr., 'Blame is Placed for Valdez spill,' *New York Times*, August 1, 1990. Lev, 'Hazelwood's Acquittal Clouds the Exxon Case.'

[7] Newsom et al, *This is PR*, 10th edn., 331.

[8] Claudia H. Deutsch, 'The Giant With a Black Eye,' *New York Times*, April 2, 1989.

[9] Regester & Larkin, *Risk Issues and Crisis Management in Public Relations: A Casebook of Best Practice*, (London: Kogan Page, 2008), 175.

[10] Advertisement: Seitel, *The Practice of Public Relations*, 8th edn., 170. Responsibility: Fearn-Banks, *Crisis Management*, 107.

[11] Newsom et al, *This is PR*, 331.

[12] Regester & Larkin, *Risk Issues and Crisis Management*, 124-125.

[13] Fearn-Banks, *Crisis Management*, 104.

[14] Seitel, *The Practice of Public Relations*, 8th edn., 2001, 169.

[15] Steven Fink, 'Learning from Exxon: Prepare for Crisis, It's Part of Business,' *New York Times*, April 30, 1989.

[16] Wilcox et al, *Public Relations*, 7th edn., 185.

[17] Fearn-Banks, *Crisis Management*, 102.

[18] Steve Coll, *Private Empire: ExxonMobil and American Power*, (London: Allen Lane, 2012), 15.

[19] William J. Small, 'Exxon Valdez: How to Spend Billions and Still Get a Black Eye,' *Public Relations Review*, Vol. 17, No. 1, (Spring 1991), 9–25.

[20] 'Most of the Decade,' *Time*, January 1, 1990.

[21] Philip Shabecoff, 'Six Groups Urge Boycott of Exxon,' *New York Times*, May 3, 1989.

[22] Keith Hearit, *Crisis Management by Apology: Corporate Response to Allegations of Wrongdoing*, (Mahwah, NJ: Lawrence Erlbaum Associates, Inc., 2006), 83.

[23] William L. Benoit, *Accounts, Excuses, and Apologies: Image Repair Theory and Research*, 2nd edn, (Albany, NY: SUNY Press, 2015), 21.

[24] The main points of crisis preparation are to write and agree a crisis plan, to include who should be on the crisis management team, with what responsibilities; training for the relevant people, including running a crisis exercise to test the plan; logistics such as a base for the crisis team, external briefing materials, and arrangements for telecommunications, social media, and the internet; and how will the organization communication with key people outside the organization and who are they, sometimes called a *message action plan*. (This last point should already have been covered as part of the strategic task of deciding who are the strategic stakeholders and focusing on them.) The organization also needs to assess where it is most vulnerable, likely to be covered as part of a risk management exercise. See literature review carried out by Jennifer L. Borda and Susan Mackey-Kallis, 'A Model for Crisis Management,' in *Responding to Crisis*, Millar & Heath (eds.).

[25] Fearn-Banks, *Crisis Management: A Casebook Approach*; Timothy L. Sellnow & Matthew W. Seeger, *Theorizing Crisis Communication*, (Chichester, UK: John Wiley & Sons, Inc., 2013), 88.

[26] Seitel, *The Practice of Public Relations*, 8th edn., 215 - Tim Wallace.

[27] Four current books by hands-on crisis communication experts are:
(1) Eric Dezenhall & John Weber, *Damage Control: Why Everything You Know About Crisis Management Is Wrong*, (New York: Portfolio, 2007).
(2) Steven Fink, *Crisis Communications: The Definitive Guide to Managing the Message*, (New York: McGraw-Hill Education, 2013) - his latest book. The first came out in 1986 - Steven Fink, *Crisis Management: Planning for the Inevitable*, (New York: American Management Association, 1986).
(3) James E. Lukaszewski, *Lukaszewski on Crisis Communication: What Your CEO Needs to Know About Reputation Risk and Crisis Management*, (Brookfield, CT: Rothstein Associates, Inc., 2013). This was the most recent of various books.
(4) Regester & Larkin, *Risk Issues and Crisis Management; a Casebook of Best Practice*. First published in 1997.
In two of the leading PR textbooks (see chapter 3) there was no mention of Dezenhall & Weber, Fink, or Regester & Larkin. In "Wilcox," (p. 241), there was one reference to Fink but that was merely to a study of Fortune 500 crisis preparedness. In an article for O'Dwyer's, Seitel wrote: "Several years ago, some nitwit wrote a book in which he posited that companies shouldn't apologize when they're confronted by crisis." (Fraser P. Seitel, 'Seitel – Cutting Your Losses – Adidas and the Shackle Shoes,' June 22, 2012.) The article linked "nitwit wrote a book" to "Damage Control" by Dezenhall & Weber. However, the latest edition of "Seitel" quoted Lukaszewski and cited the books by Dezenhall & Weber and by Regester & Larkin in a much improved selection of further reading on crisis communications (p. 363). Fearn-Banks made no mention of the above four. Sellnow & Seeger mentioned only Fink.

[28] Eric Dezenhall in Bergin, 'BP PR Blunders Carry High Political Cost.'

[29] Regester & Larkin, *Risk Issues and Crisis Management*, 124-6.

[30] James E. Lukaszewski, 'Crisis Communication Management: Protecting and Enhancing Corporate Reputation and Identity,' in *Raising the Corporate Umbrella: Corporate Communications in the 21st Century*, ed. by Philip J. Kitchen and Don E. Schultz, (New York: Palgrave, 2001), 208.

[31] Wilcox et al, *Public Relations*, 7th edn., 337.

[32] David E. Sanger & Nicole Perlroth, 'After Profits, Defense Contractor Faces the Pitfalls of Cyber Security,' *New York Times*, June 15, 2013.

[33] 'Booz Allen Statement on Reports of Leaked Information,' Booz Allen Hamilton news release, June 11, 2013.

[34] Jeffrey S. Helmreich, 'Does Sorry Incriminate? Evidence, Harm and the Protection of Apology,' *Cornell Journal of Law and Public Policy*, Vol. 21, No. 3, (2012), 567-609.

[35] This public sympathy approach is also justified by the view of social interaction as a drama in which subjects are obliged to play particular roles. See Sellnow & Seeger, *Theorizing Crisis Communication*, 181.

[36] Lukaszewski, 'Crisis Communication Management,' 234.

[37] Seitel, *The Practice of Public Relations*, 8th edn., 215.

[38] John Holusha, 'Exxon's Public-Relations Problem,' *New York Times*, April 21, 1989.

[39] Regester & Larkin, *Risk Issues and Crisis Management*, 126.

[40] Holusha, 'Exxon's Public-Relations Problem.'

[41] Teresa L. Holder, 'Constructing Response During Uncertainty: Organizing for Crisis' in *Responding to Crisis*, Millar & Heath, 51-62.

[42] 'Company Defends Chief in Bhopal Disaster,' *Associated Press*, August 2, 2009.

[43] Steven Fink, 'Learning from Exxon.'

[44] Frank M. Corrado, *Getting the Word Out: How Managers Can Create Value with Communications*, (Homewood, IL: Business One Irwin, 1993), 163.

[45] Paul A. Argenti, 'The Crisis Communications Playbook: What GM's Mary Barra (and Every Leader) Needs to Know,' Harvard Business Review Blog Network, March 11, 2014.

[46] Regester & Larkin, *Risk Issues and Crisis Management*, 147.

[47] Peter Ruff & Khalid Aziz, *Managing Communications in a Crisis*, (Aldershot, UK: Gower Publishing, 2003), 79.

[48] Regester & Larkin, *Risk Issues and Crisis Management*, 154.

[49] Bergin, *Spills and Spin*, 161.

[50] Holder, 'Constructing Response During Uncertainty,' 58. Heather Yaxley, 'Risk, Issues and Crisis Management' in *The Public Relations Handbook*, ed. by Alison Theaker, (London: Routledge, 2012), 170. Corrado, *Getting the Word Out*, 160.

[51] David M. Berg & Stephen Robb, 'Crisis Management and the Paradigm Case' in *Rhetorical and Critical Approaches to Public Relations*, ed. by Elizabeth L. Toth & Robert L. Heath, (New York: Routledge, 1992).

[52] Susan Schultz Huxman, 'Exigencies, Explanations, and Executions: Toward a Dynamic Theory of the Crisis Communication Genre,' in *Responding to Crisis*, Millar & Heath, 287.

[53] Argenti, Corporate Communication, 212.

[54] Keith Schneider, 'Exxon Is Ordered to Pay $5 Billion for Alaska Spill,' *New York Times*, September 17, 1994.

[55] Linda Greenhouse, 'Justices to Hear Exxon's Challenge to Punitive Damages,' *New York Times*, October 30, 2007.

[56] Evelyn Nieves, 'Court Overturns Jury Award in '89 Exxon Valdez Spill,' *New York Times*, November 8, 2001.

[57] Felicity Barringer, 'Appeals Panel Cuts Award in Valdez Spill by Exxon,' *New York Times*, December 23, 2006.

[58] Adam Liptak, 'Damages Cut Against Exxon in Valdez Case,' *New York Times*, June 26, 2008.

[59] Coll, Private Empire, 73.

[60] Yergin, *The Prize*, 596.

[61] John D. Francis, 'A Look Beneath the Bottom Line,' *Public Relations Journal*, Vol. 46, No. 1, (January 1990).

[62] Wilcox et al, *Public Relations*, 7th edn., 185.

[63] Gardberg & Fombrun, 'For Better or Worse.'

[64] Ruff & Aziz, Managing Communications in a Crisis, 16 & 77-9.

[65] Maribeth S. Metzler, 'The Centrality of Organizational Legitimacy to Public Relations Practice,' in *Handbook of Public Relations*, ed. by Robert L. Heath, (Thousand Oaks, CA: Sage Publications, Inc., 2001), 321.

[66] William L. Benoit, 'Image Repair Discourse and Crisis Communication,' *Public Relations Review*, Vol. 23, No. 2, (1997), 177-186.

[67] Coll, Private Empire, 603-604.

[68] Richard A. Oppel Jr, 'When Corporate Worlds Collide: Exxon's Decision on Benefits,' *New York Times*, December 8, 1999.

[69] Cohen and his colleagues gave interviews that contributed to Seitel & Doorley, *Rethinking Reputation*, chapter 10 (published 2012).

[70] Coll, Private Empire, 219 & 33.

[71] Coll, Private Empire, 72, 213-218, & 301-312.

[72] Coll, Private Empire, 45.

[73] Coll, Private Empire, 214.

[74] Eric Dezenhall, 'Why BP Didn't Plan for This Crisis,' *Daily Beast*, June 9, 2010.

[75] Seitel & Doorley, *Rethinking Reputation*, chapter 10.

[76] Rex W. Tillerson, Taking on Great Questions: Expanding the Frontiers of Saudi Leadership, King Abdullah Petroleum Studies and Research Center Lunch Keynote, (Riyadh, Saudi Arabia: November 21, 2011).

[77] Suzanne McCarron, ExxonMobil general manager of public & government affairs, quoted in Seitel & Doorley, *Rethinking Reputation*.

[78] St. John, 'Conveying the Sense-Making Corporate Persona.'

[79] F. J. Marra, 'Crisis Communication Plans: Poor Predictors of Excellent Crisis Public Relations,' *Public Relations Review*, Vol. 24, No. 4, (1998), 464.

[80] ExxonMobil Corporation, Summary Annual Report 2013, February 1, 2014.

[81] 'Fortune 500,' *Fortune*, <http://money.cnn.com/magazines/fortune/fortune500/?iid=F500_lp_header>.

[82] 'World's Most Admired Companies,' *Fortune*, March 18, 2013.

[83] Vito J. Racanelli, 'The World's Most Respected Companies,' *Barron's*, June 28, 2014.

[84] 'Profile of Ken Cohen,' The Influence 100, <http://theinfluence100.com/ken-cohen>.

[85] Jad Mouawad, 'New Culture of Caution at Exxon After Valdez,' *New York Times*, July 12, 2010.

[86] Sellnow & Seeger, *Theorizing Crisis Communication*, 91.

CHAPTER 14

BP's Incurable Crisis Misdiagnosed as PR

"For BP Oil Spill Is a Public Relations Catastrophe." — Ronald D. White, *Los Angeles Times*, April 30, 2010.

"The Gulf of Mexico Oil Spill Is Bad, But BP's PR Is Even Worse." — Jeremy Warner, *Daily Telegraph*, June 18, 2010.

The American oil spill record set by Exxon Valdez lasted 21 years, until a drilling rig exploded in the Gulf of Mexico in April 2010. When oil began to leak it became the worst kind of crisis — one that went on day after day, then week after week.

It was unclear exactly how the accident happened but BP, the majority owner of the oil well, soon came under enormous pressure to end the crisis.

In line with crisis management doctrine, BP's response to the accident was immediate, vigorous, and led by its CEO in person. And it was on a vast scale. This may have been the biggest ever clean-up, at its peak employing 48,000 people in five states, 6,885 vessels, and 125 aircraft.[1] But the leak could not be stopped quickly. With people outside the industry, who were not familiar with the science involved, this called BP's competence into question. BP was seen by them to have messed up with the original accident, with its attempts to the oil spill, and with its crisis communication.

Ultimately, the well was capped, cutting off both the flow of leaking oil and the waves of criticism breaking over BP. Government, victims and companies entered what promised to be a convoluted, expensive and long-lasting legal battle over the apportionment of blame and assessment of damages to be paid.

Quick to respond

Like the *Exxon Valdez* spill, the Gulf spill began with a single incident. On the evening of April 20, there was a blowout at the bottom of the sea on the *Deepwater Horizon* semisubmersible oil rig.[2] It was drilling for oil 41 miles off the coast of Louisiana. The blowout killed eleven workers and fire raged until the rig sank on the morning of April 22. The rig had been drilling in 5,000 feet of water, so it took an inspection by undersea robots on April 23 to discover that oil was leaking from the base of the well, at the point where it emerged from the seabed.

Whereas *Exxon Valdez* involved only one company, the destruction of the rig involved a total of eight different businesses. *Deepwater Horizon* was owned and operated by Transocean Ltd but the lease operator for Mississippi Canyon block 252 (also known as the Macondo prospect) was BP Exploration & Production, Inc., a subsidiary of BP p.l.c. Halliburton cemented the well. Cameron International designed and made the blowout preventer that failed to prevent the explosion. Weatherford US, L.P. made the float collar used in the well. And a Schlumberger subsidiary provided lubricating drilling fluid (known as mud) for the well and employed two of the workers who were killed. Finally, BP shared ownership of the lease with Anadarko Petroleum (25%) and Mitsui Offshore Exploration (10%).

The first announcement reporting the explosion was made by Transocean.[3] It said simply that there had been a fire and that Transocean and BP were caring for the crew and searching for missing crew members. Transocean provided brief updates later on April 21 and on April 22, reporting that the rig had sunk.

The April 22 announcement included wording to protect the company from legal claims or enforcement for forward-looking statements to investors. It was routine but seems ominous with the benefit of hindsight: "Statements regarding any future aspect of the incident on the *Deepwater Horizon*, the effects, results, investigation, damage assessment relating thereto mitigation of environmental impact, as well as any other statements that are not historical facts, are forward-looking statements that involve certain risks, uncertainties and assumptions…"[4] Transocean was already sensitive to the legal implications. BP immediately relayed the Transocean announcement[5] and issued its own release, offering full support "after fire caused Transocean's semisubmersible drilling rig *Deepwater Horizon* to be evacuated." Tony Hayward, BP's chief executive, was quoted: "Our concern and thoughts are with the rig personnel and their families. We are also very focused on providing every possible assistance in the effort to deal with the consequences of the incident."[6]

The first press reports included contributions from both Transocean and BP. The *New York Times* attributed information about the fate of the workers and the speed of the explosion to "an executive for Transocean, the company that owns the rig."[7] This report said any spill was minimal thanks to combustion, "'But that does have the potential to change,' said David Rainey, the vice-president in charge of the Gulf of Mexico exploration for BP, which is leasing the rig."

By its next announcement on April 22, BP had apparently decided to take charge of the crisis, already described as an oil spill, although the leak was not verified until the next day: "BP initiates response to Gulf of Mexico oil spill – April 22, 2010. BP today activated an extensive oil spill response… BP has also initiated a plan for the drilling of a relief well, if required…" The announcement gave details of a very substantial task force. "BP has mobilized a flotilla of vessels and resources that includes: - significant mechanical recovery capacity; - 32 spill response vessels including a large storage barge; - skimming capacity of more than 171,000 barrels per day, with more available if needed; - offshore storage capacity of 122,000 barrels and additional 175,000 barrels available and on standby; - supplies of more than 100,000 gallons of dispersants and four aircraft ready to spray dispersant to the spill, and the pre-approval of the US Coast Guard to use them; - 500,000 feet of boom increasing to 1,000,000 feet of boom by day's end; - pre-planned forecasting of 48-hour spill trajectory which indicates spilled oil will remain well offshore during that period; - pre-planned staging of resources for protection of environmentally sensitive areas.") Hayward said: "We are determined to do everything in our power to contain this oil spill."

From the beginning, BP's approach to the crisis was dramatically different from Exxon's in 1989. Where Exxon had been slow and ponderous, BP quickly set out clean-up plans. BP's chief executive was quoted in its first press release. He took personal charge and was on the spot in the Gulf of Mexico within two days of the accident, on April 23.

BP also admitted quickly the possibility that this was a major oil spill and one that could take several months to stop.[8] BP badly underestimated the rate at which oil was leaking from the well, initially putting it at only 1,000 barrels per day, then increased to 5,000 barrels a day,[9] but generally provided copious information about the spill and its efforts to stop the leak and clean up.[10]

BP was initially viewed as taking appropriate action. The *Wall Street Journal* reported that: "The response to the subsequent oil spill has... been exemplary. 'Our approach is to massively over-respond,' said BP chief executive Tony Hayward."[11]

The blame game

Who was to blame for the disaster? And who was going to pay?

At the end of April 2010, BP made a drastic move. It was required by law to pay the full cost of cleaning up the spilt oil but was protected from claims for economic loss resulting from the oil spill by a legal cap on liability of $75 million. There was speculation by the end of April 2010 that the oil spill might be the biggest ever.[12] And that in that case BP would ultimately be faced with costs exceeding those of Exxon, put at $4.3 billion. In spite of this prospect, at this stage, with costs spiraling as oil continued to spill, BP set aside the legal cap and offered to meet the full cost of economic losses as well. On April 30, "Hayward unveiled his bombshell...'We are taking full responsibility for the spill and we will clean it up, and where people can present legitimate claims for damages we will honor them.'"[13]

Fig. 14.1 BP: Timeline

April 20, 2010 - Explosion on the Deepwater Horizon, drilling in the Gulf of Mexico, kills eleven workers.
April 22 - The rig sinks. BP begins a large-scale response.
April 23 - Robot inspection shows oil leaking from the broken wellhead 5,000 feet down. BP CEO Tony Hayward arrives.
April 30 - Oil begins to come ashore in Louisiana. BP says it will pay for the clean-up.
May 2 - President Obama says BP will be held responsible and must pay.
May 11 - BP, Transocean and Halliburton blame each other at hearings.
June 2 - US government announces a criminal inquiry.
Mid-June - Obama meets BP the White House. BP sets up $20bn fund to cover claims from oil spill victims.
June 17 - Tony Hayward is accused of "stonewalling" a congressional inquiry.
July 16 - BP says that the leak is under control.
July 27 - Announcing quarterly results, BP says it has put aside $32.2bn to cover oil spill costs. Hayward is to step down on October 1 and be succeeded by Dudley.
September 8 - BP publishes results of internal investigation.
September 19 - The well is finally killed.
July 2, 2015 - Agreement in principle to settle federal, state and local government claims for $18.7bn, with total costs more than $50bn.

However, BP did not want to take the blame for the accident that started it all. As shown by the announcements and news report cited above, BP associated Transocean with the accident, as owner and operator of *Deepwater Horizon*. BP and Transocean were both named by the US Coast Guard as the "responsible party."[14] The US National Contingency Plan for crises such as oil spills requires the government to set up a Unified Command... "a command structure, created and implemented by the National Contingency Plan, which integrates the 'responsible party' ... with federal and state officials 'to achieve an effective and efficient response.'" And "the responsible party that caused the spill is clearly legally responsible for containing the spill and mitigating its harmful consequences."[15]

But when it came to blame, BP was pushing it toward Transocean: "'This accident took place on a rig owned, managed and operated by Transocean,' said BP spokesman Andrew Gowers." Hayward said: "This was not our drilling rig, it was not our equipment, it was not our people, our systems or our processes. This was Transocean's rig, their systems, their people, their equipment."[16]

BP's offer to pay for economic losses, intended as a bold move that would defuse a dangerous situation, was not enough to appease politicians and media critics. They were clear that, BP's argument notwithstanding, as the operator and majority owner of the Macondo prospect, BP was to blame. President Obama: "BP is responsible for this leak. BP will be paying the bill."[17]

BP ("British Petroleum") made an ideal scapegoat as it was not only Big Oil but Foreign Big Oil, and the largest company involved. The political argument for putting BP firmly in crosshairs was irrefutable. BP would be able to pay almost whatever the eventual bill. And "BP is to blame — BP must pay" was the simplest narrative that could be sold to the American people. There was no equally marketable narrative that BP could use in its defense against this ugly political onslaught.

Politicians professed to be aghast that BP did not immediately acquiesce. "BP has become increasingly blatant in attempts to deflect blame." At Senate hearings on May 11, representatives of BP, Transocean and Halliburton blamed each other for the accident.[18] On May 14, under pressure to do something about the endless oil spill, President Obama made a statement in front of television cameras and reporters, saying that BP would be held to their obligation to pay for the clean-up. He lambasted "a ridiculous spectacle during the congressional hearings into this matter. You had executives of BP and Transocean and Halliburton falling over each other to point the finger of blame at somebody else. The American people could not have been impressed with that display, and I certainly wasn't."[19]

Unstoppable public relations disaster

BP made no secret of the potential scale of the oil spill but it was only at the end of April 2010, when politicians swung into action, that the crisis came to be seen as an all-out environmental disaster. The oil spill had ceased to be just a major business crisis and become a major political issue. Investigations were launched by the Homeland Security Secretary and Interior Secretary (jointly) and by congressional committees. The Louisiana governor declared a state of emergency. President Obama visited the Gulf coast and said he would spare no effort in dealing with "a massive and potentially unprecedented environmental disaster."[20]

There was a pressing commercial, political and popular demand to bring the situation under control — to stop the leak. But there was a problem with that. The only infallible way of stopping such a leak was to drill a relief well but that takes three months.[21] BP began drilling the relief well on May 2.

It was unacceptable that the oil spill should be allowed to continue unabated for three months so BP mounted a desperate series of attempts to stop it some other way. BP tried closing the blowout preventer using remotely operated vehicles. It tried installing a 100 tonne cofferdam, a steel dome to contain and collect the oil. It tried blasting debris at the well under high pressure to stop the flow ("Junk Shot"). It tried inserting a tube into the well's broken riser (pipe) and sucking the oil up to a ship on the surface (Riser Insertion Tube Tool). It tried pumping drilling mud into the well to stop the flow ("Top Kill"). It tried the lower marine riser package cap containment system, another way of capturing leaking oil, installed on June 3. And it tried a second containment system installed on June 16.[22]

The attempts made over the course of several weeks were widely ridiculed. Facebook Folks, media and politicians, overwhelmed by the emotion of the crisis (i.e., frustration) found it hard to accept the reality that this was a problem beyond the reach of 2010 technology. After the Santa Barbara oil spill in 1969, the government's report on the incident had recommended that methods should be developed for collecting oil from subsea leaks but, four decades later, there was still no reliable method for deep water wells.[23]

The trade-off between cost and risk is sometimes acceptable to society so long as nothing goes wrong and the costs and risks are unexamined. When the risk suddenly comes out into the open, in the wake of an accident such as this, all hell lets loose and society tends to blame whoever took the risk on its behalf, in this case, an oil company.

Some took a further step away from reality by portraying BP's problem as primarily one of communication. There were headlines such as: "PR catastrophe," "Oil spill is bad, but BP's PR is even worse," and "BP faces PR disaster."[24] It was tempting to obscure the tough reality of the insoluble engineering problem by pretending that the problem is the relationship between the scapegoat and the media — its public relations. From beginning to end, the problem was the oil spill. The unstoppable oil spill caused the unstoppable PR disaster. Once it became unstoppable, BP's public utterances were little more than pegs for the criticism to hang on.

A few public relations people made more thoughtful comments in the early stages of the crisis. Tim Bell (Lord Bell) said: "I think their position — 'We'll pay but it's not our fault' — is the only position they could have taken... I would give them nine out of ten."[25] Eric Dezenhall called for our culture "to stop diagnosing oil spills as public relations problems."[26]

Reflecting on the crisis four years later, Hayward said that each time BP had attempted to stop the leak it had allowed people to believe that it would succeed. "What we should have said was: look, this is very, very bad, and the real answer is the relief well, and it's going to take four to five months. We're going to try some other things, but we don't expect them to work."[27] BP did warn that its measures might not succeed but it would have taken a very much sterner warning to stop people believing what they wanted to believe, i.e., that the leak was about to be stopped. BP fell into the trap of optimism but inadvertently rather than as a strategic decision. (Chapter 6 discusses the strategy of optimism, frequently employed but usually inadvisable.)

This was not a case of things looking bad but of things actually being bad. The unpalatable fact was that this kind of oil spill could not be stopped quickly. BP probably received more criticism and unsolicited advice than any previous crisis-hit company — on television and radio, in the press and in social media. But once it became clear that there was a major leak at the bottom of the sea, making BP look good was Mission Impossible. Really Impossible.

Leading from the front, a high risk strategy

If BP was the corporate scapegoat, the human scapegoat was its CEO, Tony Hayward. His decision to lead from the front was in line with conventional crisis wisdom, based on the Tylenol and *Exxon Valdez* paradigm cases. Hayward apparently believed that leading from the front was part of the CEO's job description. He said early on: "I'm the general and when you're the general you have to lead from the front."[28]

Hayward can't be faulted for making it but this proved to be a calamitous decision. His military analogy helps show why the crisis doctrine is flawed. On the Western Front in the first world war the most junior officers, the ones who were leading troops into battle, had the highest casualty rates of any rank. If generals literally led from the front, few who had seen active service would still be alive. And should any commander-in-chief, no matter how deadly his combat skills might be, lead Special Forces on an operation?

An organization in the vortex of a crisis needs someone to represent it in the media, someone with credibility and authority. But that someone is not necessarily the CEO. Communication roles should be allocated according to suitability, not status. For an oil major, the relevant country head or operating company head might be suitable candidates. In the case of BP, several senior executives were based in America. They had closer working knowledge of both the Gulf and this oil well. They also had the advantage of being American, more attuned to local ways. And, as Americans, they would have been more acceptable to American ears in these fraught conditions.

Even if Hayward had been the ideal candidate, it would have been unwise to deploy him because he was neither deniable nor expendable. When Hayward spoke, he established BP's official line. Nothing he said could easily be retracted. If he misspoke, the damage could not easily be repaired. He could not easily be replaced. And if he had resigned, this could have been seen as an admission of guilt.[29] In a crisis on this scale and this drawn-out, it would not have been possible for the CEO to absent himself entirely but another executive could have played the forward role.

It is difficult to see how any representative of BP could have persuaded America to be patient in the face of a seemingly un-ending stream of oil but Hayward also, perhaps unavoidably, made gaffes ("I'd like my life back," see chapter 1) and alleged gaffes. In the febrile atmosphere, these gaffes were blown out of proportion, as was to be expected, to include not only the genu-ine gaffes but reasonable statements that critics disliked. For ex-ample, in mid-May 2010, on a visit to London, Hayward gave a series of interviews. One, for *The Guardian*, led to an article that began: "Tony Hayward, the beleaguered chief executive of BP, has claimed its oil spill in the Gulf of Mexico is 'relatively tiny' compared with the 'very big ocean.'" And later on: "The amount of volume of oil and dispersant… is tiny in relation to the total water volume." He later repeated on *Sky News* that the environ-mental impact would be "very, very modest."[30] Hayward was technically correct but the Facebook Folks had lost interest in the facts and these were said to be gaffes. They became the subject of extensive media coverage that further damaged BP's credibility and provided ammunition for the company's burgeoning band of enemies.

Key points
- BP's crisis communication strategy was good in some ways, less good in others.
- The company responded quickly and massively when the Deep-water Horizon oil rig exploded in 2010.
- BP was right to take responsibility for cleaning up the oil spill but decline to take the blame.
- Best practice in crisis management called for BP to send its CEO, a foreigner, to take charge in person. By doing this, BP exacerbat-ed an extremely difficult public position.
- As the oil leak continued, becoming the largest in US history, the crisis unavoidably became a political disaster for BP, targeted by politicians as the ideal scapegoat.

The legal dilemma

There was perhaps one way for BP to have saved its reputa-tion — by saying: "We'll pay and it *is* our fault" — by apologizing, accepting total, unlimited responsibility and devoting all its resources to making good the oil spill. This would have looked good, even to its critics. But this was fantasy because of the legal position.

BP was on the horns of a dilemma. It needed political standing in order to do business in America but it needed to protect its legal position in order to survive. The reality was that it was able to make a concession, the April 30 offer of payment, but could not afford to take the blame. Taking the blame would have put it at the mercy of legal claimants and destroyed the company, damaging all stakeholders severely.

The board of a public company has a fiduciary obligation to shareholders. It would have been politically convenient for BP as the largest party to take full responsibility in every sense and admit liability for all damages. But in a situation that was less than clear-cut, it would have betrayed the interests of shareholders, whom the company has a duty to protect (and, indeed, other stakeholders such as employees). Shareholders would have sued the company. And the directors would have been personally liable for abdicating their fiduciary responsibility. The company was therefore obliged either to defend or at least reserve its position. The only realistic option for BP was the one it took: defending itself as well as it could, ultimately in the courts.[31]

As it was, when the legal battle dragged on and questions were raised about misconduct in the administration of compensation funds, hard-headed critics said BP had been too generous: "In the weeks after the *Deepwater Horizon* accident, it opened its wallet a bit too much, creating the impression that it was a soft touch... BP is right to start playing a bit of hardball on the streets of the Big Easy."[32]

The long second phase of the crisis, post-leak, was destined from the beginning to be fought in the courts but before BP could go to court it had to endure political theater. On stage were BP on one side and, on the other, the politicians who form the professional repertory company. In the audience, with participation encouraged, especially via social media and radio phone-ins, were the American people, the media and the crisis pundits. As the drama unfolded, BP squirmed. The politicians played the game they know so well. Most of the audience were ignorant of the companies' legal dilemma, ignorant of the technical problems, and ignorant of the impotence of their political leaders. Frustrated by apparent incompetence and procrastination, they simply wanted the spill to be stopped and someone to take the blame. BP was the obvious fall guy. And idealistic crisis and communication experts, also apparently ignorant of the legal dilemma, urged that BP should "tell it all" and take full responsibility.

The politicians needed to show to their constituents that they were taking a tough line. They summoned it to appear at congressional hearings. BP was trapped by the rhetorical rule that if you point out that saying something will land you in legal trouble, that makes you look bad. It was a case of "Aha, so you *are* guilty but your lawyer says you can't admit it."

So it was that on June 17, 2010, Hayward endured a seven-and-a-half hour congressional hearing that the *Washington Post* said came down to a single word: "Sorry. In a room packed with cameras and spectators, BP chief executive Tony Hayward said, 'I am deeply sorry' for the lost lives and environmental damage from his company's doomed offshore rig."[33] Still, he was accused of evasion, allegedly saying some variant of "I don't know" no fewer than 66 times.[34] "Slippery oil CEO plays dumb," said the *New York Post*: "'I wasn't involved in any of the decision-making,' Hayward calmly told chairman Henry Waxman in his clipped British accent. 'What's clear to me,' Waxman interrupted, 'is that you don't want to answer our questions.'" Waxman said he was "'amazed... You're not taking responsibility.'"[35] Facing the danger of personal legal claims, the only practical option for him was to dodge the question. But doing so risked making him look like the villain.

In mid-June, the interests of the Obama administration and BP converged on the need to do a deal: "Bam summons BP boss to White House."[36] The deal, involving a colossal down payment, simultaneously relieved the pressure on BP to stop the oil spill and the pressure on the administration to make somebody stop it. BP agreed to hand over a colossal $20 billion (four times Exxon's $5 billion punitive damages) for an independent fund to compensate victims such as fishermen and pay for the clean-up. It was "a move some politicians dubbed a 'shake down' by the White House. Others have portrayed it as a capitulation by an oil giant responsible for one of the worst environmental disasters in history. A truer picture falls somewhere between... BP didn't offer a blank check..."[37] and so mitigated the risk of shareholder lawsuits.

At last, the containment systems installed in June worked and BP was able to announce tentatively on July 16 that the well had been closed. The well was finally killed in September.[38]

It was time for the post-mortem and time for an epilogue to begin that was expected to last for many years.

Settling the accounts

With the spill over, the coast cleaned and the reputational damage done, the legal struggle began in earnest. Indeed, while BP was battling the spill and commentators were debating, stone throwing and hand wringing, lawyers for the various parties affected were already at work. Announcing its second quarter results on July 27, 2010, BP said it was "subject to a number of legal proceedings and investigations related to the incident." The US Department of Justice was looking into whether civil or criminal laws had been violated, a presidential commission was examining the causes of the incident, and investigations were also in progress by a joint US Coast Guard/Bureau of Ocean Energy Management, Regulation and Enforcement, the Securities and Exchange Commission, the US Chemical Safety and Hazard Investigation Board and others. BP said that it was the target of more than 300 private civil lawsuits. It took a pre-tax charge of $32.2 billion.[39] On the same day, BP announced that Tony Hayward would step down as CEO on October 1, to be succeeded by Bob Dudley.[40]

BP wisely got its story out first. An internal investigation by BP, published in September 2010, concluded that: "Decisions made by 'multiple companies and work teams' contributed to the accident" which arose from "a complex and interlinked series of mechanical failures, human judgments, engineering design, operational implementation and team interfaces."[41]

The President's National Commission on the BP Deepwater Horizon Oil Spill and Offshore Drilling reported in January 2011 and criticized Transocean and Halliburton as well as BP. It said that wider industry and regulatory issues had also played a part. The explosion was not "the product of a series of aberrational decisions... Rather, the root causes are systemic." It thus looked less likely that BP would be found grossly negligent, although in 2014 a court did find that the cause of the spill was gross negligence.[42]

BP in turn pursued the other businesses that were involved in *Deepwater Horizon*.[43] BP and the other defendants faced what was said to be the most complex litigation since tobacco in the 1990s with over 120,000 plaintiffs, including the US government.[44] The legal struggle stretched out over years. Disclosure in BP's 2014 annual report ran to more than 17 pages in small print.[45] BP's CEO since 2010, Bob Dudley, said: "In all of the proceedings, we are seeking fair and just outcomes while protecting the best interests of our shareholders."[46]

The story appeared to come almost to an end in July 2015, when BP announced that it had reached an agreement in principle to settle federal, state and local government claims arising from the Deepwater Horizon accident for a headline amount of $18.7 billion. The main payments were to be $5.5 billion under the Clean Water Act, $7.1 billion for "natural resource damages" and $5.9 billion for claims by the states and local government entities, over 15-18 years. BP expected the total cumulative pre-tax charge to increase by about $10 billion from $43.8 billion at the end of the first-quarter. It deferred making an estimate of the total cost but the *Financial Times* speculated that claims by businesses may cost at least $2 billion more than the $10.3 billion for which it had already provided.[47]

A long view of *Deepwater Horizon* and BP

Taking the long view of *Deepwater Horizon*, as public companies are obliged to do, it was inevitable once the oil spill assumed major proportions that the companies involved would need to protect themselves from both prosecution and civil liability. When it is unclear exactly what caused an accident that may have enormous consequences, it would be both unreasonable and unrealistic to expect a public company to admit liability. It was futile or cynical or both to urge BP and others to act in ways that would jeopardize their officers, employees, shareholders and survival.

Crisis experts believed that BP had sacrificed its reputation and BP was well aware of the problem: "The incident has damaged BP's reputation and brand, with adverse public and political sentiment evident. This could persist into the longer term, which could impede our ability to deliver long-term growth."[48]

But more important than its unpopularity was the effect of the crisis on BP's strategic (priority) stakeholders (see chapter 12). One of these was and is the investment community. BP has sometimes been the largest company listed in London and therefore a sizable component of investment portfolios and retirement funds (in the US as well as the UK). And BP depends on finance from the capital markets to fund investment in exploration. A key competitive advantage for the oil majors is access to capital. During the crisis, investors were generally supportive of the company. Since then, BP is widely considered to have rebuilt its business well, restoring its dividend.

Its other key stakeholders were the various governments that regulate and tax the oil industry and award concessions to explore and produce. Of these, the American and British were the most important for BP. In the 1960s, BP began to develop Alaskan oil to replace interests in the Middle East. Lacking downstream presence in the US, BP merged its Alaskan interests into Standard Oil of Ohio (Sohio), eventually becoming majority owner of Sohio. But it may have been a strategic mistake (with perfect hindsight) for BP to acquire the whole of Sohio in 1987. It is conceivable that if the Macondo prospect had been owned and operated by Sohio, not BP, the US government would have pursued the company less aggressively. And from BP's viewpoint, the problem would at least have been ring-fenced, whereas "at times during the past five years it has looked as though BP was on the brink of extinction."[49]

Ever since the Alaska discovery, BP's interests in America have been indispensable to the company and it has worked assiduously to be a good corporate citizen. BP produces maps that show how, although numbers are reducing, still more than 18,000

American employees, 220,000 "supported" jobs, and $22 billion "vendor spend" are distributed, state by state. In 2013, it produced 628,000 barrels of oil and natural gas in America, of which 189,000 barrels came from the Gulf.[50] All this would be at risk, it implies, if the company were put at a disadvantage. And this may be one of the reasons why the US was eventually prepared to come to an agreement.

CEO Dudley said in the 2013 annual report that: "BP has continued to meet its commitment to environmental and economic restoration in the Gulf of Mexico... [The scale of BP's costs] underlining once again that BP is living up to its responsibilities in the region and to the US as a whole. The US remains vitally important to today's BP... Nearly 40% of our shares are held in the US, and we invest more there than in any other country."[51]

Rethinking crisis communications

Despite the scale of the Gulf oil spill, that dwarfed Tylenol and *Exxon Valdez*, this has not been declared a new paradigm case for crisis communications. While there was an enormous amount of traditional and social media coverage of the crisis in progress and there has been a slew of specialist books and articles, most of the retrospectives have concentrated on how the disaster came about and how it unfolded, with a liberal dose of melodrama, as in: "BP and the Drilling Race That Took it Down."[52] The public relations and crisis communication textbooks have not been rewritten. Yet BP seems to point the way to some different conclusions about crisis communication from the textbooks, in line with the argument of chapter 13.

For the crisis industry, the most important outcome has been to underline the terrible consequences of not making adequate preparation ahead of a crisis. Surveying businesses three years after the September 11 terrorist attacks, Ian Mitroff was appalled to find that most were keeping up preparations for terrorism and other crises, "if and only if they are cost effective."[53] Yet, writing fourteen years after September 11, with no repetition of an attack on that scale in the West, this does not seem so unwise.

BP was accused of having no plan for the worst case scenario.[54] It may seem wise to crisis experts that everyone should have a plan for every imaginable bad scenario — that every business should assume it is about to be hit by the equivalent of September 11 and *Deepwater Horizon* combined. This is unrealistic. Implementing such a program of preparation would be a huge cost drag. That cost that would ultimately be borne by citizens. It is hard for Facebook Folks to accept but there must be a limit to how far it is worth society trying to eliminate risk.

Citizens, media and politicians crave simplistic cause-and-effect narratives. In this case, the perfect such narrative was: drilling rig blows up, foreign oil giant to blame.

But why should any business take the sole blame for an accident in which its decisions did no more than play a part, at worst? Contrary to the crisis consensus, taking the blame is not a no-brainer. It would not have made any sense for BP to take the blame. (See chapter 15 on blame for the *Costa Concordia* cruise ship wreck.)

Whether to tell it all and tell it fast depends on the magnitude of the crisis. If it is a genuine crisis that has already hit the headlines (like BP) it is wise to make full, fast disclosure consistent with appropriate self-protection. But it is interesting to note that between 2001 and 2010 in the Gulf of Mexico there were 858 fires and explosions, 1,349 injuries and 69 deaths. How many of these incidents were crises? In how many of these cases was it either necessary or advisable to tell it all and tell it fast? If there is a good chance that the situation will fade without a damaging story being told, do not tell it all and tell it fast. Prepare your story and put out the fire.

And, finally, the patience of BP's management and shareholders began to look as though it would pay off. The *Financial Times* concluded: "The group's public image is on the mend... US political opposition to BP is far less intense.... Piece by piece, BP's relations with the US government have normalized."[55] Another disappointment for those who believe there is no road back from "public relations catastrophe."

Key points

- BP might perhaps have redeemed itself by an unreserved and groveling apology. But this would have required the board to fail in its duty to its most important stakeholders.
- It was clear from the start that, once political pressure abated, the outcome would be settled by a legal process lasting years. At the time of writing, it seemed likely that a $50 billion plus settlement would be reached.
- BP's difficulties were so extreme because of the length of time that the crisis was unresolved at the top of the US political and media agenda. But it was right to take a long-term view and focus on its strategic stakeholders.

In Summary

- BP responded quickly and vigorously when *Deepwater Horizon* sank but it was impossible to "solve" such a crisis. It is highly unusual for a crisis to continue at high intensity for almost three months but in any crisis it is essential to have realistic expectations of what communication can achieve.

- BP said it was sorry but did not take full and sole responsibility for what went wrong. The company was heavily criticized but it had to weigh the desire to look good against protecting its stakeholders. That made taking the blame out of the question.

References

[1] 'Group Results: Third Quarter and Nine Months 2010,' BP p.l.c., November 2, 2010.

[2] National Commission on the BP Deepwater Horizon Oil Spill and Offshore Drilling, *Deep Water, The Gulf Oil Disaster and the Future of Offshore Drilling: Report to the President*, January 2011, 1-19.

[3] 'Transocean Ltd. Reports Fire on Semisubmersible Drilling Rig Deepwater Horizon,' Transocean Ltd. news release, Zug, Switzerland, April 21, 2010.

[4] 'Transocean Ltd. Provides Update on Semisubmersible Drilling Rig Deepwater Horizon,' Transocean Ltd. news release, Zug, Switzerland, April 22, 2010.

[5] 'BP Confirms that Transocean Ltd Issued the Following Statement Today,' BP p.l.c. news release, April 21, 2010.

[6] 'BP Offers Full Support to Transocean After Drilling Rig Fire,' BP p.l.c. news release, April 21, 2010.

[7] 'Search Continues After Oil Rig Blast,' *New York Times*, April 21, 2010.

[8] Sheila McNulty & Ed Crooks, 'BP Warning over Gulf of Mexico Oil Spill,' *Financial Times*, April 26, 2010. Campbell Robertson & Clifford Krauss, 'Oil Rig Sinks, Raising Fears Of a Major Spill in the Gulf,' *New York Times*, April 23, 2010.

[9] 1,000: Bergin, *Spills and Spin*, 164. 5,000: Robert Lee Hotz & Angela Gonzalez, 'Oil Spill Estimates Raised Fivefold,' *Wall Street Journal*, April 29, 2010.

[10] 'BP Reiterates Oil Spill Response Transparency,' BP p.l.c. news release, May 21, 2010.

[11] James Herron, 'Political Consequences Loom As Gulf Oil Slick Spreads Faster,' *Wall Street Journal*, April 29, 2010.

[12] Clifford Krauss, 'Oil Spill's Blow to BP's Image May Eclipse Costs,' *New York Times*, April 29, 2010.

[13] Bergin, *Spills and Spin*, 167.

[14] Matthew L. Wald, 'Clarifying Questions of Liability, Cleanup and Consequences,' *New York Times*, May 6, 2010.

[15] National Commission report, 131 & 267.

[16] Gowers: Krauss, 'Oil Spill's Blow to BP's Image May Eclipse Costs.' Hayward: Ed Crooks & Andrew Edgecliffe-Johnson, 'BP Counts High Cost of Clean-up and Blow to Brand,' *Financial Times*, May 4, 2010.

[17] Harvey Morris & Sheila McNulty, 'Obama Pledges to Spare No Effort in Oil Clean-up,' *Financial Times*, May 2, 2010.

[18] Blatant: Crooks & Edgecliffe-Johnson, 'BP Counts High Cost of Clean-up and Blow to Brand.' Senate: Steven Mufson & David A. Fahrenthold, 'In Senate Testimony, Oil Executives Pass the Blame for Massive Gulf Spill,' *Washington Post*, May 12, 2010.

[19] 'Obama's Remarks on Oil Spill Response,' *New York Times*, May 14, 2010.

[20] Morris & McNulty, 'Obama Pledges to Spare No Effort in Oil Clean-up.'

[21] 'Work Begins to Drill Relief Well to Stop Oil Spill,' BP p.l.c. news release, May 4, 2010.

[22] Harvey Morris, 'BP Plans to Use Debris to Staunch Oil Leak,' *Financial Times*, May 9, 2010; Bergin, *Spills and Spin*, 211-219; 'Update on Gulf of Mexico Oil Spill Response,' BP p.l.c. news release, June 7, 2010; 'Update on Gulf of Mexico Oil Spill Response,' BP p.l.c. news release, June 21, 2010.

[23] National Commission report, 135.

[24] Ronald D. White, 'For BP Oil Spill Is a Public Relations Catastrophe,' *Los Angeles Times*, April 30, 2010; Jeremy Warner, 'The Gulf of Mexico Oil Spill Is Bad, But BP's PR Is Even Worse,' *Daily Telegraph*, June 18, 2010; Edward Luce, 'BP Faces Public Relations Disaster,' *Financial Times*, June 2, 2010.

25 Lord Bell, quoted in Crooks & Edgecliffe-Johnson, 'BP Counts High Cost of Clean-up and Blow to Brand.'
26 Dezenhall, 'Why BP Didn't Plan for This Crisis.'
27 Guy Chazan, 'Tony Hayward, Genel Energy CEO: Now He Has His Life Back,' *Financial Times*, September 14, 2014.
28 Bergin, *Spills and Spin*, 166.
29 Bergin, *Spills and Spin*, 239.
30 Tim Webb, 'BP Boss Admits Job on the Line Over Gulf Oil Spill,' *The Guardian*, May 14, 2010. BP Boss Tony Hayward's Gaffes, <http://www.bbc.co.uk/news/10360084, June 20,2010>; Richard Wray, 'Deepwater Horizon Oil Spill: BP Gaffes in Full,' *The Guardian*, July 27, 2010.
31 Keith Hearit commented in connection with clergy abuse, "If any institution should respond out of concern and compassion, it is the Catholic Church, yet to respond too accommodatingly would bring with it almost incalculable liability costs. Because of this the church leaders face a difficult, Hobson's choice." See Hearit, *Crisis Management by Apology*, 208. Though, arguably, religious bodies should be held to higher ethical standards than businesses.
32 Lex, 'BP: Settlement Unsettled,' *Financial Times*, July 5, 2013.
33 Steven Mufson, 'Apologies and Anger Dominate Gulf Oil-Spill Hearing as BP Goes Before Congress,' *Washington Post*, June 18, 2010.
34 Bergin, *Spills and Spin*, 234.
35 Andy Soltis, 'Slippery Oil CEO Plays Dumb,' *New York Post*, June 18, 2010.
36 Leonard Greene, 'Bam Summons BP Boss to White House,' *New York Post*, June 11, 2010.
37 Jonathan Weisman, 'BP Softens Political Hit,' *Wall Street Journal*, June 21, 2010.
38 July: 'Well Integrity Test Continues on MC252 Well,' BP p.l.c. news release, July 16, 2010. September: 'BP Confirms Successful Completion of Well Kill,' BP p.l.c. news release, September 19, 2010.
39 'BP p.l.c. Group Results Second Quarter and Half Year 2010,' BP p.l.c., July 27, 2010.
40 'BP CEO Tony Hayward to Step Down and Be Succeeded by Robert Dudley,' BP p.l.c. news release, July 27, 2010
41 'BP Releases Report on Causes of Gulf of Mexico Tragedy,' BP p.l.c. news release, September 8, 2010.
42 James Herron, 'BP Likely to Avoid Harshest Penalties for Gulf Spill,' *Wall Street Journal*, January 6, 2011. BP p.l.c., Annual Report & Form 20F 2014, 36.
43 Sheila McNulty, 'Moex to Pay $1Bn to BP over Oil Spill,' *Financial Times*, May 20, 2010. 'BP Announces Settlement with Anadarko Petroleum of Claims Related to Deepwater Horizon Accident,' BP p.l.c. news release, October 17, 2011. 'BP Seeks All Costs from Halliburton over Oil Spill,' *Financial Times*, January 3, 2012.
44 Ed Crooks, 'BP Poised to Enter Legal Labyrinth,' *Financial Times*, January 22, 2012.
45 BP p.l.c., Annual Report & Form 20F 2014. See 36-38, 69-70, 107, 111-116 & 228-237.
46 BP p.l.c., Annual Report & Form 20F 2014, 9.
47 'BP to Settle Federal, State and Local Deepwater Horizon Claims for up to $18.7 Billion With Payments to be Spread Over 18 Years,' BP p.l.c. news release, July 2, 2015. Christopher Adams & Ed Crooks, 'BP: Into Uncharted Waters,' *Financial Times*, July 9, 2015. Ed Crooks, BP Braced for Billions of Dollars More in Deepwater Payments, *Financial Times*, July 12, 2015.
48 'BP p.l.c. Group Results Second Quarter and Half Year 2010,' BP p.l.c., July 27, 2010.
49 Adams & Crooks, 'BP: Into Uncharted Waters.'
50 'BP's US Economic Impact Report 2014,' BP p.l.c., 2014.
51 BP p.l.c., Annual Report & Form 20F 2013, 9.
52 Stanley Reed & Alison Fitzgerald, *In Too Deep: BP and the Drilling Race That Took it Down*, (Hoboken, NJ: John Wiley & Sons, 2011).
53 Ian Mitroff, 'Lessons from 9/11: Are Companies Better Prepared Today?' *Technological Forecasting & Social Change*, Vol. 72 (2005), 375-376.
54 Anne C. Mulkern, 'BP's PR Blunders Mirror Exxon's, Appear Destined for Record Book,' *New York Times*, June 10, 2010.
55 Adams & Crooks, 'BP: Into Uncharted Waters.'

CHAPTER 15

Carnival: Saved by low media profile

"Vada a bordo, cazzo!" ("Get on board, you prick!") —
Gregorio de Falco[1]

When the Costa Concordia cruise ship ran aground in January 2012, crisis experts were quick to pass judgment. The loss of the ship with 32 lives made a sorry tale indeed. But was the crisis communication of Carnival, the ship's owner, as poor as these experts said? Or was its communication strategy a success that confounded the experts?

The loss of RMS *Titanic* just over a century ago was neither the worst ever maritime disaster nor the biggest ship to come to grief. (More than 4,000 people lost their lives on a ferry in the Philippines in 1987.) But *Titanic* became the shipwreck of shipwrecks against which all subsequent wrecks were measured. When *Costa Concordia* came to grief, *Titanic* was the comparison that leapt to mind. *Costa Concordia* was twice as big.[2]

What did *Costa Concordia* mean for Carnival Corporation & plc, the world's largest cruise company, whose 100 plus ships served more than 10 million customers? Soon a small number of crisis and PR pundits threw up their hands in horror. Not over the accident itself but over the way Carnival handled it.

Here is a stock prescription for crises, paraphrasing pundits:

The CEO should take responsibility, get out in front of the problem and over-react to it.

This stock prescription may work in a case where the crisis event is over in a flash, like an aircraft crashing or a bomb exploding (and especially if there is no question of the protagonist

319

being at fault). In such crises, when the organization that faces the problem starts communicating, it is dealing with something that is already in the past. It is far more difficult to find the best way to deal with a crisis that unfolds over months, like the Gulf of Mexico oil spill, or even over days, like the shipwreck. Can it really be true that one simple prescription fits all crises?

"Vada a bordo, cazzo!"

Late on January 13, 2012, *Costa Concordia* was sailing from Civitavecchia to Savona in Italy with 3,200 passengers and 1,000 crew on board. 114,000 tons and 952 ft long, she was more than twice the size of *Titanic*. The ship left the normal course to sail close to the island of Giglio. She struck a rock, began taking on water and then turned to close the island, ending up aground on an underwater shelf of rock. The ship gradually listed to 70 degrees from upright. It took several hours for all the passengers to be evacuated and for the situation to become clear. Casualties were reported in the early hours of January 14 and the eventual death toll was 32.[3] There was no sign of an oil leak.

As with *Exxon Valdez*, a ship had been steered into a sharp object. Once again, the sea was calm. The sharp object was stationary and in shallow water not far from the shore. And the only actors in the drama were the people on the ship.

But what caused the accident? After the immediate horror of the shipwreck, this was the focus of media attention. Then, when the loss of life became clear, people asked whether those lost lives could have been saved if the evacuation of the ship had not been such a shambles.[4] Experts commenting on mismanagement of the evacuation pointed to factors including poor information about the extent of damage and flooding, delay in raising the alarm, and failure to coordinate and direct the crew.[5]

The behavior of the ship's captain, Francesco Schettino, quickly became a cause célèbre. He disembarked before many of the passengers and later said he fell overboard. Coast Guard Captain Gregorio de Falco ordered him over the radio to go back on board. The recording and transcript of their exchange swiftly went viral: "Vada a bordo, cazzo!" ("Get on board, you prick!")

The day after the shipwreck, Schettino was detained by the Italian authorities.[6]

Carnival's response

Costa Concordia was owned and operated by Costa Crociere S.p.A., an Italian subsidiary of Carnival. Carnival, based in Miami, Florida, delegated responsibility for dealing with the crisis to Costa. This included communicating with the media and locals. The main speaker on behalf of the company was Costa's chief executive, Pier Luigi Foschi. Costa acted promptly, making its first statement at 1.00 am local time on January 14 and issuing frequent updates.[7] As part of its emergency response, Costa activated a dark site on the internet as well as social media amplifiers that provided an outlet for company communications when the company website was swamped and became inaccessible.[8]

Micky Arison, chairman and CEO of Carnival, said in a tweet on January 13 (Eastern time): "Our thoughts are with guests and crew of the *Costa Concordia*. We are keeping them in our hearts in the wake of this very sad event." On January 14, he tweeted: "Carnival put out its own statement at 3:45 pm EST — 9:45 am in Italy — January 14."[9] The statement said that the ship had struck a rock, that the order had been given to abandon ship, and that there were reports of casualties: "This is a terrible tragedy and we are deeply saddened. Carnival Corporation & plc offers our sympathies and heartfelt condolences to all of the *Costa Concordia* guests, crew members and their families. We are working to fully understand the cause of what occurred."

The Carnival statement was exemplary in briefly reporting the facts as far as they were known at the time; expressing concern for the victims; stating its policy on safety, the number one priority; not speculating about the cause but saying work was in progress to understand what happened; and expressing gratitude to the authorities and others for their help.

On January 15, Costa issued a fuller statement.[10] It said that the company was working to find out exactly what happened but "preliminary indications are that there may have been significant human error on the part of the ship's master, Captain Francesco

Schettino." The ship appeared to have sailed too close to the shore and the captain appeared not to have followed procedures. An Italian prosecutor had made accusations against the captain.

Carnival's second statement, issued on January 16, comprised only two points.[11] Arison said the first priority must be the safety of passengers and crew, and then: "We are deeply saddened by this tragic event and our hearts go out to everyone affected by the grounding of the *Costa Concordia* and especially to the families and loved ones of those who lost their lives. They will remain in our thoughts and prayers." Carnival made its first estimate of the financial impact on the company: $40 million insurance deductibles, $85-95 million for loss of use of the ship, and other costs that could not yet be quantified.[12]

Carnival issued three more statements. On January 17, Arison reiterated Carnival's concern for the victims, said its priorities were supporting the rescue efforts and preventing any environmental impact, and thanked the crew and the authorities.[13]

On January 18, in a joint statement with Costa, Arison said: "I give my personal assurance that we will take care of each and every one of our guests, crew and their families affected by this tragic event. Our company was founded on this principle and it will remain our focus."[14] The statement said that Costa had been arranging lodging and transportation for passengers and crew, contacting passengers, crew members and their families to offer assistance, would be addressing the loss of personal possessions, and would refund all fares and costs incurred while on board. Within two weeks, Costa offered compensation to all those passengers who had not been injured of €11,000 ($14,400). It also offered a refund of the cost of the cruise, travel expenses and medical expenses, estimated to total around $4,000 per passenger.[15] For injuries up to and including loss of life, compensation would be a maximum of $71,000.

Although cruise lines are at risk from many different and unforeseeable circumstances, they have the advantage of a contractual relationship with passengers. The three largest groups require customers to sign contracts with similar terms and conditions, limiting their liabilities. These contracts contain a forum selection clause stipulating that lawsuits must be initiated in the US District Court for southern Florida or in Miami-Dade County, Florida. In the case of a Costa cruise not touching a US port, the applicable law would be Italian and the forum would be Genoa, Italy.[16]

The loss of *Costa Concordia* raised the question of the safety of the company's other ships and in its final statement on January 19, Carnival announced: "a comprehensive audit and review of all safety and emergency response procedures across all of the company's cruise lines."[17] The company had an excellent safety record, Arison said, but the incident had: "called into question our company's safety and emergency response procedures and practices." He had confidence in the ships and their crews but a review would make sure there was no recurrence.

After January 19, Carnival relied on Costa to communicate with the media.

Carnival's communication strategy

Carnival's communication strategy was of course never published. But, in the same way as a historian does not need Hannibal's personal journal to analyze his strategy in Italy, it is not necessary to read a company's internal documents to analyze its strategy, which can be deduced from its actions:

- The parent company kept a low media profile. Its statements were limited to those outlined above. The CEO gave no interviews. The CEO did not fly to the scene and did not become a focus for television and photographers.

- Carnival focused on its strategic (priority) stakeholders: regulators, investors and customers. What passed between Carnival and its regulators is not in the public domain but it spoke volumes that the authorities did not put the company in the frame. Carnival kept investors abreast of developments and, by not making a spectacle of itself, kept their potential embarrassment to a minimum.

- Carnival took steps via Costa to support affected customers (and employees) but did not take responsibility for the disaster. It encouraged the view that the cause was human error by the ship's captain. This decision was vindicated by the conviction of the captain in early 2015 for multiple manslaughter, causing a shipwreck, and abandoning ship.[18]

- The company took steps to review and then strengthen safety procedures but worked with the industry to avoid the safety of cruises becoming a general issue with the potential to put consumers off cruising.

Key points
- When Costa Concordia sank with the loss of 32 lives, Carnival, the ship's owner, responded quickly but delegated managing the crisis to its Costa subsidiary.
- Instead of conventional crisis management, Carnival adopted a communication strategy that included keeping a low media profile, focusing on its strategic stakeholders, and declining to take responsibility for a disaster that was not its fault.
- Next the chapter examines the consequences.

Investor reaction

News of the shipwreck caused Carnival shares to sell off. There was a rational argument for selling. The financial impact of the accident, quantified by the company, meant that it was worth a bit less, and there was an obvious danger of more bad news, such as the risk of some legal penalty or that bookings would dry up.

Carnival has a dual listing in New York and London, the only company to be a member of both the S&P 500 and FTSE 100 indices, with the vast majority of trading in New York. Before the shipwreck, on January 13, Carnival closed at £22.48 in London with 665,000 shares traded. In New York, they closed at $34.28, with a volume of 5.3 million shares. After the shipwreck, on Monday, January 16, the New York Stock Exchange was closed for Martin Luther King, Jr. Day. In London, 6.3 million shares were traded, ten times the usual volume, opening at £18.00 and closing at £18.78. The fall compared with Friday's closing price was 20%. When New York reopened on Tuesday, 39.95 million shares were traded, opening at $29.48 and closing at $29.60. In New York, the fall compared with Friday's close was 16%.

Fig. 15.1 Timeline — Market Verdict on Carnival (2012)

January 13 - Costa Concordia runs aground off the Italian island of Giglio.
January 14 - In the early hours, the passengers and crew abandon ship, with an eventual death toll of 32.
January 14 - Costa Crociere issues first statement at 1.00 am, followed by Carnival at 3.45 pm EST.
January 16 - Carnival quantifies estimated financial impact.
January 16 - Carnival shares fall 20% in London.
January 17 - Carnival shares touch low of $29.22 in New York.
January 19 - Carnival issues final statement.
March 6 - Carnival shares retest their low point in New York.
December 31 - Carnival shares close at $39.57 (compared with $33.47 at the opening on January 2, 2012).

These were investors selling at the first sign of bad news. The shares of competitors also fell. A little less than 10% of Carnival's shares changed hands in the first couple of days but most shareholders stayed on board. The shares retested the low of $29.22 intra-day in New York on March 6 but by June, the shares returned to where they had been as the year began and, indeed, ended the year at $39.57.

A 1999 study suggested that this pattern is not unusual. It looked at 15 "major corporate catastrophes" and found that after an initial loss of market value averaging almost 8%, the average stock made up all of the lost ground in just over 50 trading days.[19] A plausible explanation for this is that skittish investors sell on the news, sending the price down. Other investors, seeing value in the stock at a lower price, then buy, sending it back up again. The study suggested that recovery was impaired where a large number of deaths was involved and where management was seen to be responsible for safety lapses. When economic damage to the company is significant, as in the case of BP (see chapter 14), the market behaves rationally, awarding the stock a lower value over the longer term.

Analysts noted that bookings would be affected. "While these accidents are extremely rare, the extensive media coverage will likely curtail some booking activity and pressure pricing" (Tim Ramskill, Credit Suisse). They recognized that: "Costa is an important brand... and is likely to be the most badly affected by the tragic events... There will be negative short-term implications for bookings across the cruise sector as pictures of the stricken ship are flashed around the world" (Wyn Ellis, Numis Securities). It seemed possible that ships would have to be taken out of service for safety checks and that new safety procedures would mean higher operating costs. (Ian Rennardson, Jefferies.)[20]

But, "looking at booking patterns after major air crashes shows that booking patterns return to previous levels relatively quickly." (Rennardson) A 6-10% fall in cruise bookings was expected, with "more graphic and widespread" coverage than in past incidents but "there is no major passenger fear of cruising thus far." (Gregory Badishkanian, Citigroup.)[21] Analysts' comments and investor behavior both suggested that investors were sanguine about the aftermath of the crisis.

Six months later, Morgan Stanley concluded: "The Concordia disaster was a tragic human error, and while it seems to have put some people off cruising this year... the impact is unlikely to be permanent."[22]

Public reaction

This was a very modern crisis that played out with all the benefits of social media. Although they were in the process of abandoning a sinking ship, many of those on board, as well as witnesses on shore, found time to take videos and photos. These records of the dramatic event were quickly distributed around the world. In the first 48 hours, social media were buzzing, with more than 35,000 tweets, 34,000 news mentions online, 10,900 blog mentions, and 4,600 YouTube video mentions. Two journalists who happened to be traveling as passengers wrote a book including their eyewitness accounts.[23]

The main exhibit in media coverage was the huge vessel that made a shocking sight, beached on its side. The shipwreck was ideal raw material for rolling TV news. Interviews with survivors, onlookers and experts, intercut with live footage of the wreck, could use up a lot of time on channels with 24 hours to fill with "news."

The main characters were the passengers, first escaping and then reliving their ordeal, and the ship's captain. The obvious targets for public wrath — the main potential suspects who might the court of public opinion — based on the history of past crises, were:

- The captain.
- Costa, which operated and had its name on the ship.
- Carnival, Costa's parent and the owner of the ship.
- The Italian authorities.

The captain's actions, especially after the ship ran aground, looked bad. The Coast Guard captain, representing the authorities, looked good. Costa quickly pointed to the captain's "significant human error" and, rightly or wrongly, the captain came to be seen as the culprit for both the shipwreck and the fatal evacuation.[24] (He reminded one commentator of Joseph Conrad's Lord Jim.)[25]

The disaster was the subject of headlines that sensationalized it,[26] like this from the *Daily Mail*: "'Only a disgraceful man would have left all those passengers on board': Hero captain who coordinated evacuation slams Schettino..." And the ship's previous captain said that Schettino "drove the ship like a Ferrari."[27]

Costa's chief executive and spokesman, Foschi, played a minor role in English-language coverage. The company's lawyer told the *New York Times*, "Costa Cruises is an injured party... Beyond the human drama and the tragedy, the company has suffered an extensive damage."[28]

Most newspaper articles and news broadcasts did not mention Carnival. Even in those that did, it was as the owner of Costa, with no suggestion that it was in any way responsible for what happened. Comments on cruise-related websites, such as Cruise-Critic, focused on enthusiasm for cruising versus fear of cruising rather than criticism of the company.[29] The author's own research suggests that, in the days immediately following the shipwreck, less than 1% of new threads on cruise message boards mentioned Carnival's crisis role.

Carnival and Costa were wary about exposing themselves to the media. They were not about to be drawn into a debate about the legal position of cruise customers and employees would not speak to the media. The issue was the subject of an official investigation. Most of the attention was on the captain. Crisis experts criticized the company for this. They said that the story of the rogue captain was unsustainable and would turn disaster into reputational catastrophe.[30] The predicted catastrophe never happened.

When CNN made a documentary based on the *Costa Concordia* story, "Cruise to Disaster," aired in July 2012, Carnival did not grant an interview but allowed the Cruise Lines International Association, an industry association, to handle issues such as ship registration and taxation that were raised by CNN.[31]

Finally, in the immediate aftermath, there was the usual flurry of political responses. There was a suggestion of a three mile wide no go zone for cruise ships along the Italian shoreline. New official guidance was issued for onboard stability computers, new lifeboats and minimum levels of qualified staff. Questions were asked about whether regulation of cruise ships was strict enough. There was a move in the European Union to switch cruise ships to lighter fuel with a view to minimizing pollution in an accident. The 24-hour window for cruise ships to conduct safety drills was queried.[32] And the industry responded to the accident with a range of safety improvements.

Crisis experts: Where is Micky Arison?

Standard crisis advice is that the boss must immediately take center stage at the scene, take charge, and take responsibility. And one expert said there was: "A simple rule of thumb: when you put a giant piece of metal somewhere it doesn't belong, and when people have lost their lives, only your CEO can demonstrate the company's understanding of the significance and seriousness of that event"[33] — by immediately going to the scene and groveling.

Yet it seemed that, apart from the professionals, hardly anyone noticed that this had not happened. On January 18, a "communications coach" said Carnival's share price was falling and there were three things Arison must do to retrieve the situation:

1. "Go to Italy, now!"
2. "Demonstrate empathy."
3. "Be visible. Arison should be holding daily, if not twice-a-day, news conferences."[34]

After receiving this free expert advice, Arison did not rush to Italy and did not hold news conferences. But, more important, he and the Carnival board did not panic. And Carnival's share price rose, yes, *rose* in New York on January 18 (to $30.55).

However, on January 23, nudged by the crisis experts, the *Wall Street Journal* also noticed that Carnival was not sticking to the prescription for crisis management and posed the question that was bugging the experts: "Where is Micky Arison?"[35] It quoted a crisis consultant as saying: "You can't be invisible when the spotlight is shining on you, particularly if you are the CEO."

The article as a whole was not hostile to Carnival. The *Journal* noted that Carnival had kept a low profile since the accident. It said Arison had kept himself and the company "out of the spotlight," explaining that while he was in touch with the situation, Carnival's policy was that: "The unit's management is best suited to handle on-the-ground response." An unnamed source was reported as saying: "He wants to distance Carnival from this disaster." This was wise.

Crisis experts fired another broadside at Carnival via *Fox Business* on January 27: "Carnival Fails Crisis 101 in Costa Response."[36] Once again, the main criticism was that the company had stood back from the crisis rather than visibly taking charge of it. However, the article made three egregious errors. First, it said that Carnival waited four days before expressing "heartfelt condolences," whereas the company had issued such a statement within hours. Second, it said Carnival was "on the hook" for large-scale legal liabilities. Carnival's 2014 annual report acknowledged the potential for "litigation claims, enforcement actions, regulatory actions and investigations" but stated that these were not expected to make a significant impact on the "results of operations."[37] And third, the article said that Carnival now found itself under scrutiny that was likely to intensify, when scrutiny was already ebbing.

The latest edition of "Seitel" included three pages on *Costa Concordia*,[38] which included:

- A half-page photo of Arison with former President Clinton at a basketball game, taken in February 2012. (Arison owns the Miami Heat basketball team, which makes him a local celebrity.)[39] But the photo was widely published at the time and the main focus of media interest was on Clinton, not Arison.
- A claim that Carnival was "royally pilloried" in social media. Yet a *Mashable* search for "Arison" produced nothing but basketball.[40]
- And a (rumored) "tone deaf" offer by Costa of a 30% discount on cruises to survivors. Costa denied that such an offer had ever been made.[41]

Steven Fink, veteran of the Three Mile Island nuclear power station crisis, is one of the few experts who don't believe that top management should automatically swoop in person on any crisis.[42] He argued that if the CEO does not speak the local language he should stay at home and appoint a representative who does. However, he said that Arison should have been seen in the American media. But the main effect of being seen in the American media would have been to strengthen the link between Carnival and the disaster, which it was in Carnival's interest to play down.

Two months after the shipwreck, Arison gave a press interview, in which he said he did not want to become a "diversion" by going to Italy. "I have a lot of faith in Pier [Foschi] and his team. I believe they'll work their way through this. It was a terrible, terrible, terrible accident, but that's what it was."[43]

If distancing Carnival from the disaster was the company's aim, it appeared by the middle of 2012 to have been achieved.[44]

Key points
- Carnival's share price fell on the news of Costa Concordia but quickly rebounded.
- The disaster was the subject of high intensity, worldwide, but short-lived media coverage.
- Crisis experts said that the CEO should take the lead but this would have damaged Carnival, whose communication strategy enabled it to avoid being widely associated with the disaster or blamed for it.

Name brings blame

Chapter 13 argued that the most important factor determining whether an organization's crisis management succeeds or fails is whether or not it is blamed for the crisis. But in the paradigm case of *Exxon Valdez*, even if Exxon had been cleared by investigators of any contribution to the disaster, it would still have had a hard time emerging unscathed.

- First, Exxon had its name on both the ship and the company that operated the ship. Every time the incident was discussed, Exxon's name was invoked. In a crisis, *name attaches blame*.

- Second, the *Exxon Valdez* story was not really about the ship running aground but about the subsequent oil spill. A continuing problem like an oil spill evokes a public response of impatience: "Why isn't somebody putting a stop to this?" That somebody has to have a name. In this case, the obvious name was Exxon.

A strong identity may benefit the organization but also involves risk. Identity can be structured in three ways: monolithic, in which a single name dominates all parts of the organization; endorsed, in which each part of an organization has its own identity but is also presented as part of the whole; and branded, in which an organization and its parts or products have different identities and outsiders may be unaware of the links.[45] The bene-

331

fits of applying corporate branding to products and services are obvious but depend on everything that is branded either succeeding or, at worst, fading quietly away. When a vulnerable asset, such as a ship, is damaged, the whole corporate brand is put at risk.

This danger has long been recognized. David Bernstein observed in the 1980s, "A problem with one product can't be hermetically sealed if the corporate name is used."[46] But identity projects tend to be initiated at times when everything is going well and businesses are in an expansive phase, like Mobil in the 1960s (see chapter 10) or Berkshire Hathaway today. Ever since the siege of Troy, human beings have not been very good at attending to warnings of doom when the future seems bright.

Oil companies and others belatedly learned from disasters such as the *Amoco Cadiz* and *Exxon Valdez* shipwrecks that their branding needed to retrench. In the case of tankers and oil rigs, there has generally been a withdrawal from corporate branding. Instead, companies use branding that does not put the corporate name at risk. For example, Transocean used the Deepwater brand name, as in *Deepwater Horizon*, for some of its rigs and for its website, www.deepwater.com. (What a boon that the headlines in 2010 were not about the "Transocean Horizon oil spill.") Soon after *Exxon Valdez*, Exxon replaced its Exxon Shipping subsidiary with the innocuous SeaRiver Maritime, and cautiously insulates even the subsidiary by naming ships with the cryptic prefix S/R.

Beyond the oil industry, managements tend to be less risk-averse about the relationship between their corporate brands and subsidiaries. Throughout its history as a holding company, Berkshire Hathaway has operated most of its businesses at arm's length. However, it has recently made a series of moves in the opposite direction. In 2014, its MidAmerican Energy Holdings Company unit announced that it would change its name to Berkshire Hathaway Energy.[47] It said that the change of name reflected the benefits it gained from Berkshire Hathaway's ownership.

But this meant that any operating problems experienced by MidAmerican's utilities and their 8 million customers would be one step closer to rebounding on Berkshire Hathaway. It became more likely, for example, that crisis experts would expect Warren

Buffett to take personal charge in the event of a natural gas leak. Berkshire Hathaway Home Services, a real estate brokerage network, emerged from Berkshire Hathaway Energy. Then Berkshire bought the Van Tyl Group of car dealerships, to be renamed Berkshire Hathaway Automotive. Marketing people saw hidden value in the Berkshire brand.[48] Suddenly, Berkshire's corporate flag is being planted all over the map of the USA. Berkshire Hathaway's leadership has probably received (and deserved) more accolades than any other for its investment sagacity but expanding the corporate brand like this looks questionable.

Brand contamination

Carnival avoided blame for *Costa Concordia* because its name was not directly linked to the ship, because it kept a low media profile, focusing on its strategic stakeholders, and because, in the end, the captain was found to be chiefly responsible. But soon afterwards, Carnival's luck ran out. A year after *Costa Concordia*, Carnival found itself sailing in a sea of troubles, as *Carnival Triumph*, operated by Carnival Cruise Lines (CCL), was becalmed in an ordure-sullied ocean, her toilets out of action. An engine room fire on February 10, 2013, the scheduled last day of a cruise, left the ship without most power and with limited services for its 3,143 passengers. The crew put out the fire but it took four days to bring the ship into Mobile, Alabama (broadcast live on CNN and other channels). While this was happening, passengers went without mainstream toilet, air conditioning, lighting or restaurant facilities for extended periods. The breakdown of some services on the ship did not imperil life or limb but ruined vacations in a way that played out spectacularly in the media.

In the age of social media it meant that 3,000 irate people were left for days with time on their hands to complain to the mass media, complain on social media, and send their photos and videos of the mess around the world. Meanwhile, CCL put out social media updates on action it was taking to remedy the situation and compensate passengers but it was fighting a losing battle while the sewage was seeping and stinking.

Whereas the *Costa Concordia* crisis was largely contained in

Italy, this time it was Carnival's name on the ship, Carnival Cruise Lines was the operator, and it was therefore Carnival that was seen to be directly responsible for the disruption and discomfort endured by passengers. And it was a US-based cruise. Moreover, the crisis was not a single event but dragged on, like the *Deepwater Horizon* oil spill, though on a much smaller scale and for a much shorter time.

Costa Concordia spawned more media coverage, and especially more global coverage, than *Carnival Triumph*. But *Carnival Triumph* exposed the Carnival brand. And whereas, in the case of *Costa Concordia*, Carnival avoided the blame, in the case of *Carnival Triumph*, while the fire was an accident, subsequent problems were seen as entirely Carnival's responsibility to resolve.

As a result, the *Carnival Triumph* incident, though relatively trivial, had a greater impact on what the important consumer audience thought about Carnival than *Costa Concordia*. Both the Carnival operating brand and the Carnival corporate brand, insulated from *Costa Concordia*, were now in danger of serious contamination by the bad smell from *Carnival Triumph*. Investors also reacted badly. Carnival shares closed at $39.01 on February 8, before the fire. They began to fall and reached a low of $32.07 in June 2013, a decline of 17.8%.

Carnival was founded by Arison's father back in 1972. It grew to become the world's largest cruise group both organically and through the acquisitions of other cruise businesses: Holland America Line, Seabourn Cruise Line, Cunard Line, P&O Princess Cruises, and Costa Cruises. The company's policy was to retain the brands it acquired, each of which had a distinctive position in the market. Both the parent and its largest operating company, CCL, kept the Carnival name. Now Carnival paid the price for its unwise branding strategy.

The commotion over *Carnival Triumph* has faded but the Carnival group still needs a new name, which should be anything but Carnival. Carnival today is a group of cruise businesses and should have a name that reflects its scope rather than sharing the name of one of its operating companies, however dear that operating company name may be to the leadership.

In November 2014, Carnival launched "its first-ever multi-brand marketing initiative incorporating all nine of its global brands with television, digital, social and contest elements."[49] The campaign was aimed at consumers who were new to cruising, encouraging them to visit a Carnival-operated website called WorldsLeadingCruiseLines.com. "World's Leading Cruise Lines" seems a much better name for a group of leading cruise lines than one of the individual lines. Changing its name is the biggest single step Carnival could take to improve its crisis resilience.

Crisis detox

Crisis detox is a strategic step any major business should take to prepare for the worst.

Say you are running an company with vulnerable assets and products. There is a raft of measures to put in place but bear in mind that the key determinant of success in a crisis is whether you are blamed for it. Apart from not triggering a crisis, the most important single step you can take to protect your organization from the worst consequences is to detoxify your corporate identity.

Forget corporate pride. If you have operating subsidiaries that use the corporate name, consider changing their names. Or, which probably makes more sense, consider changing the corporate name. If you have trains and boats and planes with your badge on them, take the badge off and find a new badge. If your branding structure is a mish-mash that just sort of happened that way over a long period, the crisis detox is the compelling reason you need to carry out a spring clean.

There are many examples of a leading brand accumulating other businesses over time but retaining the original brand name as the corporate name. These include BMW, Carlsberg, Heineken, Hilton Worldwide, L'Oréal, Nestlé, Pepsico, Pernod Ricard, Toyota, Tui, and Volkswagen. They should probably take the path of Google, which announced in August 2015 the separation of Google, the main internet business, from its other businesses, all now part of the new holding company, Alphabet Inc.[50]

Operational issues

Cruise companies don't talk much about operational problems for the excellent reasons that the vast majority of cruises for
the vast majority of customers go according to plan and that the
resulting negative media coverage would put customers off.

But someone out there is trying to keep score.[51] The *Cruise
Junkie* website collates information about (alleged, mostly minor)
incidents that have either come to public attention via traditional
or social media, or been reported by people who claim to be witnesses. On this basis, it recorded 20 cruise ship fires in 2012.[52] It
needs to be stressed that this is not an official record. There is no
evidence that any cruise line was at fault in any of these fires or
other incidents.

The *Carnival Triumph* incident is undoubtedly the tip of an
iceberg of operational problems, mostly small, that commonly
arise in travel businesses. The *New York Times* reported that in
2011 the Centers for Disease Control and Prevention recorded 14
outbreaks of gastrointestinal illness on ten ships.[53] More seriously,
Morgan Stanley estimated that between 2002 and 2011, the cruise
industry experienced a loss of 28 lives, with 434 injuries and an
average of 15-20 serious incidents a year.[54]

It is impossible to know, without inside information, exactly
what issues each company has faced. Even in this supposed age
of transparency, when journalists and PR experts alike are urging
firms to make a full confession, no firm is likely to disclose this
information, and it would be inadvisable to do so. Any publicity
causes disproportionate concern and dents demand, at least in the
short term.

The nearest the companies come to full disclosure is the
broad statement of risks a quoted company publishes as part of
its annual reporting but this is forward-looking. And cruise lines
are practiced in managing operational issues. Carnival has a tried
and tested process that generally works well. While the company
avoids amplifying each incident, it makes clear that running a
cruise business involves numerous risks, including: "incidents, the
spread of contagious diseases and threats thereof, adverse weather conditions or other natural disasters and other incidents affecting the health, safety, security and satisfaction of guests and

crew" and "adverse publicity concerning the cruise industry in general, or us in particular."[55]

Resilience

Every year, millions of people take cruise vacations. The proportion who are seriously affected by operational issues is very small. Most receive little traditional or social media coverage. "Most persons realize that the *Costa Concordia* disaster was an accident, and statistically, cruising remains as one of the safest place to take a vacation."[56] There is no reason to believe that Carnival and its subsidiaries have been particularly accident-prone.

The travel industry is by its nature particularly prone to unforeseen incidents, some of which hit the headlines. Freak weather wreaks havoc. Airplanes fall out of the sky. Ships hit rocks, icebergs and other vessels. Buses crash. Hotels burn down. Travelers are blown up, shot and kidnapped. In my many years working in the industry, troubleshooting was sometimes a full-time job, handling issues such as bombings and hurricanes. Nevertheless, while there are always issues to manage, and some are difficult, real crises are rare. Occasionally an incident has lasting physical consequences for travel markets. The volcanic eruptions of 1995 that devastated the Caribbean island of Montserrat made the island unviable as a destination for large-scale tourism. But the physical consequences of most crises, from hurricanes to terrorist attacks to plane crashes, are limited.

Financial markets are therefore unlikely to be fazed by an incident such as loss of power or an outbreak of norovirus on a cruise ship, unless it turns into a media circus. Investors in travel stocks accept that they are subject more than most businesses to unforeseen incidents. When I handled investor relations for a large international travel firm, any time that bombs went off or extreme weather struck a destination, I would receive a slew of calls from investors and analysts. These calls were not made in panic, with threats to sell. The calls were made to help them check out the potential downside. They can mostly be reassured with relevant information such as guidance about the proportion of business potentially affected or management action to remedy the situation. The share price might wobble, buffeted by hour-by-hour gut reactions, but quickly returns to normal.

Investors separated the impact of Carnival's run of bad luck on current trading from the longer-term prospects. "Ship incidents on the Carnival and Costa brands have each cost CCL c. 200bps to 2013 group yields. As publicity subsides, pricing should recover." And by September 2013, "the Costa and Carnival brands seem to be recovering well."[57]

Key points
- The commotion over the fire on Carnival Triumph which caused no loss of life was much more damaging to Carnival than Costa Concordia.
- If a company shares its name with vulnerable assets, that exposes it to much greater risk of being blamed for a crisis.
- Operational issues are an everyday occurrence for many businesses, especially travel firms. Few of these are crises. The best policy with most operational issues is to keep media coverage to a minimum.

Learning the lessons

The accident raised a number of issues for Carnival's communication strategy:

(1) Customer confidence

In an echo of the popular reaction to the *Titanic* disaster a century ago, people were in shock that such a large, modern ship should come to grief in such circumstances. They asked: "How safe is a cruise?"[58] — and whether they might avoid the Costa brand. The issue of customer confidence in the safety of cruising was managed on three levels:

- The shift of media and public attention to the role of the captain made it more likely that this would be seen as a freak accident than a risk that might face cruise customers in future.

338

- Carnival carried out a safety review, implemented a series of safety management improvements and took part in the Cruise Industry Operational Safety Review.[59]
- Reliance on the industry as a whole to make the case that a cruise continues to be very low risk indeed.

(2) Impact on the group

What would be the impact of the accident on the Carnival group? The group largely escaped criticism for the accident or its role in handling the crisis. Such criticism as was made was in effect deflected to Costa. Carnival handled the crisis very effectively, while flouting some of the conventional advice. It also took a series of remedial actions, including safety actions, an investment program to upgrade CCL's fleet of ships, "Fun Ship 2.0," a program of roadshows to meet travel agents ("Carnival Conversations"), a new advertising campaign in America ("Moments That Matter"), and the "Great Vacation Guarantee," promising a hassle-free vacation.[60]

(3) Public face

Deciding your stance and communicating quickly and vigorously remains vital. Carnival did this. It selected the Italian head of its Costa subsidiary to be the face of the company. Given that the ship was Italian, that it ran aground in Italian waters, subject to Italian jurisdiction, that the largest number of passengers was Italian, and that the local media spoke Italian, this was a smart move. The public face of the company in the crisis cannot be selected in advance because the selection criteria depend on the circumstances. It should be someone sufficiently senior to be credible (a line manager rather than a PR person). It should be someone trained, experienced and personable in dealing with the media, particularly television interviews. And it should be someone who is at home in the country where the disaster took place.

(4) Role of the CEO

Carnival's CEO stayed in America and kept a low media profile (basketball excepted). There was no need for him to visit Italy. It is probably unwise to commit the CEO, even if he or she has the necessary personal qualities. First, the crisis may consume all the CEO's time in the front line, when the CEO needs to focus more than ever on strategy. Second, there is no walking away from the CEO. Once the CEO has been committed, the future of both CEO and organization are on the line. And it may be counterproductive for the CEO to visit the scene. If the CEO does visit, he or she should keep a low profile in the media and be statesmanlike, not rush around doing media interviews. The appropriate role model is a head of state rather than a D-list celebrity frantically plugging his or her latest gig.

(5) Responsibility

Carnival's CEO said he was sorry for what happened but wisely did not take responsibility. It is unwise to take the blame unless you are at fault. The representative of any business involved in a disaster should express sorrow over any loss of life, injury or damage — as a human being. Those who have suffered are the organization's employees, customers and/or neighbors, and it should be sorry for any harm they have suffered, but not take the blame. Carnival expressed sorrow. But the captain was widely blamed.

Conclusion

If Micky Arison had launched himself into the disaster, like Anderson of Union Carbide, the outcome would have been quite different. Carnival as a company and Arison as a face or a voice would have featured in most press reports and broadcasts. As he himself said, he would have been a "diversion." He would have been interrogated in television interviews, press interviews and at news conferences. "How did this happen?" "What are you going

340

to do about it?" "What do you say to those who have lost their loved ones on your ship?" "How can we be sure this will never happen again?" The Italian media, presented with an American billionaire who presumably does not speak Italian like a native, would have been brutal. And the adverse media coverage would have put pressure on politicians to move against Carnival.

After 34 years as CEO, in June 2013, Arison was succeeded by one of Carnival's long-serving non-executive directors, Arnold Donald. Arison remained in post as chairman. The shares ended 2013 at $41.17, up 37.5% from the January 17, 2012, low of $29.22.

Arison's valedictory comments to the *Financial Times* were a fair appraisal: "You do wake up at night fearing certain things, because you've got 100 ships out there, stuff's gonna happen." He had imagined a terrible fire or horrendous weather: "But I could never imagine a captain just driving a ship on to a rock." Regarding the impact on Costa, he said: "Within a year of the event, it turned around... You wouldn't expect it to come 100 per cent back in a year... [but] in two or three years' time, Costa will be as strong as ever."[61] Carnival reported strong performance in September 2014 and 2015.

"Concordia discors" encapsulates the philosophical idea that the elements are in ceaseless conflict but somehow bring harmony to the world. The paradox of a business like Carnival is that although it is beset by numerous, unpredictable problems, it provides vacation experiences to millions of people that are overwhelmingly enjoyable.

In Summary

- The wreck of *Costa Concordia* killed 32 people. The crisis threatened its owner, Carnival Corporation & plc, with hostile media coverage, legal action, loss of confidence and loss of business.
- Carnival's communication strategy flouted the doctrine that the boss must go to the scene and take charge in person. Carnival's boss kept a low media profile, delegating on-the-spot handling to its Costa operating company. The company expressed sympathy but blamed the ship's captain, who was later convicted for manslaughter.
- The evidence suggests that Carnival's unorthodox communication strategy worked well.

References

[1] Philip Pullella, 'Italy Enthralled by Ship's Tale of Two Captains,' *Reuters*, January 18, 2012.
[2] Stephen Brown, Pierre McDonagh & Clifford J Shultz II, 'Titanic: Consuming the Myths and Meanings of an Ambiguous Brand,' *Journal of Consumer Research*, Vol. 40, December 2013, Ahead of print. 'Death Toll in Manila Ferry Collision Rises to 34,' *New York Times*, December 3, 1994.
[3] Philip Pullella, 'Italian Cruise Ship Runs Aground, Six Reported Dead,' *Reuters*, January 14, 2012, 0550.
[4] Edward Jones, *Reckless Abandon, The Costa Concordia Disaster*, (Riverdale, MD: Jones-Mack Technical Services, 2012).
[5] Royal Institution of Naval Architects, *Costa Concordia - Passenger Evacuation*, <http://www.rina.org.uk/costa_concordia_passenger_evacuation.html>.
[6] Gaia Pianigiani & Alan Powell, 'Captain of Stricken Vessel Says He Fell Overboard in Passenger Panic,' *New York Times*, January 18, 2013. Coast Guard: Philip Pullella, 'Italy Enthralled by Ship's Tale of Two Captains,' *Reuters*, January 18, 2012. Detained: John Hooper, 'Captain Arrested Amid Growing Anger After Italian Cruise Ship Runs Aground,' *The Observer*, January 14, 2012.
[7] <http://www.costacruises.co.uk/B2C/GB/Info/ concordia_statement.htm> last updated February 17, 2012.
[8] Brendan Hodgson, #Costa Concordia Digital Crisis Analysis, Hill & Knowlton, <http://www.slideshare.net/Brendan/costa-concordia-digital-crisis-management-the-first-48-hours>.
[9] 'Carnival Corporation & plc Statement Regarding Costa Concordia,' Carnival Corporation & plc news release, January 14, 2012.
[10] 'Costa Cruises Statement on Costa Concordia Update #3,' Costa Crociere S.p.A. news release, January 15, 2012.
[11] 'Carnival Corporation & plc Required Announcement on Financial Impact of Costa Concordia,' Carnival Corporation & plc news release, January 16, 2012.
[12] Note 7, Carnival Corporation & plc, Carnival Corporation & plc 2013 Annual Report.
[13] 'Carnival Corporation & plc Chairman and CEO Statement Regarding Costa Concordia,' Carnival Corporation & plc news release, January 17, 2012.
[14] 'Costa Cruises and Carnival Corporation & plc Reiterate Commitment to Support Costa Concordia Passengers and Crew,' Carnival Corporation & plc news release, January 18, 2012.
[15] Gaia Pianigiani, 'Stricken Cruise Ship's Operator Offers Settlements to Passengers,' *New York Times*, January 27, 2012.
[16] John Schwartz, 'Cruise Lines Use Law and Contracts to Limit Liability,' *New York Times*, January 18, 2012. And see Robert H. Wilson, 'The Legal Strategy of the Cruise Line Industry: An Effective Use of Terms and Conditions to Manage Disputes,' *Cornell Hospitality Quarterly*, 2012 53: 347.
[17] 'Carnival Corporation & plc Announces Comprehensive Audit and Review of Safety and Emergency Response Across All Its Cruise Lines,' Carnival Corporation & plc news release, January 19, 2012.
[18] Gaia Pianigiani, 'Captain of Ship That Capsized Off Italy in '12 is Convicted,' *New York Times*, February 11, 2012.
[19] Rory F. Knight & Deborah J. Pretty, 'Corporate Catastrophes, Stock Returns, and Trading Volume,' *Corporate Reputation Review*, Vol. 2, No. 4, (1999), 363-378.
[20] Garry White, 'Carnival Ship Disaster: What the Analysts Say,' *Daily Telegraph*, January 16, 2012.
[21] Jad Mouawad, 'Industry Weighs Effect of Ship Accident,' *New York Times*, January 17, 2012.

[22] 'Carnival Corp & plc: Slow Steaming,' Morgan Stanley Research Europe, June 25, 2012, 3.

[23] Hodgson, #Costa Concordia Digital Crisis Analysis. Luciano Castro & Patrizia Perilli, *Concordiagate: The Cruise Ship Tragedy as Told by Two Reporters on Board: Investigations, Lies and Doubts*, (Cagliari, Italy: CUEC, 2012).

[24] Gaia Pianigiani, 'Divers Resume Search of Capsized Cruise Ship,' *New York Times*, January 21, 2012.

[25] Juliet Lapidos, 'Whoops, I Tripped Into a Lifeboat,' *New York Times*, January 20, 2012.

[26] Katarzyna Molek-Kozakowska, 'Towards a Pragma-linguistic Framework for the Study of Sensationalism in News Headlines,' *Discourse & Communication*, May 2013 vol. 7 no. 2 173-197.

[27] Nick Pisa & Lee Moran, 'Only a Disgraceful Man Would Have Left All Those Passengers on Board,' *Daily Mail*, January 18, 2012.

[28] Gaia Pianigiani & Rick Gladstone, 'With Pollutants a Peril, Italy to Seek a Buffer to Avert Future Cruise Ship Disasters,' *New York Times*, January 19, 2012.

[29] <http://boards.cruisecritic.com, CruiseCritic>.

[30] Ian Monk, 'Rogue Captain Line Could Sink Company,' *PR Week*, January 27, 2012.

[31] Diane LaPosta & Tim Lister, 'Concordia Disaster Focuses Attention on How Cruise Industry Operates,' CNN.com, International Edn., July 8, 2012.

[32] Steven Erlanger, 'Oversight of Cruise Lines at Issue After Disaster,' *New York Times*, January 16, 2012. James Kanter, 'Europe Zeroes In on Shipping Emissions,' *New York Times*, January 30, 2012. Michelle Higgins, 'So, Just How Safe Is Your Ship?' *New York Times*, February 1, 2012.

[33] Carreen Winters of MWW, quoted in *The Top 12 Crises Of 2012* by Arun Sudhaman & Paul Holmes, <http://www.holmesreport.com/featurestories-info/12970/The-Top-12-Crises-Of-2012-Part-1.aspx>.

[34] Carmine Gallo, '3 Things Carnival Must Do Now to Manage the Costa Crisis,' *Forbes*, January 18, 2012.

[35] Mike Esterl & Joann S. Lublin, 'Carnival CEO Lies Low After Wreck,' *Wall Street Journal*, January 23, 2012.

[36] Booton, 'Carnival Fails Crisis 101 in Costa Response.'

[37] Carnival Corporation & plc, Form 10-K for the Fiscal Year Ended November 30, 2014.

[38] Seitel, *The Practice of Public Relations*, 12th edn., 360-362.

[39] Elaine Walker, 'Carnival CEO Richest Florida Resident on Forbes List,' *Miami Herald*, September 19, 2012.

[40] < http://www.mashable.com> searched January 17, 2014.

[41] 'Statement 3pm CET,' Costa Crociere S.p.A. news release, January 24, 2012.

[42] Fink, *Crisis Communications*, 2013, 63 & 68-69.

[43] 'Carnival CEO Very Sorry for Shipwreck,' *UPI*, March 10, 2012.

[44] Colleen Barry & Francesco Sportelli, 'Italy: 5 Convicted for Costa Concordia Shipwreck,' *Associated Press*, July 20, 2013.

[45] Olins, *Corporate Identity*, 79.

[46] Bernstein, *Company Image and Reality*, 173.

[47] 'MidAmerican Energy Holdings Company Changes Its Name to Berkshire Hathaway Energy,' Berkshire Hathaway Energy news release, April 30, 2014.

[48] Stephen Foley, 'Warren Buffett Rolls out the Berkshire Hathaway Brand,' *Financial Times*, October 13, 2014.

[49] 'Carnival Corporation Launches Multi-Brand National Marketing Initiative Featuring TV, Digital, Social and Contest Elements,' Carnival Corporation & plc news release, November 24, 2014.

[50] 'Google Announces Plans for New Operating Structure,' Google news release, August 10, 2015.

[51] Stephanie Rosenbloom, 'How Normal Are Cruise Mishaps?' *New York Times*, May 8, 2013.

[52] 'Shipboard Fires, 1990-2013,' *Cruise Junkie*, <http://www.cruisejunkie.com/fires.html>.

[53] Higgins, 'So, Just How Safe Is Your Ship?'

[54] *Carnival Corp & plc: Downgrade to Underweight*, Morgan Stanley Research Europe, September 25, 2013, 6.

[55] Carnival Corporation & plc, Carnival Corporation & plc 2012 Annual Report, 2013, 40.

[56] Jones, *Reckless Abandon*.

[57] Pricing: 'Carnival Corp & plc: Coast Not Yet Clear,' Morgan Stanley Research Europe, May 22, 2013, 1. Recovering well: 'Carnival Corp & plc: Downgrade to Underweight,' Morgan Stanley Research Europe, September 25, 2013, 3.

[58] Michelle Higgins, 'So, Just How Safe Is Your Ship?'

[59] Carnival Corporation & plc, Carnival Corporation & plc 2012 Annual Report, 3.

[60] 'Carnival Corporation & plc Reports Fourth Quarter and Full Year Earnings,' Carnival Corporation & plc news release, December 19, 2013.

[61] Roger Blitz, 'Chairman Sees Bright Future for Carnival's Costa Brand;' 'Carnival Chairman Says Disaster Defied Imagination,' *Financial Times*, September 24, 2013.

CHAPTER 16
The Trouble with Airports

"DELIBERATION, noun. The act of examining one's bread to determine which side it is buttered on."

"INDECISION, noun. The chief element of success; 'for whereas,' saith Sir Thomas Brewbold, 'there is but one way to do nothing and divers ways to do something, whereof, to a surety, only one is the right way, it followeth that he who from indecision standeth still hath not so many chances of going astray as he who pusheth forwards' a most clear and satisfactory exposition on the matter."

— Ambrose Bierce, "The Devil's Dictionary"[1]

The biggest passenger terminal at Europe's biggest airport keeps a low profile. Heathrow Terminal 5 is a huge building by any standards, 1,312 feet by 558 feet under its main roof alone, on seven floors, each two or three times normal height.[2] Except from the air, there is not much to see. But then it is in the middle of an airport, between the runways, and much of it is below ground level.

And large new airport developments are highly controversial. Then when Terminal 5 (T5) opened there was a shameful burst of publicity over teething troubles. Then it faded into the welcome obscurity of daily, unthinking use by many thousands of people.

The battle over T5 is largely forgotten now because the war has moved on — the long war between those who want to develop airports and those who want to stop them. The future of London's airports remains mired in controversy amid government aversion to difficult decisions. Beyond airports, similar controversies surround projects such as the Keystone XL pipeline from Canada to the Gulf of Mexico, Britain's first long-distance high speed railway (HS2), and the rail tunnel to carry the TGV from France to Italy deep beneath the Alps. However, the battle over T5 and the longer story of London's airports is one of those stories that "are worth telling and... worth learning from."[3]

The story of airports can be told in different ways. One narrative is heroic. "Freedom to travel lies at the heart of our way of life," wrote Margaret Thatcher, introducing one such narrative.[4] As Europe's largest city and a world financial center, London acquired the world's busiest city airport system (by passenger traffic).[5] The number of people flying increased rapidly almost every year after the second world war as flying went from the luxury of a few to routine for the majority. In a 1999 British survey, 85% of people said they had flown, compared with 61% of their parents and only 29% of their grandparents.[6]

This heroic history is the narrative that I helped craft and communicate as director of corporate affairs at BAA plc, the company that owned the London airports and built most of the facilities in use today.

But, as projects that damage the environment for the sake of economic benefits, airports are often unpopular, especially in densely populated areas. An alternative, tragic history, according to their antagonists, tells of airports defiling the countryside with concrete, aircraft noise, and road traffic to and from the airports.

An education in airport development

The war gave aviation a boost — now there were new planes and a surfeit of trained pilots. For the first and only time, in 1946, London was ready. The government had expanded an airfield at Heathrow under cover of wartime. Post-war growth in air traffic was so rapid that at the end of the 1940s, thoughts were already turning to providing additional airport capacity and, in July 1952, the UK government said it had decided to develop a small airfield at Gatwick as a "southern alternative" to Heathrow.[7]

Local residents formed a protest committee. It complained to the press that local government had been kept completely in the dark and called for a public inquiry "into all the circumstances attendant upon so vast an upheaval." Controversy raged in Parliament and in the press. Details of the government's plan were released at last in October 1952 after a meeting with local authorities. There were to be two 7,000 ft. runways and a passenger terminal, with the first stage to be completed by 1956. Flights in the London area were forecast to double between 1951 and 1960, and Heathrow would be unable to meet future demand, even at its maximum development. Officials said that Gatwick would not be "another London Airport" but merely an "alternate" to Heathrow.[8]

In July 1953, the government acceded to pressure for a public but not independent inquiry. At an "extremely rowdy" public meeting in November 1953 there was "distrust of the way in which the whole project had been handled." For four weeks, lawyers for the government, local authorities and opponents presented arguments for and against developing the airport that were reported in the press.[9]

The inquiry concluded that the site was suitable but suggested that Gatwick should have been compared with other potential sites. Still, the government gave the go-ahead in October 1954. The protesters had not been able to change the decision but had delayed the project for two years.

Queen Elizabeth II opened the airport on June 9, 1958. Her Majesty reflected in diplomatic terms on the problem of finding somewhere to put airports: "This is a particularly difficult problem in this small island... I sympathize with all those people whose lives are going to be affected by this airport," but she hoped there would also be advantages from having an airport nearby. She added: "My husband and I travel by air often enough to realize" that it would be impossible to fly without adequate facilities being made available on the ground.[10]

Shape of the debate is set

The main arguments for and against airport development became clear at Gatwick in the 1950s. Opponents highlighted:

- Aircraft noise, initially around the airport site.
- The risk of from flying accidents, though this objection receded as the safety record improved.
- The destruction of homes and farmland.
- Pressure on surface transport facilities.
- The disadvantages of whatever target site was being proposed, such as foggy weather, poor drainage and a low hill near one end of the runway, compared with other sites far away.

Among the opponents, local people were to the fore. They are often labeled "NIMBY" — "Not In My Backyard," also known as "Not in my neighborhood."[11] They tend to be disparaged for the supposed hypocrisy of being in favor of projects so long as they are located at a safe distance, in someone else's neighborhood. The NIMBY community control movement is usually dated to the 1980s[12] but it can be traced back much farther, to airport opposition in the 1950s. Arguably, it goes back even to the proto-NIMBY towns that fought against railways entering or crossing their centers in the 19th century.

The strength of feeling against development is directly proportional to its impact on the wellbeing of the citizen. Gatwick set the pattern. It was personal. The Gatwick scheme threatened to erase the home of the protest committee chairman from the landscape.[13] The government's remote, utilitarian arguments left such victims unmoved. NIMBY may be a term of abuse for some but it is also a political reality. As the man running the airports in 1967 admitted: "None of us would like to have an airport stuck down in our back garden."[14]

Supporters of development stressed the importance of air transport to commerce and industry, stressed the number of existing and potential jobs dependent on the airport, and raised concerns about international competition. One airline chairman pointed out in 1952 that the rival metropolis of New York already had three airports — Idlewild (now Kennedy), La Guardia, and Newark — while London had only one.[15]

The government's original, flawed approach was to plan in secret, revealing as little as possible for as long as possible and deceiving those outside the magic circle about its real intentions and their consequences. It failed to consult properly with those who would be affected for fear that consultation would encourage opposition and delay development. It took clandestine action, such as acquiring real estate, to progress development before announcing its plans. The planning process was designed to exclude those affected and those who might object. The only element of democracy was that the ultimate decision would be taken by a democratically elected national legislature. The flagrant unfairness of this approach led directly to independent public inquiries. But these proved to be unsatisfactory in a different way. It was hoped that public inquiries would make planning more open and consultative. However, each public inquiry became more expensive and time-consuming as it was hijacked by opponents, who saw that the inquiry might not resolve the issue but could be used to delay any decision.

London's third airport

Gatwick 1958 was on a small scale compared with what would be needed as North America and Europe entered the age of the jet and mass tourism. In Britain, passenger traffic was set to rise from 1 million to 15 million in 15 years.[16] But new runways for aircraft to take off and land could not be built at the existing airports without major disruption including demolishing homes. This raised the question of a third London airport, in addition to Heathrow and Gatwick.

In 1963, a government committee settled on Stansted, an airfield in countryside about 35 miles northeast of London where the US Air Force had already built a runway that could take the largest aircraft.[17] The idea was inherited by the Labour government that was elected in 1964. The new government first set up the British Airports Authority (BAA) to run the airports in public ownership at arm's length. Then it backed Stansted — and began a struggle that would last ten years and descend into farce.

When an inquiry at first rejected the government's Stansted plan, the government was undaunted and used its large majority to vote a revised proposal through the House of Commons without further public scrutiny in 1967. But opposition intensified, with a demand for the issue to be reopened and a full public inquiry.[18] Meanwhile, the need for new runway capacity had abated. The prospect of the first wide-body aircraft (the Boeing 747, which came into service in 1970) meant that the number of seats per aircraft could be increased rather than the number of flights. A new minister, Antony Crosland, now added to a "long series of botched or badly presented decisions" and sly government maneuvers by halting Stansted.[19]

The issue had become too hot for the politicians to handle and Crosland ducked it by setting up the Third London Airport Commission to produce a solution. The Roskill Commission, as it was known, was chaired by a judge and composed of technocrats. Starting work in 1968, it attempted to use the latest pseudo-scientific methodology, cost-benefit analysis, to determine the best possible site for the airport. After cost-benefit-analyzing for a year, it announced a shortlist of four possible sites: not Stansted but the Thames estuary (Maplin, off Foulness) and three villages far to the north of London.[20]

To many outside the aviation industry, Maplin was the obvious answer — an airport distant from either centers of population or picturesque villages, on land (or mud) that was for the birds. Local governments, countryside organizations, the press and, probably, the majority of citizens of the London region all backed the distant estuary location.[21] The Thames Estuary Development Company, supported by the Port of London Authority, volunteered to build an airport and deep-water port. Maplin came to seem the obvious choice: "In view of the enormous outcry over any inland site, [the estuary] will almost certainly be chosen."[22]

However, the aviation industry was opposed to the estuary because of its inaccessibility, its proximity to foreign air traffic control systems, the danger of bird strikes, and bad weather.[23] Then, as now, the most commercially attractive option (not shortlisted) was to expand Heathrow instead.

The Roskill Commission of technocrats was not concerned with public opinion. After 74 days of sittings, hearing 160 witnesses, consuming three million words and 350 documents, cost-benefit analysis awarded the decision to Cublington, a site in deep countryside north-west of London.[24]

There was a mutiny on the Commission. Colin Buchanan, one of the commissioners, dissented, saying: "It would be nothing less than an environmental disaster if the airport were to be built at any of the inland sites," and argued for the estuary. Buchanan caught the prevailing public mood.

The Roskill report appeared in January 1971, after an election had replaced the Labour government with the Conservatives, and the new government decided to overrule the Commission and build in the estuary.[25] The country needed an airport, the government wanted a showpiece project, and the public wanted the whole business of airports, aircraft and noise moved far away from human habitation.

Until the energy crisis. In the ensuing struggle between government and coal miners, a general election was called and Labour narrowly returned to power. Labour regarded this pet airport project of the Conservatives as an expensive white elephant. Between two close elections (February and October 1974), it was economically and politically expedient to decide to do nothing. In the politically fragile summer of 1974, the government announced that Maplin had been abandoned, saying: "Up to 1990 no further main runways will be required."[26]

More than twenty different ministers were in charge of aviation between 1945 and 1976.[27] Most of them were closet but steadfast NIMTOOs — "Not In My Term Of Office."[28] Encouraged by the knowledge that their own tenure was likely to be very short, they became adept at deferring unpopular decisions. There was no danger that any individual would be called to account for the damage done by the delays. The long term could look after itself.

Key points
- Current intractable issues in transport infrastructure development date back many years to the immediate post-war period.
- The shape of the debate about providing airports for London was set at Gatwick in the 1950s.
- London's third airport was a fiasco.

The airport business: BAA's challenge

In 1987, Margaret Thatcher's Conservative government sold the BAA with its seven airports through an initial public offering as part of its privatization program. This had the fringe benefit of putting more distance between politicians and hassle. Thus the BAA metamorphosed into BAA plc, owned by and generating a return for its shareholders, mainly institutions but including more than 400,000 citizens who were encouraged to buy shares by the government.

BAA excelled at a range of business activities including facilities management, real estate, retail, security, and construction. The company even built and operated the first private rail line in decades to help people travel to and from Heathrow (Heathrow Express). Yet, fundamentally, there were two ways for an infrastructure company like BAA to make higher profits. First, it could earn more from users of its facilities. It did this primarily by pioneering high quality retail attractions at its airports. Second, it could increase throughput, principally by expanding the facilities. In addition, BAA was subject to a permanent government requirement that it must provide enough airport capacity for the regions it served. It was understood that, if it was unable to achieve this, it risked losing its licence. And London would run out of airport capacity unless something was done, since passenger traffic was forecast to almost double by 2015, to 168 million passengers a year.[29]

BAA owned three London airports. Heathrow was the world's busiest international airport (until now), and made most of its profits. But the airport was well within the expanding built-up area of the London conurbation, so that no new runway could be built without property demolition. Three of its four terminals were between the runways, on a site that was in effect an island, accessible only through tunnels (the Central Terminal Area). See fig. 16.1. The airport had been "laid out in ramshackle fashion over decades, making it difficult to achieve any kind of design consistency."[30] And it was impossible for it to operate without an impact on large numbers of local residents. For these reasons, any development at Heathrow would be fraught with difficulty.

Fig. 16.1 Heathrow in the Early 1990s and with Terminal 5

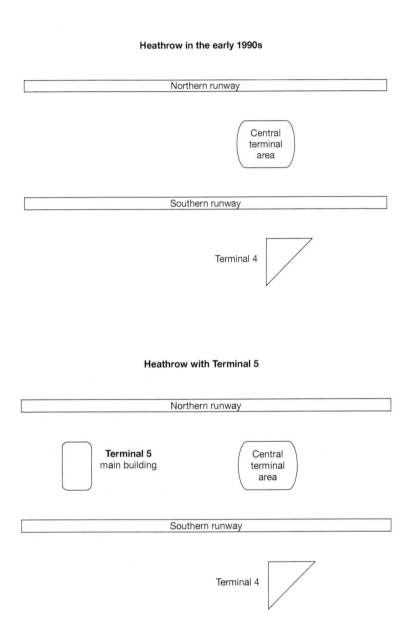

Airlines used a "hub and spoke" business model, with passengers from outlying cities taking feeder flights to a hub airport, from which they could fly to a wide range of destinations, perhaps on another continent. This model made it much more profitable and less risky for airlines to fly from a hub airport, with lots of connecting flights, than a small one. Heathrow was and remains "the only significant hub airport in... the UK."[31]

Gatwick, much smaller than Heathrow, and with many fewer scheduled flights, was much less attractive to airlines. In the mid-1980s, 14 million passengers used it, almost entirely for leisure travel. Some feared that its single runway would be unable to cope with even the predicted 25 million passengers.[32] Adding a runway at Gatwick was off the table, because the BAA had made an agreement with the local council not to seek one before 2019 in return for council approval of a second passenger terminal in 1979.

At Stansted, two decades after the ill-fated 1963 plan, a small passenger terminal was finally approved and opened in 1991. This coincided with the first Gulf War and recession in North America and Western Europe causing passenger traffic to turn down for the first time since the second world war. Stansted was empty. To schedule flights from a new, untested and empty airport was a major risk. BAA ingeniously used the spare capacity to encourage the development of airlines such as Ryanair. These "low-cost," "low fare," or discount airlines operated a different business model, pioneered by Southwest in America, flying people from point to point with no frills, using flexible labor, and seeking reduced airport charges. By attracting low cost flights and passengers through the 1990s, Stansted was serving 11.9 million people a year by 2000.[33]

It was occasionally suggested that BAA might abandon Heathrow and build a completely new airport somewhere else but this was never a commercial proposition either for BAA or the airlines. It would have been impossible for BAA to build a giant airport without destroying shareholder value on an equally gigantic scale. It would have been impossible to borrow enough without government help. Why should investors bet on a new airport without any customers, whose capital cost would far exceed the market value of the company building it?

An airport for the 21st century

Eschewing expansion at Heathrow in favor of Stansted, Gatwick or even a greenfield airport made no business sense. BAA therefore decided to concentrate on expanding Heathrow to the maximum extent possible using the existing two runways. It would seek planning permission for a fifth terminal. This would be not just another terminal but a mega-terminal that would be as large as most existing airports. It would not only expand but transform the airport. By relieving congestion, it would enable airline accommodation to be configured more efficiently and old facilities to be rebuilt. In this way, the entire airport could be upgraded. For the first time since the doomed third airport project, there was a vision of airports fit for London as the 21st century loomed. See fig. 16.1.

The company announced its plan in May 1992 (although plans had originally been considered years earlier.)[34]

Over the years, the BAA and government departments working hand-in-hand had fought three small passenger terminals through the planning process. But each time had taken longer as political conditions deteriorated. Now Sir John Egan, the prominent executive who had just sold Jaguar to Ford, took over as CEO at the beginning of the 1990s. Egan backed the Heathrow expansion plan that his new company already had on the drawing board but, attending a public meeting held in order to educate residents of one district about the plan, he was shaken by the strength of feeling:

- First, the impact of the airports had grown as numbers had risen, so that more people were affected and the "enough is enough" case had become more persuasive."[35]
- Second, special interest groups were better organized. Instead of the amateur Gatwick Protest Committee of 1952, BAA faced an alliance of thirty organizations, run in a professional way by experienced campaigners. Worse, all the local governments around Heathrow opposed the expansion and banded together to campaign against it.

- Third, aviation had become a more contentious issue than ever, of concern to environmental interests on a global level.

The company could no longer count on winning solely through a robust technical case and the support of government officials. Egan needed help and hired Des Wilson, the virtuoso campaigner, putting him in charge of winning the political case. Hard liners saw joining BAA as a betrayal of environmentalism but Wilson was unabashed. It was the time when globe-trotting, globe-warming environmentalists were overtaking champagne socialists up the league table of hypocrites. Wilson, by contrast, was genuine and open about his love of travel. A champion of citizens' rights as well as the environment, he recognized that in-sufficient airport capacity would logically mean rationing travel, presumably by price. But to travel was virtually a human right and he was not going to deny it to others: "Terminal Five is the most environmentally friendly way of meeting the growth in air traffic: 'Trying to stop people flying is just not on.'"[36]

Pre-empting the public inquiry

The traditional approach called for planners to devise a scheme and make the case for it, tediously, in the courtroom-like arena of the public inquiry. At Wilson's instigation, BAA took its case instead to the local people who would be directly affected by its proposals. It came up with a new narrative. It said it was committed to growing the airports *with the support and trust of its neighbors.* (This corporate neighborliness harked back to an ap-proach taken by some American corporations from the 1920s onwards.)[37]

The company held many local meetings to discuss the plan and commissioned Gallup to carry out an opinion poll, publish-ing the results.[38] More local people, defined as those living within the airport's noise footprint and a five-mile radius of the airport, supported T5 than opposed it.

The decisive factor was probably jobs. The airport was by far the largest source of employment in the area, with an estimated 68,000 people working for the airport, airlines and services such as shops, hotels and restaurants.

The poll clearly identified the main public concerns about T5: first, that the new terminal was a Trojan horse to prepare the way for a third runway at Heathrow; second, a government project to widen London's orbital superhighway, the M25, to 14 lanes; and third, a feared increase in the number of flights at night. BAA tackled each of these concerns, aiming to eliminate them from the debate before the public inquiry.

- RUNWAY. The wartime plans had called for additional runways to the north of the Heathrow site. A 1993 government study (RUCATSE) said that there was a strong case for a new runway in south-east England within twenty years, stressing the advantages of Heathrow as its site. And the majority of local people believed that T5 would lead to a third runway. BAA believed that a third runway was unacceptable and bent over backward to try to convince people that it should and could never happen, publicly asking the government to rule it out.[39]

- ROAD. BAA took a similar approach to the issue of highway widening. The company had originally supported widening — "because the government asked us to."[40] Now it withdrew its support, the argument for 14 lanes disintegrated, and the plan was discarded. More selective widening would suffice.

- NIGHT FLIGHTS. The issue of night flights was cleared up through clear communication of the facts. People had assumed that a new terminal would mean more flights at night. This was incorrect. In fact, the flights in question, arriving at Heathrow in the very early morning, would no longer be necessary with the additional capacity the new terminal would provide.

BAA won the argument before the inquiry opened.

Time stands still

The only hitch was that it took six years for the victory to be accepted and declared.

The T5 public inquiry opened on May 16, 1995. BAA arranged for a letter from Egan to be delivered to 500,000 homes on the first morning. He promised to deal with the concerns of the recipients, ("our neighbors,") to take steps to minimize the airport's impact on its neighbors, and to provide them with an annual progress report.[41]

At Gatwick in 1954, the opposite had happened. There the public inquiry was the first opportunity for the issues to be properly aired. Every day something happened at the inquiry that was new and unpredictable. As a result, the inquiry proceedings were news, covered throughout by the media. At Heathrow, all the arguments were aired beforehand, so the media coverage was like a very dull firework display. After some orchestrated sound and fury on opening day, there was an occasional wisp of smoke followed by a long darkness.

But, in the darkness, while millions of people slumbered, the inquiry worked like an infernal machine. Once it had been set in motion, it could neither be stopped nor speeded up because it would have been politically impossible for a government, even if it had wanted to, to be seen to truncate or tamper with the "democratic process." Teams of lawyers convened at an airport hotel, commandeered for the duration, and slogged through the evidence in mind-numbing, hair-greying detail for nearly four years, consuming time and money on a scale never seen before or since. There were 525 days of hearings, 734 witnesses, 27,500 written representations and 21 million words of evidence.[42] Once the lawyers had finished, it took a year-and-a-half for the inspector (chairman) to submit his report.

It was then another eleven months, until November 20, 2001, before the government (which had changed from Conservative to Labour half-way through the inquiry in 1997) could bring itself to pronounce — and approve T5.[43]

Government policy-making about airports has long proceeded at a glacial pace. This is neither systemic lethargy nor attention to detail but a feature of the politics of awkward topics such as airports. Uncontroversial decisions can be made, even by a bureaucratic state, in a jiffy. When an official commission recommended the popular move to lead-free fuel, the government announced its agreement within half-an-hour of the commission reporting.[44] But if the government is not seen to consider a contentious decision with exhaustive care, the decision is likely to be challenged in the courts, potentially causing additional years of delay.

The inquiry had been an epic filibuster by the anti-airport lobby. Speaking for the Conservatives on approval day, Eric Pickles said there was "a deep tragedy about parts of the announcement. Instead of its being a triumph for the aviation industry and for addressing the environmental concerns of local people, T5... will be remembered as the last hurrah of a cumbersome planning system." He pointed out that while T5 had been stuck in the planning process, numerous new terminals and runways had been built elsewhere in Europe.

Construction began and the queen opened the new terminal in March 2008. This was 16 years since BAA announced its plan and 50 years since she had opened Gatwick.

A new approach

T5 and the associated improvements at Heathrow was the only major airport expansion project to go forward in the London region in more than two decades. This was achieved in a political atmosphere that ranged from indifference, at best, to open hostility. (Terminal 2 at Heathrow, opened in 2014, rebuilt existing facilities.) That it did was thanks to Egan, Wilson and team radically changing the company's approach.

What lessons for communication strategy could be learned from the victory?

BAA had become a "stakeholder company." This strategic narrative (see chapters 9 and 17) was crucially important both to BAA's victory and its approach to doing business. BAA's communications at the time, a retrospective by Egan and Wilson, and Sharon Doherty's review of the T5 project all agree.[45] One of the principles underlying a new "Contract with the Community" was: "Pursue a stakeholder partnership approach to the decision-making process on new developments and other issues affecting the wider community, listening to and understanding the concerns of stakeholders, and developing practical programs of action to address them." It tried to put "reporting to stakeholders" on an equal footing with reporting to shareholders. BAA's approach was widely praised outside the company.

Proclaiming that it was a stakeholder company put BAA in a strong position rhetorically. It was not a purely commercial organization, run for the sole benefit of shareholders. It was a new kind of public-private business run for the benefit of all its stakeholders. Having worked inside the company at a senior level at the time, I am in no doubt that this was all sincere. And Des Wilson, whose brainchild it was, consistently advocated the same position in his memoir a decade later.[46]

Who exactly were BAA's stakeholders? Egan and Wilson said it was: "Every individual or group that has either a specific direct interest or an indirect interest in the activities of a company." This definition was almost as broad as Freeman's (chapter 12): "Any group or individual who can affect or is affected by the achievement of a corporation's purpose." The stakeholder company, Egan and Wilson argued, should be "communicating, cooperating and combining with them to the benefit of company and stakeholder alike."[47] And BAA's mission included: "Growing with the support and trust of our neighbors."[48]

But stakeholders may not be in accord. "The role of the board is to… ensure that the company meets its responsibilities to shareholders, customers, neighbors and other stakeholders," said BAA.[49] But how should these conflicting interests be reconciled?

If there was one criticism that could be leveled at the company, it was that it was unclear how this was to be done in practice. Consensus among its "stakeholders," broadly defined, was likely to be elusive.

BAA's published business strategy was a vague hotch-potch of good intentions that did not express clearly where the company was trying to go and how it was going to get there: "Concentrate on the core airport business, be prudently financed, continuously improve quality and cost effectiveness, become excellent in information technology, fully develop our property and retail potential, achieve world class standards in capital investment and develop an international business which enhances the quality and growth prospects of the Group."[50]

This gave no hint of choices having been made and resources allocated, and left so many questions unanswered that it would be necessary to examine actions rather than words. Judging by actions, an important element of the strategy was to develop the airports. Increasing profits depended on putting more traffic through its facilities, either by building or higher utilization and exploiting the traffic commercially.

BAA had not taken up two-way symmetric communication. The company genuinely wanted to serve its stakeholders but it was absolutely committed to winning approval for T5 as its primary way of expanding facilities. This required a campaign of persuasion. Some stakeholders were implacably opposed to T5. Approval could not be won by symmetry. Instead, BAA appealed when necessary over the heads of stakeholders such as the local authorities, direct to the people.

This targeted the enabling stakeholder that was affected by BAA's proposal, the usually dormant public of local residents, whose support would ensure that there was popular majority support for T5. Although the time taken by the inquiry was tiresome, absence from the news took the steam out of the opposition. BAA campaigned hard in advance of the inquiry, then kept a relatively low profile on the issue while the inquiry was in progress.

It also played well with BAA's principal enabling stakeholder, the government. The government might no longer own the company but it was still the ultimate arbiter of BAA's fate. For BAA to be seen to be working with public opinion was helpful to politicians.

Through the years between the inquiry opening and government approval being granted, there was a danger of legal challenges that could potentially halt the process part way through and cause a restart. Any deviation from the case presented to the inquiry may have risked opponents saying that plans had changed. In such a situation, tight control of all communications, along the lines set out in chapter 17, is essential.

Public acceptance

Once the T5 inquiry was under way, BAA followed a strategy of community acceptance to bring smaller projects to fruition, using the same narrative of "growing with the support and trust of our neighbors." These projects would be less contentious and could be delivered through a process of persuasion and negotiation.

BAA obtained approval for developments at Gatwick and Stansted in this way. One of its methods was to begin a dialog with local representatives before plans were completed. "All the time, it stressed that the plans were drafts. Gatwick needed to grow, it said, but how this was to happen was open to discussion; in some cases several options were put before local people."[51] If a business wanted to develop an infrastructure project it should explain its plans, discuss them, listen to local concerns and make modifications to suit its neighbors. It was an effective campaign of persuasion that focused on those who mattered.

This was not completely novel. It had been used, for example, for infrastructure projects in New Jersey in the 1980s.[52] Community acceptance strategies work well when infrastructure projects are acceptable in principle to local residents. But in the difficult cases, conflict is unavoidable and cannot be resolved to the satisfaction of all parties. In the case of the 1965-66 public inquiry into London's planned third airport at Stansted, it was observed at the time that: "No objectors were interested in suggesting modifications; they quite simply did not want an airport at Stansted at all. This is likely to happen wherever an airport is proposed."[53] In this respect, nothing has changed in four decades. This is a different world from what *The Economist* once called the "Hollywood vision of liberal politics in which entrenched conflicts are simply misunderstandings that can be resolved through personal contact and (bogus) emotional catharsis."[54]

Key points
- The state agency running London's airports was privatized in 1987 as BAA plc. It inherited the challenge of providing for room for the world's busiest international airport system to grow.
- But gaining political approval for large-scale airport developments around London had become almost impossible by the early 1990s.
- BAA fought a shrewd campaign to build a new terminal at Heathrow so large that it would be the equivalent of a whole new airport. The campaign involved targeted communications, periodically keeping shtum, and a strategic narrative that cast BAA as a stakeholder company working in the interests of local people.

Pyrrhic victory

BAA won but its victory was Pyrrhic because the long delay led directly to the demise of the company.

For most of the 1990s and 2000s, conditions at Heathrow for travelers and airlines were difficult. The airport became more and more overcrowded. If, somehow, T5 could have opened in the mid-1990s rather than the late 2000s, BAA could have transformed users' experience and hence their view of the company. As it was, a rising tide of dissatisfaction broke over the company. Who else to blame? The politicians who failed to approve the necessary works were too distant. They had craftily insulated themselves from popular dissatisfaction.

By the mid-2000s, infrastructure investment was in vogue. The reliable cash flow from infrastructure over a term of many years was particularly desirable for pension funds with their long-term liabilities. Aggressive investors saw that London's airports were ripe for leveraging up. BAA's prime assets and steady cash flow could be used to finance far more debt than the company then carried. It became a takeover target as £11 billion ($17.5 billion) of debt for BAA began to seem manageable, although some wondered whether a leveraged company would still have the ability to invest in improving facilities.[55]

BAA could have carried out the leveraging itself and converted itself from a transport operator into an infrastructure fund with exceptional knowledge of airports. Despite the global financial crisis, the leading infrastructure funds have fared well. But, in the event, after the company had been in play for some time, the shareholders accepted an offer for the company at a considerable premium to the market price. It was acquired by a Spanish-led consortium, the snappily named FGP TopCo Limited.

As a construction project, T5 was a tour de force displaying the expertise in construction BAA had developed under Egan. It was rare among projects of its size in being completed on time and on budget. Its opening in 2008 should have been a triumph. But, at the last moment, disaster struck. The new baggage handling arrangements seized up, causing flights to be canceled.[56]

BAA's monopoly ownership of the major London airports was periodically investigated by regulators to ensure that it was not stifling competition. Indeed, such an investigation was under way when T5 opened. Whatever the correct apportionment of blame for the opening fiasco, it was the last nail in the airport operator's coffin. Past reviews had found "no public interest reason to question BAA's management of Heathrow, Gatwick and Stansted as a single airport system."[57]

But BAA II was no longer a blue chip British company, so no longer enjoyed the political cover BAA had always worked hard to secure. With service standards crippled by overcrowding at Heathrow, and widely believed to have presided over a debacle, BAA II was in line for the guillotine.

Delivering its verdict, the Competition Commission referred to "widespread criticism of BAA's management of several of its airports, most particularly Heathrow." The unkindest cut was noting that a principal political objective of the 1987 privatization "was the provision of adequate airport capacity to meet the expected growing demand and to support airline competition." More than 20 years after privatization, the Commission dismissed the immense effort BAA had made to provide capacity, despite government lethargy, and said it was inadequate.[58] BAA II was broken up, with the consortium forced to sell both Gatwick and Stansted.

Repeating the 1960s

In more than 14 years since T5 was approved, not a single major piece of new airport infrastructure for London has been approved, let alone begun to be built. In 2016, the number of runways remains the same as in the 1960s. Two runways at Heathrow and one each at Gatwick, Stansted and Luton, a smaller, non-BAA airport north of London, proved to be capable at a stretch of handling as many as 135 million passengers in 2013.[59]

But words have been spoken and written by the torrent, falling naturally into two phases. First, the 13-year Labour administration which came to office in 1997, approved T5 in 2001, and ended in 2010. Second, the Conservative-Liberal Democrat coalition administration 2010-15.

Once T5 was approved, the Labour government started thinking again about new runways. It fancied a second runway at Stansted and a third runway at Heathrow — the "political and environmental non-runner" that had been "ruled out" in 1995. It envisaged that both would be built and financed by BAA, using the income stream from Heathrow to subsidize the development of Stansted.[60] The Stansted runway was firmly proposed in December 2003, to open in 2012, with a later runway at Heathrow.[61] BAA announced its plan for the new Stansted runway in 2005, to a chorus of disapproval,[62] and the plan was subsequently abandoned as BAA II was being broken up. The government lost a legal challenge to eventual plans for a new Heathrow runway in March 2010[63] and political interest in aviation evaporated in view of the May 2010 election.

The coalition government then took office on a promise of no Heathrow third runway. It was not initially prepared to back a new runway anywhere.[64] There were already enough difficult decisions to take in the wake of the global financial crisis without becoming bogged down in battles over airports. What to do now? Back to 1968. For the new government decided in 2012 to set up the Third London Airport Commission Version 2.0, which it named the Airports Commission. Sir Howard Davies, former executive chairman of the UK Financial Services Authority, was appointed chairman.

But the Davies Commission (Roskill Redux) was not due to make its final recommendations until 2015, enabling the 2010-15 government to avoid making any decisions about new runways or airports. It all went into the big tray marked Only After 2015 Election.

The future of the city is at stake

A megalopolis tends to outgrow its system of government. Greater New York may be one of the world's great citities and most important economic regions but officially it is merely a statistical area. Sprawling across parts of four states, its arrangements for government are a shambles. But at least it has airports, even if New Yorkers have complained bitterly about the condition of La Guardia for many years.

Similarly, London long ago burst through county boundaries. Even today's Greater London Authority, with an elected mayor and assembly, supposedly covering the whole city, actually covers only the central area of this vast conurbation. The problem is partly that: "The city scale – even the metropolitan city scale – is too small to capture the appropriate economic processes. Economies and labor markets operate over larger areas that are not contiguous with administrative boundaries."[65] (Tony Travers.)

But metropolitan cities need airports. "Cities with a high degree of accessibility... are at special advantage... Major hub airports have acted as major magnets for new activities: alike in Europe, North America and in Australia, there is a clear relationship between major business centers as measured by international activity, and the presence of major airports."[66] (Peter Hall)

London used often to be contrasted with Paris. London's airports offered accumulating delay and congestion, whereas a new state-of-the-art four-runway airport was being built for Paris at Roissy-en-France. "While we are still talking, the French have been getting on with the job,"[67] *The Times'* Arthur Reed said in 1970. Nothing has changed in more than 45 years. "The comparison between London Heathrow and Paris Charles de Gaulle shows how far national characteristics can infuse airport design... the latter is grandly conceived, beautifully executed and infused with Gallic pomp."[68] (Brian Edwards)

The London-Paris comparison no longer seems the most compelling. Instead, look at the Gulf. The vision of Dubai was to build a major hub airport not just to serve an existing city but as the catalyst for a whole new city. In 1999, Dubai's population was estimated to be less than a million yet Dubai International handled 10.7 million passengers. By 2014, while the population had more than doubled, the airport's throughput had multiplied to 71 million passengers, overtaking Paris Charles de Gaulle, Frankfurt and finally Heathrow to become the world's busiest international airport.[69]

But Dubai is thinking even bigger, building a completely new airport 70 kilometers from Dubai International. Al Maktoum International at Dubai World Central is designed to handle 150-200 million passengers.[70] "Aviation is at the heart of Dubai's economic strategy. The government of Dubai clearly recognizes that aviation is not only an important driver of growth in its own right, but that it underpins growth in other key sectors."[71] A short distance along the coast, Tony Douglas, the executive who was responsible for constructing Heathrow Terminal 5 and became CEO of Abu Dhabi Airports, contrasted the time taken for T5 to be approved with the quick decisions made by Abu Dhabi. He was able to start work in 2013 on its new terminal, expecting to handle 30 million passengers a year only four years later in 2017.[72]

In the meantime, while the great recession briefly reduced demand for air travel, the long-term trend for air travel to grow much faster than GDP shows no sign of changing. London's airports are becoming ever more congested, with all that implies for service, delays and frayed tempers but not, unfortunately, political commitment to change.

The Davies plan

In December 2013, the Davies Commission said: "Decisions on airport location and capacity are among the most important strategic choices a country or city can make, influencing the economic, environmental and social development of cities and regions more than almost any other single planning decision. They are also among the most contentious."[73] It made the broad case for more airport capacity and "shortlisted" runway options at Heathrow and Gatwick. (In September 2014 the Commission also said that it was definitely opposed to an estuary airport.)[74] After the May 2015 election, it published its final report as promised, recommending a new runway at Heathrow, the most economically attractive but contentious option.

At the time of writing it remained to be seen whether the new Conservative government would muster the strength to make a firm decision, even in the knowledge that it will probably have four-and-a-half years for the resulting commotion to die down before it has to face the voters again. In December 2015, the government said it needed to do further work before making a decision in the summer of 2016.[75]

Key points
- Delayed by a legal logjam and political pusillanimity, Heathrow Terminal 5 did not open until 2008.
- The airport company was sold to a consortium at the top of the market. Blamed for poor conditions caused by the overcrowding it had worked to relieve, it became an easy target for competition authorities to break up.
- A new commission was set up in 2012, whose recommendation of a new runway at Heathrow awaits government consideration.
- At the time of writing, no large-scale airport development is in progress for London despite continuing and forecast rapid growth in passenger numbers.

Answers

Like Roskill before it, the Davies Commission served more than one purpose. It is a fair assumption that it was intended partly to answer the airport question and, just as important, both to distance the airport question from the government and to build support for a conclusion.

Davies narrows down the options, yet with a greater variety of airlines and with each London airport in separate ownership, the range of views about what should be done is wider than ever. Most recent argument has been about *where* a new runway should be built. Any airport owner wants to develop its airport. Heathrow Airport Holdings Limited, the rump of BAA II, now believes that the solution is a third runway at Heathrow — the one that its ancestor once asked to be ruled out. Deep down, business interests probably share the sentiments of Michael O'Leary, the plain speaking boss of Ryanair, who said in 2013: "They don't have a policy on aviation because they're so busy pandering to the bloody environmental lunatics. You need three more runways in the south-east — one at Heathrow, one at Gatwick, one at Stansted. That would solve the problem and make the UK competitive."[76] But that is just a dream.

Notwithstanding Davies, the options are numerous and can be plotted on a spectrum from centrally planned to free-for-all.

At one end of the spectrum is the comprehensive answer offered by a single giant airport. Boris Johnson, the charismatic Mayor of London, is the most prominent advocate of a new airport in the Thames estuary. This would be a variation on the grand project of the early 1970s. There are technical difficulties but London would not be the first to reclaim land from the sea for its airport. New York, Hong Kong and Nice are among those who have already done it without dire consequences. What makes it improbable is not technical difficulty but the immense cost and the absence of political commitment such a project would require.

Adding a runway to Heathrow (or alternatively Gatwick) is in the middle of the spectrum. This is currently being presented as The Answer. What makes it less likely than it looks is the need for a government not only to make a decision but to make the decision stick. Previous governments have made "decisions" but either failed to follow through or been succeeded and had their decisions overturned. The sole major airport project of the past thirty years to succeed, Terminal 5, did so partly thanks to skilful management by BAA and partly because, uniquely, one government which supported the project was succeeded by another government which also supported the project. The election which changed governments took place in 1997, two years into the T5 inquiry. BAA facilitated government policy continuity by keeping the airport political climate around the time of the election cool — by *keeping shtum.*

Heading for the far end

At one end of the spectrum is a new airport in the estuary — unlikely. In the middle is a new runway at Heathrow or Gatwick — presented as most likely. At the far end of the spectrum is no major development at all. If history is a guide, doing nothing big is the most likely answer.

Environmental and local opposition will fiercely oppose whatever building plan the government finally proposes. 2015 election night reports suggested that current Mayor Boris might lie in front of bulldozers to stop a third runway at Heathrow.[77] Short of putting an airport out at sea on "Boris Island," any new runway would affect people on the ground across large swathes of London and south-east England who will object. When planners were looking at possible sites for London's third airport in the 1960s, it was estimated that a new airport would create an "oppressive zone" 45 miles by six miles, affecting many thousands of people,[78] although the noise footprint would be smaller today, thanks to quieter aircraft, and will progressively shrink as the aircraft of the future become quieter still.

The Conservative government has only a slim majority in the House of Commons. Assume that the opposition parties will oppose the government's scheme. A significant number of Conservative MPs represent constituencies where there is a strong lobby against aircraft noise but little direct economic benefit from the airport. These MPs are in a position to exert considerable influence. How likely is it that the government will confront them in the summer of 2016?

The answer could instead be a fudge, that is an appearance of action, in the form of various small projects, without any large scale action to upset people, and especially no new runway. This does not mean constraining air travel but leaving it to the market. Each airport could independently advance its own small schemes, on the tacit understanding that major projects are out but small projects that are not too contentious can go ahead. BAA showed how this could be done with its projects at Gatwick and Stansted, as discussed above. Consumers from the London region could travel longer distances to reach airports which have spare capacity. Airlines could offer consumers ways round the capacity constraint, connecting to airports in cities such as Amsterdam, Dublin, Frankfurt and Paris. Others will do for London what London is seemingly unable to do for itself.

In Summary

- Large infrastructure projects that make uncomfortable neighbors tend to be controversial and divisive.
- Astute communications enabled BAA, the world's leading airport company, to win approval to build Terminal 5, London's only major airport expansion in more than two decades. But it took 16 years from proposal to completion.
- The political impossibility of redeveloping Heathrow's jumble of inadequate facilities quickly enough led indirectly to BAA's break-up. London airport infrastructure remains inadequate, with no clear way forward.

Note on confidentiality

This book advocates respect for confidentiality. In line with that position, no confidential information has been disclosed in it. The author was involved in some of the events described, especially in the chapter about BAA, but all the facts, figures and cited opinions in the book are in the public domain. The aim has not been to reveal confidential information but to analyze what happened.

References

[1] Bierce, *The Devi's Dictionary*, 159 & 68.

[2] Tom Dyckhoff, 'Cattle Queues Give Way at Last to Civil Aviation,' *The Times*, March 15, 2008.

[3] Sir John Egan, foreword to Sharon Doherty, *Heathrow's Terminal 5: History in the Making*, (Chichester, UK: John Wiley & Sons, Ltd, 2008).

[4] Michael Donne, *Above Us The Skies*, (Whitley, UK: Good Books/BAA plc, 1991).

[5] London (Heathrow, Gatwick and Stansted): 121.7m, 2012 (Civil Aviation Authority, UK Airport Statistics: 2012, 2013, Table 01). New York (Kennedy, Newark, La Guardia): 109.0m, 2012 (The Port Authority of New York and New Jersey, *Airport Traffic Report: 2012*, 2013, Table 2.1.1).

[6] BAA plc, Annual report 1999-2000, 2000, 36.

[7] Wartime: See Philip Sherwood, *Heathrow: 2000 Years of History*, (Stroud, UK: Sutton Publishing, 1999), 63-64. Post-war: 'Gatwick Airport Derequisition Deferred,' *The Times*, Aug. 23, 1949. Southern alternative: Donne, *Above Us The Skies*, 49-50.

[8] Inquiry: 'Gatwick Airport Expansion: Residents' Anxiety,' *The Times*, Aug. 14, 1952. Local authorities: 'Gatwick Airport Extension,' *The Times*, Oct. 7, 1952. Alternate: 'Objections To Gatwick Plan,' *The Times*, Oct. 11, 1952.

[9] Inquiry: 'Modified Plan For Gatwick,' *The Times*, July 23, 1953. Meeting: 'Gatwick Airport Inquiry Terms Defined by Minister,' *The Times*, Nov. 6, 1953. Four weeks: 'Expert's View on Fog at Gatwick,' *The Times*, April 2, 1954.

[10] 'The Queen at Gatwick,' *The Times*, June 10, 1958.

[11] Jon D. Hull, 'Not In My Neighborhood,' *Time*, Jan. 25, 1988.

[12] Lisa S. Nelson, 'Community Control,' in *International Encyclopedia of Public Policy and Administration*, ed. by Jay M. Shafritz, (Boulder, CO: Westview Press, 1998), 440.

[13] 'Airport Plans at Gatwick,' *The Times*, Oct. 8, 1952.

[14] David McKie, *A Sadly Mismanaged Affair: A Political History of the Third London Airport*, (London: Croom Helm, 1973), 112.

[15] Lord Douglas of Kirtleside, chairman of British European Airways, 'Letter to the Editor,' *The Times*, Oct. 24, 1952.

[16] Anthony Sampson, *Empires of the Sky*, (London: Coronet Books, 1985), 140.

[17] McKie, *A Sadly Mismanaged Affair*, 49-76.

[18] Majority: Arthur Reed, 'Stansted Best Of All Alternatives,' *The Times*, May 13, 1967. Opposition: McKie, *A Sadly Mismanaged Affair*, 91-103 & 124-136.

[19] McKie, *A Sadly Mismanaged Affair*, 106.

[20] 'New Battles Loom over Third London Airport,' *The Times*, March 4, 1969.

[21] 'GLC Wants Foulness as Airport,' *The Times*, Aug. 6, 1970. Arthur Reed, 'Survey Sees Foulness as Best Site,' *The Times*, March 20, 1970. Arthur Reed, 'New Sites Worse for Noise than Heathrow' *The Times*, April 8, 1970.

[22] Arthur Reed, 'London's Third Airport - It Looks Like Foulness,' *The Times*, Aug. 8, 1970.

[23] 'Third Airport Vote for Cublington,' *The Times*, May 12, 1970; 'Airlines Oppose Foulness,' *The Times*, March 28, 1970.

[24] 'Airport Inquiry Ends Sittings,' *The Times*, Aug. 13, 1970. Arthur Reed, 'Why Roskill Prefers Cublington Site,' *The Times*, Dec. 19, 1970.

[25] Buchanan: Colin Buchanan, 'Note of Dissent,' *Report of the Commission on the Third London Airport*, HMSO, 1971, paragraph 56, page 159. Cublington: McKie, *A Sadly Mismanaged Affair*, 191 & 199. Estuary: 'Foulness Chosen for Third Airport on Environment Grounds,' *The Times*, April 27, 1971.

[26] The Secretary of State for Trade and President of the Board of Trade (Mr Peter Shore), HC Deb 18 July 1974, Vol. 877, cc675-92, <http://hansard.millbanksystems.com/commons/1974/jul/18/maplin>.

[27] Arthur Reed, 'Doubt over Direction Airlines Should Go,' *The Times*, Nov. 29, 1976.

[28] Larry S. Luton, 'Acronym,' in *International Encyclopedia of Public Policy and Administration*, Shafritz (ed.), 18.

[29] The Heathrow Terminal Five and Associated Public Inquiries, Report by Roy Vandermeer QC, November 21, 2000, Chapter 7.2.1, 59.

[30] Michael Skapinker, 'Heathrow Trails Behind,' *Financial Times*, Sep. 14, 2004.

[31] BAA Airports Market Investigation: A Report on the Supply of Airport Services by BAA in the UK, Competition Commission, March 19, 2009.

[32] 'Airports policy,' *The Times*, July 6, 1985.

[33] Civil Aviation Authority, *UK Airport Statistics: 2000 - annual*, 2001, <http://www.caa.co.uk/default.aspx?catid=80&pagetype=88&sglid=3&fld=2000Annual>.

[34] 'Plans for Fifth Heathrow Terminal Confirmed,' *Associated Press*, May 12, 1992; Peter Masefield & Bill Gunston, *Flight Path, the Autobiography of Sir Peter Masefield*, (Shrewsbury, UK: Airlife Publishing, 2002), 297.

[35] John Egan & Des Wilson, *Private Business... Public Battleground: The Case for Twenty-First Century Stakeholder Companies*, (Basingstoke, UK: Palgrave, 2002), 35 & 83-84.

[36] Christian Wolmar, 'Big Guns Line up for Battle of Heathrow,' *The Independent*, Sep. 25, 1994.

[37] Marchand, *Creating the Corporate Soul*, 361-363.

[38] Heathrow Residents' Survey, Executive Report, Gallup Poll Limited, April 1995.

[39] The Heathrow Terminal Five and Associated Public Inquiries, Chapter 8.1.5, 70.

[40] Des Wilson, *Memoirs of a Minor Public Figure*, (London: Quartet Books Limited, 2011), 325.

[41] A letter to our Heathrow neighbours from Sir John Egan, Chief Executive, BAA plc, BAA plc, May 16, 1995.

[42] 'Heathrow's Fate,' *The Economist*, March 18, 1999.

[43] Secretary of State for Transport, Local Government and the Regions (Mr Stephen Byers), HC Deb 20 Nov. 2001 Vol. 375, cc177-93, <http://hansard.millbanksystems.com/commons/2001/nov/20/heathrow-terminal-5#S6CV0375P0_20011120_HOC_159>.

[44] John McCormick, *British Politics and the Environment*, (Abingdon, UK: Earthscan, 2009), 138.

[45] Egan & Wilson, *Private Business... Public Battleground*, Doherty, Heathrow's Terminal 5.

[46] Wilson, *Memoirs of a Minor Public Figure*, 322-332 & 390-391.

[47] Egan & Wilson, *Private Business... Public Battleground*, 69.

[48] BAA plc, Annual report 1998-99, 1999.

[49] BAA plc, Annual report 1998-99, 1999, 39.

[50] BAA plc, Annual report 1997-98, 1998.

[51] Egan & Wilson, *Private Business... Public Battleground*, 103-112.

[52] Nancy Blethen, 'NIMBY: Defining and Dealing with the Not-In-My-Backyard Syndrome,' in *Corporate Communication: Theory and Practice*, ed. by Michael B. Goodman, (Albany, NY: State University of New York Press, 1994), 103-109.

[53] Ronald E. Wraith, 'The Public Inquiry into Stansted Airport,' *The Political Quarterly*, Vol. 37, No. 3, 1966, 265-280.

[54] 'Vicky Cristina Jerusalem,' *The Economist* blog, Jan. 31, 2014, <http://www.economist.com/blogs/democracyinamerica/2014/01/scarlett-johansson-and-sodastream>.

[55] 'On the runway,' *The Economist*, June 8, 2006.

[56] See for example: 'Terminal Disgrace: Poor Training and Computer Failings to Blame for T5 Chaos as Flights Fiasco to Last into the Weekend,' *London Evening Standard*, March 27, 2008. Tim Brady & Andrew Davies, 'From Hero to Hubris - Reconsidering the Project Management of Heathrow's Terminal 5,' *International Journal of Project Management*, 28 (2010) 151-157.

[57] 'MMC Report Reflects Quality Company; No Public Interest Reason to Break up BAA London Airport System,' BAA plc news release, July 16, 1996.

[58] Competition Commission, BAA Airports Market Investigation: Provisional findings report, Aug. 20, 2008, 5.

[59] Civil Aviation Authority, UK Airport Statistics: 2014, <http://www.caa.co.uk/docs/80/airport_data/201401/Table_01_Size_of_UK_Airports.pdf>.

[60] 'No stopping Heathrow,' The Economist, Aug. 14, 2003.

[61] 'Insatiable Demand for Air Travel,' The Economist, Dec. 4, 2003.

[62] 'Plans to Expand Airports,' The Economist, Dec. 14, 2005.

[63] Philip Pank & Steve Bird, 'Heathrow Third Runway Plan in Tatters After Ruling, Claim Opponents,' The Times, March 27, 2010.

[64] Bob Sherwood, 'Plans for Third Heathrow Runway Scrapped,' Financial Times, May 13, 2010.

[65] Tony Travers, The Politics of London: Governing an Ungovernable City, (Basingstoke, UK: Palgrave Macmillan, 2004), 4.

[66] Peter Hall, Cities in Civilization, (London: Weidenfeld & Nicholson, 1998), 964.

[67] Arthur Reed, 'An Inquiry on the Site of London's Third Airport Opens Today. In Paris the Problems Have Been Overcome,' The Times, April 6, 1970.

[68] Brian Edwards, The Modern Airport Terminal: New Approaches to Airport Architecture, (Abingdon, UK: Spon Press, 2005), 28.

[69] Joel Lewin, 'Dubai Replaces Heathrow as Busiest Airport,' Financial Times, Jan. 12, 2015.

[70] Kari Lundgren, 'Dubai Airport Has Heathrow in Its Sights After Eclipsing Paris,' Bloomberg, Jan. 29, 2014.

[71] Dubai Airports, Connecting the World Today and Tomorrow: Strategic Plan 2020, 2011, 12.

[72] Andrew Parker, 'Abu Dhabi Enters the Slipstream,' Financial Times, Dec. 9, 2013.

[73] Airports Commission, Airports Commission: Interim Report, 2013, 6.

[74] 'Airports Commission Announces Inner Thames Estuary Decision,' Airports Commission news release, Sep. 2, 2014.

[75] 'Government Confirms Support for Airport Expansion in the South-East,' Department for Transport announcement, December 10, 2015.

[76] Michael O'Leary, on Bloomberg Surveillance, Bloomberg Television, May 20, 2013, 1256 CET.

[77] Fiona Keating, 'Boris Johnson Prepared to Lie Down in Front of Bulldozers to Stop Construction of Third Runway at Heathrow,' International Business Times, (UK edn.), May 12, 2015.

[78] McKie, A Sadly Mismanaged Affair, 35.

PART IV

Communication Strategy

In Part IV

How to create a communication strategy — in 100 days. Chapter 17 puts together the elements of communication strategy examined in Part II in the form of a program that could be accomplished in 100 days. This program could be used by someone taking up a senior executive role, whether at the top or as a divisional or functional head. Or it could be used as a reference at any time on how to do communication strategy.

Chapter 18 concludes the book by stressing the importance of focus.

CHAPTER 17

100 Days: For a communication strategy

"When Metellus Pius was in Spain and was asked what he was going to do the next day, he replied: 'If my tunic could tell, I would burn it.'" — Sextus Julius Frontinus, "Strategemata,"[1] on the important of concealing intentions.

In the first 100 days of Franklin D. Roosevelt's presidency, he launched the New Deal, a vigorous burst of initiatives to tackle the Depression. Two centuries ago, the "Hundred Days" stood for the astonishing comeback of Napoleon from Elba.

In the first hundred days, a new leader has a great opportunity to bring about change. This chapter is addressed to you as that leader. It assumes that your aim is not to be a caretaker but to make an impact — to move your organization from where it is now to where it should be in the future.

Urgency

Following the example of the most effective presidents of the US, communication direction should be set with a sense of urgency.

Once Ronald Reagan was elected in 1980, but before he took office, he tasked aides with writing an "Early Action Plan" for the first 100 days of the presidency. For this plan, David Gergen made a study of the first 100 days of each of the first time presidents from Roosevelt onwards (Roosevelt, Eisenhower, Kennedy, Nixon and Carter). He looked at what each man had done and how it had been received — not ideology but whether it worked well. He concluded that the public has a fresh look at each president when he ceases to be a candidate or a president-elect and takes office. And the new president has an opportunity to set the tone of the administration, giving clear leadership.[2] The most successful presidents were the ones who quickly set and pursued a clear and simple agenda.

Reagan concentrated on four issues in his legislative program, rapidly establishing the direction of his presidency, which was widely regarded as a success by friend and foe alike.[3] Gergen became Reagan's director of communications. He was considered to have been so good at the job that Bill Clinton appointed Gergen, a Republican, as his own director of communications in 1993.

Three steps

You need to take these three steps to set your strategic direction in communication:

1. Take control of communications without delay.

2. Quickly analyze and take stock of the situation you face.

3. Set the agenda, the new communication strategy.

These three stages are laid out in fig. 17.1, Communication Strategy Process:

Fig. 17.1 Communication Strategy Process

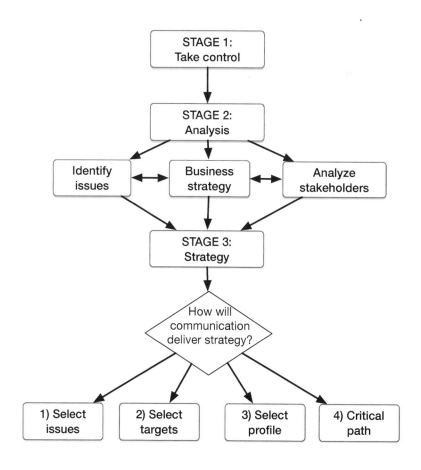

STAGE 1: Take Control

"When you walk into a company as chief executive, what do you do? How do you take charge?"

That was the theme of a speech I wrote twenty-five years ago for a well-known CEO to deliver at a management forum. The speech said that this problem was peculiar to chief executives. But actually how to take charge is a problem for any incoming senior executive, not just the CEO. A new divisional or functional head is part of the management team but also needs to be a leader and take charge of his or her new responsibility. This applies to all leaders.

Tactically, people frequently mess up their communications by making gaffes, by saying too much, and by speaking out when they should keep their own counsel, but there is a strategic solution that is the essential first step. Before you can decide what and how to communicate, you have to take control. If you don't have control, anything you do is going to be undermined by other people doing their own thing. The perils of being out of control were discussed in chapter 1. And chapter 8 showed the importance of control at Apple. Taking control was a priority for Steve Jobs when he made his comeback as Apple CEO.

The White House provides a fascinating case study of taking charge because each new president starts from scratch, in the public eye. When Richard Nixon took office in January 1969, he set up the White House Office of Communications. Its purpose was to resolve the problem of government departments speaking with multiple voices and impose unity. Nixon's chief of staff, H. R. Haldeman, designated a select few to speak in public. He sent memos to all other White House staff banning television interviews, press briefings or other public appearances without approval. Nixon's move was a milestone in the shift from loose coordination to control.[4]

In Britain, conspicuous control arrived with Tony Blair at the head of a group of realists in the Labour Party in the mid-1990s that included Peter Mandelson and Alastair Campbell (see also chapter 18). Reams have been written about the Blair era, usually employing the catchword "spin," but my favorite is Gerald Kaufman's brief admonition to his colleagues: "Keep your trap absolutely shut."[5]

Haldeman was no slouch yet his measures were only part of what is required to be in control of communication. This is not the place for a comprehensive manual but these are some steps that can't be left out:

(1) Designate speakers

Authorize people with the right credentials and skills to do the job of speaking for the organization on a given subject.

Authorized speakers should be few. For example, at one company, only three people were authorized to speak on corporate and financial matters — the CEO, the CFO and the communications director (me). When Apple launched the iPhone, only five people were authorized to speak (see chapter 8). The more people are allowed to speak, the more effort it takes to co-ordinate them, to keep them briefed and to stop things going out of control.

Be clear about the conditions under which speakers are authorized to speak. No freelancing — all arrangements should have to be made through the agreed communication channels. Above all, there should be no speaking when in an inappropriate physical or mental state — see chapter 1.

(2) Stop everyone else speaking

Invoke legal arrangements to stop unauthorized people speaking about the organization.

Contracts of employment often prohibit employees from speaking to the media about their employment, (and this should include identifying themselves as employees), or limit their ability to speak. Separate non-disclosure agreements with certain employees may be needed to cover sensitive issues such as mergers and acquisitions. Employees need to be aware of the securities regulations that restrict disclosure. You should check that all these legal barriers are up and being thoroughly policed.

This might seem heavy-handed but it is in the interest of everyone in the organization. The aim is not to curtail the liberty of particular employees but to protect the rights of the employees as a whole. The organization does not just take account of the personal interest of an employee. It is the commonwealth of employees. Even WikiLeaks, a body that is widely believed to be devoted to the truth, the whole truth and nothing but the truth, allegedly makes its employees sign non-disclosure agreements.[6] It is not a problem for junior employees to speak to the media about their personal interests and concerns, as long as they are neither breaking the law nor identified as employees. Employees can be encouraged to use controlled intranets and dedicated web-based services for communication among themselves.

Depending on the strength or weakness of your commercial position, you may also be able to persuade suppliers to limit their communications. As described in chapter 8, Apple has enforced controls over what suppliers disclose, particularly to prevent information about new products being revealed. Even if your position is relatively weak, it may be possible to negotiate with suppliers for their help. There could be common ground over material neither party wants in the public domain.

Keep people who are close to you personally out of the public eye. If the opinions and activities of your partners, family members and close friends are eccentric, journalists are likely to take an interest in them. You may believe they are irrelevant and private; they will be inclined to believe that these matters affect your suitability for office, your performance and your policy positions. They usually believe it is in the public interest to publish them. Don't leave it to chance.

(3) The Party Line

Stick to the script. That is standard advice to executives giving media interviews or making other public appearances. For a senior executive to remember the key messages when speaking to the media is essential (and without committing the faux pas of saying something like, "The key message is..."). But this is only the most basic level of performance — essential but not suffi-cient. CEO performance in interviews is the apex of the pyramid that is the public presence of the organization.

Where does the script come from? The script is the party line — or just "line." In an ideal world, the leadership of an organiza-tion would take the time to discuss and decide the line on the main issues it faces. But properly considering policy positions comes more naturally to political leaders than it does to business people and others in public life. Briefing the board of directors ahead of the annual general meeting at which they will be facing their shareholders can be a fractious affair.

In a less than ideal world, other methods may have to be used to engineer the setting of a line. There are work-arounds. At one major company, the process of preparing quarterly results or the annual report and accounts involved a "verification commit-tee." The aim was to ensure that every word and figure that went into the results announcement was not only accurate but verifia-ble. The process was time-consuming, with considerable scope for debate, but it was time well spent, not only for the sake of accuracy but also to establish the line. The final document, debat-ed, verified, and subsequently signed off by the leadership and announced to the world, became the bible to which anyone in the organization could later be referred, in the interest of keeping control of communications. It was then relatively easy to insist, "You can't say it's black. We said in the results announcement it's white." It is routine for similar precautions to be taken in connec-tion with formal documents such as circulars to shareholders or important presentations.

The line can be distributed to those who need to know, be-cause they are authorized to speak, as often as required. When I was responsible for communications at a FTSE 100 company, I edited and distributed a "Current Issues Brief" that set out the line with briefing material (facts and figures). Then it was fre-quently updated and reissued; now it would be live and interac-tive. (The party line has a long pre-digital history.)[7]

(4) Take precautions against a crisis

Taking control includes preparing for a possible crisis. Chapter 11 argues that anxiety about crises may be overdone and that often a crisis can be avoided through effective management of issues. But if a crisis is always possible, even in the best-run organization, it is necessary to get fit — to put the organization in the best condition to cope with a crisis. Part III covers what needs to be done, with a summary at the end of chapter 13.

(5) Controlled disclosure

Comply fully with securities regulations but resist blanket calls for transparency. Adopt a policy of controlled disclosure, with the aim of disclosing information in line that is helpful to achieving strategic objectives. See chapter 3.

Key points
- Designate people to speak for the organization.
- Stop everyone else speaking in public.
- Set and enforce the party line.
- Take precautions against a crisis.
- Practise controlled disclosure.

STAGE 2: Analysis

Three pieces of analysis need to be carried out before the communication strategy can be formulated:
1. Understand the business strategy.
2. Identify the issues facing the organization.
3. Analyze the organizations stakeholders.

Is it possible to do all this within 100 days? Yes, easily, with a focused approach. A million dollar work-up is unnecessary and delays the process of formulating strategy.

(1) Understand the strategy

As discussed in chapter 7, the communication strategy must have the sole purpose of supporting the overall objectives. The question is going to be: "How will communication deliver the strategy?" It would obviously be impossible to answer without being familiar with and understanding the strategy.

Strategies in their rough state are not always easily comprehensible. I have seen strategies that are really detailed business plans, running to hundreds of pages, from which it can be difficult even for an insider to distinguish the forest from the trees. Assuming that the official strategy document is not just bullshit, and that the strategy is hiding in there somewhere, it may be possible to pull it out with the help of conversations with key executives. The output from such an exercise is likely to prove very useful when it comes to selling the strategy (see below).

What if the overall strategy has not yet been formulated? In that case, communication has a contribution to make.

"The dirty little secret of the strategy industry is that it doesn't have any theory of strategy creation," wrote Gary Hamel in 1997.[8] This has since become one of the most quoted sayings about strategy. (See Stage 3 for communication strategy creation.) However, he did not say that the strategy industry has no theory of strategy formulation. Every textbook and every consultancy has its own model and, although there are different views about where strategy comes from and how to do it, there is a broadly agreed model of strategy formulation. But there is no need to buy a proprietary model, though a consultancy may be a great help in working through it.

Fig. 17.2 shows such a process for strategy formulation that illustrates the contribution of communication. One of the building blocks of a strategy is a scan of the environment for opportunities and threats. Communication experts can contribute to this by identifying issues and analyzing stakeholders. At a later stage in the process, the possible strategic options are considered. This involves evaluating options against the most important issues. And the strategic (priority) stakeholders need to be considered. What is the impact of each strategic option on these stakeholders and which options will they be likely to support?

Fig. 17.2 Interaction of Communication with Formulation of Overall Strategy

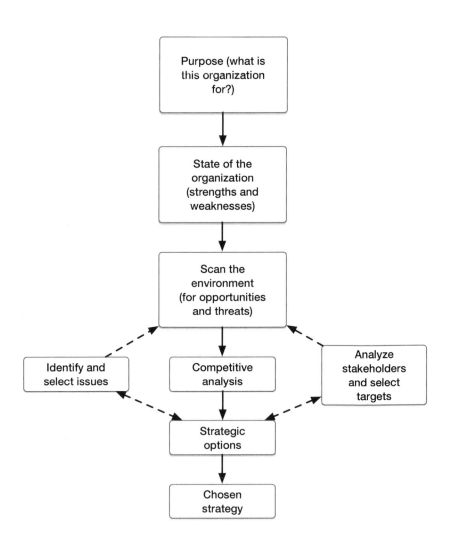

(2) Identify issues

If there is no existing issues management process, a list of issues can be compiled by scanning the environment and asking senior executives.

The quick way of scanning the environment for issues is to search recent media coverage of the organization, its competitors, and its industry. There is no need to be concerned about social media for this exercise. Journalists use social media as a resource. The chances of a monster issue simmering on social media without any journalists noticing are small indeed.

Competent legal counsel, HR directors, heads of operating units and the like also have a good idea of the public issues facing their areas of responsibility.

There is a well-known acronym for the issues to be surveyed — PEST — political, economic, social and technological. Other factors that have been proposed for inclusion in this analysis, resulting in the proliferation of rival acronyms, include cultural, ecological, educational, environmental, ethical, demographic, legal, regulatory, religious and security.

Whatever, remember that the purpose of this exercise is not to produce an exhaustive account of every issue that that could possibly impact the organization. It is merely the raw material for selecting which of these issues really matter in Stage 3.

(3) Analyze stakeholders

As discussed in chapter 12, there are many competing versions of stakeholder theory and many different analyses of stakeholders. Applying conventional prescriptions for stakeholder management is likely to generate a long list of stakeholders. This list would then need to be prioritized somehow. And professional communicators may advise in-depth research before any direction can be set. They would regard skipping the research as "shooting in the dark."[9]

Professionals may have been trained to use the four stage public relations planning process mentioned in chapter 7, Situation (Research) - Objectives – Program – Evaluation. It is second nature to many not to embark on any action without research and it would be natural, but incorrect, to assume that since communication strategy is at the highest level, it needs to be even more thoroughly researched. This is wrong because good communication strategy is mainly the product of insight, not data. This is not "shooting in the dark" because the choice of strategic stakeholders is determined by the business strategy, not by the views of stakeholders.

There will always be many different candidates for the role of stakeholder. Scholars compete to devise lists of groups it could be argued deserve management attention and communication. In stakeholder theory, these lists could include everyone who has an interest in the organization, from the local government where a facility is located to the person who delivers milk or newspapers to the offices.

It is not hard to see that the application of normative stakeholder theory to this problem is anti-strategic.

A sensible, strategic process for selecting targets was set out in chapter 12. Start by listing all the stakeholders in the organization. But don't take it to the point of absurdity. Only include those which are genuine stakeholders.

Stage 3 moves on to the task of decluttering the list of stakeholders to keep as strategic stakeholders only those which really matter.

Key points
- Understand the strategy, since the whole purpose of the communication strategy is to help deliver it.
- Identify the issues that could affect whether objectives are achieved or not.
- Identify all the (genuine) stakeholders.
- Now go to Stage 3.

STAGE 3: Setting Communication Strategy

There is a process for strategy formulation (see above, fig. 17.2). But strategy formulation does not necessarily produce great strategy. And generic strategy certainly does not produce great strategy. A great strategy is unique and requires creativity.

That is why possibly Napoleon resisted the notion of a theory of strategy. He did offer some practical advice but it didn't amount to a theory. He believed that great strategy was the product of military genius. He could always ignore the rules if it was necessary for some stroke of genius. That view was flattering to himself but he was probably right. When Napoleon failed to dazzle, it was not because he failed to follow some formula but because he was out of sorts and inspiration failed.

It was a problem even for Napoleon. How are the rest of us supposed to create a great strategy?

The parable of the boring strategy

Once upon a time, someone was promoted to be CEO of an established, profitable company which faced no obvious threats to its existence. He realized he was expected to have a strategy. But he didn't naturally see the big picture. He thought that a strategy formulation process would paint the big picture for him. He appointed a strategy director but the strategy director was just a project manager.

The strategy director appointed a management consultancy, which sold the company their branded, elaborate version of fig. 17.2. The entire corps of senior managers was mobilized and assigned to strategy working groups. The end product was an expanded revision of the existing business plan but it arrived in a glossy binder.

For the strategy director, it was job done — look at the binder. The HR director saw nothing wrong with the new strategy, which involved a lot of benchmarking, the fancy term for finding out what the best organizations are doing and copying it. He shared the view of many professionals that his role was to benchmark everything against the competition and then do the same. Label it best practice and few will criticize.

The communications director agreed. His only reservation was that it was turgid, and the CEO handed over the binder to him to be cleaned up, dressed up and presented to the outside world. The communication director hired outside help to turn it into an attractive presentation. The resulting rhetoric-enhanced PowerPoint helped the CEO past his first hurdle. When he and his top team presented it to investors, analysts and journalists, they looked as though they knew and understood the business, even if it was all firmly "inside the box." Few noticed that the painting of the strategy had been very much painting by numbers.

It was a strategy of improvement through benchmarking. In day-to-day operations, emulating the best is a good idea but, as Lafley and Martin put it, "Sameness isn't strategy. It is a recipe for mediocrity."[10] It is impossible to win anything just by copying someone else, no matter how good they are. Benchmarking is good but it's not a strategy.

The communication plans of this organization didn't amount to much either. The communication director and the CEO saw eye to eye. His job was merely to help an established organizations cope with things as they are. He was content to benchmark. This suited a fundamentally complacent organization with little interest in change or motivation to change. And so long as the organization's position in reputation surveys was satisfactory, everyone thought he was doing a good job. But the organization was strategically exposed.

No two communication strategies should be the same. Generic strategies are useful for inspiration and comparison but are not prescriptions to be followed. John Kay was rightly critical of the use of generic strategies. "There are no recipes... for corporate success. There cannot be, because if there were their general adoption would eliminate any competitive advantage which might be derived." And he was scathing about what he called "copycat strategy."[11]

Several generic communication strategies have been examined in this book, including the personality strategy, optimistic strategy, strategy of truth, and strategy of surprise. But these are not whole strategies. Adopting a strategy of truth, say, may be appropriate but is not sufficient. Generic strategies have only been discussed here as a way of exploring aspects of the subject.

There is no off-the-shelf communication strategy because the communication direction has to fit the overall corporate or business strategy. And you can't take that off the shelf.

Helping creativity along

We have been told that the dirty little secret of the strategy industry is having no theory of strategy creation. But that is a bit like complaining that the literary world doesn't have a theory of novel creation. There is no series of steps to follow that will result in the creation of a great novel. It is hard to see how there could ever be such a theory. There is a lot of information about how to put a novel together, the equivalent of strategy formulation, but no one can tell you how to produce the great creative idea. Creative writing courses seem to consist of repeated attempts by the students to write pieces that are critiqued by a master, then they try again.

That is not to say that no help is available. The technique of mind mapping, pioneered by Tony Buzan, is the tip of an iceberg of work on thinking more productively. William Duggan has investigated where strategic ideas come from. To some extent, as in "Strategic Intuition,"[12] this has been a study of the work of great innovators, from Napoleon to Pablo Picasso to Bill Gates, which is interesting but no solution. However, in his recent "Creative Strategy,"[13] Duggan provides practical guidance on how to produce creative ideas for strategy. The method still comes with no guarantee that it will generate a great idea but it is worth an attempt.

Surprise

The most powerful creative idea in communication strategy is surprise.

The twin concepts of stealth and deception have always been central to strategy — ever since David stunned Goliath and Odysseus tricked the Trojans. At the opposite extreme of time and culture, David Bowie crowned a career fueled by twists and turns with an unexpected death. This last surprise ensured that his final album, released two days earlier, shot to the top spot in the American chart — a first achieved only posthumously.[14]

The concept of surprise has been much more openly discussed in military strategy than in business strategy. However, Eric Clemons and Jason Santamaria urged business to pay attention to recent developments in military strategy. They analyzed surprise, distinguishing between stealth (preparing actions in secret), deception (misleading others about intentions), and ambiguity (acting so that others don't know what to expect). They suggested that Microsoft employs ambiguity when announcing upgrades so that competitors never know which features will finally be changed.[15]

At various points throughout this book there have been instances of a communication strategy of surprise. For example, the introduction told the story of one of Apple's great surprises, the first mass market tablet. Chapter 3 began with a reminder of the Reagan administration's surprise invasion of Grenada. Chapter 8 pointed out that Apple is not the only leading technology company whose innovations disrupt through surprise. Chapter 9 discussed Napoleon's great strategy of surprise leading up to and at Austerlitz.

Surprise has never played a larger part in business strategy than it does today. New and/or nimble businesses have tapped the potential of the communication network to "spring surprises" such as file-sharing systems, Wikipedia and Facebook.[16] This makes it all the more bizarre that the consensus among professional organizational communicators is firmly opposed to surprise — another case of excessive regard for norms, as discussed in chapter 12. Abstaining from surprise as a strategic option, on the ground that some people (self-styled "stakeholders") won't like being surprised, is too idealistic.

In fact, surprise is often the crucial contribution communication makes to the success of a strategy. It is not only a common element in strategy but central to *communication strategy*. For example, as suggested in chapter 3, the strategy could be to occupy market space where there is no existing competition (blue ocean strategy). The communication strategy is to do so while keeping shtum about it — or even deliberately misleading competitors about what is going on.

The bold communication strategist will make a contrarian call and embrace the disruption of surprise.

Selling the strategy

Strategy has to be sold. Strategy has to be shared (in some form) with the people who carry it out. It surely has to be sold to allies. One writer on strategy spoke of "the never-ending selling of strategic thinking" to all those whose support is needed.[17] The best way to sell strategy is in narrative form — something that has been called organizational storytelling. Storytelling is a way for the leader to "take this organization by the scruff of the neck and hurl it into the future, so that everyone wants to be part of that future."[18]

Strategy is also confidential. In Frontinus' example, Metellus Pius would not reveal his plan for the next day. Next he cited Crassus. Someone asked what time he intended to break camp. Crassus replied, "Why do you need to know? Are you afraid you won't hear the trumpet?" But these were examples of commanders keeping their immediate intentions to themselves, perhaps on the eve of battle. To gain its full effect, the spirit of a strategy has to be shared. The paradox can be resolved. Strategic thinking can be sold — the story can be told — without revealing a strategy fully.

The primary job of the strategic narrative is to set out a version of the business strategy. Many firms make some sort of public statement of it but that does not mean that they are candid. The strategy statement may be incomplete, vague, or so detailed that it is hard to work out what the firm's real strategy is — or indeed whether it has one. It is better not to publish the strategy itself, both because it should be confidential to the leadership and to preserve flexibility. Strategy is naturally subject to change at any time. Don't promise to keep everyone up to date with the latest thinking in case you later have a game-changing idea.

And few say much about their communication strategy. This is because wise firms prefer not to give their competitors any help. "The strategy for a public relations program usually includes proprietary information, for example a company or product's competitive market position. So rather than publish information of value to a firm's competitors, the underlying analysis that supports a public relations program isn't divulged."[19]

For example, Apple's strategy, which depended on surprise, could not be made public. We now know that its strategy in the 2000s came to include conquering a whole new category, the tablet computer. But success relied on confining this to those who needed to know — a small number of people inside Apple. There was no Apple presentation to an auditorium full of investors or journalists at which a tablet strategy was spelt out and discussed. But there was a strategic narrative that renewed and updated a version of Apple's strategy for public consumption every time Steve Jobs made one of the presentations for which he was famous. Facebook, Alphabet (Google) and Amazon similarly keep their strategies to themselves while also telling strategic stories that enable investors, customers and others to glimpse and share aspects of their strategies (chapter 8).

Thus the strategic narrative is closely related to the strategy but not the same as the strategy. It gives an idea of how the company is planning to develop, minus its confidential elements.

It should be possible for any business to sum up its strategy very briefly. It may take dozens of slides, pages and spreadsheets to explain all the details — to set out the business plan in full. But the basic plan should be simple and succinct. If not, there is something badly wrong.

Aristotle bequeathed a model that is suitable for the strategic narrative, in the shape of his three-act formula for drama:

- Act I — The beginning, which is the set-up or status quo. For strategic narrative, this is the state of the organization today, with its potential and shortcomings.

- Act II — The middle, the part of the drama when the status quo is disturbed, when the existing order of things is subject to disruption. In the strategic narrative, this is the stage that sets out what action management intends to take and what is expected of employees and partners.

- Act III — The end, when the issues raised in the second act are resolved and a new equilibrium is reached. In strategic narrative, this is the bright future that awaits once the strategy is implemented in full. (And then the cycle begins again.)

Sonata form, the most influential structure in music, echoes Aristotle with its tripartite pattern of exposition, development and recapitulation.

Narratives are so effective that a health warning is necessary. For the story to work, it has to be convincing. But the authors of the narrative need to be able to maintain an inner detachment from it and keep the big picture in perspective, as the big picture is composed of thousands of brushstrokes.

Falling in love with your own narrative is a mistake. I knew one CEO who fell in love with his narrative and handed it out in the form of a one-page printed manifesto. He refined the wording of his manifesto obsessively but lost sight of the strategy. He was like the character in "La Peste" by Albert Camus who never advances beyond the opening paragraph of the novel he is trying to write.

If detachment sounds difficult, it's what great storytellers do. Their stories are spellbinding but they don't lose touch with reality in their personal lives.

3.1 Select issues

Stage I included identifying the issues facing the organization. Now the first step in setting the communication strategy is deciding what issues to focus on.

Fig 17.3 Issues management process 2.0

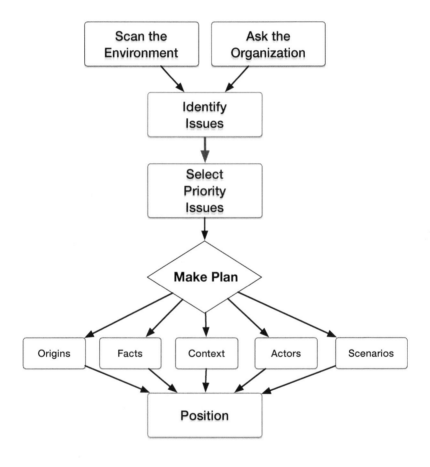

The key is prioritizing so you can decide what resources should be allocated. The priority issues are different in every situation and change over time.

In deciding which of the issues to focus on there are three considerations. The first is by far the most important:

- STRATEGIC RELEVANCE. Which of the issues is likely to affect the delivery of the strategic objectives? It may be necessary to redefine an issue to answer this question. For example, maybe climate change is identified as an issue. The question is exactly how such a broad issue would manifest itself as a challenge to delivering the strategy.

- TOTAL IMPACT ON THE COMPANY. Issues whose impact is likely to be small don't matter. And the timescale is important. Issues that will have no material impact in the foreseeable future should not be a priority.

- INFLUENCE. To what extent does the organization have the power to do something about the issue, either alone or in concert with others?

Once the key issues have been chosen, plans can be made for managing them while they are constantly monitored. The plan for each key issue needs to take into account:

- ORIGINS. How did the issue arise and how has it developed historically? The history can be an important factor in the way an issue evolves. Take the question of how to provide sufficient airport capacity for London. It would be reasonable to expect local communities affected by airport development to be skeptical toward any official promises because there is a history of promises being broken.

- THE FACTUAL BACKGROUND.

- CONTEXT. How does this issue fit into the political, social and economic environment in the relevant jurisdiction? Staying with the airport case, how does climate change, for example, affect the prospects for airport expansion?

- ACTORS. Who are the relevant decision-makers and influential groups and individuals? Where do they stand and what have they already said publicly?

- SCENARIOS. How is the issue likely to play out over the timescale of the overall strategy?

3.2 Select targets (strategic stakeholders)

How should you decide which groups to communicate with? As discussed in chapter 12, everyone in public life takes this strategic decision. Many take it by default, allowing their priorities and profile to be dictated by events or by pressure from outside.

Focus on gaining and keeping the support of indispensable allies (strategic stakeholders) is a common feature of successful communication strategies including those of Apple (Introduction & chapter 8), ExxonMobil (chapter 13) and BAA (chapter 16). The strategic (priority) stakeholders of any organization should be the groups who are critical to its success. These must be the focus of communication.

As previously discussed, the targets for a communication should be the people who make or influence a decision. This was a lesson from campaigning but the same applies to communication strategy.

Fig 17.4 Target Selection

Who will make or influence decisions affecting your strategic objectives? Forget the bystanders and focus on the people with real power and influence. There is no need to be open and transparent about this. No one, including the key decision-makers, need ever know about your process. (See also chapter 13 on Exxon.)

Bearing in mind the overall strategy, ask the following questions:

- What business is the firm in?
- Where is it in its life cycle?
- Which stakeholder groups can influence achievement of the strategy?
- Within each stakeholder group, who are the key decision-makers?

To do this requires a judgment, not a research exercise. You tell me the business strategy; I'll tell you who the strategic (priority) stakeholder groups should be.

As an example, Chapter 8 sets out the strategic stakeholders of Apple. Chapter 13 sets out the strategic stakeholders of ExxonMobil. Chapter 15 sets out the strategic stakeholders of Carnival. Identifying these companies' strategic stakeholders was a matter of analysis, not inside information or research. It may be worth carrying out detailed research into stakeholders' attitudes and opinions but only after the strategic stakeholders or indispensable allies have been selected.

3.3 Profile

What kind of profile do you need?

How do you decide how to communicate? And how do you decide how loudly to communicate? There are many tactical reasons for communicating or keeping shtum but deciding the who, when and how of communication is also a strategic decision. The third piece of the communication strategy is deciding how, and how loudly, to communicate.

A high profile is often taken for granted. Textbooks and scholarly works pay little attention to profile because of the unstated assumption that the higher the profile the better. But a high profile is just one option. Do you sincerely want a high profile?

"Public Relations for Dummies" opened with this: "When I was a young man of 24 and almost a complete beginner at public relations, I got on the front page of *USA Today* with a feature story about the baseball strike..."[20] The author wanted a high profile to publicize his new PR agency. If all you want is publicity, and you don't care about bad publicity, perhaps because you are a start-up, you need a high profile. If your strategy is to go all out for a high profile, "Public Relations for Dummies" could be the book for you.

Chapter 10 looked at the high profile advocacy strategy employed by Mobil. If you share Mobil's views on the need to speak out, the benefits of confrontation and so on, the high profile advocacy strategy could be for you and you might start by reading "Goodbye to the Low Profile" by Herb Schmertz.

If you don't need a high media profile to execute your strategy, you need to think carefully about what your profile should be. You have already decided who should be your targets (allies or strategic stakeholders). For organizations that don't have any mass strategic stakeholders, a high public profile may be unnecessary and counter-productive. Even for organizations with a consumer audience, their profile should be carefully planned and controlled, like Apple's, not a free-for-all.

This means not equating profile with media profile. Some public relations people believe that public relations *is* media relations.[21] That is understandable given that, ever since the development of mass media in the 19th century and the earliest days of public relations as a business, PR has been in a symbiotic relationship with the media. The largest part of the workload of a government or private sector PR department or a generalist PR consultancy is likely to be dealing with the media. The media (including social media) are the natural channel for broadcast communication.

But this is most likely to be the case when an organization or client has failed to decide who its targets (strategic stakeholders) should be and is trying to communicate with everyone.

And the key point is that your profile should be a strategic decision, not something that just happens. The targeted profile aligns your profile with your targets, on the basis that there is no point in achieving a high profile with non-targets.

Handling criticism

What about the high profile that is accidental? What about finding you have a high profile because you are under attack?

How to handle criticism is a question that has arisen time and again in the course of this book. For instance:

- What should you do when you are fired? (Chapter 2.)
- What should you do when interest groups, say on the environment, single you out for criticism? (Chapter 3.)
- What should you do when information is leaked against you? (Chapter 5.)
- What should you do when directors of the company are defamed? (Chapter 10.)

These were particular instances but what is the right overall approach to handling criticism?

In his memoir-manifesto, Herb Schmertz, Mobil's high profile and combative public affairs chief, posed a similar question. He took an example: "Let's say... a prominent politician publicly attacks your company." And he offered a number of alternative responses:

- Saying nothing in the hope that it would all "blow over."
- Immediately issuing a "strong rebuttal."
- Calling a "news conference to discuss your views."[22]

It is not hard to guess what manner of response Mobil might have made, especially since he went on to tell the story of two public quarrels with the president of the US (Jimmy Carter).

Mobil's intention, partly enabled by its great wealth, was to give as good as it got. The company wanted its enemies to know that nobody was going to have a pop at Mobil without feeling the full force of its disagreement. And it believed that this deterrent was more likely to eliminate criticism than less pugnacious approaches. However, as discussed in chapter 10, whether Mobil's high profile advocacy strategy was a net benefit to its position is debatable.

For some, responding by launching a counter-attack is prompted by the emotional response of going ballistic. "Going ballistic" means a communication that is a hot-tempered reflex rather than a calm, logical argument. Going ballistic is a common cause of gaffes. And in an organizational setting, going ballistic sometimes involves a close-knit group of people losing all sense of perspective when dealing with the media.

The natural response to being attacked is to hit back, hard. But, in the public eye, hitting back can just make matters worse.

Options

When it comes to significant public criticism, there are four main ways to respond:

- RETALIATION. The aim of retaliation is to punish and deter critics but it can be a poor deterrent and counter-productive. Whereas in warfare retaliation may tend to degrade the enemy's ability to attack, in the public arena, as discussed in chapter 10, the high profile response publicizes the criticism and breeds new critics.

- APPEASEMENT. Giving in to criticism both helps them and harms you. And, as the detractors of this approach have pointed out in cases of appeasement going back at least as far as Ethelred the Unready, the problem is that, after you have once appeased your enemy, it is difficult to stop making concessions.

- TALKING TO THE CRITICS. Whether this is likely to work depends on the circumstances and the nature of the critics. Reasonable people are particularly susceptible to believing that other people will be reasonable too, if only they are treated right. But some people are simply not reasonable, as in the encounter between the gentleman Chamberlain and the thug Hitler. Some of the critics of institutions today are ideological and fanatical. Trying to convert such critics through reason and kindness is futile. As Eric Dezenhall said: "One of the great myths of public relations is that you can get hostile audiences to like you."[23]

- PATIENT, TARGETED RESISTANCE. If a significant criticism threatens your vital interests, you have no alternative but to defend yourself, with a response calibrated to the level of threat. Deal with criticism on social media promptly and firmly but without overreacting. You don't need to mount a big corporate stage to do so. Indeed, that could be counter-productive. Respond to social media communications through the same channels and keep it low key. Otherwise, focus on keeping your strategic stakeholders on your side and ignore pygmy critics. Accept that in the age of social media a certain level of criticism is tolerable background noise. Nothing can or should be done about it. Follow the example of innovators who accept that there will always be a few objectors, like those who hated the iPad because it reminded them of sanitary products. Ignore them, focus on your priority targets and move on.

The case of the critical politician

Returning to Schmertz's example, how to respond to a critical politician depends on whether there is any substance to the attack. It depends on whether the attack is part of a pattern or a one-off. And it depends on who the politician is.

If the attack is a serious threat to your business, you need to fight. Otherwise, you need to keep the damage to a minimum. The best way to do that could indeed be to say little or even nothing. (Chapter 5 looked at the case of Goldman Sachs and its critics, and the option of saying less.)

Suppose the politician is unelected and comes from a country that is a byword for corruption, your best move probably is to say nothing publicly, while reassuring any strategic stakeholders who need reassurance. If you come out immediately with a strong rebuttal or, heaven forbid, call a news conference, you merely ensure that the unfounded criticism receives additional publicity. Don't forget that some media organizations believe that every story has at least two sides, and in always telling both sides, even when the other side's argument depends on the belief that the moon is made of green cheese.

And it depends on your profile. If your profile is high, all other things being equal, the media and the public will notice the attack and react. If your profile is low, unless your alleged fault is particularly heinous, it may well be that few notice, few react, and it does indeed "blow over." Unless you are confident that the overwhelming majority will come in on your side, responding in kind is a high-risk strategy.

- Hitting back can sustain and amplify public awareness of the original attack.
- It invites third parties to jump into what has now become a public debate.
- It distracts the organization from pursuing its original objectives (which may be part of the critics' plan).

Policy

The number of possible criticism scenarios is legion and there are numerous possible responses. You cannot plan for all of them, nor should you try. But you should have a broad policy. Otherwise, there is a greater danger that you will over-react in the heat of the moment. Your response to events might be geared to looking tough in front of colleagues and people you know, rather than geared to defending the long-term interests of the company. There is a danger, in short, that you will be in the "out of control" territory explored in chapter 1.

You cannot plan for the exact circumstances but you can decide in advance what shape your response is likely to take. And how loud is your voice is likely to be?

If you decide on a low profile, or a targeted profile, it is not simply a question of saying nothing. But the best policy for handling criticism is the measured response of patient resistance. Ignore criticisms that don't threaten the organization. Keep to the profile you have planned. If you need to defend yourself, concentrate on your strategic stakeholders.

3.4 Critical path

Like PR people, journalists are officially on the side of telling the truth. As professional gatherers and distributors of information, they have a vested interest in being told the truth by their sources. It is therefore not surprising to see journalists opining in favor of telling the truth in public relations.

But problems of coordination and timing can be misconstrued as questions of truth.

J.C. Penney

In September 2013, Lex in the *Financial Times* fastened onto an incident involving J. C. Penney Company, Inc. (JCP), the American retailer, as the peg for a homily entitled "We can handle the truth."[24]

The series of events that offended Lex was as follows. JCP held a conference call with analysts on August 20, 2013, to discuss its second quarter results. On the call, its CFO said in answer to a question: "As we look through the end of the year, the $1.5 billion of liquidity that we have projected we are not assuming that we need any additional financing."[25]

Fig. 17.5 Timeline: J. C. Penney's Critical Path

August 20 – Q2 call with analysts – "we are not assuming that we need any additional financing."
September 20 – Press speculation – "exploring fundraising."
September 25 – Goldman Sachs initiates coverage – "likely that management will look to build a bigger liquidity buffer."
September 26 – Company statement does not mention fundraising.
September 26 – Stock offering raises $782m gross.

A month later, there were press reports that JCP would raise funds. For example, it was said to be "in talks to potentially raise more cash... The chain doesn't have immediate cash needs, and is exploring fundraising amid shareholder pressure to take advantage of cheap financing."[26]

On September 25, Goldman Sachs initiated coverage of the company's debt with an "underperform" rating. The *Wall Street Journal* quoted it as saying that: "Weak fundamentals, inventory rebuilding, and an underperforming home department will likely challenge J. C. Penney's liquidity levels in 3Q. In order to safeguard against a potentially poor 4Q holiday season, it is likely that management will look to build a bigger liquidity buffer, as has been suggested by recent press reports."[27]

The next day (September 26), the company issued a statement "in response to inquiries," saying "J. C. Penney said today that it is pleased with its progress thus far," etc., but making no reference to liquidity. The same day (September 26), the company announced a public offering of stock, underwritten by Goldman Sachs, that raised $786.2 million before expenses, diluting shareholders.[28]

Lex commented: "Any half-competent flack knows the drill. Own the bad news. Make sure colleagues and partners are prepared; go public quickly, clearly, and completely; be accountable, be available; candor is a sign of respect."

It surely could not have been a deliberate plan all along for the company to raise funds from a stock offering but deceive the market about its intentions, even on the very day of the fundraising, until the offer was made. That would simply have been pointless. Most likely, what JCP said on August 20 was honest. It did not believe, at that time, that it would need additional financing. Any prudent management might also have been preparing a capital raising, just in case, as one option. Then, as time passed, the situation changed. Perhaps it changed as daily results came in from the business. Perhaps it changed as investors urged the company to raise cheap funds. Perhaps it changed as management discussed the opportunities and threats facing the company. And perhaps the final catalyst was the stock price plummeting after Goldman Sachs' report. Whatever the exact course of events, a capital raising gradually became a more attractive or necessary option for JCP and that option was finally taken.

JCP's behavior was not a case study in poor ethics. The only moral to be drawn was that appearing to say or imply something

is black one day and then white the next (regardless what the col-
or really is) is going to make you look foolish. And may land you
in legal trouble. After the stock offering, JCP received lawsuits
from shareholders and the SEC announced that it was looking
into the offering.[29]

In such a scenario, in which conditions change rapidly and
different options become more or less attractive, (as with the executive health issues discussed in chapter 3), it is not practical or
desirable to update the market with each twist and turn. That can
make it difficult to avoid a jolt between "we have no need to raise
capital" and "we're raising capital." The more closely in touch
with the market a company keeps, the harder it is to change tack
without a jolt. This is why many companies choose to observe a
quiet or close period in the run-up to results declarations.

The best advice is therefore usually to lie low in turbulent
times. Keeping a low or targeted profile enables the organization
(or person) to say the situation is x, say the opposite several
weeks later and, fairly and accurately, put the switch down to
changes in conditions.

However, avoiding the twists and turns requires careful timing and close coordination — the same degree of planning large
businesses would routinely employ for projects, for everything
from putting a man on the moon downwards.

Focus on critical path

Breakdowns of coordination and timing in communication
can be avoided by borrowing the concept of the "critical path"
from project management. The idea is that the timing of different
pieces of work that contribute to the achievement of a project is
crucial. Similarly, one of the key elements of communication
strategy is ensuring that the focus is on those actions that are critical to the organization — that they are done, done well, and
done in the right order.

Whereas a project has a beginning, a middle and an end, the
implementation of strategy is continuous. Communication is not
a project but a continuing important aspect of all major developments. But it can still be useful to analyze it like a project. The

fundamental insight of project management is that a project involves a number of tasks that are interdependent and usually carried out in a number of streams of work. Because they are
interdependent, if there is a failure of coordination, the result will
be chaos. Coordination is the role of a project manager, who typically uses charts such as Program Evaluation and Review Technique (PERT), to keep track of the project's tasks, resources,
specifications and time.

Most people use project management for simple projects in
their daily lives without thinking. It is obvious to the domestic
project manager that before attempting to cook eggs for breakfast
it is necessary to acquire the eggs, other materials and cooking
facilities. It is obvious in corporations that project management
has to make similar arrangements on a grand scale for a new car
to be developed, a new airport to be built, or a new drug brought
to market. It is equally imperative but, apparently, less obvious,
that corporate activities and their accompanying disclosures also
require project management.

The need for certain tasks to be performed in a certain order
is sometimes overlooked. To avoid such snafus, project managers
carry out critical path analysis. This involves making a list, usually
in the form of a diagram or flow chart, of everything that has to
be done, and noting which tasks depend on other tasks. It must
be stressed that this is not just a linear timetable but a plan that
takes account of dependencies. From such a chart it is possible to
see the shortest route from start to finish and hence the minimum time required for the project. The chart also reveals which
tasks are essential for the project to go forward from stage to
stage. The critical path is the sequence that connects all the activities in the right order. The critical path for strategy includes
communication.

The engineers working on a new car or airport or software
may not naturally regard communications as very important. But
"sometimes, a relatively unimportant component on its own can
be the critical dependency that prevents true priority 1 work from
being completed. Without doing critical path analysis, you might
never recognize this until it is too late."[30] Where the project is a
corporate action, whether that is discrete, such as a project to acquire another company, or more open-ended, such as a turna-

round, some of the activities required will be communications such as announcements to the capital markets, circulars to shareholders or holders of other securities, and presentations to key audiences.

Take the example of an announcement that one company has agreed to buy another. Such an announcement forms the tip of an iceberg of work. Critical path communications are those communications that are required for the corporate action to be completed successfully, that is, those communications without which it cannot go forward.

Falling off the critical path

Omitting critical path analysis frequently leads to communication problems, as these two further examples show:

- In March 2015, Ryanair told the *Financial Times*, without making an announcement, that its board had approved plans to start a transatlantic airline. Three days later, it announced: "In the light of recent press coverage, the Board of Ryanair Holdings Plc wishes to clarify that it has not considered or approved any transatlantic project and does not intend to do so." Referring to the original report, it told the *FT*, "It was a miscommunication."[31]

- Benoît Coeuré, an executive board member at the European Central Bank (ECB), spoke at a private conference dinner in London in May 2015. He mentioned at the dinner that the ECB intended to increase its bond purchases in May and June. This meant those who attended the dinner accidentally receiving a head start on the next day's likely fall in the euro. The information only became public when the ECB published the speech on its website the following morning. The ECB blamed a procedural error and subsequently issued new guidelines for external communication for its top executives.[32]

It is impossible to be sure in cases like these whether some game is being played behind the scenes but, in principle, these are problems that can and should be avoided through critical path planning.

Managers are well used to discrete projects such as new buildings or new vehicle models requiring project management that includes the use of critical path analysis. Managing the critical path for communications is just as important if the strategy is to be implemented effectively. The top communication executive must have, as well as a good understanding of the strategy, a clear view of what communications are on the critical path.

Focusing on the critical path ensures that:

- Communications follow the strategy rather than being buffeted by developments either down the organization or in the outside world.

- Disclosure is made at the right time, in line with the right process, and in the right order. This should avoid denials that the organization will do precisely what it is about to do.

Key points
- Focus on issues which are critical to delivering your strategic objectives.
- Focus on gaining and keeping the support of indispensable allies — the stakeholders which can make a major impact on whether strategy succeeds or not.
- Don't seek a high profile without good reason. And don't confuse your media profile and your profile with strategic stakeholders.
- There is a critical path for the delivery of a strategy. Communications need to focus on this critical path.

In Summary

The first 100 days in a senior role are crucial. Looking at what needs to be done in that initial period captures the essentials of communication strategy:

Stage 1. Take control:
- Define who can speak for the organization.
- Stop everyone else speaking.
- Set and enforce the party line.
- Take precautions against a crisis.
- Implement controlled disclosure.

Stage 2. Analyze and take stock of the situation:
- Understand the business strategy.
- Identify the issues facing the organization.
- Analyze the organization's stakeholders.

Stage 3. Set the communication strategy:
- How will communication help to deliver strategy?
- Select the key issues that may impact achievement of strategic objectives.
- Select the key targets (strategic stakeholders).
- Select the profile — both what profile is desired and how to handle criticism.
- Focus communications on the critical path.

References

[1] Sextus Julius Frontinus, *Strategemata*, 84-96, (London: William Heinemann, 1925), I. I. 12.

[2] David A. Gergen, *Eyewitness to Power: The Essence of Leadership, Nixon to Clinton*, (New York: Simon and Schuster, 2000), 166-168.

[3] Joseph A. Pika & John Anthony Maltese, *The Politics of the Presidency*, (Washington, DC: CQ Press, 2010), 102.

[4] Maltese, *Spin Control*, 26, 35 & 109.

[5] John Kampfner, 'The Nod and a Wink Spins Out of Control,' *Financial Times*, October 22, 1997.

[6] James Ball, 'Exclusive: Former WikiLeaks Employee James Ball Describes Working With Julian Assange,' *Daily Beast*, May 30, 2013 - <http://www.thedailybeast.com/articles/2013/05/30/exclusive-former-wikileaks-employee-james-ball-describes-working-with-julian-assange.html>.

[7] I treasure an original copy of a political party national campaign guide from the 1970s. (*The Campaign Guide 1977*, Conservative and Unionist Central Office, 1977.) This runs to 789 pages and includes "speaking notes" (i.e., the line) on the major issues of the day. It was first published in 1892. And note that the campaign guide, for internal consumption, and the manifesto, for external consumption, are separate documents.

[8] Gary Hamel, 'Killer Strategies That Make Shareholders Rich,' *Fortune*, June 23, 1997.

[9] Ronald D. Smith, *Strategic Planning for Public Relations*, 2nd edn., (Mahwah, NJ: Lawrence Erlbaum Associates, 2005), 15.

[10] Lafley & Martin, *Playing to Win*, 23.

[11] John Kay, *Foundations of Corporate Success: How Business Strategies Add Value*, (Oxford University Press, 1993), vi & 350.

[12] William Duggan, *Strategic Intuition: The Creative Spark in Human Achievement*, (New York: Columbia University Press, 2007).

[13] William Duggan, *Creative Strategy: A Handbook for Innovation*, (New York: Columbia University Press, 2013).

[14] Ben Sisario, 'David Bowie Hits No. 1 on Billboard Chart with "Blackstar," a First,' *New York Times*, January 17, 2016.

[15] Eric K. Clemons & Jason A. Santamaria, (2002). 'Can Modern Military Strategy Lead You to Victory?' *Harvard Business Review*, April 2002, 56-65.

[16] John Naughton, *From Gutenberg to Zuckerberg: What You Really Need to Know About the Internet*, (London: Quercus, 2012), 51.

[17] Colin White, *Strategic Management*, (Basingstoke, UK: Palgrave Macmillan, 2004), 678.

[18] Stephen Denning, 'Using Narrative as a Tool for Change,' in *Storytelling in Organizations: Why Storytelling Is Transforming 21st Century Organizations and Management*, ed. by John Seely Brown, Stephen Denning, Katalina Groh, & Laurence Prusak, (Burlington, MA: Elsevier Butterworth–Heinemann, 2005), 129.

[19] Bill Cantor, 'Special Comment on Gerald Hickman's Chapter,' in *Experts in Action*, Cantor & Burger, (eds.), 350.

[20] Yaverbaum, *Public Relations for Dummies*, 9.

[21] Grunig & Hunt, *Managing Public Relations*, 223.

[22] Schmertz & Novak, *Goodbye to the Low Profile*, 13.

[23] Eric Dezenhall & John Weber, *Damage Control: Why Everything You Know About Crisis Management Is Wrong*, (New York: Portfolio, 2007), 72.

[24] Lex, 'Public Relations: We Can Handle the Truth,' *Financial Times*, September 27, 2013.

[25] J C Penney Co. Inc., Q2 2013 Earnings Conference Call, Edited Transcript, *Thomson Reuters Streetevents*, August 20, 2013.

26 Jodi Xu, Lauren Coleman-Lochner & Beth Jinks, 'J.C. Penney Said in Talks to Raise More Money for Turnaround,' *Bloomberg*, September 20, 2013.

27 Steven Russolillo, 'Goldman Blasts J.C. Penney; Shares Tumble to 13-Year Low,' *Wall Street Journal*, September 25, 2013.

28 'JCPenney Responds to Inquiries,' J. C. Penney Company, Inc. news release, September 26, 2013. 'J. C. Penney Announces Proposed Public Offering of Common Stock,' J. C. Penney Company, Inc. news release, September 26, 2013. Matt Townsend & Chris Burritt, 'J.C. Penney Investor Glenview Joins Hayman Cutting Stake,' *Bloomberg*, November 15, 2013.

29 Wites & Kapetan, 'P.A. Announces That Class Action Lawsuits Have Been Filed against J.C. Penny Company,' *BusinessWire*, October 16, 2013. 'Wolf Haldenstein Adler Freeman & Herz LLP Commences Class Action Lawsuit on Behalf of J.C. Penney Co., Inc. Investors,' *Business-Wire*, October 23, 2013. Suzanne Kapner, 'SEC Seeks Details of Penney Stock Sale,' *Wall Street Journal*, December 5, 2013.

30 Scott Berkun, *The Art of Project Management*, (Sebastopol, CA: O'Reilly Media, Inc., 2005), 241.

31 Jane Wild, 'Ryanair Board Approves Plan for Transatlantic Airline,' *Financial Times*, March 16, 2015. 'Ryanair Statement 19 March 2015, Dublin,' Ryanair Holdings Plc news release, March 19, 2015. Jane Wild & Peggy Hollinger, 'Ryanair in U-turn on Plans for Transatlantic Airline,' *Financial Times*, March 19, 2015.

32 Laurence Fletcher & Paul Hannon, 'Benoît Coeuré Gives Diners Sneak Peek at ECB Move,' *Wall Street Journal*, May 19, 2015. Dave Shellock, 'Prospect of Increased European Central Bank Bond Buying Hits Euro,' *Financial Times*, May 19, 2015. Claire Jones & Sam Fleming, 'Benoît Coeuré Speech Highlights Central Bank Links to Financiers,' *Financial Times*, May 20, 2015. 'ECB Publishes Guiding Principles for Speeches and Meetings,' ECB press release, October 6, 2015.

CHAPTER 18

Focus

"Without selective interest, experience is an utter chaos."
— William James, "The Principles of Psychology"[1]

What would Martians make of the art or science of public communication on Earth? They would be astounded by the complexity.

From troubleshooting to focus

Much of this book has been about avoiding trouble or getting out of trouble.

Part I discussed what happens when communications are out of control; the social pressure to communicate in ways that go against your interests, and therefore against your strategy; how public relations thinking often has different agendas, other than effectiveness; and the confusion about truth and the temptations of institutionalized optimism.

Part II looked at the elements of communication strategy and various different communication strategies, with chapter 7 examining the nature of communication strategy, and chapter 17 setting out how a leader can quickly devise and carry out a sound strategy.

Part III examined how Exxon, BP, Carnival, BAA, and others have handled strategic problems, issues and crises.

In every case, it was necessary to focus on what really matters. Some, such as Apple, HSBC and MyTravel, have done this well. Some have not. So how should it be done?

Let's return to the visiting Martians.

Elusive simplicity

On this planet, a focused communication strategy is unusual. Campaigns may be focused but, at the strategic level, most public relations people seem to believe in trying to be all things to all people or, as some might put it, developing mutually beneficial relationships with all stakeholders.

Even campaigns often suffer from unnecessary complexity. The danger of getting lost in the detail has never been greater because there has never been more detail to get lost in. Social media can be powerful. Access to big data is a huge advantage. But as *The Economist* pointed out, in 2007-08, Hillary Clinton, with her micro-policies for micro-electorates, made possible by big data, was defeated by Barack Obama, who focused on the big picture, not on big data. "The winning slogans were vague and broad ('hope' and 'change')."[2]

There are a number of perfectly understandable reasons why both scholars and professional communicators have piled complexity upon complexity rather than trying to reduce what needs to be said about public communication to its essentials:

- The desire of textbook authors to make their books relevant to many types of organization and sectors facing many different issues.
- The multiplicity of activities that come under the umbrella of public relations. One expert enumerated no fewer than 31 "core competencies of a public relations practitioner," from "conferences" to "internet communications."[3] And these were just the core.
- The extraordinarily large number of social groups (stakeholders) with which experts suggest that an organization should try to have a relationship (chapter 12). They recommend that organizations try to manage their reputations by reference to broad measures that tend to include popularity contests and assessments by critics, rather than concentrating on the people who really matter.
- The range of issues that may pose some threat or opportunity for an organization. The unexpected disruption of European aviation by a volcanic eruption (chapter 11)

makes plain the difficulty of being sure which issues are important. Often the de facto solution is to try to manage them all.

Reduction to the essentials

Where PR often adds complexity, the best advertising is simple.

The power of simplicity is widely recognized in the advertising industry. When the advertising greats, all experts in distilling the essence of a product into an advertising campaign, wrote books on how they did it, they frequently preached the gospel of simplicity. An advertising campaign that thoroughly explains all 27 reasons why a product is superior to its competitors, with supporting evidence, is going to flop. (Unless, of course, the simple idea is that the product is superior in so many ways, it would take a book to explain them all properly.)

Ken Segall, who worked on Apple advertising over many years, summed up their approach as "Insanely Simple."[4] Apple is only the most obvious example of a successful business that was built on and evangelized for simplicity and focus.

Leo Burnett received this tribute from Jerry Della Femina: "He produces very simple advertising, so simple that it's deceptive. You almost think it isn't good. It isn't sophisticated, and it doesn't make you laugh. But boy, it sells goods." Della Femina himself was likely to say: "Let's pull it down to its simplest form."[5] Let's reduce the case to its essentials.

"If you want your work to achieve the impossible, you will need Brutal Simplicity of Thought," said M&C Saatchi.[6] And Dave Trott said: "The best writing takes complicated things and makes them simple. So everyone can understand them."[7]

Is it fair to read across from advertising? Admittedly, advertising usually operates at the campaign level, within an overall strategy that has already been set. But then so does most PR.

PR people have many core competencies but the ability to make things simple does not seem to be among them.

Does it help to achieve objectives?

A few hundred of the world's most famous people (and some not so famous) contribute to an up-market bulletin board on LinkedIn, branded "Influencers." Some of them are CEOs. And LinkedIn has said: "We have a long list of CEOs who are asking to get in."[8]

LinkedIn offers a way of communicating with hundreds of millions of business people all over the world. By contributing to Influencers, CEOs have the possibility of reaching many of LinkedIn's 300 million members. Using LinkedIn could potentially both encourage people to think of you as a "thought leader" and generate sales leads.[9] It sounds tempting, so how should someone, perhaps a CEO, assess this opportunity and decide whether or not to become an Influencer?

The quality of the posts is variable. People have wondered: "Why Is LinkedIn Emailing Us About Mark Cuban's 6-Year-Old Colonoscopy?"[10] But, in principle, there is nothing wrong with CEOs posting articles on Influencers. Some of the world's most famous business leaders are said to have millions of followers on LinkedIn. That is a big number and helps to sustain their celebrity status — and their personality strategies (chapter 2) — and their egos.

There is nothing wrong with it but is it strategic? Does it help you achieve a strategic objective?

There may be firms for whom the members of LinkedIn, eminent as they may be, (including the author, tongue in cheek), are a key audience — perhaps those whose customers or raw materials are business executives, like Manpower or Adecco. For the rest, the rationale for those who take part in Influencers could be something like this: "It won't take a lot of effort and it may even do some good."

Now imagine thousands of people in a large corporation, at all levels up to and including the CEO, saying to themselves every day, as the basis for their decisions — it won't take a lot of effort and it may even do some good. This is beginning to sound like Jane Austen's Lydia Bennet, who said: "Look here, I have bought this bonnet. I do not think it is very pretty; but I thought I might as well buy it as not."[11]

In this scenario, a vast effort is being expended on activity that is irrelevant or marginally relevant to the strategic objectives. Suddenly, the large corporation looks unfocused.

And now try to imagine Steve Jobs saying: "It won't take a lot of effort and it may even do some good, so let's do it!"

Not enough resources

The fundamental reason for strategic focus is the inescapable shortage of resources. There are never enough. There is never enough money, people and time to achieve more than strictly limited, sharply focused objectives.

This applies to everyone everywhere, both people and organizations. Even at the personal level. For example, there will never be enough time to do everything you want to do by bedtime — unless you set an objective that is attainable and focus on achieving it.

Therefore it is vital to focus on what really matters and make choices. These choices are the essence of strategy: choices between different actions and therefore choices between different allocations of resources.[12]

As with any strategy, a communication strategy is a commitment to one set of actions rather than another. Yet many managers, communication professionals and academics behave as though communication is somehow exempt from resource constraints. (Reputation management is no help in resource allocation. Reputation management and stakeholder theory, especially when wielded as arguments by critics, are a demand for resources.) They argue that organizations both should and can communicate with everyone who comes under the elastic stakeholder umbrella (even perhaps if that means uncontacted peoples or trees – see chapter 12).

The essence of communication strategy is facing up to the difficult decisions that result from resource constraint.

Fatal distraction

The opposite of focus is confusion, compounded by distraction. A good communication strategy depends on a clear corporate strategy. But people and organizations sometimes make a mess of their strategies by losing sight of what they are trying to achieve.

Focus is partly a question of deciding the strategy and partly a question of execution. Michael Porter was uncompromising when he identified three generic approaches to competitive strategy, saying that to implement one of them effectively would require total commitment.[13]

There will always be outside interests – stakeholders (stakeseekers) – who want resources to be reallocated in their favor. But the more dangerous source of distraction is the groups or individuals within an organization who pursue their own agendas, in conflict with the strategy. Sometimes this is flagrant, like a trade union seeking more pay. But often it is concealed. When leadership is weak and the culture permits or even encourages rival views of what the strategy should be, internal interest groups can easily disguise their agendas as being in the interest of the whole.

The larger and more complex the organization, the more likely it is that internal groups will develop and promote their own agendas. England's National Health Service (the NHS), which has the burden of employing 1.3 million people, is the most blatant example of internal interest groups dragging an organization down by distracting it from its purpose. (Leaving aside armed forces, only Wal-Mart, McDonald's and a couple of Chinese state corporations are larger.)[14]

The stated objective of the NHS is: "High quality care for all."[15] But, on the contrary, the quality of care provided varies from very high to poor or non-existent. (Quality may be variable and health care may be impaired by bureaucracy in other countries but these problems are less intractable when the customer has power and choice, rather than having to accept what is provided.)

Like all Western health systems, the NHS must cope with an aging population that needs more care. Costs are out of control in a system with limited incentives to balance income (from subsidies) and expenditure. Bureaucrats can always demand billions more in funding, especially when the politicians who distribute the funds come up for re-election.

But apart from sheer size, its biggest problem is distraction from its only proper purpose of providing its customers with high quality care.

It is distracted by the vested interests of employee groups such as surgeons, doctors and nurses, (and numerous sub-groups) as well as multifarious organizational units. These all tend to resist less rigid working practices and press their own agendas. Expensive facilities stand idle for much of the time because to put them to use would require employees working inconvenient hours. Professionals are in a particularly strong political position because their technical expertise is often mistaken for managerial expertise and strategic insight, though of course medical knowledge and managerial ability don't go hand in hand. The net result is that the agenda that is supposed to focus on care for customers often focuses on employees.

In addition, the organization is internally fragmented and in a state of flux as a result of continual restructuring. Successive political masters have found it easier to rearrange the organization chart than tackle the fundamental problem of strategy. Managers' energy is consumed by the bureaucratic struggle – fighting with other units, budgeting, collecting and reporting mountains of data, and addressing issues such as sustainability and diversity that are irrelevant to the strategic objective. One symptom is that Florence Nightingale would feel at home with the way much information moves around the NHS today. Basic modern technologies such as email have not been rolled out. Documents travel through the mail or by hand. Hospitals and medical centers are full of paper files.

Quality is highly variable. The critical factor determining whether the care is satisfactory or not is which individual employee(s) the customer sees, in which town, in which unit, on which day of the week and at which time of day. Management, in the sense of a hierarchy of people directing and controlling what happens, is largely missing. Collection of more and more data and internal regulators are work-arounds to make up for the absence of conventional line management.

There is rarely a straight answer in the NHS to the simple question: who is in charge here?

The status quo is maintained by popular ignorance and fear. The English tend to be under the illusion that their health system is the best in the world, and are tormented by the fear that someone will deprive them of a service they believe is uniquely "free." (They pay for it through taxes, giving up control over how their money is spent to the bureaucrats.)

Until a way is found to bring strategic focus to the universal health care system in England, its quality will remain uneven and unreliable with frequent scandals and crises. And the idea that the NHS will be able to embrace the new era of personalized medicine will continue to seem far-fetched.

The answer is no

Two of the best television dramas of the 2000s – "The West Wing" and "The Thick of It" – have helped non-insiders to gain a better idea of what really goes on in modern politics.[16] "The West Wing" was ostensibly the more realistic of the two but it was more genteel than real life.

Despite its satirical intentions, "The Thick of It" took a more clear-eyed look into the snakepit. Here the prime minister's communications director, Malcolm Tucker, became the de facto central character. Its black humor arose largely from foolish but believable behavior such as hapless politicians and officials blurting out previously undisclosed, awkward facts to journalists, announcing new policies or initiatives in damaging circumstances, or using dodgy language in broadcast interviews. The plots of their ineffectual staffs tend only to increase their embarrassment while Tucker, the realist, cleans up. They come up with foolish schemes and Tucker tries to stop them.

The publicity campaign for the movie spin-off, "In The Loop," included a poster. President Obama's 2008 election campaign was encapsulated by a portrait poster entitled "Hope," also used with the slogan "Yes We Can." The poster for the film shows Tucker in the same style as Obama, saying: "No You F-----

Can't."

Focus has a foundation in psychology, where experts talk about attention, which William James said was "the taking possession by the mind, in clear and vivid form, of one out of what seem several simultaneously possible objects or trains of thought. Focalization, concentration, of consciousness are of its essence. It implies withdrawal from some things in order to deal effectively with others."[17]

Focus is not a question of taking a moment or having a flash of inspiration that gives birth to a brilliant idea, fully formed, but continuing concentration. One learning point from "Mad Men," another great TV show about the Sixties advertising industry, is the time, effort and teamwork required even for Don Draper, a "genius," to produce effective advertising. "Born to Run," Bruce Springsteen's first major hit single, sounds spontaneous. It lasts four and a half minutes but took Springsteen six months to perfect.[18] Francis Poulenc said that it took him four years to write his song, "Montparnasse."[19]

Apple once again shows the way. Focus saved Apple from failure[20] and has become part of the essence of the company and its products. Apple has incorporated simplicity into its brand personality, with the implied promise of helping people to remove complexity from their lives.[21]

One of many stories about Steve Jobs, via Walter Isaacson's biography, put him at a conference for Apple's top 100 people. He set up a debate about what its ten priorities should be. With the list of ten, he gave them the strategic reality check: We can only do three of them.[22] Many leaders would have attempted all ten. Jobs recognized that to be sure of accomplishing the really important tasks and doing them well, Apple only had enough brainpower, time and money for a few. He was making the point that it was necessary to say no to many good ideas.[23]

On his return to Apple in 1997, Jobs cut its product range from 350 to 10, with only four computers – consumer and business versions of a desktop and a laptop.[24] "Deciding what not to do is as important as deciding what to do. That's true for companies, and it's true for products."[25]

Focus is a hallmark of great businesses. ExxonMobil is said to have been unrelenting in its focus on core business issues.[26]

MyTravel, where I served as communications director, was unrelenting in its focus on turning around and restructuring the company.

Achieving focus requires not only removing what is superfluous but things which have real value. The issue is not whether something is valuable or not. The issue is relative value. The issue is finite resources. The issue is that allocating resources to achieving something of relatively low value means there are not enough resources to achieve something of high value really well.

In communication, the problem is most obvious with stakeholders (audiences). Many organizations want to communicate with everyone but are unable to choose, unable to eliminate the less important, and finish by failing to give enough attention to the ones that really matter.

The best communication strategy is the one that focuses on what is really important to deliver the strategic objectives.

In Summary

- Communication strategy is beset by layers of complexity. Advertising seems to be the only branch of communication that fully grasps the power of simplicity. As the amount of data multiplies, it becomes ever more vital to focus not on data but on the big picture.

- Resources are always limited. Strategy is fundamentally a decision about how to deploy resources. No is often the right answer.

References

[1] James, *The Principles of Psychology*, 402.

[2] 'Schumpeter: Building with Big Data,' *The Economist*, May 28, 2011.

[3] Sandra Cain, *Key Concepts in Public Relations*, (Basingstoke, UK: Palgrave Macmillan, 2009), 48.

[4] Ken Segall, *Insanely Simple: The Obsession That Drives Apple's Success*, (London: Penguin Group, 2012).

[5] Jerry Della Femina, *From Those Wonderful Folks Who Gave You Pearl Harbor: Front-Line Dispatches from the Advertising War*, (New York: Simon & Schuster, 2010), 150 & 178.

[6] M&C Saatchi, *Brutal Simplicity of Thought: How It Changed the World*, (London: Ebury Press, 2013).

[7] Dave Trott, *Predatory Thinking*, (London: Macmillan, 2013).

[8] Daniel Roth, LinkedIn, quoted in Leslie Kaufman, 'LinkedIn Builds Its Publishing Presence,' *New York Times*, June 16, 2013.

[9] Allyson Scott, 'How to Get Executives Excited about LinkedIn,' *Ragan's PR Daily*, October 10, 2014.

[10] Patricia Clark, 'Why Is LinkedIn Emailing Us About Mark Cuban's 6-Year-Old Colonoscopy?' *BetaBeat.com*, February 11, 2013 - <http://betabeat.com/2013/02/ why-is-linkedin-emailing-us-about-mark-cubans-6-year-old-colonoscopy/>.

[11] Austen, *Pride and Prejudice*, 272.

[12] Sharon M. Oster, *Modern Competitive Strategy*, (Oxford University Press, 1999), 2.

[13] Porter, *Competitive Strategy*, 35-40.

[14] NHS England, 'About the NHS,' <http://www.nhs.uk/NHSEngland/thenhs/about/Pages/overview.aspx>. 'Defending Jobs,' *The Economist*, September 12, 2011.

[15] NHS England, <http://www.england.nhs.uk/about/our-vision-and-purpose/>.

[16] *The West Wing*, created by Aaron Sorkin, Warner Bros. Television, 1999-2006. *The Thick of It*, created by Armando Iannucci, BBC, 2005-2012. See also Iannucci's movie, *In the Loop*, (BBC Films/UK Film Council/ Aramid Entertainment, 2009), in which the Tucker character also appeared.

[17] James, *The Principles of Psychology*, 403-4.

[18] Louis P. Masur, *Runaway Dream: Born to Run and Bruce Springsteen's American Vision*, (New York: Bloomsbury Press, 2009), 47.

[19] Carl B. Schmidt, *Entrancing Muse: A Documented Biography of Francis Poulenc*, (Hillsdale, NY: Pendragon Press, 2001), 299.

[20] Isaacson, *Steve Jobs*, 339.

[21] Eric Viardot, 'Achieving Market Leadership for Innovation Through Communication,' in *Strategies and Communications for Innovations: An Integrative Management View for Companies and Networks*, ed. by Michael Hüelsmann & Nicole Pfeffermann (Heidelberg, Dordrecht, London & New York: Springer, 2011), 251.

[22] Isaacson, *Steve Jobs*, 378.

[23] Steve Jobs at Apple Worldwide Developers Conference, 13-16 May 1997, quoted in George Beahm, *I, Steve: Steve Jobs In His Own Words*, (Chicago: B2 Books, 2011), 43.

[24] Arthur, *Digital Wars*, 7.

[25] Walter Isaacson, 'The Real Leadership Lessons of Steve Jobs,' *Harvard Business Review*, April 2012.

[26] Coll, *Private Empire*, 125.

Executive Summary

Seven Things to Focus On

Communication strategy is the use of communication to achieve the strategic objectives through a combination of policies, plans, positions and ploys.

It answers the questions, What is our story? When, how and to whom should we tell it? And when is it better to say less or nothing?

To formulate a communication strategy:

Objectives

- Focus on setting a communication strategy that supports the overall corporate or business strategy. The biggest shortcoming of conventional public relations is neglecting strategic objectives in favor of tactics – day-to-day publicity and skirmishing.
- Strategy is competitive. Bear in mind ploys such as surprise to disrupt competitors.

Control

- Focus on taking control of your communications. Loss of control greatly reduces the chances of achieving your objectives.
- Transparency is an illusion. The strategic alternative to transparency is controlled disclosure.

Narrative

- Focus on being ready to tell your story in the form of a strategic narrative. This explains your strategy, your heritage, how you are making the world a better place, and your commitment to safety.

Profile

- Focus on designing your profile to suit your strategy.
- Don't assume that a high profile is a good thing. It is often better to say less in the media and be less exposed.

Issues

- Focus on the issues most likely to affect delivery of your strategic objectives.
- When something goes wrong, don't overreact.

Allies (strategic stakeholders)

- Focus on the audiences (stakeholders) that really matter. These are the ones whose support you need in order to achieve your strategic objectives.
- Ignore normative stakeholder theory and reputation scores in public surveys.

The big picture

- Focus on strategy rather than tactics. Pay attention to detail but avoid distraction from the strategy.

Select Bibliography

Agle, Bradley R. Nandu J. Nagarajan, Jeffrey A. Sonnenfeld & Dhinu Srinivasan, 'Does CEO Charisma Matter? An Empirical Analysis of the Relationships among Organizational Performance, Environmental Uncertainty, and Top Management Team Perceptions of CEO Charisma,' *The Academy of Management Journal*, Vol. 49, No. 1, (Feb. 2006), 161-174.

Alleyne, Brian, *Narrative Networks: Storied Approaches in a Digital Age*, (London: Sage Publications Ltd, 2015), 106.

Argenti, Paul A., *Corporate Communication*, 4th edn., (New York: McGraw-Hill/Irwin, 2007).

Arthur, Charles, *Digital Wars: Apple, Google, Microsoft and the Battle for the Internet*, (London: Kogan Page, 2012).

Barnouw, Eric, (ed.), *International Encylopedia of Communications*, ed. by (Oxford University Press, 1989).

Barthes, Roland, 'Introduction to the Structural Analysis of Narratives' in *The Narrative Reader*, ed. by Martin McQuillan, (London: Routledge, 2000), 109-114.

Barton, Laurence, *Crisis in Organizations II: Managing and Communicating in the Heat of Chaos*, (Cincinnati: South-Western, 2000).

Barzun, Jacques, *From Dawn to Decadence: 500 Years of Western Cultural Life*, (New York: HarperCollins, 2000).

Baylis, John, James J. Wirtz & Colin S. Gray (eds.), *Strategy in the Contemporary World: An Introduction to Strategic Studies*, (Oxford University Press, 2013).

Benoit, William L., 'Image Repair Discourse and Crisis Communication, *Public Relations Review*, Vol. 23, No. 2, (1997), 177-186.

——*Accounts, Excuses, and Apologies: Image Repair Theory and Research*, 2nd edn, (Albany, NY: SUNY Press, 2015).

Bergin, Tom, *Spills and Spin: The Inside Story of BP*, (London: Random House Business Books, 2011).

Bernays, Edward L., *Propaganda*, (New York: Horace Liveright, 1928).

——*Public Relations*, (Norman, OK: University of Oklahoma Press, 1952).

——*Crystallizing Public Opinion*, (New York: Liveright Publishing Corporation, 1961).

Bernstein, David, *Company Image and Reality: a Critique of Corporate Communications*, (Eastbourne, UK: Holt, Rinehart and Winston, 1986).

Bettinghaus, Erwin P., & Michael J. Cody, *Persuasive Communication*, (Fort Worth, TX: Harcourt Brace College Publishers, 1994).

Blohowiak, Donald W., *No Comment! An Executive's Essential Guide to the News Media*, (New York: Praeger, 1987).

Boorstin, Daniel J., *The Image: A Guide to Pseudo-Events in America*, (New York: Vintage Books, 1992).

Bostdorff, Denise M., & Steven L. Vibbert, 'Values Advocacy: Enhancing Organizational Images, Deflecting Public Criticism, and Grounding Future Arguments,' *Public Relations Review*, Vol. 20, No. 2, (1994), 141-158.

Botan, Carl H. & Maureen Taylor, 'Public Relations: State of the Field,' *Journal of Communication*, Vol. 54, No. 4, (2004).

Botan, Carl, & Vincent Hazleton (eds.), *Public Relations Theory*, (Hillsdale, NJ: Lawrence Erlbaum Associates, 1989).

——*Public Relations Theory II*, (Mahwah, NJ: Lawrence Erlbaum Associates, 2006).

Bowen, Shannon A., Brad Rawlins, & Thomas Martin, *An Overview of the Public Relations Function*, (Business Expert Press, LLC, 2010).

Broom, Glen M., & Bey-Ling Sha, *Cutlip and Center's Effective Public Relations*, 11th (international) edn.), (Harlow, UK: Pearson, 2013).

Brown, John Seely, Stephen Denning, Katalina Groh, & Laurence Prusak, (eds.), *Storytelling in Organizations: Why Storytelling Is Transforming 21st Century Organizations and Management*, (Burlington, MA: Elsevier Butterworth–Heinemann, 2005).

Brown, Peggy Simcic, 'Communication Managers as Strategists? Can They Make the Grade?' *Journal of Communication Management*, Vol. 5, No. 4, (2001), 313-326.

Brown, Robert E., 'St. Paul as a Public Relations Practitioner: A Metatheoretical Speculation on Messianic Communication and Symmetry,' *Public Relations Review*, Vol. 29, No. 2, (2003), 229-240.

——'Myth of Symmetry: Public Relations as Cultural Styles,' *Public Relations Review*, Vol. 32 (2006), 206–212.

——'Sea Change: Santa Barbara and the Eruption of Corporate Social Responsibility,' *Public Relations Review*, Vol. 34 (2008), 1-8.

Bunker, Matthew D., 'Takin' Care of Business: Confidentiality under the Business Exemption of the FOIA,' *Public Relations Review*, Vol. 21 No. 2, (1995), 137-149.

Cain, Susan, *Quiet: The Power of Introverts in a World that Can't Stop Talking*, (New York: Crown Publishers, 2012).

Campbell, F. E., R. A. Herman, & D. Noble, 'Contradictions in Reputation Management,' *Journal of Communication Management*, Vol. 10, No. 2, (2006), 191-196.

Cantor, Bill, & Chester Burger, (eds.), *Experts in Action: Inside Public Relations*, (New York: Longman, 1989).

Carroll, Archie B., & Ann Buchholtz, *Business & Society: Ethics and Stakeholder Management*, (Stamford, CT: Cengage Learning, 2015).

Carroll, Craig E., (ed.), *The Handbook of Communication and Corporate Reputation*, (Chichester, UK: John Wiley & Sons, Inc., 2013).

Castro, Luciano, & Patrizia Perilli, *Concordiagate: the Cruise Ship Tragedy as Told by Two Reporters on Board: Investigations, Lies and Doubts*, (Cagliari, Italy: CUEC, 2012).

Caywood, Charles L., (ed.), *The Handbook of Strategic Public Relations & Integrated Communications*, ed. by (New York: McGraw-Hill, 1997).

Christensen, Clayton, *The Innovator's Dilemma: When New Technologies Cause Great Firms to Fail*, (Harvard Business Press, 1997).

Clarkson, Max B. E., 'A Stakeholder Framework for Analyzing and Evaluating Corporate Social Performance,' *The Academy of Management Review*, Vol. 20, No. 1 (Jan., 1995), 92-117.

Clausewitz, Carl von, edited & translated by Michael Howard & Peter Paret, *On War*, (Princeton University Press, 1989).

Clegg, Stewart, Chris Carter, Martin Kornberger & Jochen Schweitzer, *Strategy: Theory & Practice*, (London: SAGE Publications Ltd, 2011).

Clemons, Eric K., & Jason A. Santamaria, (2002). 'Can Modern Military Strategy Lead You to Victory?' *Harvard Business Review*, April 2002, 56-65.

Cole, Benjamin Mark (ed.), *The New Investor Relations: Expert Perspectives on the State of the Art*, (Princeton, NJ: Bloomberg Press, 2004).

Coll, Steve, *Private Empire: ExxonMobil and American Power*, (London: Allen Lane, 2012).

Coombs, W. Timothy, & Sherry J. Holladay, (eds.), *The Handbook of Crisis Communication*, (Oxford, UK: Blackwell Publishing Ltd, 2010).

Corrado, Frank M., *Getting the Word Out: How Managers Can Create Value with Communications*, (Homewood, IL: Business One Irwin, 1993).

Cowley, Don, (ed.), *Understanding Brands: by 10 People Who Do*, (London: Kogan Page, 1991).

Crable, Richard L., & Steven L. Vibbert, 'Mobil's Epideictic Advocacy: 'Observations' of Prometheus-Bound,' in *Public Relations Inquiry as Rhetorical Criticism: Case Studies of Corporate Discourse and Social Influence*, ed. by William L. Elwood, (Westport, CT: Praeger, 1995), reprinted from *Communications Monographs*, 380-394 (Dec. 1983).

Cull, Nicholas J., David Culbert & David Welch, (eds.), *Propaganda and Mass Persuasion: A Historical Encyclopedia*, (Santa Barbara, CA: ABC-CLIO, Inc., 2003).

Cutlip, Scott M., & Allen H. Center, *Effective Public Relations*, 1st edn., (New York: Prentice-Hall, Inc., 1952).

Cutlip, Scott M., *The Unseen Power: Public Relations. A History*, (Hillsdale NJ: Lawrence Erlbaum Associates, 1994).

——*Public Relations History: From the 17th to the 20th Century. The Antecedents*, (Hillsdale NJ: Lawrence Erlbaum Associates, 1995).

Dallek, Robert, 'The Medical Ordeals of JFK,' *The Atlantic*, Dec. 1, 2002.

Davies, Gary, Rosa Chun, Rui Vinhas da Silva, & Stuart Roper, *Corporate Reputation and Competitiveness*, (London: Routledge, 2002).

Della Femina, Jerry, *From Those Wonderful Folks Who Gave You Pearl Harbor: Front-Line Dispatches from the Advertising War*, (New York: Simon & Schuster, 2010).

Deutschman, Alan, *The Second Coming of Steve Jobs*, (New York: Broadway Books, 2000).

Devereux, Eoin, (eds.), *Media Studies: Key Issues and Debates*, ed. by (London: Sage, 2007).

Dewey, John, *The Public and Its Problems*, (Chicago: Swallow Press, 1927).

Dezenhall, Eric, & John Weber, *Damage Control: Why Everything You Know About Crisis Management Is Wrong*, (New York: Portfolio, 2007).

Doherty, Sharon, *Heathrow's Terminal 5: History in the Making*, (Chichester, UK: John Wiley & Sons, Ltd, 2008).

Donaldson, Thomas, & Lee E. Preston, 'The Stakeholder Theory of the Corporation: Concepts, Evidence, and Implications', *The Academy of Management Review*, Vol. 20, No. 1 (Jan. 1995), 65-91.

Donne, Michael, *Above Us The Skies*, (Whitley, UK: Good Books/BAA plc, 1991).

Donsbach, Wolfgang, (ed.), *The International Encylopedia of Communication*, (Malden, MA: Blackwell, 2008).

Doorley, John, & Helio Fred Garcia, *Reputation Management: The Key to Successful Public Relations and Corporate Communication*, (New York: Routledge, 2007).

Dozier, David M., Larissa A. Grunig, & James E. Grunig, *Manager's Guide to Excellence and Public Relations and Communication Management*, (Mahwah, NJ: Lawrence Erlbaum Associates, Inc., 1995).

Drucker, Peter F., *The Effective Executive*, (New York: HarperBusiness, 1993).

Egan, John, & Des Wilson, *Private Business... Public Battleground: The Case for Twenty-First Century Stakeholder Companies*, (Basingstoke, UK: Palgrave, 2002).

Ewen, Stuart, *PR!: A Social History of Spin*, (New York: BasicBooks, 1996).

Fearn-Banks, Kathleen, *Crisis Management: A Casebook Approach*, (New York: Routledge, 2011).

Fink, Steven, *Crisis Communications: The Definitive Guide to Managing the Message*, (New York: McGraw-Hill Education, 2013).

——*Crisis Management: Planning for the Inevitable*, (New York: American Management Association, 1986).

Fisher, Walter R., *Human Communication as Narration: Toward a Philosophy of Reason, Value, and Action*, (Columbia, SC: University of South Carolina Press, 1987).

Fiske, John, *Introduction to Communication Studies*, (London & New York: Routledge, 1990).

Fitzpatrick, Kathy R., 'Public Relations and the Law: A Survey of Practitioners,' *Public Relations Review*, Vol. 22 No. 1, (1996) 1-8.

Flippen, J. Brooks, *Jimmy Carter, the Politics of Family and the Rise of the Religious Right*, (Athens GA: University of Georgia Press, 2011).

Fombrun, Charles J., ' Indices of Corporate Reputation: An Analysis of Media Rankings and Social Monitors' Ratings,' *Corporate Reputation Review*, Vol. 1, No. 4, (1998), 327-340.

——*Reputation: Realizing Value from the Corporate Image*, (Harvard University Press, 1996).

Fombrun, Charles, & Mark Shanley, 'What's in a Name? Reputation Building and Corporate Strategy,' *The Academy of Management Journal*, Vol. 33, No. 2, (June 1990), 233-258.

Franklin, Bob, Mike Hogan, Quentin Langley, Nick Mosdell, & Elliot Pill, *Key Concepts in Public Relations*, (London: Sage, 2009).

Freedman, Lawrence, *Strategy: A History*, (Oxford University Press, 2013).

Freeman, R. Edward, *Strategic Management: A Stakeholder Approach*, (Marshfield, MA: Pitman Publishing Inc., 1984).

Friedman, Andrew L., & Samantha Miles, *Stakeholders: Theory and Practice*, (Oxford University Press, 2006).

Gaines-Ross, Leslie, *Corporate Reputation: 12 Steps to Safeguarding and Recovering Reputation*, (Hoboken, NJ: John Wiley & Sons, 2008).

Gardberg, Naomi A., & Charles J. Fombrun, 'For Better or Worse — USA The Most Visible American Corporate Reputations,' *Corporate Reputation Review*, Vol. 4, No. 4, (1 Jan. 2002), 385-391.

Gergen, David A., *Eyewitness to Power: The Essence of Leadership, Nixon to Clinton*, (New York: Simon & Schuster, 2000).

Gibbon, Edward, *The History of the Decline and Fall of the Roman Empire*, ed. by J. B. Bury,1776-1788, (New York: Fred de Fau & Company, 1906).

Gleick, James, *The Information: a History, a Theory, a Flood*, (New York: Pantheon Books, 2011).

Goodman, Michael B., (ed.), *Corporate Communication: Theory and Practice*, (Albany, NY: State University of New York Press, 1994).

Goodman, Michael B., & Peter B. Hirsch, *Corporate Communication: Strategic Adaptation for Global Practice*, (New York: Peter Lang Publishing, Inc., 2010).

Girona, Ramon, & Jordi Xifra, 'The Office of Facts and Figures: Archibald MacLeish and the Strategy of Truth,' *Public Relations Review*, Vol. 35 (2009) 287-290.

——'From the Strategy of Truth to the Weapon of Truth: The Government Information Manual for the Motion Picture Industry, 1942,' *Public Relations Review*, Vol. 36 (2010) 306-309.

Graves, Samuel B., & Sandra A. Waddock, 'Beyond Built to Last...: Stakeholder Relations in Built-to-Last Companies,' *Business and Society Review*, Vol. 105, No. 4, (2000), 393-418.

Gray, Colin S., *Modern Strategy*, (Oxford University Press, 1999).

Grunig, James E., & Todd Hunt, *Managing Public Relations*, (Orlando FL: Harcourt Brace Jovanovich, 1984).

Grunig, James E., (ed.), *Excellence in Public Relations and Communication Management*, (Mahwah, NJ: Lawrence Erlbaum Associates, Inc., 1992).

Grunig, Larissa A., James E. Grunig, David M. Dozier, *Excellent Public Relations and Effective Organizations: A Study of Communication Management in Three Countries*, (Mahwah, NJ: Lawrence Erlbaum Associates, 2002).

Gurman, Mark, 'Seeing Through the Illusion: Understanding Apple's Mastery of the Media,' *9TO5Mac*, Aug. 29, 2014.

Haig, Matt, *Brand Royalty: How the World's Top 100 Brands Thrive & Survive*, (Philadelphia, PA: Kogan Page, 2004).

Hall, Peter, *Cities in Civilization*, (London: Weidenfeld & Nicholson, 1998).

Hallahan, Kirk, Derina Holtzhausen, Betteke van Ruler, Dejan Vercic, & Krishnamurthy Sriramesh, 'Defining Strategic Communication,' *International Journal of Strategic Communication*, Vol. 1, No. 1, (2007), 3-35.

Hamel, Gary, 'Killer Strategies that make Shareholders Rich,' *Fortune*, June 23, 1997.

Hansen, Morton T., Herminia Ibarra, & Urs Peyer, 'The Best Performing CEOs in the World,' *Harvard Business Review*, Jan. 2010.

Hart, Norman A., (ed.), *Effective Corporate Relations: Applying Public Relations in Business and Industry*, (London: McGraw-Hill, 1987).

Hart, Roderick P., *Campaign Talk: Why Elections Are Good for Us*, (Princeton University Press, 2000).

Heath, Robert L., (ed.), *Strategic Issues Management: How Organizations Influence and Respond to Public Interests and Policies*, (San Francisco, CA: Jossey-Bass Publishers, 1988)

——'Issues Management: Its Past, Present and Future,' *Journal of Public Affairs*, Vol. 2, No. 4, (2002), 209-214.

——*Encyclopedia of Public Relations*, (Thousand Oaks, CA: Sage, 2005).

——*Handbook of Public Relations*, (Thousand Oaks, CA: Sage Publications, Inc., 2001).

——*Sage Handbook of Public Relations*, (Thousand Oaks, CA: Sage Publications, Inc., 2010).

Heath, Robert L., Elizabeth L. Toth & Damion Waymer, (eds.), *Rhetorical and Critical Approaches to Public Relations II*, (New York: Routledge, 2009).

Hendrix, Jerry A., *Public Relations Cases*, (Belmont, CA: Wadsworth Publishing Company, 1988).

Herskovitz, Stephen, & Malcolm Crystal, 'The Essential Brand Persona: Storytelling and Branding,' *Journal of Business Strategy*, Vol. 31, No. 3, (2010), 21-28.

Holtzhausen, Derina, & Ansgar Zerfass, (eds.), *The Routledge Handbook of Strategic Communication*, (New York: Routledge, 2015).

Huang, Yi-Hui, 'Is Symmetrical Communication Ethical and Effective?' *Journal of Business Ethics*, Vol. 53, No. 4 (Sep. 2004), 333-352.

Hutton, James G., Michael B. Goodman, Jill B. Alexander, & Christina M. Genest, 'Reputation management: The New Face of Corporate Public Relations?' *Public Relations Review*, Vol. 27, No. 3, (2001), 247-61.

Ihlen, Øyvind, Betteke van Ruler, & Magnus Fredriksson, (eds.), *Public Relations and Social Theory: Key Figures and Concepts*, (New York: Routledge, 2009).

Isaacson, Walter, *Steve Jobs*, (London: Little, Brown 2011).

James, William, *The Principles of Psychology*, (London: Macmillan and Co., Ltd., 1890).

Jones, Edward, *Reckless Abandon, The Costa Concordia Disaster,* (Riverdale, MD: Jones-Mack Technical Services, 2012).

Jowett, Garth S., & Victoria O'Donnell, *Propaganda and Persuasion,* 3rd edn., (Thousand Oaks, CA: Sage Publications, Inc., 1999).

Kahneman, Daniel, *Thinking, Fast and Slow,* (New York: Farrar, Straus and Giroux, 2011).

Keegan, John, *Intelligence in War: Knowledge of the Enemy from Napoleon to Al-Qaeda,* (New York: Alfred A. Knopf, 2003).

―― *The Second World War,* (London: Arrow Books, 1990)

Kerr, Robert L., *The Rights of Corporate Speech: Mobil Oil and the Legal Development of the Voice of Big Business,* (New York: LFB Scholarly Publishing, 2005).

Khurana, Rakesh, *Searching for a Corporate Savior: The Irrational Quest for Charismatic CEOs,* (Princeton University Press, 2002).

Kim, W. Chan, & Renée Mauborgne, *Blue Ocean Strategy: How to Create Uncontested Market Space and Make the Competition Irrelevant,* (Harvard Business School Press, 2005).

Kitchen, Philip J., & Don E. Schultz, (eds.), *Raising the Corporate Umbrella: Corporate Communications in the 21st Century,* (New York: Palgrave, 2001).

Klein, Ross A., *Cruise Ship Blues: The Underside of the Cruise Ship Industry,* (Gabriola Island, Canada: New Society Publishers, 2002).

Knight, Rory F., & Deborah J. Pretty, 'Corporate Catastrophes, Stock Returns, and Trading Volume,' *Corporate Reputation Review,* Vol. 2, No. 4, (1999), 363-378.

Lafley, A. G., & Roger L. Martin, *Playing to Win: How Strategy Really Works,* (Boston, MA: Harvard Business Review Press, 2013).

Lamme, Margot Opdycke, & Karen Miller Russell, 'Removing the Spin: Toward a New Theory of Public Relations History,' *Journalism and Communication Monographs,* Vol. 11, No. 4, (Winter 2010).

Lange, Donald, Peggy M. Lee, & Ye Dai, 'Organizational Reputation: A Review,' *Journal of Management,* Vol. 37, No. 1, (Jan. 2011), 153-184.

Lashinsky, Adam, *Inside Apple,* (New York: Business Plus, 2012).

Lasswell, Harold D., Daniel Lerner, & Hans Speier, (eds.), *Propaganda and Communication in World History,* (Honolulu, HI: East-West Center, 1979).

Lerbinger, Otto, *Corporate Public Affairs: Interacting with Interest Groups, Media, and Government,* (Mahwah, NJ: Lawrence Erlbaum Associates, Inc., 2006).

Lippmann, Walter, *Public Opinion,* (New Brunswick, NJ: Transaction Publishers, 1991), originally published 1922.

Loewenstein, George, 'Out of Control: Visceral Influences on Behavior,' in *Advances in Behavioral Economics,* ed. by Colin F. Camerer, George Lowenstein & Matthew Rabin, (Princeton University Press, 2004), 689-723.

Lukaszewski, James E., *Lukaszewski on Crisis Communication: What Your CEO Needs to Know about Reputation Risk and Crisis Management*, (Brookfield, CT: Rothstein Associates, Inc., 2013).

Macdonald, Scott, *Propaganda and Information Warfare in the Twenty-First Century: Altered Images and Deception Operations*, (Abingdon, UK: Routledge, 2007).

Maltese, John Anthony, *Spin Control: The White House Office of Communications and the Management of Presidential News*, (Chapel Hill, NC: University of North Carolina Press, 1994).

Manheim, Jarol B., *All of the People, All the Time: Strategic Communication and American Politics*, (Armonk, NY: M. E. Sharpe, Inc., 1991).

Manning, Martin J., *Historical Dictionary of American Propaganda*, (Westport, CT: Greenwood Press, 2004).

Marchand, Roland, *Creating the Corporate Soul: The Rise of Public Relations and Corporate Imagery in American Big Business*, (Berkeley, CA: University of California Press, 1998).

Marcus, Bruce W., *Competing for Capital: Investor Relations in a Dynamic World*, (Hoboken, NJ: John Wiley & Sons, Inc., 2005).

Marra, F. J., 'Crisis Communication Plans: Poor Predictors of Excellent Crisis Public Relations,' *Public Relations Review*, Vol. 24, No. 4, (1998), 461–74.

Martin, Dick, 'Gilded and Gelded: Hard-Won Lessons from the PR Wars,' *Harvard Business Review*, (Oct. 2003), 44-54.

McKie, David, *A Sadly Mismanaged Affair: A Political History of the Third London Airport*, (London: Croom Helm, 1973),

McQuail, Denis, *McQuail's Mass Communication Theory: An Introduction*, (London: Sage Publications Ltd, 2010).

McQuail, Denis, & Sven Windahl, *Communication Models for the Study of Mass Communication*, (New York: Longman, 1993).

Michie, David, *The Invisible Persuaders: How Britain's Spin Doctors Manipulate the Media*, (London: Bantam Press, 1998).

Miles, Samantha, 'Stakeholder: Essentially Contested or Just Confused?' *Journal of Business Ethics*, Vol. 108, No. 3, (2012), 285-298.

Millar, Dan Pyle, & Robert L. Heath, (eds.), *Responding to Crisis: A Rhetorical Approach to Crisis Communication*, (Mahwah, NJ: Lawrence Erlbaum Associates, 2004).

Miller, Katherine, *Organizational Communication: Approaches and Processes*, (Boston, MA: Wadsworth, Cengage Learning, 2012).

Mitchell, Ronald K., Bradley R. Agle & Donna J. Wood, 'Toward a Theory of Stakeholder Identification and Salience: Defining the Principle of Who and What Really Counts,' *The Academy of Management Review*, Vol. 22, No. 4 (Oct., 1997), 853-886.

Mitroff, Ian, 'Lessons from 9/11: Are Companies Better Prepared Today?' *Technological Forecasting & Social Change*, 72 (2005), 375-376.

Moore, Simon, & Mike Seymour, *Global Technology and Corporate Crisis: Strategies, Planning and Communication in the Information Age*, (New York: Routledge, 2005).

Moritz, Michael, *Return to the Little Kingdom: Steve Jobs, the Creation of Apple, and How It Changed the World*, (London: Duckworth Overlook, 2009).

Morris, Trevor, & Simon Goldsworthy, *PR - A Persuasive Industry? Spin, Public Relations and the Shaping of the Modern Media*, (London: Palgrave Macmillan, 2008).

Moss, Danny, & Gary Warnaby, 'Communications Strategy? Strategy Communication? Integrating Different Perspectives,' *Journal of Marketing Communications*, Vol. 4, No. 3, (1998), 131-140.

Munter, Mary, *Guide to Managerial Communication: Effective Business Writing and Speaking*, (Upper Saddle River, NJ: Prentice Hall, 2006).

Nairn, Alasdair, *Engines That Move Markets: Technology Investing from Railroads to the Internet and Beyond*, (New York: John Wiley & Sons, Inc., 2002).

Newsom, Doug, Judy VanSlyke Turk, & Dean Kruckeberg, *This Is PR: The Realities of Public Relations*, 11th edn., (Boston MA: Wadsworth Cengage Learning, 2012).

Ogilvy, David, *Ogilvy on Advertising*, (New York: Vintage Books, 1985).

O'Hair, Dan, Gustav W. Friedrich & Lynda Dee Dixon, *Strategic Communication in Business and the Professions*, (London: Pearson, 2011)

Olins, Wally, *Corporate Identity*, (London: Thames & Hudson, 1989).

Ollard, Richard, *The Image of the King: Charles I and Charles II*, (London: Pimlico, 1993).

Oster, Sharon M., *Modern Competitive Strategy*, (Oxford University Press, 1999).

O'Sullivan, Tim, John Hartley, Danny Saunders, Martin Montgomery & John Fiske, *Key Concepts in Communication and Cultural Studies*, 2nd edn., (London: Routledge, 1994).

Packard, Vance, *The Hidden Persuaders*, (Brooklyn, NY: IG Publishing, 2007).

Paret, Peter, 'The Genesis of On War,' in *On War*, by Carl von Clausewitz, edited & translated by Michael Howard & Peter Paret, (Princeton University Press, 1989).

Parsons, Patricia J., *Ethics in Public Relations: A Guide to Best Practice*, (London: Kogan Page Limited, 2008).

Pauchant, Thierry C., & Ian I. Mitroff, *Transforming the Crisis Prone Organization*, (San Francisco, CA: Jossey-Bass Publishers, 1992).

Pauly, John J., & Liese L. Hutchison, 'Moral Fables of Public Relations Practice: The Tylenol and Exxon Valdez Cases,' *Journal of Mass Media Ethics*, Vol. 20, No. 4, 231–249

Pearson, Christine M., & Judith A. Clair, 'Reframing Crisis Management', *The Academy of Management Review*, Vol. 23, No. 1, (1998), 59-76.

Peters, Thomas J., & Robert H. Waterman, *In Search of Excellence: Lessons from America's Best-Run Companies*, (New York: Harper & Row, 1982).

Bibliography

Porter, Michael E., *Competitive Strategy: Techniques for Analyzing Industries and Competitors*, (New York: The Free Press, 1998).

Powell, Anton, (ed.), *Roman Poetry & Propaganda in the Age of Augustus*, (London: Bristol Classical Press, 1992).

Price, Stuart, *Communication Studies*, (Harlow, UK: Addison Wesley Longman Ltd, 1996).

Raupp, Juliana, & Olaf Hoffjann, 'Understanding Strategy in Communication Management,' *Journal of Communication Management*, Vol. 16, No. 2, (2010), 146-161.

Rawlins, Brad L., Kenneth D. Plowman & Elizabeth Stohlton, 'A Comprehensive Approach to Prioritizing Stakeholders: A Synthesis of Stakeholder and Public Relations Literature on Identifying and Prioritizing Stakeholders for Strategic Management,' Institute for Public Relations, 2005, <http://hdl.handle.net/123456789/814>.

Rawlins, Brad L. 'Prioritizing Stakeholders for Public Relations,' Gold Standard paper of the Commission on Public Relations Measurement & Evaluation, Institute for Public Relations, 2006.

Reed, Stanley, & Alison Fitzgerald, *In Too Deep: BP and the Drilling Race That Took it Down*, (Hoboken, NJ: John Wiley & Sons, 2011).

Regester, Michael, & Judy Larkin, *Risk Issues and Crisis Management in Public Relations; a Casebook of Best Practice*, (London: Kogan Page, 2008).

Ruff, Peter, & Khalid Aziz, *Managing Communications in a Crisis*, (Aldershot, UK: Gower Publishing, 2003).

Rumelt, Richard P., *Good Strategy/Bad Strategy: The Difference and Why it Matters*, (New York: Crown Business, 2011).

Saatchi, M&C, *Brutal Simplicity of Thought: How It Changed the World*, (London: Ebury Press, 2013).

Sachs, Sybille, Edwin Rühli, & Isabelle Kern, *Sustainable Success with Stakeholders: The Untapped Potential*, (Basingstoke, UK: Palgrave Macmillan, 2009).

Sampson, Anthony, *The Seven Sisters: The Great Oil Companies & the World They Shaped*, (London: Bantam Books, 1974).

Sanford, George, *Katyn and the Soviet Massacre of 1940: Truth, Justice and Memory*, (Abingdon, UK: Routledge, 2005).

Schlender, Brent, & Rick Teztzeli, *Becoming Steve Jobs: The Evolution of a Reckless Upstart Into a Visionary Leader*, (London: Sceptre, 2015).

Schmertz, Herb, & William Novak, *Goodbye to the Low Profile: The Art of Creative Confrontation*, (London: Mercury Books, 1986).

Schmidt, Eric, & Jonathan Rosenberg, *How Google Works*, (New York: Grand Central Publishing, 2014).

Schnee, Christian, 'Augustus – Public Relations and the Making of an Imperial Reputation,' The Proceedings of the International History of Public Relations Conference, Bournemouth University, 2011, 427-443.

Schoenfeld, Gabriel, *Necessary Secrets: National Security, the Media and the Rule of Law*, (New York: W. W. Norton & Company, 2010).

Schultz, Majken, Mary Jo Hatch & Mogens Holten Larsen, (eds.), *The Expressive Organization: Linking Identity, Reputation and the Corporate Brand*, (Oxford University Press, 2000).

Scott, Mark C., *Achieving Fair Value: How Companies Can Better Manage Their Relationships with Investors*, (Chichester, UK: John Wiley & Sons Ltd., 2005).

Sedereviciute, Kristina, & Chiara Valentini, 'Towards a More Holistic Stakeholder Analysis Approach. Mapping Known and Undiscovered Stakeholders from Social Media,' *International Journal of Strategic Communication*, Vol. 5, No. 4, (2011), 221–239.

Seitel, Fraser P., *The Practice of Public Relations*, 12th edn., (Upper Saddle River, NJ: Pearson Education, 2013).

Seitel, Fraser P., & John Doorley, *Rethinking Reputation: How PR Trumps Marketing and Advertising in the New Media World*, (New York: Palgrave Macmillan, 2012).

Sellnow, Timothy L., & Matthew W. Seeger, *Theorizing Crisis Communication*, (Chichester, UK: John Wiley & Sons, Inc., 2013).

Shafritz, Jay M., (ed.), *International Encyclopedia of Public Policy and Administration*, (Boulder, CO: Westview Press, 1998).

Sherwood, Philip, *Heathrow: 2000 Years of History*, (Stroud, UK: Sutton Publishing, 1999)

Siegel, Alan, & Irene Etzkorn, *Simple: Conquering the Crisis of Complexity*, (New York: Random House Books, 2013).

Simon, Hermann, *Hidden Champions of the Twenty-First Century: Success Strategies of Unknown World Market Leaders*, (New York: Springer, 2009).

Simons, Herbert W., with Joanne Morale, & Bruce Gronbeck, *Persuasion in Society*, (Thousand Oaks, CA: Sage Publications, Inc., 2001).

Small, William J., 'Exxon Valdez: How to Spend Billions and Still Get a Black Eye', *Public Relations Review*, Vol. 17, No. 1, (Spring 1991), 9–25.

Smith, Gerri L., & Robert L. Heath, 'Moral Appeals in Mobil Oil's Op-ed Campaign,' *Public Relations Review*, Vol. 16, No. 4, (Winter 1990), 48-54.

Smith, Ronald D., *Strategic Planning for Public Relations*, 2nd edn., (Mahwah, NJ: Lawrence Erlbaum Associates, 2005).

Smith, Terry, *Accounting for Growth: Stripping the Camouflage from Company Accounts*, (London: Century Business, 1992).

Smythe, John, Colette Dorward, & Jerome Reback, *Corporate Reputation: Managing the New Strategic Asset*, (London: Century Business, 1992).

Spring, Joel H., *Images of American Life: A History of Ideological Management in Schools, Movies, Radio and Television*, (State University of New York Press, 1992).

Sriramesh, Krishnamurthy, Ansgar Zerfass, & Jeong-Nam Kim, *Public Relations and Communication Management: Current Trends and Emerging Topics*, (New York: Routledge, 2013).

445

St. John III, Burton, 'Conveying the Sense-Making Corporate Persona: The Mobil Oil "Observations" Columns, 1975-1980,' *Public Relations Review*, Vol. 40, No. 4, (Nov. 2014), 692-699.

Strachan, Hew, *The Direction of War: Contemporary Strategy in Historical Perspective*, (Cambridge University Press, 2013).

Taithe, Bertrand, & Tim Thornton, (eds.), *Propaganda: Political Rhetoric and Identity 1300-2000*, (Stroud, UK: Sutton Publishing, 1999).

Taylor, Philip M., *Munitions of the Mind: A History of Propaganda from the Ancient World to the Present Day*, (Manchester, UK: Manchester University Press, 2005).

Tench, Ralph, & Liz Yeomans, *Exploring Public Relations*, (Harlow, UK: Pearson Education, 2006).

Theaker, Alison, (ed.), *The Public Relations Handbook*, (London: Routledge, 2012).

Thompson, Arthur A., Margaret A. Peteraf, John E. Gamble, A. J. Strickland III, Alex Janes & Ciara Sutton, *Crafting and Executing Strategy: The Quest for Competitive Advantage*, (Maidenhead, UK: McGraw-Hill Education, 2013).

Toth, Elizabeth L. & Robert L. Heath, (eds.), *Rhetorical and Critical Approaches to Public Relations*, (Hillsdale, NJ: Lawrence Erlbaum Associates, 1992).

Toth, Elizabeth L., (ed.), *The Future of Excellence in Public Relations and Communication Management: Challenges for the Next Generation*, (Mahwah, NJ: Lawrence Erlbaum Associates, 2007).

Travers, Tony, *The Politics of London: Governing an Ungovernable City*, (Basingstoke, UK: Palgrave Macmillan, 2004).

Trott, Dave, *Predatory Thinking*, (London: Macmillan, 2013).

Ulmer, Robert R., Timothy L. Sellnow, & Matthew W. Seeger, *Effective Crisis Communication: Moving from Crisis to Opportunity*, (Thousand Oaks, CA: Sage Publications, Inc., 2014).

Vickers, Brian, *In Defence of Rhetoric*, (Oxford: Clarendon Press, 1988).

Waller, David S. & Michael J. Polonsky, 'Multiple Senders and Receivers: A Business Communication Model,' *Corporate Communications: An International Journal*, Vol. 3, No. 3, (1998), 83-91.

Watson, Peter, *Ideas: A History of Thought and Invention, from Fire to Freud*, (New York: HarperCollins, 2005).

Westbrook, Ian, *Strategic Financial and Investor Communication: the Stock Price Story*, (Abingdon, UK: Routledge, 2014).

Whetten, David A., 'Theory Development and the Study of Corporate Reputation,' *Corporate Reputation Review*, Vol. 1, No. 1, (1997).

White, Colin, *Strategic Management*, (Basingstoke, UK: Palgrave Macmillan, 2004).

Wilcox, Dennis L. & Glen T. Cameron, *Public Relations: Strategies and Tactics*, 10th edn., (Harlow, UK: Pearson Education Limited, 2013).

Wilson, Des, *Campaigning: The A to Z of Public Advocacy*, with Leighton Andrews, (London: Hawksmere, 1993).

——*Memoirs of a Minor Public Figure*, (London: Quartet Books Limited, 2011).

Windahl, Sven, Benno H. Signitzer & Jean T. Olson, *Using Communication Theory*, (London: Sage, 2009).

Woodward, Gary C., & Robert E. Denton, *Persuasion and Influence in American Life*, (Long Grove, IL: Waveland Press, Inc., 2014).

Yergin, Daniel, *The Prize: The Epic Quest for Oil, Money, and Power*, (New York: Simon & Schuster, 1991).

——*The Quest: Energy, Security, and the Remaking of the Modern World*, (New York: The Penguin Press, 2011).

Index

Index